STANDARD REFERENCE LIBRARY

THROUGH-THE-BIBLE COMMENTARY

OLD TESTAMENT VOLUME TWO

The History of Israel

compiled by Douglas Redford

Standard®
PUBLISHING
Bringing The Word to Life

Cincinnati, Ohio

Library of Congress Cataloging in Publication data:

Redford, Doug, 1953-
  The history of Israel / compiled by Douglas Redford.
      p. cm. -- (Standard reference library. Old Testament ; v. 2)
  Includes bibliographical references and index.
  ISBN 978-0-7847-1905-3 (casebound : alk. paper)
  1. Jews--History. 2. Bible. O.T.--History of Biblical events. I. Title.

DS116.R43 2008
222'.07--dc22
                              2007039830

Published by Standard Publishing, Cincinnati, Ohio.
www.standardpub.com

Printed in China.

Table of Contents

Introduction

The Class That's Always in Session

"You've been teaching history for over 35 years," a college student said to her professor one day as they chatted in his office. "Doesn't it ever get tiring? How do you stay so fresh and so interesting in class?"

The professor thought for a moment then replied, "The fact that I teach history is only one side of the coin. The other side is that history teaches me—and continues to teach me every day. And there are always new lessons to learn and to pass on to others."

This same observation could be made of Old Testament history. In the introduction to the previous volume in this series, comprising studies on the Pentateuch, some general observations that many people hold about the Old Testament were noted. One of these was that the Old Testament is often viewed as including "too much history." How could so much ancient history possibly be relevant to life in the 21st century? Some skeptics might even echo the oft-quoted observation of Henry Ford: "History is more or less bunk."

Perhaps one reason that so many people have a negative opinion of history is that history is often taught as an endless series of persons, places, events, and dates. In some cases, students are not taught the meaning of these facts for the time when they took place, let alone their significance for modern times. As you proceed through the studies that are part of this volume covering the historical books of the Old Testament (Joshua through Esther), you will encounter a sizable, and possibly intimidating, number of persons, places, events, and dates. Various charts and maps have been included in this book to assist you in becoming better acquainted with this information.

However, the divinely inspired writers who recorded all of this information have not merely provided information for information's sake. These writers saw more than just random events that comprised human experience; they saw the hand of God himself involved in these events, interweaving them in just the manner he wanted to achieve the desired result. They saw human beings receiving either God's favor and blessing because of their obedience to him, or his judgment and wrath because of their refusal to listen to his law and his messengers. It may well be helpful to consider the Old Testament's record of history under the two important headings of God's sovereignty and humanity's accountability to him.

GOD IS SOVEREIGN

Although God's people may have believed that they found freedom whenever they turned from him and removed his "yoke" and his "bonds" (Jeremiah 2:20, 31), they were only deluding themselves. God's plan was always carried out in spite of his people's stubbornness. For example, when the tragic split of the kingdom occurred following Rehoboam's acceptance of some very foolish advice from his peers, the inspired writer offers this insight: "So the king did not listen to the people, for this turn of events was from the Lord, to fulfill the word the Lord had spoken to Jeroboam son of Nebat through Ahijah the Shilonite" (1 Kings 12:15). This did not remove Rehoboam's accountability for his ego-centered actions. The writer of the biblical record is letting the reader know that a higher purpose was served through those actions—what Peter described on the Day of Pentecost (regarding Jesus' crucifixion) as "God's set purpose and foreknowledge" (Acts 2:23).

The same could be said of the fall of Jerusalem and the destruction of the temple in 586 BC, which without question had a devastating impact on the people of Judah. In the ancient Near Eastern mindset, the destruction of a god's temple reflected quite negatively on that god. If he were truly a superior god, why would he not come to the defense of his "house"? He would never allow it to be ravaged by outsiders—unless, of course, he was too weak and impotent to defend it. The presence of such a perspective is the reason that the Old Testament is so emphatic that God allowed the events of 586 BC to occur as an act of judgment against his people. Second Chronicles 36:15-17 provides the following summation of what happened to God's people and, more important, *why* it happened.

> The Lord, the God of their fathers, sent word to them through his messengers again and again, because he had pity on his people and on his dwelling place. But they mocked God's messengers, despised his words and scoffed at his prophets until the wrath of the Lord was aroused against his people and there was no remedy. He brought up against them the king of the Babylonians, who killed their young men with the sword in the sanctuary, and spared neither young man nor young woman, old man or aged. God handed all of them over to Nebuchadnezzar.

Far from reflecting poorly on Judah's God, the events of 586 BC demonstrated his power and his sovereign purpose. That purpose included more than judgment for Judah; it included hope and restoration. Second Chronicles does not end on the sad note described above; the book concludes with the account of how "the Lord moved the heart of Cyrus king of Persia to make a proclamation throughout his realm and to put it in writing" (36:22). That proclamation was what became the Jews' "Emancipation Proclamation," allowing them to return and rebuild their temple and their lives. Their real King was still on the throne; indeed, he had never vacated it.

HUMANITY IS ACCOUNTABLE

While Old Testament history teaches God's sovereignty, it does not teach it to the exclusion of an individual's responsibility for his or her actions. As noted in the previous section, however, that responsibility should not be looked at solely from the standpoint of God's bringing judgment on people for their sins. That God holds humanity responsible means that every person also has the privilege of cooperating with him in carrying out his purpose for the world. Whenever we see wrongdoing on the rise among God's people in the Old Testament, God always has his person or persons in place to make a difference and to speak and act on his behalf.

When "everyone did as he saw fit" during the time of the judges (Judges 21:25), there were individuals such as Deborah, Gideon, and Ruth providing a spiritual "breath of fresh air."

When Ahab and Jezebel attempted to make Baal worship "the law of the land" in the northern kingdom, God raised up Elijah and Elisha to counter their wicked intentions.

When Ahab and Jezebel's daughter Athaliah seized power in the southern kingdom and attempted to wipe out the entire royal family, God used a priest, Jehoiada, to protect one remaining member of the house of David (Joash) and establish him as king.

When Haman attempted to wipe out the Jews throughout the Persian Empire, God had a young Jewish girl, Esther, in place along with her courageous uncle Mordecai "for such a time as this" (Esther 4:14).

Whenever we read such accounts as these, we as Christians need to do some serious self-examination. Here is where Scripture must be allowed to serve its purpose as a "mirror" (James 1:22-25), challenging us to take a good hard look at ourselves in light of the times in which we live.

We live in a very Judges-like day, when everyone is doing as he or she sees fit. Terms such as *moral relativism, post-modernism,* and *post-Christian* are used to describe the spiritual landscape of the 21st-century. Will we be the Deborahs, the Gideons, and the Ruths who provide the needed breath of fresh air?

We live in a time when numerous false gods and religions are embraced in the name of tolerance. People scoff at or in some cases are outraged at the idea that Christianity is the only way to God. Will we be the Elijahs and Elishas who stand firm for the truth?

Often it seems that wrongdoing has gotten the upper hand in our world. We wonder whether or not our efforts are having any impact on anyone. It is easy to let our morale weaken and to neglect the spiritual disciplines that are necessary for keeping ourselves fit for the spiritual battle in which we are engaged. Will we be the Jehoiadas, the Esthers, and the Mordecais— determined not to be overcome by evil but to overcome evil with good (Romans 12:21)?

What the professor told the student in his office is true: history *is* meant to teach us, but we have to be willing students. The study of Old Testament history is indeed a class that is always in session and one from which a person never really "graduates." That is not meant to be a discouraging thought but an encouraging one. After all, according to Paul, "everything that was written in the past [and he was describing the Old Testament with these words] was written to teach us, so that through endurance and the *encouragement* of the Scriptures we might have hope" (Romans 15:4).

May the studies in this volume give you a fresh appreciation, not only of the history of God's people but of the God who guided that history—and guides ours as well.

Chapter 1

Conquering the Promised Land: Studies in Joshua

Joshua 1:1-11; 3:7-17; 6:1-5, 15-20; 24:1, 14-24

THE LORD INSTRUCTS JOSHUA (JOSHUA 1:1-11)

Establishing the Groundwork

The book of Joshua opens upon a new Israel having a new opportunity to possess Canaan. Thirty-eight years had passed since an unbelieving and fearful people refused to enter that promised land, and by refusing forfeited both their inheritance and their lives. God would have given the former generation the land of promise had they proved faithful, even as he was ready to give it to the new generation. The Israelites, however, had to realize that the land was indeed a gift and that they would receive it only if they followed the Giver's terms. They would not gain the land by their own power; they would not inherit Canaan because they were especially worthy, or because they had earned it. They would gain it by the grace and power of God, who had promised it centuries earlier to Abraham and his descendants.

Another promised land awaits Christians who are faithful to the Lord. It is described in Revelation, chapters 21 and 22. There God will dwell with his people. Sorrow, pain, death, and tears will not be found. We will not receive such a home because of our great achievements or possessions. Indeed, we cannot begin to earn such a place or claim that we are worthy of it. We can receive it only by the grace of God given to us through his beloved Son.

Examining the Text

I. Preliminary Concerns (Joshua 1:1-4)
A. Death of Moses (vv. 1, 2a)

¹After the death of Moses the servant of the LORD, the LORD said to Joshua son of Nun, Moses' aide:

The book of Deuteronomy closes with a record of the death of Moses and also with a description of him as *the servant of the Lord* (Deuteronomy 34:5). Thus we can see how the book of Joshua picks up where Deuteronomy ends and that even though we have moved in our study from one section of the Bible (the Pentateuch, or the books of law) to another (the books of history), there is no break in the "flow" of the record.

Joshua son of Nun was originally named Hoshea, but his name had been changed by Moses (Numbers 13:16). The name *Hoshea* means "salvation"; *Joshua* means "the Lord saves." A summary of his service prior to this significant moment, including his role as *Moses' aide*, may be found in the comments under Deuteronomy 34:9 in chapter 13 of the previous volume.

²ᵃ**"Moses my servant is dead.**

Although Joshua knew this, it was important for the Lord to preface his words to Joshua with a reference to the man whose position of leadership he had been commissioned to assume.

B. Description of the Land (vv. 2b-4)

²ᵇ**"Now then, you and all these people, get ready to cross the Jordan River into the land I am about to give to them—to the Israelites.**

At this point, Joshua and the *Israelites* were camped in the plains of Moab on the east side of the *Jordan River*. There Moses had declared to them the words found in the book of Deuteronomy (Deuteronomy 1:5). Some of the territory east of the Jordan had already been allotted to the tribes of Reuben, Gad, and half of Manasseh (Joshua alluded to this in verses 12-15 of this chapter). *Now* it was time for the *people* to *get ready to cross the Jordan* and possess the *land* of Canaan. Again the Lord emphasized (as he had throughout the Pentateuch and as he did in the next verse) that he was about to *give* this land to the Israelites. Canaan was his gift to them and could be received only by adherence to his conditions.

³**"I will give you every place where you set your foot, as I promised Moses.**

Although Moses was dead, what the Lord had *promised* him was no less valid than it had been when he was alive. The people could walk through the length and breadth of the land of Canaan, and every place they traveled would be theirs.

⁴**"Your territory will extend from the desert to Lebanon, and from the great river, the Euphrates—all the Hittite country—to the Great Sea on the west."**

To the south of Moab, where Joshua and the Israelites were at this point, was *the desert*, a part of which was the territory where the Israelites had been wandering. This desert country (which today comprises part of the Arabian Desert) formed the southern and eastern borders of the promised land.

To the north were the peaks of *Lebanon*, but the promised land stretched northward beyond them and touched the upper part of *the Euphrates* River. The western boundary was *the Great Sea*, the Old Testament designation for the Mediterranean Sea. The eastern boundary was the desert east of the plains of Moab. It should be noted that the extent of the Israelites' conquests to these limits was reached only during the time of David and Solomon (1 Kings 4:21).

The Hittites were descendants of Heth, a son of Canaan, who was a grandson of Noah (Genesis 10:6, 15). Here their name seems to be used to refer to all the people living in the land of Canaan. More specific listings of the various peoples may be found in Deuteronomy 7:1 and Joshua 3:10. For many years the Hittites were unknown outside of the Bible, and certain critics of the biblical record asserted that there was no truth in the statements concerning them. Then the hieroglyphic writings of ancient Egypt and the cuneiform records of ancient Assyria were deciphered, and scholars were confronted with an amazing amount of material related to this people. The biblical record was once again proven accurate and trustworthy.

II. Personal Challenge (Joshua 1:5-9)
A. Call to Courage (vv. 5, 6)

⁵*"No one will be able to stand up against you all the days of your life. As I was with Moses, so I will be with you; I will never leave you nor forsake you.*

There is always a sense of loss when a dynamic leader such as Moses dies. But the power of Moses was not inherent in him. Rather it was in the fact that he was sustained by God. Now God promised Joshua that *no one* would *be able to stand up against* him during his entire lifetime. The reason was that God would be *with* him, just as he *was with Moses*. The same promise of God's never-failing presence is made to Christians (Hebrews 13:5).

⁶*"Be strong and courageous, because you will lead these people to inherit the land I swore to their forefathers to give them.*

The divine promises are never intended to offset the need for development of proper spiritual attitudes. The qualities of leadership had to be possessed by Joshua, although they would be enhanced by the motivation provided by God. A part of that motivation was that God had sworn to the Israelites' *forefathers* (the patriarchs) *to give* the *land* to them. God would never renege on such a promise.

B. Call to Obedience (vv. 7, 8)

7"Be strong and very courageous. Be careful to obey all the law my servant Moses gave you; do not turn from it to the right or to the left, that you may be successful wherever you go.

Victory was not going to be given unconditionally to Joshua. He needed to *be careful to obey all the law* given by God's *servant Moses*. He must not turn from it in any way; only then could he and the people be *successful* as they advanced into the promised land.

8"Do not let this Book of the Law depart from your mouth; meditate on it day and night, so that you may be careful to do everything written in it. Then you will be prosperous and successful.

The *Book of the Law* had been written down by Moses and delivered to the priests (Deuteronomy 31:9). As noted in the comments on Deuteronomy 31:9, the phrase *Book of the Law* may have included only Deuteronomy or it may have embraced the entire Pentateuch (Genesis—Deuteronomy). However, it was not enough simply to possess the book. The contents had to be the subject of constant thought and deliberation and then had to be translated into one's daily conduct. The ultimate purpose of meditation upon God's Word is to enable one to obey more fully *everything written in it*. Our spiritual progress is dependent upon this, and God's blessing is conditioned upon it.

C. Assurance of God's Presence (v. 9)

9"Have I not commanded you? Be strong and courageous. Do not be terrified; do not be discouraged, for the LORD your God will be with you wherever you go."

God had given the order to advance and take the land of Canaan. That was reason enough to *be strong and courageous*. When God's people are obeying his orders, there is no reason to be *terrified* of giants or to be *discouraged* by formidable city walls. When you are committed to his will, *the Lord . . . will be with you wherever you go*. The enemy may be too strong for you alone, but he cannot stand against you and the Lord.

III. People's Cooperation (Joshua 1:10, 11)
A. Command to the Officers (v. 10)

10So Joshua ordered the officers of the people:

Soon after the Israelites had left Egypt, Moses had followed the advice of his father-in-law Jethro and had organized the people thoroughly, delegating responsibility so as to lighten his load (Exodus 18:24-26). Whether or not the organization of the people was still the same at this point some 40 years later, we do not know. But clearly there were *officers* who could convey Joshua's orders *to the people* and see that they were carried out.

B. Command to the People (v. 11)

¹¹"Go through the camp and tell the people, 'Get your supplies ready. Three days from now you will cross the Jordan here to go in and take possession of the land the LORD your God is giving you for your own.'"

The command was to prepare to march. The people had been camped in one place through the month of mourning for Moses (Deuteronomy 34:8), so their possessions were no longer packed for travel.

At this point, the time of the Passover was near (Joshua 5:10). The rainy season was ending, but the Jordan was still at flood stage, overflowing its banks (Joshua 3:15). It was not hard for two men (Joshua 2:1) to swim that swollen river, perhaps with the help of a floating log, and then travel on to Jericho. But millions of men, women, and children, loaded down with their goods and limited in travel by their livestock—how could they hope to cross that river? The call to prepare and *cross the Jordan* was a call to have faith. The people obeyed and got ready for whatever was to take place *three days from now.*

CROSSING THE JORDAN (JOSHUA 3:7-17)

Establishing the Groundwork

From where they were camped east of the Jordan River, the Israelites perhaps could see the city of Jericho located among the palm trees across the river. It was known as the "City of Palms," according to Deuteronomy 34:3. Jericho was strongly walled, but the Israelites, encouraged by Joshua, who had in turn been encouraged by the Lord, were enthusiastic in their support of Joshua and their recognition that he deserved the same measure of respect and obedience that Moses had received (Joshua 1:16-18). One wonders if Joshua had any reservations about the sincerity of the people's claim, given their previous record of inconsistent obedience. The Lord had previously warned Joshua of the people's tendency toward rebellion (Deuteronomy 31:14-18).

Possibly following the example of Moses, Joshua sent spies to Jericho on a reconnaissance mission (Joshua 2:1). Some students have found it interesting that only two spies were sent. They suggest that Joshua recalled the problems that resulted from sending a larger number (12) to explore the land of Canaan and wisely chose fewer men for this mission. Such students have forgotten that God commanded Moses to send 12 spies (Numbers 13:1-3), so no error in judgment can be attributed to Moses or to the method employed for the reconnaissance. The problem at Kadesh was not an excess of spies, but a lack of faith.

The two men crossed the Jordan and came to Jericho, where they found lodging with a prostitute named Rahab. When the men's presence in the city became known, she hid them on the roof of her house and sent the men who were looking for them on a false trail.

Later, before the spies had settled down for the night, Rahab acknowledged to them that the city of Jericho was greatly alarmed at the presence of the Israelites; for they had heard of the Lord's mighty acts on their behalf. Rahab herself expressed her own convictions about Israel's God in declaring, "I know that the Lord has given this land to you" (Joshua 2:9) and "the Lord your God is God in heaven above and on the earth below" (v. 11). Rahab asked for mercy from the spies because of her kindness to them, and they assured her that she and her family would be spared from the coming destruction of the city. The spies also asked that Rahab place a scarlet cord in the window of her house so that the Israelites would know where she lived (vv. 12-21).

When the spies returned to the Israelite camp, they reported that Jericho was ripe for conquest: "The Lord has surely given the whole land into our hands; all the people are melting in fear because of us" (Joshua 2:24). The Israelites moved closer to the Jordan (Joshua 3:1), and after three days had passed, the officers told the people to prepare for the crossing and to follow the lead of the priests as they carried the Ark of the Covenant (v. 3). Joshua himself told the people, "Tomorrow the Lord will do amazing things among you" (v. 5). A spirit of eager expectation must have permeated the camp.

Examining the Text

I. God's Words (Joshua 3:7-13)
A. For Joshua (v. 7)

7And the LORD said to Joshua, "Today I will begin to exalt you in the eyes of all Israel, so they may know that I am with you as I was with Moses.

Ultimately the people of Israel owed their allegiance to *the Lord,* not to *Joshua* alone. They would accept Joshua as their leader if they knew the Lord was *with* him. All through the past 40 years the Lord had been *with Moses* and had demonstrated that fact in unmistakable ways. For example, at one time there had been a rebellion against Moses. To show that the Lord was on Moses' side, the earth had opened up and swallowed the rebels (Numbers 16:1-33).

Now Joshua was beginning his leadership of Israel, and the Lord was about to show how he would be with Joshua just as he had been with Moses. He would do this, not by having rebels destroyed, but by enabling Joshua to foretell and carry out a great miracle (v. 13). This miracle would indicate that God was with all the people and would do great things for them (v. 10); Joshua's prediction would demonstrate that God was with Joshua. Thus God would *exalt* Joshua and make him great *in the eyes of all Israel.*

B. For the Priests (v. 8)

8"Tell the priests who carry the ark of the covenant: 'When you reach the edge of the Jordan's waters, go and stand in the river.'"

The priests carrying *the ark of the covenant* were to lead the march directly into the flooded river. As they waded into the shallow water at the edge, they were to *stand in the river.* The water would then vanish before them (v. 13). Verse 17 adds that the priests carrying the ark would then go to the middle of the river and remain standing there until all the people had crossed over.

C. For the People (vv. 9-13)

9Joshua said to the Israelites, "Come here and listen to the words of the LORD your God.

Joshua wanted *the Israelites* to *come* as close as they could so that all of them could hear him. He began by declaring that they must *listen to the words of the Lord,* not merely the words of Joshua.

10"This is how you will know that the living God is among you and that he will certainly drive out before you the Canaanites, Hittites, Hivites, Perizzites, Girgashites, Amorites and Jebusites.

Seven warlike peoples lived in the country west of the Jordan—the land that the Lord had promised to Israel. It would take courage to march into that country—more courage than the fathers of those Israelites had exhibited 38 years earlier. Intimidated by giants and high city walls, that previous generation had balked at the border of the promised land, refusing to capture the land God had given them.

Now, as the new generation of Israelites was gathered before the Jordan, the giants and the high city walls were still present. The seven peoples listed by Joshua were the same ones mentioned by Moses in Deuteronomy 7:1. The coming battle was not one for Israel to undertake alone. They would need *the living God* to be *among* them. Joshua proceeded to give the people a sign to prove that this was so.

> ¹¹"See, the ark of the covenant of the Lord of all the earth will go into the Jordan ahead of you.

The *ark of the covenant* was a symbol of God's presence and favor. It held the Ten Commandments engraved on enduring stone—the symbol of God's enduring and unchanging authority. He was leading the way into the flooded *Jordan* and into the battles beyond it. Israel could confidently follow without fear.

> ¹²"Now then, choose twelve men from the tribes of Israel, one from each tribe.

What these *twelve men* were to do is not described at this point, but it would be a part of the miracle that was soon to take place.

> ¹³"And as soon as the priests who carry the ark of the LORD—the Lord of all the earth—set foot in the Jordan, its waters flowing downstream will be cut off and stand up in a heap."

Now Joshua described the convincing sign promised in verse 10. The *priests* would wade into the *Jordan*, carrying *the ark of the Lord*. At the touch of their feet, the water in front of them would flow on down toward the Dead Sea; but the *waters* upstream would *be cut off and stand up in a heap*, forming a growing mountain of water somewhere to the north. In front of Israel would be a dry riverbed. The people would walk across it without getting their feet wet.

Can you imagine a more convincing proof of the presence and power of the Lord? The similarity of this miracle to the crossing of the Red Sea would assure the people that the Lord who had brought the previous generation safely out of Egypt would bring them safely into the promised land and allow them to possess it.

II. God's Actions (Joshua 3:14-17)
A. The Trusting Start (vv. 14, 15)

> ¹⁴So when the people broke camp to cross the Jordan, the priests carrying the ark of the covenant went ahead of them.

Slowly the huge caravan was formed. The *priests carrying the ark of the covenant* led the way. The *people* left their campsite and followed at a respectful distance (Joshua 3:4). All Israel *broke camp* and prepared to approach the flooded *Jordan*, though not one of them could possibly wade across it.

15Now the Jordan is at flood stage all during harvest. Yet as soon as the priests who carried the ark reached the Jordan and their feet touched the water's edge,

This was the crucial moment in the promised sign of God's presence and power. Once the priests' *feet touched the water's edge*, it was time for the miracle to begin (v. 13). The fact that the *Jordan is at flood stage all during harvest* is mentioned to underscore the magnificence of the sign.

B. The Opened Way (v. 16)

16. . . the water from upstream stopped flowing. It piled up in a heap a great distance away, at a town called Adam in the vicinity of Zarethan, while the water flowing down to the Sea of the Arabah (the Salt Sea) was completely cut off. So the people crossed over opposite Jericho.

What happened was so unusual and marvelous that it was hard to find words to describe it. Some details of the record are not clear, but the main facts are indisputable. The water *from upstream* simply *piled up in a heap*. That heap was upstream from Israel, of course, but it is hard to tell just where. The text describes the place as being *a great distance away, at a town called Adam in the vicinity of Zarethan.*

All of this would be somewhat less confusing if we knew where Adam and Zarethan were, but their exact locations are uncertain. The scene becomes more dramatic if we suppose that the people could see the waters rising swiftly into a mountain north of them, but the record does not make it clear whether the mound was in sight. At the same time, the waters right in front of Israel were *cut off*, or separated, and kept on flowing down toward the Dead Sea. (*The Sea of the Arabah* and *the Salt Sea* are two ancient names of the body of water we now call the Dead Sea. The term *Arabah* describes that part of the Jordan Valley that included the region around the Dead Sea.)

As a result of all of this, in front of the people of Israel was no water at all—only the empty bed of a river! Very easily the people *crossed over* that waterless ground, going straight toward the city of *Jericho*, which was just a few miles west of the river.

C. The Safe Arrival (v. 17)

17The priests who carried the ark of the covenant of the LORD stood firm on dry ground in the middle of the Jordan, while all Israel passed by until the whole nation had completed the crossing on dry ground.

Carrying *the ark of the covenant of the Lord*, the priests proceeded forward until they came to the middle of the dry riverbed. There the priests *stood firm* while *all Israel passed by* and went on to the west bank of the river. The ark was the symbol of God's presence and authority. Positioned there in the middle of the *dry ground*, it pictured God holding back the flooded Jordan while his people crossed to the other side.

When all the Israelites were gathered safely on the high ground west of the river, Joshua called to the priests; and they too finished crossing the river. Then the mountain of water came down with a rush, filling the wide channel, covering the banks, and spreading over the plain; but it did not reach the spot that Israel had chosen for a new campground. (See Joshua 4:15-18.)

What happened to the 12 men mentioned earlier in verse 12? Their work was not finished. They were to get 12 stones from the middle of the river and carry them to the west bank. There Joshua would build the stones into a monument in memory of the miraculous crossing (Joshua 4:1-7).

Over the course of many generations, that monument would be seen by travelers, including family groups who would eventually go to Jerusalem for the annual feasts. Parents would tell their children of the miraculous crossing, and those children would repeat the story years later to their children. That story would lead to others: the crossing of the Red Sea, the providing of manna in the desert, the miraculous supplying of water from dry rock, and the giving of the Ten Commandments from Sinai. Thus through many centuries this simple monument would help to perpetuate the knowledge of God's power and God's care for his people.

THE CONQUEST OF JERICHO (JOSHUA 6:1-5, 15-20)

Establishing the Groundwork

After the Israelites crossed the Jordan River through the Lord's miraculous provision, they set up camp at Gilgal, which is described as being "on the eastern border of Jericho" (Joshua 4:19). Archaeological discoveries of what is believed to be ancient Gilgal place it approximately two miles northeast of Jericho. Here four significant events occurred that helped solidify the preparation of Joshua and the Israelites for the conquest of Canaan that lay ahead.

1) All of the Israelite males were circumcised (Joshua 5:2). Why this covenant sign had not been administered when the males were eight days old as God had prescribed (Genesis 17:12) is not known. But it was vital that this matter be taken care of as the people prepared to receive the blessing of the land that God had promised in establishing his covenant with the patriarchs and their descendants.

2) The Passover was observed (Joshua 5:10). The day Israel crossed the Jordan River was the tenth day of the first month (Joshua 4:19). That was the very day when each family was to select a lamb to be eaten four days later as part of the first Passover feast (Exodus 12:1-8). Forty years after that first Passover, Israel celebrated its first Passover in the promised land.

3) The produce of the promised land was eaten, and the manna ceased (Joshua 5:11, 12). The day after the Passover was celebrated, the Israelites ate "unleavened bread and roasted grain" that had grown west of the Jordan. At that point, the manna was no longer provided for them. God would still be the source of their food, but not in the way he had been in sending the manna.

4) An individual described as the "commander of the army of the Lord" appeared to Joshua (Joshua 5:13-15). This may well have been an angel, perhaps similar to the one God had promised to guide the Israelites in Exodus 23:20-23. The individual had a drawn sword in his hand (Joshua 5:13), possibly indicating his preparedness to lead Joshua and the Israelites into battle. He commanded Joshua to remove his sandals because the place where Joshua was standing was holy (v. 15)—a command similar to the one Moses received at the burning bush (Exodus 3:5). Apparently this was another step in the process of preparing Joshua for his leadership role and assuring him that he would carry out the task originally given to Moses— taking the Israelites into Canaan.

Examining the Text

I. A Plan Outlined (Joshua 6:1-5)

In God's own time he gave the order for Israel to advance to battle. With the command he provided a battle plan. Joshua passed it on to the Israelites, and they obeyed—even though they must have been quite mystified. This was a strange plan for conquering a city.

A. Jericho's Apprehension (v. 1)

¹Now Jericho was tightly shut up because of the Israelites. No one went out and no one came in.

Before the Israelites crossed the Jordan, their two spies had learned that the people west of the river bank were terrified of them. People of that region had heard how Israel had crossed the Red Sea 40 years earlier, and how they had recently destroyed two nations east of the Jordan (Joshua 2:9-11).

The residents of *Jericho* must have panicked when another miracle brought the invaders across the Jordan, for it looked as if Jericho would be next.

The frightened inhabitants of Jericho took refuge in the city and kept the gates *tightly shut up* day and night. *No one went out and no one came in.* They could only hope that the city walls would keep them safe.

B. The Lord's Assurance (v. 2)

²Then the LORD said to Joshua, "See, I have delivered Jericho into your hands, along with its king and its fighting men.

Already *the Lord* had determined the outcome of the battle of *Jericho.* Both *its king and its fighting men* would be helpless before the onslaught of Israel. God had *delivered* them into Joshua's *hands.*

C. The People's Assignment (vv. 3-5)

³"March around the city once with all the armed men. Do this for six days.

Having assured the Israelites of victory, the Lord proceeded to outline how that victory was to be achieved. *For six days* no blow was to be struck, either against the walls of stone or against a human enemy. The *armed men* (the fighting men of Israel) were simply to *march around the city once.*

This reference to a specific group of Israelites *(the armed men)* makes it doubtful that all the Israelites marched around the city (which would have involved around two to three million people). Verses 9 and 13 tell us that the armed men along with a "rear guard" marched around Jericho. According to one estimate, ancient Jericho would have covered no more than four or five acres.

⁴"Have seven priests carry trumpets of rams' horns in front of the ark. On the seventh day, march around the city seven times, with the priests blowing the trumpets.

The *ark* of the covenant was to be carried in the great procession. To call attention to the ark, *seven priests* were to march in front of it, *blowing the trumpets* as they went. Perhaps the people of Jericho knew that it was the symbol of Israel's God—the God who had made the water of the Red Sea stand up like walls, and made the water of the Jordan pile up in a heap—or perhaps their pagan minds supposed that the ark actually was that God.

On the *seventh day*, that great procession would *march around the city seven times.* The frequency of the number *seven* in these instructions highlighted their sacred significance (*seven* often symbolizes completeness in the Bible).

What was the point of all this marching? God did not explain, but we may suppose that these actions served to create a sense of panic and foreboding within the residents of Jericho. Probably they would not sleep well at night, as they wondered about that army marching outside their walls each day. On the seventh day they would grow more apprehensive as the marching went on and on and on. By the time the walls came down, they would have been weakened by a week of fitful sleep and daily anxiety; so their defense was not what it might have been when the Israelite soldiers stormed the city.

Perhaps, too, it was a lesson to Israel. What good is marching around a walled city? None, if that is all there is. But when their marching was an act of obedience to God, it was extremely valuable. This method may have been chosen for the same reason God later chose to deliver Israel through Gideon and only three hundred men: "in order that Israel may not boast against me that her own strength has saved her" (Judges 7:2).

> [5]**"When you hear them sound a long blast on the trumpets, have all the people give a loud shout; then the wall of the city will collapse and the people will go up, every man straight in."**

We are not told what sound the trumpeters were making prior to the seventh circuit; but when that final round of the city was completed, they would *sound a long blast*. The marchers were to remain silent through the week (v. 10), but that long blast would be the signal for *all the people* to *give a loud shout*. Such a deafening roar would alarm the frightened defenders even more. Then, before any Israelite even came near it, *the city wall* would *collapse*. Panic would seize all in Jericho as *every man* among Israel's fighting men would charge over the fallen stones *straight in* to the city. Probably those men were numerous enough to reach all the way around small Jericho, so they could enter the city from all directions.

II. A Plan Obeyed (Joshua 6:15-20)

Verses 6-14 tell how God's battle plan was carried out for six days. The armed men led the way in marching around Jericho. Then came seven priests blowing their trumpets, followed by other priests carrying the ark of the covenant in the middle of the marching column. The rest of the armed men (or "rear guard") followed at the end. We now move to the events of the critical seventh day.

A. Circling the City (v. 15)

> [15]*On the seventh day, they got up at daybreak and marched around the city seven times in the same manner, except that on that day they circled the city seven times.*

We know the people of Jericho were afraid of the Israelites (Joshua 2:11). Their fears and anxiety must have escalated when the marchers did not stop after one circuit as they always had done before, but *marched around the city seven times.*

B. Claiming the City (vv. 16-20)

*¹⁶The seventh time around, when the priests sounded the trumpet blast, Joshua commanded the people, "Shout! For the L*ORD *has given you the city!*

Following the loud *trumpet blast* of the *priests, Joshua* repeated the command to *shout.* That shout was the Israelites' battle cry. When it was given, the wall would collapse and they would rush into the city (v. 5). Joshua assured the people, *The Lord has given you the city!* Victory would be quick and complete.

*¹⁷"The city and all that is in it are to be devoted to the L*ORD*. Only Rahab the prostitute and all who are with her in her house shall be spared, because she hid the spies we sent.*

Now came additional instructions concerning the treatment of *the city* once it was captured. Jericho and all the people, animals, and objects in it were to be *devoted to the Lord* and designated as his property. Just as the firstfruits of every harvest belonged to the Lord (Deuteronomy 26:1-4), so this first city taken from the pagans on the west bank was to be the Lord's.

In the case of Jericho, the setting apart was not so that these people and items could be used in God's service; it was so that they could be objects of his righteous judgment. The peoples living in the promised land were ripe for such judgment because of their idolatry and utter wickedness. Israel, in contrast, was to be "holy," or set apart, as God's obedient people. The difference between these two kinds of setting apart is clear from a study of Deuteronomy 7:1-6.

Verses 18 and 19 tell more about these instructions concerning Jericho, but the last part of verse 17 tells of an exception to the destruction. *Rahab* and her family were to be *spared* because she had saved the lives of Israel's *spies* when they went to Jericho (Joshua 2).

¹⁸"But keep away from the devoted things, so that you will not bring about your own destruction by taking any of them. Otherwise you will make the camp of Israel liable to destruction and bring trouble on it.

No one in Israel was to be enriched by any of the wealth of Jericho; all of it was the Lord's. Anyone who violated this order would be doomed to *destruction* along with the city. In addition, he would *bring trouble* upon the entire *camp of Israel*. Read Joshua 7 to see how this tragically came to pass when one man (Achan) ventured to steal some of the spoil of the city.

> *¹⁹"All the silver and gold and the articles of bronze and iron are sacred to the LORD and must go into his treasury."*

Every living thing in Jericho, human or animal, was to be killed (v. 21). The city was to be burned (v. 24), including the houses and their contents, in a huge sacrifice to the Lord. The metals that could not be destroyed by fire were to be put *into* the Lord's *treasury*.

Eventually other cities in the promised land would be conquered. Then the children of Israel would be permitted to live in the houses, eat the wheat and barley, use the animals, and collect the plunder (see, for example, Joshua 11:14). This first captured city, however, belonged to the Lord.

> *²⁰When the trumpets sounded, the people shouted, and at the sound of the trumpet, when the people gave a loud shout, the wall collapsed; so every man charged straight in, and they took the city.*

The plan of battle was carried out exactly as God had given it. *The trumpets sounded* a long blast, *the people shouted* at the top of their voices, the city *wall collapsed*, the men of Israel swarmed into Jericho from every side, *and they took the city*.

The citizens of Jericho had been demoralized already by a week of fear. The collapse of the wall must have brought them to utter despair. Women and children were killed along with the men. So were cattle, sheep, and donkeys (v. 21).

Many have wondered why God would permit and even command the kind of total destruction described in the account of the conquest of Canaan. To consider what occurred as the eradication of one people in order that God might give the land to another people is to see only one part of the picture. The conquest of Canaan must be seen also as an act of God's righteous judgment upon a wicked nation. The moral degeneracy of the various peoples who inhabited Canaan is almost without parallel. It was not for false religion alone that they were condemned, but for the nature of that religion. Its practice included the most disgusting brand of cruelty and unnatural crimes of the greatest depravity. (See Leviticus 18:20-24.) Their cup of iniquity was full and overflowing. God had been patient with them, telling Abraham that he had not yet judged these peoples because their sin had "not yet reached its full measure" (Genesis 15:16).

Two other observations may be included here. The first is that God used other peoples to judge his chosen people when they disobeyed him and refused to repent. The northern kingdom of Israel was conquered by the Assyrians, and the southern kingdom of Judah was brought under control by the Babylonians. Both of these peoples were pagan. However, God did not totally destroy his chosen people because to do so would have thwarted his plan to bring his chosen person (Jesus, the Messiah) into the world.

Another question often raised deals with the innocent children who died in this destruction. Why did they have to suffer in this way? This is a difficult question to answer adequately, but it may be suggested that in God's eyes it was far better for these children to die in their innocence and thus be taken into his presence than to grow up and die in sin.

JOSHUA'S FINAL CHALLENGE (JOSHUA 24:1, 14-24)

Establishing the Groundwork

The book of Joshua can be divided into two sections of twelve chapters each. The first twelve record the conquest of the promised land, and the last twelve tell how the land was allotted to the tribes of Israel. (See the map on page 32.) Joshua 13:1 begins with the description of Joshua as "old and well advanced in years." The verse also records God's message to him that there were still "very large areas of land to be taken over." It appears that Joshua's efforts, outlined in chapters 1–12, accomplished the defeat of various coalitions of kings that aligned themselves against Joshua and the Israelites. Each tribe then had the responsibility of conquering the portion of land that was assigned to it and driving out the inhabitants. In some cases the people succeeded, as illustrated by Caleb, who showed the same faith and enthusiasm in conquering a part of the promised land as he did when he had earlier encouraged the first generation of Israelites to trust God and enter the land (Numbers 13:30; 14:6-9; Joshua 14:6-15). Caleb even succeeded at passing that same faith on to his daughter, as Joshua 15:13-19 indicates. But in other instances, the Israelites were not able to complete the task given them, and as a result some of the pagan peoples continued to live alongside God's people (Joshua 15:63; 16:10).

Like his predecessor Moses, Joshua could not be expected to lead the Israelites forever. (Joshua 24:29 tells us that Joshua died at the age of 110.) Before his death, Joshua called the leaders of the people together for an assembly that is recorded at the beginning of Joshua 23. Joshua encouraged these leaders to be strong and obedient, much as the Lord had encouraged him (Joshua 1:6-9). There were also unmistakable warnings against disobedience.

Joshua 24 records another gathering—this one involving "all the tribes of Israel" (Joshua 24:1). Here, much as Moses his predecessor had done, Joshua renewed the Lord's covenant with them and challenged them to take their commitment to the Lord seriously.

Examining the Text

I. A Call to Choose (Joshua 24:1, 14, 15)

Shechem was an appropriate place for a national gathering such as this one. It was located near the center of Israel's territory, making it easier for people throughout the land to attend. In addition, Shechem had already played a significant part in Israel's history, as one of Abraham's first altars had been built there (Genesis 12:6, 7).

Shechem was situated in a narrow valley between Mount Gerizim and Mount Ebal, where Moses had commanded the people to gather and renew their commitment to obey God (Deuteronomy 27:9-13). Israel had gathered there earlier under Joshua's leadership to do this (Joshua 8:30-35). The rising terrain on either side of the valley provided a natural amphitheater.

A. A Choice for Everyone (v. 1)

¹Then Joshua assembled all the tribes of Israel at Shechem. He summoned the elders, leaders, judges and officials of Israel, and they presented themselves before God.

All the tribes of Israel, a huge throng, met *at Shechem.* An appeal was given to the prominent men of every tribe, clan, and family. Perhaps they came forward and stood with *Joshua* as he spoke. Thus they would show that they agreed with what he was saying. Previously he had consulted them and enlisted their support (Joshua 23:2). Together, then, *they presented themselves before God.*

B. The Right Choice (v. 14)

¹⁴"Now fear the LORD and serve him with all faithfulness. Throw away the gods your forefathers worshiped beyond the River and in Egypt, and serve the LORD.

In verses 2-13, we read that Joshua began his farewell address by giving the people a history lesson and summarizing what God had done for them to this point. Joshua reminded his hearers that God had faithfully helped

Abraham and his descendants and had brought them to this moment of triumph. Therefore these people ought to *fear* and *serve* him, not in mere form and ritual, but with with complete and exclusive *faithfulness.* To do that they would have to *throw away* idols of all kinds. The real God must be the only God in their minds and hearts.

The *River* in this verse is the Euphrates River. Abraham had come from Ur of the Chaldeans (Genesis 15:7), *beyond* (east of) the Euphrates in what we now call Iraq. In that land Abraham's *forefathers* had worshiped idols (Joshua 24:2). More recently the forefathers of the Israelites had lived in *Egypt,* a land of many false *gods.* Joshua urged that no worship or service should be given to any god but *the Lord,* the true God—the one who had blessed and helped Israel abundantly.

C. Wrong Choices (v. 15a)

¹⁵ᵃ"But if serving the LORD seems undesirable to you, then choose for your-selves this day whom you will serve, whether the gods your forefathers served beyond the River, or the gods of the Amorites, in whose land you are living.

Joshua realized that he could not compel his fellow Israelites to do what he was urging. To serve the Lord was costly. But they ought to remember that the Lord was the one who had helped and blessed them continually ever since the time of Abraham.

Here the word *Amorites* is a general name for all the hostile people who had lived in the promised land before the Israelites came. Not all of these peoples had been totally destroyed at this point, as God had commanded (Deuteronomy 7:1, 2). There was still the possibility that their *gods* could seduce the Lord's people.

D. Joshua's Choice (v. 15b)

¹⁵ᵇ"But as for me and my household, we will serve the LORD."

Joshua's mind was made up; his choice had been made, and he would never waver. Only *the Lord* is worthy of worship. Joshua announced that he and his family would *serve* him.

II. A Reasonable Choice (Joshua 24:16-18)
A. Israel's Response (v. 16)

¹⁶Then the people answered, "Far be it from us to forsake the LORD to serve other gods!

Vigorously *the people* declared their choice: they agreed with Joshua. They too would serve *the Lord.*

B. Israel's Reasoning (vv. 17, 18)

¹⁷"It was the Lord our God himself who brought us and our fathers up out of Egypt, from that land of slavery, and performed those great signs before our eyes. He protected us on our entire journey and among all the nations through which we traveled.

The people of Israel were indebted to the Lord for many blessings. They acknowledged all his deeds that had been mentioned earlier (vv. 5-11). Simple gratitude ought to lead them to give all their worship to the One who had done so much for them.

¹⁸"And the Lord drove out before us all the nations, including the Amorites, who lived in the land. We too will serve the Lord, because he is our God."

As noted under verse 15, *Amorites* is a general name for all the hostile peoples who had *lived in the land* of Canaan before the Israelites came. The Lord had given Israel victory over all of these. That was one more good reason for Israel to *serve the Lord.* It seems that there was no dissenting voice as the people expressed their desire to make the same choice that Joshua had made.

III. A Concluding Challenge (Joshua 24:19, 20)

The people made the right choice and gave sound reasons for making it. But no doubt wise old Joshua could see that they had made it too lightly, not realizing all it implied. Instead of praising their choice, he issued a strong challenge.

A. A Demanding Choice (v. 19)

¹⁹Joshua said to the people, "You are not able to serve the Lord. He is a holy God; he is a jealous God. He will not forgive your rebellion and your sins.

Joshua's response may seem at first like an effort to discourage the people. But his purpose was to remind them of the seriousness of what they were committing themselves to. They needed to understand clearly some important truths about the Lord.

God is *holy.* He is altogether good, separated from anything that is bad or even questionable. His word to the people was, "Be holy because I, the Lord your God, am holy" (Leviticus 19:2). Were the people of Israel ready for that? Are we?

God is *jealous.* He will not tolerate a rival in the minds and hearts of his people (Exodus 20:3-6). He wants their total devotion. Were the people of Israel ready for that? Are we?

God *will not forgive your rebellion and your sins.* That jolts us, and it must have jolted those who heard Joshua say it. The law describes several offerings to atone for sin and bring forgiveness (Leviticus 4:1–6:7). What could Joshua have meant?

Perhaps he meant that God will not forgive a person's sins if that one treats lightly the issue of sin in his or her life. God will not forgive one's transgressions while that one keeps on transgressing, thus showing that he prefers to do wrong rather than right. Were the people of Israel ready to serve so demanding a God? Are we?

B. A Dire Caution (v. 20)

²⁰*"If you forsake the L*ᴏʀᴅ *and serve foreign gods, he will turn and bring disaster on you and make an end of you, after he has been good to you."*

Joshua had used part of his address to review all the *good* that God had done for his people. But he would not always do them good, regardless of what they would do. They were promising to serve him. If they broke that promise, then he would do them harm instead of good—and it would be no trivial harm. God would *bring disaster on* them *and make an end of* them.

Were the people ready to pledge themselves to God under these conditions? Are we? It is easy even for "seasoned" Christians to become complacent in their dedication, to take for granted that "we all know and believe" certain truths. But our fervor can die down, our zeal can diminish, and our commitment can waver. Paul's warning to the Corinthians is one we must take to heart: "So, if you think you are standing firm, be careful that you don't fall!" (1 Corinthians 10:12).

IV. A Solemn Pledge (Joshua 24:21-24)

Too lightly, too easily the people of Israel had pledged to serve God (vv. 16-18). Joshua had made them stop and think. It was a demanding commitment, and failure to meet its demands would be tragic (vv. 19, 20). Were the people still ready to make that pledge?

A. Affirming the Pledge (v. 21)

²¹*But the people said to Joshua, "No! We will serve the L*ᴏʀᴅ*."*

Joshua had said, "You are not able to serve the Lord" (v. 19). To that the people responded, *No:* it is not so! They said, *We will serve the Lord.* They were pledging to meet all the demands of such service, to be holy and obedient to God.

B. Acting on the Pledge (vv. 22, 23)

*²²Then Joshua said, "You are witnesses against yourselves that you have chosen to serve the L*ORD.*"*

"Yes, we are witnesses," they replied.

Joshua knew how easy it was to affirm one's convictions in a public setting such as this. He also knew how easily such verbal commitments melt away in the face of opposition. He let his hearers know that their words would later come back to testify against them if they proved unfaithful to the Lord. Once more the people gave voice to their convictions, and in so doing they indicated that they were entering the covenant with eyes wide open.

²³"Now then," said Joshua, "throw away the foreign gods that are among you and yield your hearts to the Lord, the God of Israel."

Twice the people had promised to serve the Lord, to worship and obey him (vv. 18, 21). Now they had to demonstrate, immediately and tangibly, their sincerity about this promise. Joshua challenged them to get rid of any pagan *gods*, or idols, that they still possessed.

During their recent years of war, the Israelites had destroyed several towns in the promised land and taken the possessions of those towns as spoils. No doubt those spoils included some pagan idols. Also, the Israelites who had lived in Egypt had brought many items of value from that land (Exodus 12:35, 36). Perhaps some of the Egyptian idols were included. Every idol of any kind had to go, for the Lord said, "You shall have no other gods before me" (Exodus 20:3).

C. Reaffirming the Pledge (v. 24)

*²⁴And the people said to Joshua, "We will serve the L*ORD *our God and obey him."*

The *people* had made this pledge twice before (vv. 18, 21). Each time Joshua had responded by helping them understand what they were promising. Now, with a fuller understanding, they voiced their pledge the third time.

We sometimes speak of "mountaintop experiences"—those occasions when our consciousness of God is raised to a high level and we are emotionally stirred to take our commitment to God more seriously. But sooner or later we have to come down from the mountain into the valley, where we must face two daunting threats to our faith: the aggressive attacks of Satan and his cohorts on the one hand and the faith-dulling routine of everyday living on the other.

The Israelites were in much the same position as they were gathered before Joshua on this occasion. It was easy to declare good intentions in a setting where everyone was on the same side. That is the reason Joshua offered the stern challenges that we have seen in the verses just examined. Sadly, subsequent events would prove his concerns to be valid, as Israel fell into the spiritual chaos that typified the period of the judges.

How to Say It

ABRAHAM. *Ay*-bruh-ham.

ACHAN. *Ay*-kan.

AMORITES. *Am*-uh-rites.

ARABAH. *Ar*-uh-buh.

ARABIAN. Uh-*ray*-bee-un.

ASSYRIA. Uh-*sear*-ee-uh.

BABYLONIANS. Bab-ih-*low*-nee-unz.

CALEB. *Kay*-leb.

CANAAN. *Kay*-nun.

CHALDEANS. Kal-*dee*-unz.

CUNEIFORM. kyoo-*nee*-uh-form.

EBAL. *Ee*-bull.

EUPHRATES. You-*fray*-teez.

GERIZIM. *Gair*-ih-zeem or Guh-*rye*-zim.

GILGAL. *Gil*-gal (G as in *get*).

GIRGASHITES. *Gur*-guh-shites.

HIEROGLYPHIC. *high*-(uh)-ruh-*glih*-fik (strong accent on *glih*).

HITTITE. *Hit*-ites or *Hit*-tite.

HIVITES. *Hi*-vites.

HOSHEA. Ho-*shay*-uh.

JEBUSITES. *Jeb*-yuh-sites.

JERICHO. *Jair*-ih-co.

JETHRO. *Jeth*-ro.

JOSHUA. *Josh*-yew-uh.

LEBANON. *Leb*-uh-nun.

MANASSEH. Muh-*nass*-uh.

MEDITERRANEAN. *Med*-uh-tuh-*ray*-nee-un (strong accent on *ray*).

MESSIAH. Meh-*sigh*-uh.

MOAB. *Mo*-ab.

PATRIARCHS. *pay*-tree-arks.

PENTATEUCH. *Pen*-ta-teuk.

PERIZZITES. *Pair*-ih-zites.

REUBEN. *Roo*-ben.

SHECHEM. *Shee*-kem or *Shek*-em.

SINAI. *Sigh*-nye or *Sigh*-nay-eye.

SOLOMON. *Sol*-o-mun.

ZARETHAN. *Zair*-uh-than (*th* as in *thin*).

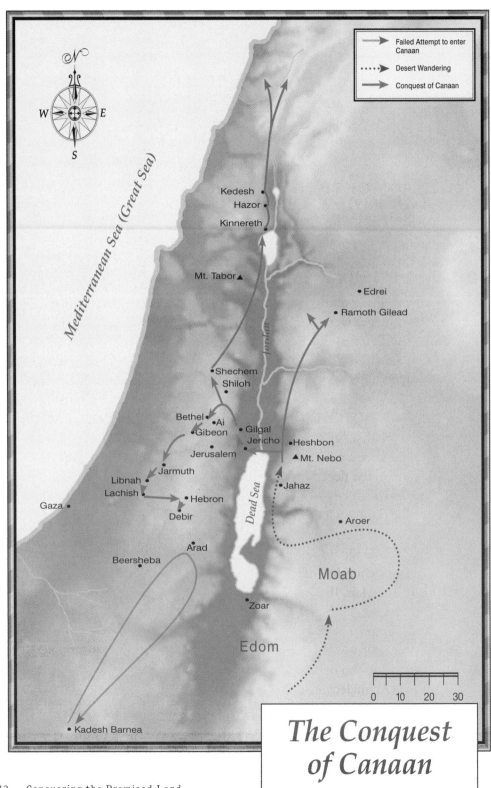

Failed Attempt to enter Canaan
Desert Wandering
Conquest of Canaan

N
W E
S

Mediterranean Sea (Great Sea)

Kedesh
Hazor
Kinnereth

Mt. Tabor

Jordan

Edrei

Ramoth Gilead

Shechem
Shiloh

Bethel
Ai
Gibeon
Jerusalem

Gilgal
Jericho

Heshbon
Mt. Nebo

Jarmuth
Libnah
Lachish
Hebron
Debir

Gaza

Dead Sea

Jahaz

Aroer

Arad
Beersheba

Moab

Zoar

Edom

0 10 20 30

Kadesh Barnea

The Conquest of Canaan

Chapter 2

Israel's Dark Ages:
Studies in Judges

Judges 2:11-19; 4:1-9, 14, 15; 6:11-14;
7:1-7, 20, 21; 16:4, 5, 16, 17, 19-22, 28-30

SUMMATION OF THE PERIOD OF THE JUDGES
(JUDGES 2:11-19)

Establishing the Groundwork

The book of Judges records the history of Israel from the time of Joshua's death until the time of Samuel, who guided Israel as it moved from living under judges to living under kings. The period of the judges covers (roughly) 1370-1070 BC. Judges were men and women who arose providentially during times when God's people were being invaded and oppressed by their pagan neighbors and delivered the people from their oppressors. In several cases the Bible records how these individuals were endowed with the Spirit of God in a special way (Judges 3:10; 6:34; 11:29; 13:24, 25; 14:6, 19; 15:14). However, even in cases where such power is not specifically mentioned, one may be assured that the Lord was still "with the judge" (Judges 2:18).

The judges were a colorful cast of characters, including the woman-warrior Deborah, the fleece-man Gideon, the left-handed assassin Ehud, and the well-known "superman" Samson. In all, 12 judges are mentioned by name in the book of Judges. They are often divided into two groups of six "major" judges and six "minor" judges, based on the amount of space given in the biblical record to describe their ministries. The major judges are Othniel, Ehud, Deborah, Gideon, Jephthah, and Samson. The minor judges are Shamgar, Tola, Jair, Ibzan, Elon, and Abdon. Eli and Samuel also served as judges (1 Samuel 4:18; 7:15) but are not included in the book of judges. (See the chart on page 38 for further information about the judges.)

Judges were not like kings in that there was no hereditary succession of judges. The one son of a judge who tried to succeed his father in this manner failed (Abimelech, son of Gideon, whose account is recorded in Judges 9). Furthermore, the judges of Israel did not function like kings by imposing taxes or negotiating treaties with other nations—functions frequently expected of kings. Israel's judges had no standing army but relied on the tribal leaders of Israel to provide men when military action was necessary. The judges did not have grand palaces or any of the other luxuries often associated with royalty. They may be considered as ordinary citizens empowered by God to carry out extraordinary responsibilities.

Chapter 2 of Judges gives a preview of the book and outlines a "vicious cycle" that was repeated many times in the period before Israel had a king. This cycle was tragically repetitive: apostasy led to crisis, which led to repentance, which led to deliverance, which faded back to apostasy. (The alliterative terms *sin, slavery, supplication,* and *salvation* may also be used to summarize this period.) The moral chaos of this period is captured in the final verse of the book: "In those days Israel had no king; everyone did as he saw fit" (Judges 21:25). And yet, we shall find within this dark and ugly period shafts of faith and mercy that penetrated the gloom like searchlights. It was indeed a time when "sin increased" but also a time when "grace increased all the more" (Romans 5:20).

Examining the Text

I. Israel's Apostasy (Judges 2:11-15)
A. Sin Described (vv. 11-13)

11Then the Israelites did evil in the eyes of the LORD and served the Baals.

"Baal" is a Hebrew word meaning "master" or "lord." The word *Baals* describes the various representations of the god Baal; for each town could have a Baal of its own, probably represented by a crude image in a shrine of some sort. While the myths about the god Baal may have differed from town to town, it was generally believed that Baal controlled the fertility of people, animals, and crops. As a result, Baal worshipers often engaged in "religious" prostitution in order to induce Baal to grant fertility to themselves or their farms.

Of course, the Baals had no Ten Commandments by which their followers should live. They did not teach people to be unselfish, helpful, kind, or forgiving. People who *served the Baals* naturally *did evil* more and more as they became more oblivious to the Lord and his ways. Such is the consequence of making God in man's image.

12They forsook the LORD, the God of their fathers, who had brought them out of Egypt. They followed and worshiped various gods of the peoples around them. They provoked the LORD to anger

Judges 1 tells that, in many cases, certain tribes of Israel failed to destroy the Canaanite inhabitants of the territories that had been allotted to them under Joshua. (God had clearly told them to do this, as Deuteronomy 7:1-5 states.) In the course of time, Israelites of the generations following Joshua's became acquainted with some of the pagans living near them. Perhaps those pagans did not seem to be as terrible as they had been reported to be. After all, they were farmers and shepherds just like the Israelites. Wouldn't it be better for all concerned to try to work together?

The problem was that the Israelites began to turn from the true God to the *various gods of the peoples around them*. As noted earlier, these gods had no moral standards. As the worship of them increased among the Israelites, so did all kinds of wrongdoing; and so did the anger of the Lord. He had warned the people of this very danger (Deuteronomy 7:4). Now his words were proving true.

13 . . . because they forsook him and served Baal and the Ashtoreths.

The *Ashtoreths* included imaginary goddesses that were associated with the various Baals (usually as their lovers). By serving such gods, the Israelites were violating the first Commandment: "You shall have no other gods before me" (Exodus 20:3), and the second: "You shall not make for yourself an idol" (v. 4). They needed a drastic "wake-up call."

B. Sin Disciplined (vv. 14, 15)

14In his anger against Israel the LORD handed them over to raiders who plundered them. He sold them to their enemies all around, whom they were no longer able to resist.

God's wake-up call came in the form of *raiders*, who originated from the pagan peoples nearby. They came to steal cattle, sheep, or grain as soon as it was threshed—and did not hesitate to kill anyone who was in their way. The peoples who posed the most significant threat to the Israelites are cited on the map on page 56.

In Joshua's time the army of Israel, with the help of God, had swept across the land, capturing cities and villages as it did so. But now the people of Israel had no such army. The men of the various tribes had settled in their towns and villages. They were not organized, trained, or equipped to resist these bands of raiders. Most significant, God no longer helped them; and for that reason, they *were no longer able to resist* their oppressors. That God *sold them* is a way of describing how he handed the Israelites over to *their enemies* as if they had been bought.

*15Whenever Israel went out to fight, the hand of the LORD was against them
to defeat them, just as he had sworn to them. They were in great distress.*

The hand of the Lord signifies God's power at work. We observed in the
previous chapter of studies how that power had allowed the Israelites to
cross the Jordan River (Joshua 4:23, 24). Now it worked *against them* to defeat
them. The bands of raiders were the weapon in God's hand to punish his
people. Such punishment was designed to prevent a far greater tragedy—the
people's continued descent into paganism and wickedness.

The Israelites could not claim that this punishment came without
warning. Plainly and in clearest detail the Lord had promised this very
punishment (and others) if the people disobeyed him (Deuteronomy 28:15-
68, especially v. 25). That promise was as certain as the promise of blessings
for obedience (Deuteronomy 28:1-14). This was no mere slap on the wrist;
the people *were in great distress*. But neither was it total rejection by the Lord;
his purpose was to turn the Israelites back to him.

II. The Lord's Answer (Judges 2:16-19)
A. Act of Deliverance (v. 16)

God's punishment accomplished its intended purpose: the distressed
Israelites realized that they had turned away from God. In their misery they
turned back to him and begged him for help. As we progress through the
book of Judges, we see this same plea to the Lord recorded again and again
(Judges 3:9, 15; 4:3; 6:6; 10:10, 15). The Lord's wondrous patience is seen
in his response to these cries, for each time he provided the deliverance for
which his people prayed.

*16Then the Lord raised up judges, who saved them out of the hands of these
raiders.*

How did God rescue his people from oppression when they turned to
him with cries for help? He *raised up judges*. A judge was a leader—one from
among the people—who rallied them to take a brave stand against the enemies
who were plundering them. Since the judge represented God's presence with
the people, their resistance was successful and their oppression ended. This
happened again and again over approximately 300 years (Judges 11:26).

B. Act of Defiance (v. 17)

*17Yet they would not listen to their judges but prostituted themselves to other
gods and worshiped them. Unlike their fathers, they quickly turned from the way
in which their fathers had walked, the way of obedience to the Lord's commands.*

When an enemy had been defeated and robbery and oppression were ended, the judge who had led the people to victory would urge them to keep living in obedience to God so that peace and prosperity would continue. But the people *would not listen*. All too soon they lapsed again into idolatry and sin. As an unfaithful wife turns away from a good husband to seek pleasure with other men, unfaithful Israel turned away from the true God and *prostituted themselves* to the *gods* of the pagans. In so doing, they violated their covenant as God's people just as an unfaithful spouse violates the sacred covenant of marriage. *Their fathers* (a term that included all of their faithful ancestors) had gone in the way of righteousness—*the way of obedience to the Lord's commands*. In contrast, *they quickly turned from the way*.

C. Repeated Deliverance and Defiance (vv. 18, 19)

18Whenever the LORD raised up a judge for them, he was with the judge and saved them out of the hands of their enemies as long as the judge lived; for the LORD had compassion on them as they groaned under those who oppressed and afflicted them.

What is told briefly in verses 16 and 17 is now repeated in more detail. It is something that happened repeatedly in the approximately three centuries that we call the time of the judges. *Whenever the Lord* provided a leader for the Israelites, their *enemies* were defeated. The result was that "the land had peace" (Judges 3:11; 3:30; 5:31) until the people strayed from God once again. According to this verse, the slide into idolatry and sin was not as swift as we might think from verse 17. The Lord *was with the judge . . . as long as the judge lived*. The influence of the judge kept the people obedient. Sometimes the "peace" he provided lasted for 40 years (Judges 3:11; 5:31; 8:28). In one case it lasted for 80 years (Judges 3:30).

19But when the judge died, the people returned to ways even more corrupt than those of their fathers, following other gods and serving and worshiping them. They refused to give up their evil practices and stubborn ways.

Peace, prosperity, and happiness might last forty years or eighty; however, *when the judge died* and when his influence no longer was present in the land, gradually *the people* began again to join in pagan worship. Incredibly and tragically, they engaged in practices *even more corrupt than those of their fathers*. Stubbornly they continued in such *evil practices* until God withdrew his protection and allowed an enemy to conquer them. It seems, however, that with each succeeding generation the spiritual conditions of Israel did not improve; if anything, they grew darker.

Judges of Israel

Judge	Major Oppressor	Years as Judge
Othniel (Judges 3:8-11)	Mesopotamia (Cushan-Rishathaim)	1373-1334 BC
Ehud (Judges 3:12-30)	Moabites (Eglon)	1319-1239 BC
Shamgar (Judges 3:31)	Philistines	1300 BC
Deborah (Judges 4, 5)	Canaanites (Jabin)	1239-1199 BC
Gideon (Judges 6-8)	Midianites	1192-1152 BC
Abimelech (Judges 9)	Period of Civil War	1152-1150 BC
Eli (1 Samuel 1-4)	Ammonites and Philistines	1150-1110 BC
Tola (Judges 10:1, 2)	Ammonites and Philistines	1149-1126 BC
Jair (Judges 10:3, 5)	Ammonites and Philistines	1126-1104 BC
Jephthah (Judges 10:6-12:7)	Ammonites	1112-1106 BC
Ibzan (Judges 12:8-10)	Philistines	1106-1099 BC
Elon (Judges 12:11, 12)	Philistines	1099-1089 BC
Abdon (Judges 12:13-15)	Philistines	1089-1081 BC
Samson (Judges 13-16)	Philistines	1110-1090 BC
Samuel (1 Samuel 7-10)	Philistines	1110-1050 BC

THE MINISTRY OF DEBORAH (JUDGES 4:1-9, 14, 15)

Establishing the Groundwork

Because of the abundance of godly men whose accounts fill the pages of the Old Testament, we can easily overlook the crucial and inspirational roles played by women in the history of Israel. At times we find them in supporting roles as mothers, sisters, and wives of important men. Consider Moses, whose leadership of God's people has already been highlighted. His life was influenced significantly by the efforts of both his mother (Jochebed) and his sister (Miriam). Exodus 2:1-10 relates the story of Jochebed's daring actions to save her baby from the Pharaoh's death edict. God providentially rewarded her by allowing her to keep her baby and nurse him before turning him over to the Egyptian princess.

Also involved in this incident was Moses' sister, Miriam. This brave young girl (the Bible does not indicate her age at this time) hid near her baby brother along the Nile River and had the presence of mind to suggest to Pharaoh's daughter her mother as a nurse. Later, Miriam played a key leadership role during the exodus. After the destruction of Pharaoh's army in the Red Sea, she led the women of Israel in a celebration of singing and dancing (Exodus 15:20, 21). In this passage she is referred to as a prophetess, although we have no record of her specific prophetic activities. Centuries later, the prophet Micah remembered the leaders of the exodus as three: Moses, Aaron, and Miriam (Micah 6:4).

Other prophetesses mentioned in the Bible besides Miriam include Huldah, in the days of King Josiah (2 Kings 22:11-20), and the four daughters of Philip the evangelist (Acts 21:8, 9). Another was the woman who is the subject of our next study from Judges: Deborah. Not only was this woman a prophetess (Judges 4:4) and a judge who settled disputes among the people (Judges 4:5), but she approached Barak and urged him to lead an army against Israel's oppressors. Such was the respect in which Deborah was held that Barak refused to go into battle unless she was present during the conflict.

Certain women in Old Testament history were involved with matters of state, both in a positive and a negative way. The beautiful queen Esther comes to mind as a positive influence, while the wicked queen Athaliah of Judah certainly belongs in the negative category. Yet no woman besides Deborah is said to have gone into battle along with men. She was an example of faith and courage to the people of her era. She remains an example of how gifted women, even in unusual and unfavorable circumstances, can accomplish great things when they are yielded to God and willing to use the special talents he has given them.

Examining the Text

I. Severe Oppression (Judges 4:1-3)
A. Its Cause (vv. 1, 2)

¹After Ehud died, the Israelites once again did evil in the eyes of the LORD.

Ehud was a judge of Israel prior to the time described in this passage. His efforts on behalf of God's people are told in Judges 3:12-30. As indicated in Judges 2:18, 19, Ehud's strong influence kept the nation faithful to God as long as he lived. But *after Ehud died,* there was no one of like faithfulness and influence to take his place. In time *the Israelites once again did evil in the eyes of the Lord.*

²So the LORD sold them into the hands of Jabin, a king of Canaan, who reigned in Hazor. The commander of his army was Sisera, who lived in Harosheth Haggoyim.

King Jabin's capital was located at *Hazor,* far north in Israel's land (approximately nine miles north of the Sea of Galilee; see the map on page 56) in the territory belonging to the tribe of Naphtali. This means that we should understand *Canaan* in this verse to include, not the entire promised land (sometimes referred to as the land of Canaan), but the northern region of Canaan where the Canaanites were particularly strong. That Jabin is described as *a king of Canaan* likely means that he ruled one of the city-states that were located within this northern region.

Apparently a large part of Jabin's army was stationed in *Harosheth,* located farther south in the plain of Jezreel. The troops there were commanded by *Sisera.* The word *Haggoyim,* which is attached to Harosheth, means "of the Gentiles" and may indicate that peoples of different nationalities lived there.

B. Its Continuance (v. 3)

³Because he had nine hundred iron chariots and had cruelly oppressed the Israelites for twenty years, they cried to the LORD for help.

With his impressive array of *iron chariots,* Sisera easily terrorized the farmers of the valley and took whatever share of their harvests and livestock he chose to demand. In the days when Joshua was leading and God was helping Israel, Joshua had promised two of the tribes a victory over the Canaanites in spite of their intimidating iron chariots (Joshua 17:17, 18). But now there was no godly leader like Joshua, and God was giving victory to Israel's enemies rather than to Israel. Thus the people of Israel did not have the capability to oppose those chariots. *They cried to the Lord for help*, but he left them in their distress *for twenty years*.

II. Surprising Developments (Judges 4:4-9)
A. Deborah's Introduction (vv. 4, 5)

⁴Deborah, a prophetess, the wife of Lappidoth, was leading Israel at that time.

Like the other judges, *Deborah* was not elected by the people or appointed by anyone. God raised her up to help his people, and that is the reason she *was leading Israel at that time*. Here she is also described as a *prophetess*. Thus Deborah was not only the only judge who was a woman, but also was one of only two who are described as having the gift of prophecy. (Samuel is the other; 1 Samuel 3:19, 20.) Under the influence of the Spirit of God with which she was blessed, she settled disputes and directed the people in God's ways.

⁵She held court under the Palm of Deborah between Ramah and Bethel in the hill country of Ephraim, and the Israelites came to her to have their disputes decided.

We cannot pinpoint the exact location of this palm tree, but it would have been somewhere in the hilly country near the middle of Israel's territory and within the land belonging to the tribe of Benjamin. The phrase *the hill country of Ephraim* came to designate a mountain range that ran through central Palestine and included territory (such as that of Benjamin) that was not allotted to the tribe of Ephraim. *Ramah* was about six miles north of Jerusalem, and *Bethel* was about five miles farther north. This location would have been approximately 80 miles from the place where the eventual battle with the Canaanites was fought. Thus, where Deborah *held court* was far enough away from the Canaanites' center of activity that she could do her work undisturbed by them. Here she regularly dispensed justice to those who *came to her to have their disputes decided*. Apparently this location became so familiar that it was known as *the Palm of Deborah*.

B. Deborah's Instructions (vv. 6, 7)

⁶She sent for Barak son of Abinoam from Kedesh in Naphtali and said to him, "The Lord, the God of Israel, commands you: 'Go, take with you ten thousand men of Naphtali and Zebulun and lead the way to Mount Tabor.

Barak lived in *Naphtali*, closer to the territory where the Canaanites were active. It appears that he came promptly when Deborah *sent for* him. When he arrived, Deborah first made it clear that she was giving him the message of *the Lord, the God of Israel*, not her own. God wanted Barak to assemble an army of *ten thousand men* from the neighboring tribes of *Naphtali* (Barak's own tribe) and *Zebulun*. He was to lead that army to *Mount Tabor*, a mountain (1,843 feet high) overlooking the valley of Jezreel. The Kishon River, mentioned in the next verse, flowed through that valley.

7"'I will lure Sisera, the commander of Jabin's army, with his chariots and his troops to the Kishon River and give him into your hands.'"

As mentioned in verse 2, *Jabin's army* was stationed at Harosheth, several miles to the west of Mount Tabor where the valley of Jezreel widened into a plain. The Lord promised to *lure* his army from that location and down the river to a point near Barak's position on Mount Tabor. *Sisera*, commander of that army, would bring his aforementioned 900 iron *chariots* (v. 3). Probably *his troops* included a large force of infantry that would accompany the chariots. The Lord planned to *give* those men *into* Barak's *hands*: that is, he promised victory to Barak and his army.

C. Deborah's Involvement (vv. 8, 9)

8Barak said to her, "If you go with me, I will go; but if you don't go with me, I won't go."

It is to Barak's credit that he recognized Deborah's credentials as someone who could convey the word of the Lord. He did not intend to be caught on Mount Tabor with 10,000 men and without God's guidance as to what to do next. If God's prophetess would not *go with* him on this mission, then he also would not *go*.

Still, there appears to have been some limitation in Barak's faith that he would set conditions on which he would obey what the Lord had commanded him to do (v. 6). As in the later case of Gideon and his fleece (Judges 6:36-40), it seems the Lord responded on the basis of the faith that was expressed in spite of the clear need to grow in that faith.

9"Very well," Deborah said, "I will go with you. But because of the way you are going about this, the honor will not be yours, for the Lord will hand Sisera over to a woman." So Deborah went with Barak to Kedesh.

Thus the leadership team was formed. God would be the commander; Deborah would convey his orders to Barak; Barak would command the army. However, Deborah warned Barak that he would not receive the primary credit for Israel's victory. That would be given to *a woman*. At this point in the story, we might expect Deborah to be that woman, but she would not be.

That heroine would be Jael, who enticed Sisera into her tent, then drove a tent peg into his head while he lay asleep (Judges 4:17-22).

Quickly Barak enlisted 10,000 men and led them to Mount Tabor, and "Deborah also went with him" (v. 10). Such a mobilization could not be kept secret, and Sisera soon learned about it (v. 12). To him it must have had all the appearances of an armed revolt among the Israelites. Sisera readied his chariots and infantry and set out from Harosheth to put the impudent rebels in their place. From his position on Mount Tabor, Barak and his men could see them coming.

III. Supernatural Deliverance (Judges 4:14, 15)
A. Deborah's Faith (v. 14a)

14aThen Deborah said to Barak, "Go! This is the day the LORD has given Sisera into your hands. Has not the LORD gone ahead of you?"

It is noteworthy that Deborah mentioned *the Lord* twice and *Sisera* only once. Sisera represented an imposing enemy, with his armies and his iron chariots. But the Lord represented the many deliverances and victories achieved in Israel's past and the present assurance of a victory that the prophetess of God said would belong to his people.

B. Barak's Action (v. 14b)

14bSo Barak went down Mount Tabor, followed by ten thousand men.

Encouraged by Deborah's assurance, Barak led his *ten thousand men* down the slope of *Mount Tabor* and across the valley floor to meet the chariots and infantry by the river. It should be noted that this strategy seemed to favor Sisera, for it allowed him to fight where his iron chariots could be used to their greatest advantage—in the level valley rather than on the slopes of the mountain. Perhaps Sisera anticipated an easy victory at little cost to himself or his men. The Lord, of course, had other plans.

C. Sisera's Defeat (v. 15)

15At Barak's advance, the LORD routed Sisera and all his chariots and army by the sword, and Sisera abandoned his chariot and fled on foot.

The Lord routed Sisera. For more about the Lord's action in this conflict, we can consult the song of victory in the next chapter of Judges. There we read that the Lord caused a spectacular cloudburst to come from the south (Judges 5:4, 5). Without being told all the details, we can imagine that such a rain would have produced a flash flood on the Kishon. Quickly the river would have come forth from its banks. The soft ground turned to mud; the chariots bogged down to their axles. The rising flood overwhelmed both horses and men, drowned them, and swept their dead bodies away (5:21).

Those men who managed to make their way to dry ground above the flood were met with the edge of *the sword*—10,000 vengeful swords in the hands of men smarting from 20 years of severe oppression. The Canaanites who did not die immediately raced back by the way they had come, but the men of Israel chased them all the way to Harosheth and killed every one of them (Judges 4:16).

GIDEON DEFEATS THE MIDIANITES (JUDGES 6:11-14; 7:1-7, 20, 21)

Establishing the Groundwork

Following the defeat of the Canaanites through the leadership of Deborah and Barak, "the land had peace forty years" (Judges 5:31). By the end of that time, most of the Israelites under 60 years old had no memory of the terrible oppression that had come because Israel had disobeyed God. They had not been involved in the momentous battle against the Canaanites. So the members of this new generation began their own path of disobedience. For that reason, for seven years the Lord "gave them into the hands of the Midianites" (Judges 6:1).

The Midianites were nomads from the deserts east and south of Israel. They crossed the Jordan in great numbers, bringing countless thousands of sheep and cattle to pasture on the young barley and wheat in Israel. Thus deprived of their harvests, the Israelites found it hard to survive. Desperately they "cried out to the Lord for help" (Judges 6:6). And once again, the Lord raised up a deliverer to rescue his people from their oppressors—an unlikely hero named Gideon.

Examining the Text

I. Recruiting a Leader (Judges 6:11-14)
A. An Angel's Assurance (vv. 11, 12)

11The angel of the Lord came and sat down under the oak in Ophrah that belonged to Joash the Abiezrite, where his son Gideon was threshing wheat in a winepress to keep it from the Midianites.

An *Abiezrite* was a member of one of the families of the tribe of Manasseh. *Ophrah* probably was located in the hills southeast of the plain of Jezreel, where Barak and the Israelites had routed the Canaanites. Here *Joash and his son Gideon* had been able to grow and harvest a little *wheat*. Gideon was secretly *threshing* some of it in order to provide food.

A *winepress* usually consisted of a pit cut into the limestone rock that was common throughout Israel. There grapes were trampled to crush the juice out of them for wine—only now the pit also served as a hiding place. No doubt Gideon was actually *in* the winepress—down in the pit and out of sight as much as possible, since the Midianites would steal his wheat if they saw it. As Gideon worked, *the angel of the Lord came and sat down under the oak* nearby.

12When the angel of the Lord appeared to Gideon, he said, "The Lord is with you, mighty warrior."

For Gideon to hear himself described as a *mighty warrior* must have sounded like cruel sarcasm. Some warrior—hiding in a winepress to thresh a bit of wheat! *The Lord is with you* must have sounded unbelievable, too. Gideon had an immediate response to that claim.

B. Gideon's Anxiety (v. 13)

13"But sir," Gideon replied, "if the Lord is with us, why has all this happened to us? Where are all his wonders that our fathers told us about when they said, 'Did not the Lord bring us up out of Egypt?' But now the Lord has abandoned us and put us into the hand of Midian."

The Lord had indeed brought the people of Israel *out of Egypt by* means of *his wonders*. Gideon, however, had seen no wonders in his own time. He was quite right in saying, *The Lord has . . . put us into the hand of Midian.* Judges 6:1 tells us exactly the same thing. But Gideon was wrong in saying, *The Lord has abandoned us.* The Lord had delivered his people to the Midianites to turn them away from idolatry and other sins and to bring them back to worshiping him alone and obeying his commands.

C. The Lord's Assignment (v. 14)

14The Lord turned to him and said, "Go in the strength you have and save Israel out of Midian's hand. Am I not sending you?"

Here, as in several places in the Old Testament, there appears to be no clear distinction between the angel of the Lord and the Lord himself. Someone has suggested that the angel was God "in one particular phase of his self-revelation." That seems to explain a concept that is difficult to understand fully.

Hiding in the winepress, Gideon must have wondered how he could have possessed any *strength* of his own. How could someone like him *save Israel?* His family was a poor one in its tribe, and he was the least in his family (v. 15). But the Lord had a ready answer for him: "I will be with you" (v. 16). The answer to Gideon's inquiry about God's wonders was simple: Gideon himself would become a "wonder," demonstrating God's power to use someone who saw himself as useless.

After some further convincing, and at God's command, Gideon began to display his might. He destroyed an altar used in the worship of the imaginary god Baal (vv. 25-27). Men of the city wanted to kill Gideon for destroying Baal's altar, but his father dissuaded them (vv. 28-32).

Events moved swiftly after that. The Midianites assembled in a huge camp in the valley of Jezreel (v. 33). Gideon called for volunteers, and men from his tribe and three others responded (vv. 34, 35).

II. Reducing an Army (Judges 7:1-7)
A. From 32,000 to 10,000 (vv. 1-3)

¹Early in the morning, Jerub-Baal (that is, Gideon) and all his men camped at the spring of Harod. The camp of Midian was north of them in the valley near the hill of Moreh.

Jerub-Baal was a nickname Gideon was given when he destroyed Baal's altar. When the people of the city came for Gideon, his father said, "Are you going to plead Baal's cause? Are you trying to save him? . . . If Baal really is a god, he can defend himself" (Judges 6:31). So from that day Gideon was also known as Jerub-Baal, meaning "let Baal plead" (v. 32).

Gideon and his men made their camp on an elevated area where *the spring of Harod* provided an ample water supply. Since this spring was located at the northern foot of Mount Gilboa, this is most likely where Gideon and his men were camped. From this position they could look down on the enemy camp *in the valley* that was *north* of them.

²The Lᴏʀᴅ said to Gideon, "You have too many men for me to deliver Midian into their hands. In order that Israel may not boast against me that her own strength has saved her,

The Lord explained why the army must be reduced in size. The battle must be won by a force so small that everyone would know without question that God had given the victory.

*3"... announce now to the people, 'Anyone who trembles with fear may
turn back and leave Mount Gilead.'" So twenty-two thousand men left,
while ten thousand remained.*

The proclamation went out through the camp of Israel: *anyone who trembles
with fear* may be excused. More than two-thirds of the men happily left *Mount
Gilead* (most likely another name for Mount Gilboa). Now Gideon had an
army of 10,000 men—the same number of men with which Barak had faced
Sisera at the Lord's command (Judges 4:6, 14).

B. From 10,000 to 300 (vv. 4-7)

*4But the LORD said to Gideon, "There are still too many men. Take them down
to the water, and I will sift them for you there. If I say, 'This one shall go with
you,' he shall go; but if I say, 'This one shall not go with you,' he shall not go."*

There were *still too many men* in Gideon's army to serve the Lord's
purpose. The number had to be reduced again. A small stream flowed from
the bigger spring near the camp. The men were to go down there for a drink,
and God would make known to Gideon which ones should be selected for
the coming battle.

*5, 6So Gideon took the men down to the water. There the LORD told him,
"Separate those who lap the water with their tongues like a dog from those
who kneel down to drink." Three hundred men lapped with their hands to
their mouths. All the rest got down on their knees to drink.*

There are different ways of drinking from a running stream. Some men
would *lap the water with their tongues like a dog*. This action is further explained in
verse 6. One man would cup the palm of his hand to dip a little water from
the stream; then he would lap it from his hand with his tongue. Another man,
however, would *kneel* on both knees and bend forward, bringing his lips to
the surface of the stream.

Some suggest that these ways of drinking showed something about the
attitudes of the men. The Israelites were camped in sight of the enemy, an
enemy that greatly outnumbered them. At any time that enemy might decide
to attack rather than wait to be attacked. A man who lifted a little water with
his hand showed himself to be more alert and watchful, and more concerned
about the possibility of sudden attack. In contrast, one who knelt and put
his face down to the water showed himself to be overconfident or careless,
unaware of the potential danger.

Others note that God's intention in assembling this army was to
highlight Israel's weakness rather than its strength. They call attention to

the comparison of the 300 to dogs. Dogs (with apologies to dog lovers) are one of the most despised creatures in the Bible. They are used to symbolize false teachers (Philippians 3:2), male prostitutes (Deuteronomy 23:18, with the footnote in the *New International Version*), and fools (Proverbs 26:11). By choosing individuals who acted like such an animal to carry out his mission, perhaps God was once again choosing "the weak things of the world to shame the strong" (1 Corinthians 1:27).

A third explanation suggests that the 300 men were neither better, more alert soldiers nor careless "dogs." The Lord simply chose the smaller group to show that it was his power and not theirs at work (v. 2). This explanation removes the emphasis from the men and puts it on the Lord.

> **7The Lord said to Gideon, "With the three hundred men that lapped I will save you and give the Midianites into your hands. Let all the other men go, each to his own place."**

At this point, let's try to imagine what the *Midianites* were thinking in their camp in the valley. They had seen 32,000 men of Israel gather on the hill above them. Then they had seen most of those Israelites go away. They must have wondered where all those men were going, and why. Were they planning to meet with other Israelites—thousands of them? Were they preparing to surround the camp of Midian with an overpowering army? When the number of men on the hillside shrank to *three hundred*, the thousands of Midianites possibly felt more uneasy rather than more secure.

That was confirmed when later, under cover of darkness, Gideon and an aide sneaked near the enemy camp and heard the men of Midian talking. They learned that the Midianites indeed were apprehensive, fearing a devastating attack by Gideon and his men (Judges 7:9-14).

Encouraged by this information, Gideon went back to his own camp to prepare to carry out God's plan. The Midianites were to be routed by clever strategy rather than by force of arms. Gideon divided his three hundred men into three groups. Each man lighted a torch but hid its flame in a clay jar. Each man also took a trumpet. The three groups crept away silently in the darkness to their assigned places.

III. Routing an Enemy (Judges 7:20, 21)
A. Battle Tactics (v. 20)

> **20The three companies blew the trumpets and smashed the jars. Grasping the torches in their left hands and holding in their right hands the trumpets they were to blow, they shouted, "A sword for the Lord and for Gideon!"**

Three hundred *torches* gleamed in the darkness. Three hundred breaking *jars* shattered the silence. Three hundred *trumpets* blared, and three hundred voices shouted the battle cry to let the Midianites know what was upon them: *"A sword for the Lord and for Gideon!"*

B. Beaten Throng (v. 21)

²¹While each man held his position around the camp, all the Midianites ran, crying out as they fled.

The men of Israel did not need to draw their swords and charge. *Each man held his position.* They waved their torches; they blew their trumpets; they shouted their battle cry—as they had been instructed to do.

In the dark camp of Midian, uneasy sleepers woke to the sound of 300 trumpets and looked out at 300 torches like a line of fire around them. The startled Midianites must have thought that countless thousands of angry Israelites were upon them. Panic-stricken, they *ran, crying out as they fled.* No one paused to light a lamp; no one took time to pack his belongings. Some did pick up their swords.

Charging out of their tents, the Midianites saw dark figures coming swiftly toward them. Swinging their swords in blind horror, they cut down their own comrades. In darkness and terror they ran screaming until they were out of breath and only faintly could hear the sound of the 300 trumpeters, each of whom remained steadfast in his place. With scarcely a pause for rest, the Midianites pushed on toward the Jordan River and their homeland to the east of it (v. 22).

The rout of Midian was under way. Probably those men who had left the camp of Israel earlier now returned to chase the fleeing enemies, and other men of Israel joined in the pursuit (v. 23). Men from the tribe of Ephraim were alerted to intercept the fugitives (vv. 24, 25). Gideon then led his troops across the Jordan and defeated the Midianite army that remained there (Judges 8:10-12).

SAMSON AND THE PHILISTINES
(JUDGES 16:4, 5, 16, 17, 19-22, 28-30)

Establishing the Groundwork

The account of Samson records yet another instance where the Lord used a pagan people to discipline his chosen people. On this occasion he delivered the Israelites into the hands of the Philistines, who lived along the southern Mediterranean coast. These oppressors harassed Israel, stealing the people's livestock and harvests for forty years (Judges 13:1).

Once more God set in motion a plan to rescue his people from their enemies. This plan, however, was quite different from what he had done in previous instances. He sent his angel to tell a childless couple that they would have a son who would be a Nazirite all his life. This meant that he would remain dedicated to the service of God. The sign of his dedication would be that his hair must never be cut. (Read more about the Nazirite vow in Numbers 6:1-21.) When the promised baby was born, he was named Samson (Judges 13:2-25).

As he grew to manhood, Samson began to demonstrate incredible strength. On one occasion, when a lion was about to attack him, Samson tore the beast apart with his bare hands (Judges 14:5, 6). In spite of Samson's failure to demonstrate a wisdom to match his strength, God repeatedly used his recklessness to punish the Philistines. During a conflict that followed Samson's marriage to a Philistine girl, he twice put to death some of the Philistines and once set fire to their ripened grain fields (Judges 14:10–15:8). When the Philistines came in great numbers to capture Samson, he picked up the jawbone of a donkey and killed 1000 more of them (Judges 15:9-20).

The record of Samson and his exploits is the longest of any of the judges, covering chapters 13–16 in the book of Judges. Some have suggested that what happened to Samson represents the failures of Israel as a nation. Samson had great strength but did not use it to its full potential because of his sinful behavior. In the same way, Israel had great potential as the chosen people of God; but the people often failed to live up to it because of their disobedience. Samson also had great difficulties in dealing with the pagan influence around him, and this was true of Israel as well. Instead of having the impact they were intended to have, God's people were all too often more influenced by their pagan surroundings than their pagan neighbors were influenced by them.

Examining the Text

I. Samson Seduced (Judges 16:4, 5, 16, 17)

It seems that Philistine women held a "fatal attraction" for Samson, but in the providence of God this proved fatal to his enemies. As noted above, when Samson married a Philistine girl, the resulting conflict brought death to Philistines, not Samson. When he visited another Philistine girl in Gaza, the Philistines shut and locked the gates of the city, planning to trap and kill him. But Samson simply pulled up the gates with the gateposts and carried them away (Judges 16:1-3). The following passage describes Samson's pivotal encounter with the infamous Delilah.

A. Evil Plot (vv. 4, 5)

⁴Some time later, he fell in love with a woman in the Valley of Sorek whose name was Delilah.

The Valley of Sorek extended from near Jerusalem to the Mediterranean Sea, about eight and a half miles south of Joppa. From the little that is told of *Delilah,* we suppose she was a Philistine woman of charming personality and pagan moral standards. Some students think Samson married her. Whether he did or not, it seems clear that he often came to spend time with her, but was away long enough to let the Philistines plot with her in his absence.

⁵The rulers of the Philistines went to her and said, "See if you can lure him into showing you the secret of his great strength and how we can overpower him so we may tie him up and subdue him. Each one of us will give you eleven hundred shekels of silver."

The phrase *rulers of the Philistines* describes the five men (Judges 3:3) who ruled the key cities situated in different parts of the Philistines' territory. They wanted to find out two things: what gave Samson his *great strength* and how that strength could be overcome.

Vengeful as they were, these angry men did not want to kill Samson. They wanted to *tie him up and subdue him:* they wanted to see him suffer in retaliation for all the suffering he had brought upon the Philistines. The bribe they offered Delilah totaled 5,500 *shekels of silver.* The fact that during the time of the judges someone could be hired at a salary of ten shekels a year (Judges 17:10) indicates the enormous sum that was being offered to Delilah. That the Philistine rulers were willing to pay it shows their determination to rid themselves of Samson.

It appears that Samson, despite his unruly behavior, was something of a joker and a creator of riddles (see Judges 14:10-14). Here he teased Delilah three times, pretending to reveal to her the secret of his strength. Delilah tried each way and found it would not work (Judges 16:6-15). Urged on by thoughts of a lucrative reward, she kept on trying.

B. Endless Nagging (v. 16)

16With such nagging she prodded him day after day until he was tired to death.

Delilah had reproached Samson for lying to her (vv. 10, 13) and had complained that he did not love her (v. 15). Now she resorted to ceaseless *nagging* until Samson could stand it no more.

C. Earnest Admission (v. 17)

17So he told her everything. "No razor has ever been used on my head," he said, "because I have been a Nazirite set apart to God since birth. If my head were shaved, my strength would leave me, and I would become as weak as any other man."

Finally Samson gave in. The phrase *told her everything* is literally, in the Hebrew text, "told her his heart." Samson explained to Delilah the simple truth: if his hair was cut, his tremendous *strength* would be gone. Three times this woman had revealed her purpose to turn Samson over to the enemy (vv. 6-14), and now he was letting her know how it could be done. How could he be so blind to her intentions?

Apparently Samson had become accustomed to irresistible power. It seems that he really could not imagine himself weak and powerless, even when he divulged how he could be reduced to that state. At the moment, he could think only of putting an end to Delilah's continual nagging. That was the part of Samson's character that constantly led him into trouble: his desire to live for the moment and satisfy the desires of the flesh.

II. Samson Subdued (Judges 16:19-22)

At last Delilah had the truth! Once more she sent word to the Philistine conspirators, confident that she could now deliver Samson into their hands (v. 18).

A. A Helpless Man (vv. 19-21)

19Having put him to sleep on her lap, she called a man to shave off the seven braids of his hair, and so began to subdue him. And his strength left him.

Now the woman displayed nothing but tender affection for her man. She stroked and soothed him until he fell asleep *on her lap*. There he lay undisturbed, oblivious to what proceeded to take place. Long and flowing, Samson's *hair* had been tied or woven into *seven braids*. *A man* was summoned to remove them all. Thus Delilah *began to subdue* Samson, for *his strength*, which had kept him from being subdued, *left him*.

²⁰*Then she called, "Samson, the Philistines are upon you!"*
He awoke from his sleep and thought, "I'll go out as before and shake
*myself free." But he did not know that the L*ORD *had left him.*

Samson expected to overcome his attackers as he had always done before, for *he did not know that the Lord had left him.* Samson's strength was not really from his hair; it was from the Lord (Judges 14:6, 19; 15:14, 15). Samson had been devoted to the Lord by his parents' vow before he was born. His uncut hair was the sign of that vow (Judges 13:3-5). When Samson recklessly let the sign be removed, the Lord departed. Samson was now "as weak as any other man" (v. 17).

²¹*Then the Philistines seized him, gouged out his eyes and took him down to*
Gaza. Binding him with bronze shackles, they set him to grinding in the prison.

Imagine the delight of the Philistines. Samson was in their power, and they lost no time in adding to his misery. First, they *gouged out his eyes*. Then they *took him down to Gaza,* one of their principal cities, and bound him *with bronze shackles.* While his superhuman power was gone; his human power seems to have remained rather extraordinary. Samson was put to work turning a heavy millstone in order to grind wheat for his captors' food—a task sometimes given to an ox or a donkey.

B. A Hopeful Man (v. 22)

²²*But the hair on his head began to grow again after it had been shaved.*

The sign of the vow was returning. Would Samson renew the vow itself? Would the Lord come back to him? Would Samson be strong again?

III. Samson Strengthened (Judges 16:28-30)

The capture of Samson called for a celebration. The Philistines gathered to rejoice and to give thanks to Dagon, their supposed god. When the hearts of the revelers were merry, Samson was brought from the prison to entertain them (vv. 23-25). We can only guess what cruelties were involved in this "entertainment."

It is hard for us to imagine the shape of the "temple" (v. 26) in which the celebration was held. Probably it was dedicated to the worship of Dagon, in whose honor the Philistines had assembled. Verse 27 tells us that about 3,000 people were gathered on the roof of the structure to watch Samson.

At some point Samson asked to be led to the pillars that supported the temple so that he could lean against them (v. 26). The stage was set for the final scene.

A. Samson's Plea (v. 28)

28Then Samson prayed to the LORD, "O Sovereign LORD, remember me. O God, please strengthen me just once more, and let me with one blow get revenge on the Philistines for my two eyes."

Blinded by his enemies and abused to amuse them, Samson thirsted for vengeance as he once had thirsted for water: *please strengthen me . . . and let me with one blow get revenge on the Philistines for my two eyes*. However, though Samson was making a request for himself, the vengeance that answered his prayer gave Israel freedom from Philistine oppression for some time.

B. God's Provision (vv. 29, 30)

29Then Samson reached toward the two central pillars on which the temple stood. Bracing himself against them, his right hand on the one and his left hand on the other,

As noted earlier, the design of this *temple* is not made clear to us in the biblical record. What is clear is that Samson was guided to *the two central pillars on which the temple stood*. The stability of the entire structure depended on those two. In some way Samson braced *himself against them*.

30 . . . Samson said, "Let me die with the Philistines!" Then he pushed with all his might, and down came the temple on the rulers and all the people in it. Thus he killed many more when he died than while he lived.

Blinded, imprisoned, and tormented, Samson no longer cared to live. He wanted only for the Philistines to *die*, too. In answer to Samson's prayer, God gave him the strength he needed. With one great final effort he pushed the two main pillars out of place, and the building came tumbling down. *Thus he killed many more when he died than while he lived.* The five *rulers* of the Philistines died in that catastrophe, and probably their subordinates as well. Eventually, however, the Philistines regained strength and again became a force capable of threatening Israel, which they did during the reigns of Saul and David.

The Bible adds a touching postlude in verse 31. Members of Samson's family came to dig his body from the rubble and take it home for an honored burial. More important, the inspired writer gives Samson an honored place in God's book. With all his faults and follies, this man is worthy of honor. Among the heroes of Israel he stands alone. In the New Testament, the writer of Hebrews cites Samson as an example of faith in action (Hebrews 11:32).

How to Say It

ABDON. *Ab*-dahn.

ABIEZRITE. *A*-by-*ez*-rite (strong accent on *ez*).

ABIMELECH. Uh-*bim*-eh-lek.

ASHTORETH. *Ash*-toe-reth.

ATHALIAH. Ath-uh-*lye*-uh.

BAAL. *Bay*-ul.

BARAK. *Bair*-uk.

CANAAN. *Kay*-nun.

DAGON. *Day*-gon.

DELILAH. Dih-*lye*-luh.

EHUD. *Ee*-hud.

ELON. *Ee*-lahn.

EPHRAIM. *Ee*-fray-im.

GIDEON. *Gid*-e-un (G as in *get*).

HAGGOYIM. Huh-*goy*-im.

HAROSHETH. Huh-*roe*-sheth.

HAZOR. *Hay*-zor.

HULDAH. *Hul*-duh.

IBZAN. *Ib*-zan.

JABIN. *Jay*-bin.

JEPHTHAH. *Jef*-thuh (*th* as in *thin*).

JEZREEL. *Jez*-ree-el or *Jez*-reel.

JOCHEBED. *Jock*-eh-bed.

JOPPA. *Jop*-uh.

JOSIAH. Jo-*sigh*-uh.

LAPPIDOTH. *Lap*-ih-doth.

MEDITERRANEAN. *Med*-uh-tuh-*ray*-nee-un (strong accent on *ray*).

MIRIAM. *Meer*-ee-um.

NAPHTALI. *Naf*-tuh-lye.

NAZIRITE. *Naz*-ih-rite.

OTHNIEL. *Oth*-ni-el.

PHARAOH. *Fair*-o or *Fay*-roe.

PHILISTINES. Fuh-*liss*-teens or *Fill*-us-teens.

SHAMGAR. *Sham*-gar.

SISERA. *Sis*-er-uh.

SOREK. *So*-rek.

TOLA. *Toe*-lah.

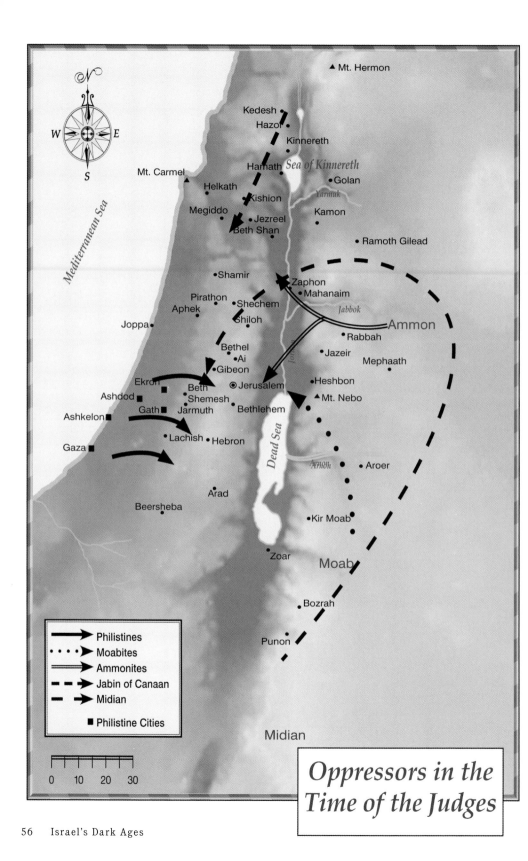

Oppressors in the
Time of the Judges

Chapter 3

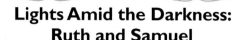

Lights Amid the Darkness:
Ruth and Samuel

Ruth 1:3-9, 14-18; 2:1-3, 8-12; 4:13-17;
1 Samuel 1:20, 24-28; 3:1-10, 19-21

RUTH'S LOYALTY TO NAOMI (RUTH 1:3-9, 14-18)

Establishing the Groundwork

The book of Ruth has been compared to a beautiful, delicate flower that emerges from the ground and survives amidst an abundance of worthless, unsightly weeds. Or one could think of it as a breath of fresh air, providing some relief from a smog-filled, polluted atmosphere. The first verse of the book gives us the setting: "in the days when the judges ruled." As we have already noted, these days were not part of Israel's "golden age"; rather, they were the time characterized by the far from flattering assessment that appears at the conclusion of the book of Judges: "In those days Israel had no king; everyone did as he saw fit" (Judges 21:25).

In contrast, the book of Ruth highlights the exemplary faith and devotion of a Moabite woman—an individual outside the "chosen nation" of Israel. Yet she demonstrated the kind of loyalty to the Lord that was sadly missing from God's own people at this time in their history. What Jesus said of a certain centurion could also be spoken of Ruth: "I have not found anyone in Israel with such great faith" (Matthew 8:10).

The author of the book of Ruth is not given anywhere in the text. A Jewish tradition names Samuel as the author, but that is only a suggestion. We can be certain that whoever he was, he was an individual "carried along by the Holy Spirit" (2 Peter 1:21).

Examining the Text

I. Family's Disasters (Ruth 1:3-5)

While the book of Ruth provides a welcome exception to the generally depressing tone of the book of Judges, it does not begin that way. The opening verse mentions a famine that had struck the land, a famine that became so severe as to cause a man named Elimelech to move his family from Bethlehem of Judah to Moab, a mountainous region east of the Dead Sea. This would have been a journey of 50 or 60 miles.

A. Death of Naomi's Husband (v. 3)

³Now Elimelech, Naomi's husband, died, and she was left with her two sons.

Sometime after the move (the exact time is not given in the text), a tragedy far worse than famine occurred: *Elimelech . . . died.* The text gives no details as to the cause. All we are given is the consequence of his passing: *Naomi,* Elimelech's widow, *was left with her two sons,* Mahlon and Kilion (v. 2). One can only imagine how devastated these three individuals felt. Perhaps they questioned the wisdom of their move and wished they had remained in Judah. Some Bible students today do as well, believing Elimelech's death (as that of his two sons, v. 5) was the result of divine judgment. Scripture is silent on the subject.

B. Death of Naomi's Sons (vv. 4, 5)

⁴They married Moabite women, one named Orpah and the other Ruth. After they had lived there about ten years,

Whether or not the family discussed returning to Judah after Elimelech's death is not known. Mahlon and Kilion took wives from the women of Moab. That these two Israelite men *married Moabite women* may seem questionable in light of earlier restrictions given in the law of Moses regarding the marriage of foreigners (see Deuteronomy 7:1-4). But marriage with Moabites was not specifically forbidden in the law. The only restriction involving Moabites is found in Deuteronomy 23:3: "No Ammonite or Moabite or any of his descendants may enter the assembly of the Lord, even down to the tenth generation." Certainly there was a kind of stigma attached to the Moabites, part of it perhaps stemming from the rather sordid account of their origin (Genesis 19:30-38).

Apparently there was not yet any relief from the famine in Judah, so Mahlon, Kilion, and their wives, along with Naomi, dwelt in Moab *about ten years.* Exactly when in the ten-year stay Mahlon and Kilion married is not stated. That neither had any children suggests they married only late in that period. Perhaps they had assumed their stay would be temporary and planned to marry after they returned to Judah. But as the famine dragged on, they gave up hope of returning. Kilion married a woman named *Orpah,* while Mahlon married a woman named *Ruth* (Ruth 4:10).

5 *. . . both Mahlon and Kilion also died, and Naomi was left without her two sons and her husband.*

After the ten-year period mentioned in verse 4 passed, *Mahlon and Kilion also died.* While Ruth and Orpah no doubt grieved over their respective losses, the deaths of these two men constituted an especially crushing blow to Naomi. Again, she *was left* (as in verse 3)—only now she was left *without her two sons and her husband.*

Naomi was thus both widowed and childless, a doubly disastrous condition in the ancient world. The first situation left her vulnerable to being taken advantage of—a problem that had not improved by Jesus' day (Luke 20:46, 47) and is still evident at times in today's society. The second situation left Naomi in a position that carried with it a sense of dishonor or disgrace. (Note that when the long-time barren Elizabeth became pregnant, she said, "The Lord . . . has taken away my disgrace"; Luke 1:25.) Naomi had no sons and thus no means of continuing the family line of her husband Elimelech. In a sense, she had lost her identity.

II. Naomi's Decision (Ruth 1:6-9)

Once more one can only surmise the barrage of questions and doubts that flooded Naomi's mind following the deaths of her sons. Why did her family leave Judah to begin with? Was all of this a punishment from God for leaving the promised land and residing with foreigners? Was it only a matter of time until Naomi herself died?

A. Concerning Her Dwelling (vv. 6, 7)

6 *When she heard in Moab that the Lord had come to the aid of his people by providing food for them, Naomi and her daughters-in-law prepared to return home from there.*

Eventually news arrived from back home—good news, for a change. For the first time in the book of Ruth, *the Lord* is mentioned, perhaps an indication that Naomi's plight would begin to improve (though slowly at first). Specifically, the Lord had *come to the aid of his people by providing food for them.* The famine was over.

7 *With her two daughters-in-law she left the place where she had been living and set out on the road that would take them back to the land of Judah.*

The picture set forth in this verse is a touching one. Here were three women united by the common bond of tragedy. All three had lost their husbands. Perhaps they determined, at first, that they would try to survive together in Naomi's homeland of *Judah*. Certainly there was something to be said for such companionship; people who have gone through a similar tragedy or crisis can often lend encouragement to one another by forming a kind of "support group."

B. Concerning Her Daughters-in-law (vv. 8, 9)

⁸Then Naomi said to her two daughters-in-law, "Go back, each of you, to your mother's home. May the Lᴏʀᴅ show kindness to you, as you have shown to your dead and to me.

At some point Naomi seemed to realize that it was really not in the best interest of her *daughters-in-law* for them to travel to Judah with her. They would be much more apt to find husbands (and therefore security) in their homeland of Moab. So Naomi urged them to return, each to her *mother's home*. In some instances in the ancient Near East, the mother's house seems to have served as a kind of bridal chamber. Genesis 24:67 tells how Isaac brought Rebekah to the tent of his mother, Sarah.

Naomi concluded her plea to her daughters-in-law with a blessing: *May the Lord show kindness to you, as you have shown to your dead and to me.* Naomi thus committed these two women, though they were Moabites, to the Lord's care. Her words reflected her desire that the Lord would reward them for being so kind to her during the tragedies that had befallen them all. She knew that they had already made a genuine sacrifice by being willing to come with her this far.

⁹"May the Lᴏʀᴅ grant that each of you will find rest in the home of another husband."
Then she kissed them and they wept aloud.

Again, Naomi expressed her wish that *the Lord* would provide each of her daughters-in-law with *rest* by allowing each to settle down in Moab with a *husband*. The concept of rest included the sense of security and well-being that would be missing from their lives if they remained widows.

From a practical standpoint, Naomi's advice was sound. Actually carrying it out was another matter entirely. The bonds that had been forged from the tears of grief and sorrow were not easy to break. Now came new tears as the three women prepared to part company.

III. Ruth's Decision (Ruth 1:14-18)

Verses 10-13 tell how Ruth and Orpah both voiced their loyalty to Naomi and stated their desire to accompany her to Judah. Naomi then tried to persuade the two of them to look at their situation realistically. She herself had nothing to offer Ruth and Orpah in the way of providing the "rest" mentioned in verse 9. Naomi's advanced age made childbearing an impossibility for her. Even if through some means she was able to become pregnant and bear sons, it did not make sense for Ruth and Orpah to wait until these sons became old enough to marry. It was far better for both of the younger women to resettle in Moab.

Naomi concluded her appeal by declaring, "The Lord's hand has gone out against me!" (v. 13). From her viewpoint, her current situation appeared hopeless. She had resigned herself to the fact that the Lord had determined to bring disaster upon her.

Yet it is out of such seemingly hopeless scenarios that the Lord often does his greatest work. In his time his hand would provide abundant blessings to Naomi. That thought, however, gave no comfort to her at this particular moment. In fact, it was the farthest thought from her mind.

A. Naomi's Plea (vv. 14, 15)

14At this they wept again. Then Orpah kissed her mother-in-law good-by, but Ruth clung to her.

Naomi's counsel to the daughters-in-law made perfect sense, but that did not make it any easier to obey. More weeping followed. Finally, *Orpah* decided to bid farewell and *kissed her mother-in-law* one last time. *Ruth,* however, refused to do so. She *clung to* Naomi.

15"Look," said Naomi, "your sister-in-law is going back to her people and her gods. Go back with her."

By mentioning that Orpah was *going back* to both *her people and her gods,* Naomi highlighted two crucial marks of a person's identity in the ancient world. Was Ruth really willing to sever ties with these?

The Hebrew word here translated "gods" is *Elohim.* Though it is actually a plural form in Hebrew, it is also one of the primary names in the Old Testament for the one true God. The Moabites worshiped many gods, including a chief god known as Chemosh (1 Kings 11:7). In 2 Kings 3:26, 27 the king of Moab sacrificed his firstborn son (apparently to Chemosh) in an effort to turn the tide of a battle with the Israelites in his favor.

Perhaps Naomi's plea reflected her earlier lament in verse 13: "The Lord's hand has gone out against me." Was she expressing her own frustration with the Lord by encouraging Ruth to go back to the gods of her homeland?

B. Ruth's Pledge (vv. 16-18)

16But Ruth replied, "Don't urge me to leave you or to turn back from you. Where you go I will go, and where you stay I will stay. Your people will be my people and your God my God.

If Naomi was determined that her daughters-in-law return to Moab, Ruth was even more determined to travel on to Judah with Naomi. She told Naomi that she may as well "save her breath," because Ruth had her mind made up. For her, there was no turning back.

Ruth's statement of devotion in this verse may be considered a kind of "Good Confession" from the Old Testament point of view. She was expressing a firm decision to break ties with the two primary sources of her identity: her *people* and her gods. No longer would she see herself as a Moabite; she would be an Israelite. No longer would she honor Chemosh, whose worship included the sacrifice of children; she would worship the *God* of Israel through the "sacrifice" of her heart and mind. Note that in spite of Naomi's claim that the hand of her God had gone out against her (v. 13), Ruth was still willing to acknowledge him as her God!

17"Where you die I will die, and there I will be buried. May the LORD deal with me, be it ever so severely, if anything but death separates you and me."

The words *Where you die, I will die, and there I will be buried* reflect the uncompromising commitment that Ruth was making. One's place of burial testified to one's sense of identity and belonging. Thus Joseph, just before he died in Egypt, requested that his bones be carried from Egypt to Canaan when the Lord delivered his people from bondage there (Genesis 50:24, 25). In the same way, Joseph's father Jacob had insisted that Joseph not bury him in Egypt, but in "the cave in the field of Machpelah, near Mamre in Canaan" (Genesis 47:29-31; 49:29, 30).

Although Ruth had been unquestionably clear in her statement of loyalty, she concluded her words with an oath, using the name of Naomi's God: *May the Lord deal with me, be it ever so severely, if anything but death separates you and me.* Her pledge could be considered the equivalent of the phrase "till death do us part" in modern marriage vows. Ruth was making herself accountable to the Lord himself. If she should in any way break the promise of loyalty she was voicing to Naomi, she would be willing to pay whatever consequences the Lord would determine.

18When Naomi realized that Ruth was determined to go with her, she stopped urging her.

What could Naomi say in rebuttal to such a thorough declaration of devotion? Similar to Jesus, who "resolutely set out for Jerusalem" (Luke 9:51), Ruth *was determined to go with* Naomi. Naomi knew that there was nothing she could do to dissuade Ruth from her intentions, so *she stopped urging her.*

BOAZ'S KINDNESS TO RUTH (RUTH 2:1-3, 8-12; 4:13-17)

Establishing the Groundwork

Following Ruth's passionate declaration of her intent to accompany Naomi back to her homeland in Judah, the two women journeyed on to Bethlehem. A rather "odd couple," they both faced a future of uncertainty: Naomi, bereft of her husband and her sons, and Ruth, a young widow and a stranger in a foreign land, perhaps apprehensive of her reception by the citizens of Bethlehem. Upon their arrival, Naomi voiced her frustration to the women of Bethlehem, telling them, "The Lord has afflicted me; the Almighty has brought misfortune upon me" (Ruth 1:21). But "the barley harvest was beginning" (Ruth 1:22), and that time of harvest would become, in God's providence, the beginning of the end of Naomi's "misfortune."

Examining the Text

I. Ruth's Request (Ruth 2:1-3)
A. Relative Introduced (v. 1)

¹Now Naomi had a relative on her husband's side, from the clan of Elimelech, a man of standing, whose name was Boaz.

Boaz is the fourth man introduced in the book of Ruth. (The first three, *Elimelech* and his two sons, died in Moab.) The description of Boaz indicates that he was respected, wealthy, and (of particular significance) related to the family of *Elimelech*. While the term *relative* is used in this verse to describe Boaz, later in the book of Ruth a special expression is used, in both noun and verb forms, to describe the relationship of Boaz to Naomi and Ruth. That term is translated in the *New International Version* as "kinsman-redeemer." In Israelite society, this individual had the responsibility to care for his extended family, particularly the poor, the widows, and the orphans. In addition, he was responsible for buying back any land that had passed from the family's possession (Leviticus 25:25-28). Boaz's duty toward Naomi and Ruth will become more significant as the account unfolds.

B. Request Made (v. 2)

²And Ruth the Moabitess said to Naomi, "Let me go to the fields and pick up the leftover grain behind anyone in whose eyes I find favor."
Naomi said to her, "Go ahead, my daughter."

The Lord's plan for assisting the poor in Israel resembled what some today call "workfare." Reapers were to leave the edges of the *fields* unharvested, and they could not pick up any *grain* that they had dropped. These were to be left so that "the poor and the alien" could have something to gather (Leviticus 19:9, 10; 23:22). Ruth fit both of these categories, and she apparently knew (perhaps as a result of conversations with Naomi as they traveled to Bethlehem) about this special arrangement. The note that Ruth was *the Moabitess* emphasizes her status as a stranger. With that observation, this fact also puts Boaz in a favorable light: he showed kindness to Ruth in spite of the fact that she was not a native Israelite.

That Ruth took the initiative in going into the fields is commendable. She was willing to work in order to put food on the table for her mother-in-law and herself. Before going, however, she respectfully sought permission for what she proposed to do. As noted earlier, the leftover grain would have been barley (Ruth 1:22), which was harvested during our months of March and April.

C. Reaping Begins (v. 3)

³So she went out and began to glean in the fields behind the harvesters. As it turned out, she found herself working in a field belonging to Boaz, who was from the clan of Elimelech.

All of us would do well to reflect on events of the past that seemed coincidental at the time but were used of God in a special way to provide the people or the circumstances that became a pivotal part of our lives. Often some time must pass (in some cases, even years) before we become aware, like Joseph, that God meant certain circumstances for good (Genesis 50:20). That is the case in this narrative; a reminder is provided that Boaz was related to Ruth's deceased father-in-law, *Elimelech*, but the significance of this connection will become apparent only later.

II. Ruth's Recognition (Ruth 2:8-12)

After Ruth had begun gleaning in Boaz's field, Boaz himself came from Bethlehem and greeted the workers cordially. (This is another example of God's providence at work in these events.) Noticing Ruth, Boaz inquired of his foreman as to who she was. The foreman identified her as "the Moabitess who came back from Moab with Naomi" (v. 6). He also noted that she had worked very hard all day and had taken only a brief rest (v. 7). Boaz then approached Ruth and spoke to her. His kindness to her at this first meeting was based on the fact that he had already heard about Ruth's kindness to Naomi (v. 11).

A. Boaz's Compassion (vv. 8, 9)

8So Boaz said to Ruth, "My daughter, listen to me. Don't go and glean in another field and don't go away from here. Stay here with my servant girls.

Boaz addressed Ruth as *My daughter*, which is usually understood to mean that he was older than Ruth. His kindness compelled him to give special considerations to her in order to make her situation easier: she was not to *go and glean in another field*; she was to *stay* close to his own *servant girls*.

Some have suggested that the women in a harvest crew were the ones who tied the stalks of grain that the men had cut. Those such as Ruth who gleaned the leftover grain would follow the harvesting crew as it moved from field to field.

9"Watch the field where the men are harvesting, and follow along after the girls. I have told the men not to touch you. And whenever you are thirsty, go and get a drink from the water jars the men have filled."

Boaz expanded his gracious provisions toward Ruth. He encouraged her not to go to any other fields except those where his servant girls were working. The *men* who were working were charged *not to touch* Ruth, which meant that they should not harm her in any way. The fact that she was a foreigner and had no husband made her more vulnerable to such treatment. Boaz's final provision was that Ruth could satisfy her thirst from the *water jars* that the other workers had brought with them. She would not have to be burdened with bringing her own supply of water. Boaz was thus practicing what his descendant, Jesus, would later advocate: the principle of going the second mile or doing more than is required (Matthew 5:41). The Mosaic law required only that the edges of the field be left unharvested and that dropped stalks of grain not be picked up by the reapers.

B. Ruth's Gratitude (v. 10)

10At this, she bowed down with her face to the ground. She exclaimed, "Why have I found such favor in your eyes that you notice me—a foreigner?"

When Ruth left Naomi that morning, there was probably some uncertainty in her mind about how the events of the day would unfold. Now the kindness of Boaz overwhelmed Ruth: a place to glean, water, and the promise of safety. She responded in the manner that is still typical in that region: she fell to her knees and touched her *face to the ground*.

Not only was Ruth moved by this unexpected kindness, but she also wanted to know *why* she was the object of *such favor*. Such treatment was not what she expected, for she was aware that she was a *foreigner* in Judah.

C. Boaz's Blessing (vv. 11, 12)

11*Boaz replied, "I've been told all about what you have done for your mother-in-law since the death of your husband—how you left your father and mother and your homeland and came to live with a people you did not know before.*

Boaz's answer indicated that he was aware of recent events in his community. Someone had informed him fully concerning Ruth's decision to leave her *father and mother* and the land of her birth to become part of a *people* with whom she had had little if any prior contact. It takes a special faith and courage to leave behind the things and people that are a part of one's identity in order to take on what amounts to a new identity. Ruth's commitment is reminiscent of that of Abraham, whom God instructed to move to a distant land (Genesis 12:1).

12*"May the Lord repay you for what you have done. May you be richly rewarded by the Lord, the God of Israel, under whose wings you have come to take refuge."*

Boaz then included a formal blessing that he pronounced in the name of *the Lord*—the God whom Ruth had chosen to accept as her own (Ruth 1:16). Boaz desired that Ruth would *be richly rewarded* for all she had done. The final phrase in this verse emphasizes Ruth's decision to leave behind the god of her Moabite upbringing and to cast herself upon the Lord. Boaz used a particularly striking word picture—a young bird's taking *refuge* by placing itself *under* the *wings* of its mother. This symbol is found in the book of Psalms (Psalms 36:7; 63:7; 91:4), and it was used by Jesus when he wept over the city of Jerusalem not long before his crucifixion (Matthew 23:37).

III. Ruth's Reward (Ruth 4:13-17)

The remainder of Ruth 2 tells how Ruth's gleaning continued through barley harvest and into wheat harvest (v. 23), which occurred during our months of May and June. Chapter 3 then records how Naomi re-entered the picture as a "matchmaker." She intended to find a husband for Ruth (v. 1).

She gave instructions to Ruth on how she should propose to Boaz, whom she described as "a kinsman of ours" (v. 2).

Behind this plan for marriage was a command of God in the law of Moses that the brother of a man who had died childless was to marry the deceased man's widow and raise up children for him (Deuteronomy 25:5-10). In the case of Ruth, since there was no brother of the deceased for her to marry, it was the kinsman's or kinsman-redeemer's duty to assume this responsibility.

Ruth did propose to Boaz, and Boaz responded in an appropriate way. He was aware that there was a "kinsman" or "kinsman-redeemer" who was more closely related than he (Ruth 3:12), and that that person should be given first choice concerning Ruth. (Boaz's tact and consideration in this sensitive matter are in keeping with his character as seen throughout the book of Ruth.) The closer relative, however, chose not to marry Ruth (Ruth 4:5, 6). Boaz was then free to purchase all that belonged to Elimelech (Naomi's late husband), which included his land and the responsibility to marry Ruth, the widow of one of Elimelech's sons. Ruth 4:7-12 describes the procedure that was followed to make this transfer of responsibility official before those gathered as witnesses.

A. Boaz's and Ruth's Son (v. 13)

13So Boaz took Ruth and she became his wife. Then he went to her, and the Lord enabled her to conceive, and she gave birth to a son.

The verse before us is very simple. Left unmentioned are the emotions that must have been experienced by Naomi, Ruth (who apparently had no children from her former marriage), and Boaz. Most important is the statement that the conception of Boaz and Ruth's child (*a son*) was of *the Lord*.

B. The Women's Blessing (vv. 14, 15)

14The women said to Naomi: "Praise be to the Lord, who this day has not left you without a kinsman-redeemer. May he become famous throughout Israel!

Most likely the *women* of Bethlehem recalled the statement that Naomi made when she returned from Moab: she requested to be called Mara (meaning "bitter"), not Naomi (meaning "pleasant"). She added that she had left Bethlehem "full," but the Lord had brought her back "empty" (Ruth 1:20, 21). This praise to God from the women noted that he had made Naomi's life full again.

Bible students debate the identity of the *kinsman-redeemer* in this verse. Does it refer to Boaz or to the son of Boaz and Ruth? A good case may be made for either position. The special kindnesses of Boaz highlighted in the book of Ruth seem to suggest that he is being described; on the other hand, the next verse calls attention to the son. No doubt both Boaz and his son Obed became *famous throughout Israel,* and both of them are included in the ancestry of Jesus (Matthew 1:5). Ultimately it makes little difference which of the two is specifically in mind. Of greater importance is the fact that *the Lord* raised up a redeemer.

> ¹⁵*"He will renew your life and sustain you in your old age. For your daughter-in-law, who loves you and who is better to you than seven sons, has given him birth."*

The women's pronouncements of blessing upon Naomi continued. They provided her with a confidence that the days ahead would be much brighter. Her *old age* would be a time of joy. One should note the high praise that is given to Ruth in the women's words: *your daughter-in-law . . . loves you and . . . is better to you than seven sons.* Since seven is often symbolic of perfection or completeness in the Bible, to have seven sons was a unique blessing indeed. Thus the women highlighted the superiority of Ruth's love for and devotion to Naomi.

C. Naomi's Care (v. 16)

> ¹⁶*Then Naomi took the child, laid him in her lap and cared for him.*

Naomi had the privilege of caring for this *child,* who continued the line of her husband and son and thus would be considered her grandson.

D. A Special Genealogy (v. 17)

> ¹⁷*The women living there said, "Naomi has a son." And they named him Obed. He was the father of Jesse, the father of David.*

The *women* of Bethlehem *named* the baby and called him *Obed.* While this was unusual (the parents generally named the child), it may simply reflect the unusual circumstances behind the marriage of Boaz and Ruth. The name *Obed* means "servant." The reference to his being Naomi's *son* should be understood according to the word's biblical usage, for *son* may describe any male descendant or successor. Again, it highlighted the fact that Naomi was no longer "empty."

Obed was *the father of Jesse* and thus became the grandfather of *David,* Israel's second king. The mention of David indicates that the book of Ruth was written after David had become king over Israel. It also helps to give one reason why the book of Ruth was written—to give more details of the genealogy of Israel's most famous king. Since the book begins with a reference to "the days when the judges ruled" (Ruth 1:1), the reference to David may also foreshadow him as the answer to the chaos of those days, which is attributed to the fact that "in those days Israel had no king" (Judges 21:25). David will be the king who will be "a man after [God's] own heart" (1 Samuel 13:14).

BIRTH OF SAMUEL; FULFILLMENT OF HANNAH'S VOW (1 SAMUEL 1:20, 24-28)

Establishing the Groundwork

Two Old Testament books bear the name of Samuel. Samuel was the last of the judges (1 Samuel 7:6, 15-17) and the beginning of a long line of prophets who would call Israel to turn from sin and follow the Lord (1 Samuel 3:19-21). In so doing, he would also, as his successors in the prophetic ministry did, foretell of the coming of the Messiah and his impact (Acts 3:24). As mentioned in a previous study, the period of the judges lasted roughly 300 years, from about 1373 to 1050 BC. Samuel's prophetic ministry began during the latter part of those deplorable years, during the time when Israel had no king and everyone did as he pleased. He guided the nation during a time of transition as it moved from the leadership of judges to the leadership of kings. In fact, Samuel anointed the first two kings of Israel—Saul and David.

The story of Samuel, like that of Samson, begins before his birth. Elkanah, Samuel's father, had two wives, Hannah and Peninnah. And while Peninnah had children (the Bible does not indicate how many), Hannah was barren. To make matters worse, Peninnah would mercilessly taunt Hannah because of her barrenness (1 Samuel 1:1-8).

The tabernacle had been at Shiloh (about 20 miles north of Jerusalem) since the days of Joshua (Joshua 18:1). Each year Elkanah would go there and offer a sacrifice. On one of these occasions, Hannah's bitterness over her barren condition made her especially distraught. She approached the tabernacle and prayed that God would allow her to have a child. She included a vow with her prayer, stating that if God would give her a son, she would "give him to the Lord for all the days of his life, and no razor will ever be used on his head" (1 Samuel 1:11). Apparently Hannah was placing her son under a Nazirite vow for life, since this included never cutting one's hair (Numbers 6:1-21; Judges 13:2-5).

Eli, the high priest at the time, who is also described as having "led" (literally, "judged") Israel for 40 years (1 Samuel 4:18), thought that Hannah was drunk when he watched her praying. When he learned otherwise, he gave Hannah his blessing and told her, "May the God of Israel grant you what you have asked of him" (1 Samuel 1:17). Hannah left, encouraged by what she heard, "and her face was no longer downcast" (v. 18). As with other notable women of the Bible who faced the challenge of barrenness (Genesis 11:30; 25:21; 29:31; 30:22; Judges 13:2), Hannah depended on the mercy of the Creator of life for her plea to be answered.

Examining the Text

I. A Son's Arrival (1 Samuel 1:20)
A. Hannah Gives Birth (v. 20a)

20a So in the course of time Hannah conceived and gave birth to a son.

After Hannah's prayer, she and her family returned home. Sometime later, as verse 19 tells us, "the Lord remembered" Hannah and answered her prayer uttered at the tabernacle. The words *in the course of time* may be similar to the words "as it turned out," which describe Ruth's coming to glean in the field of Boaz (Ruth 2:3). God in his providence and according to his time answered Hannah's plea for a *son.*

B. Hannah Gives a Name (v. 20b)

20b She named him Samuel, saying, "Because I asked the LORD for him."

Hannah named her precious gift from the Lord in such a way as to recognize the true source of her blessing. The name *Samuel* has been interpreted to mean "name of God" or "asked of God." In either case, there is a play on words that is appropriate because Hannah had *asked the Lord for* Samuel.

II. A Vow's Accomplishment (1 Samuel 1:24-28)
A. Samuel Brought to Shiloh (v. 24)

24 After he was weaned, she took the boy with her, young as he was, along with a three-year-old bull, an ephah of flour and a skin of wine, and brought him to the house of the LORD at Shiloh.

In the ancient Near East, children were usually *weaned* at the age of two or three years. No doubt Hannah treasured these short years with the son she had devoted to the Lord.

When the time came for Hannah to fulfill her vow and to take Samuel to the tabernacle, she made the journey to *Shiloh* with the necessary sacrifice. There is a question as to whether the sacrifice was a *three-year-old bull* (as the *New International Version* text has) or "three bulls," (as in the *King James Version* and also suggested in a footnote in the *NIV*). If the family traveled with three bulls, the first may have been for a special burnt offering, while the other two could have served as Elkanah's yearly sacrifice to the Lord (1 Samuel 1:3). If the phrase describes just one bull that was three years old, and that is more likely, then the family was sacrificing a bull in its prime.

An *ephah of flour* was the equivalent of about three-fifths of a bushel. A *skin of wine* reflects the fact that such containers in the ancient world were made from animal skins. (Jesus referred to old and new wineskins in Matthew 9:17.) Both of these items were probably taken along for use in the sacrificial rituals. Grain offerings and drink offerings were a part of the sacrifices offered at "the Lord's appointed feasts" that were celebrated by the Israelites (Leviticus 23:37, 38).

The reference to Samuel's being *young* dramatizes the sacrifice to which Hannah had committed herself, as well as the unusual decision that permitted a young child to be given for service at the tabernacle. Hannah fulfilled her promise to the Lord, even though it undoubtedly was painful to let go of her son. In both the Old and New Testaments, vows were not taken lightly (Judges 11:30-40; Proverbs 20:25; Ecclesiastes 5:4-6; Matthew 14:6-10).

B. Samuel Brought to Eli (vv. 25-27)

25 When they had slaughtered the bull, they brought the boy to Eli,

The term *they* indicates that others were involved in this procedure, most likely Elkanah and other members of the family. The *bull* was *slaughtered* by the altar and dismembered. Then parts of it were burned on the altar. Some of the blood was sprinkled on the altar, signifying the dedication of the child Samuel to God. (Note the "sprinkling" of blood that occurred when Moses confirmed God's covenant with the Israelites, according to Exodus 24:5-8.) Then Samuel was formally placed in the care of *Eli*, the high priest who had comforted Hannah earlier (1 Samuel 1:17).

Presenting a *boy* to the tabernacle at this young age was out of the ordinary: a Levite's son was usually not presented for such service until he had reached an age of at least 25. He would then continue in office until retiring at age 50 (Numbers 8:23-26). Samuel was beginning his lifelong service some 22 years ahead of schedule!

> *26 . . . and she said to him, "As surely as you live, my lord, I am the woman who stood here beside you praying to the LORD.*

Hannah reminded the high priest Eli of the incident a few short years earlier when she stood before the tabernacle in prayer asking for a child. The phrase *as surely as you live* was a common oath formula (see 1 Samuel 17:55; 20:3; 25:26; 2 Samuel 11:11; 14:19). Her purpose in using this oath was to guarantee to Eli that whether or not he could recall the incident in which she had prayed for a child (four years or so had passed since then: nine months for the pregnancy, and then about three years to the age of weaning), she was speaking the truth about the matter.

> *27"I prayed for this child, and the LORD has granted me what I asked of him.*

We can only imagine Hannah's joy and excitement as she gave her testimony to answered prayer: *I prayed for this child*—and here he is! Hannah's words to Eli corresponded with his own words to her earlier, according to 1 Samuel 1:17.

C. Samuel Brought to the Lord (v. 28)

> *28"So now I give him to the LORD. For his whole life he will be given over to the LORD." And he worshiped the LORD there.*

Hannah now expressed her intentions regarding the destiny of young Samuel: she would leave him at the tabernacle to begin a lifetime of service to the Lord. This was her way of giving back *to the Lord* who had so richly blessed her. For now, Samuel's role would be to serve in the tabernacle as one of the assistants under Eli's supervision (see 1 Samuel 2:11). But Hannah did not allow Samuel to escape her thoughts. Each year she made clothing for him, and she delivered these items when she traveled with her husband to Shiloh for their annual worship (1 Samuel 2:19). The Lord blessed Hannah's dedication of her son to the Lord by allowing her the privilege of being a mother to five additional children (v. 21).

The word *he* in the statement *he worshiped the Lord there* most likely refers to Samuel rather than Eli or Elkanah, since the immediate context addresses the ministry of young Samuel. Perhaps the statement conveys how quickly Hannah's son took up his role in a very serious way. Already he was demonstrating a sensitivity to the things of God that would characterize his later ministry to God's people.

THE LORD CALLS SAMUEL (1 SAMUEL 3:1-10, 19-21)

Establishing the Groundwork

The previous study ended with a reference to the spiritual sensitivity that Samuel seemed to demonstrate even at a very early age. And such sensitivity was desperately needed in Israel, given the sorry spiritual condition of the nation at this time. One must keep in mind that Samuel was born during the latter portion of the period of the judges. Even the tabernacle—the dwelling place of God—was not immune from the "everyone did as he saw fit" mentality that characterized life during the time of the judges (Judges 21:25). Eli's own sons, Hophni and Phinehas, abused their sacred privilege of the priesthood by taking portions of the sacrifices by force from the worshipers and by sleeping with some of the women who served at the entrance to the tabernacle (1 Samuel 2:12-22). When Eli spoke to them about their actions, he noted, "I hear from all the people about these wicked deeds of yours" (v. 23). One can only wonder whether Samuel's parents were aware of the actions of Eli's sons when they brought their son to the tabernacle to serve there. If they were, it may be an indication of the high degree of faith they possessed that they would fulfill the vow Hannah had made and bring their son to the tabernacle even amidst such sorry surroundings.

Despite the presence of Eli's wicked sons, Samuel maintained his devotion to the Lord (1 Samuel 2:18, 21, 26). The description of Samuel's youth (v. 26) closely resembles a description of Jesus in Luke 2:52 when it says, "And the boy Samuel continued to grow in stature and in favor with the Lord and with men."

Our next passage takes up the account of Samuel while he was still a boy (1 Samuel 3:1), but we are not told how old he was. Josephus, a noted Jewish historian who lived during the first century, says that he was 12.

Examining the Text

I. The Lord Speaks to Samuel (1 Samuel 3:1-10)
A. The Conditions (vv. 1-3)

¹The boy Samuel ministered before the Lord under Eli. In those days the word of the Lord was rare; there were not many visions.

That *the boy Samuel ministered before the Lord* was noted earlier in the record (1 Samuel 2:11). Thus Samuel's service to the Lord remained consistent and exemplary, despite the presence of Eli's evil sons. This verse reminds us that the nation was still reeling from the spiritual havoc associated with the times of the judges: *the word of the Lord was rare; there were not many visions.*

²One night Eli, whose eyes were becoming so weak that he could barely see, was lying down in his usual place.

Eli was "very old" (1 Samuel 2:22). Part of Samuel's duties as he "ministered" may well have been assisting Eli with responsibilities that Eli had become too frail to carry out. Perhaps the weakness of Eli's *eyes* is mentioned at this point to explain why the boy Samuel appears to have been at his call, night or day. Now it was *night,* and Eli had gone to bed.

³The lamp of God had not yet gone out, and Samuel was lying down in the temple of the Lord, where the ark of God was.

As noted earlier, the tabernacle had been set up at Shiloh soon after Israel had conquered the promised land and had divided it among the 12 tribes (Joshua 18:1). But here we read of the *temple* rather than the tabernacle, and verse 15 mentions "the house of the Lord." These differences in terminology should not confuse us. In our own time a historic building is sometimes enclosed within a larger structure to protect it from the weather. Perhaps something similar had been done for the tabernacle.

Inside the tabernacle itself was *the lamp of God,* the seven-branched golden lampstand that gave light to the Holy Place (Exodus 25:31-40). In the Holy of Holies rested *the ark of God,* often called the ark of the covenant. Of course, Eli and Samuel did not sleep in the Holy of Holies or even in the Holy Place, where the lampstand was. They must have had bedrooms elsewhere in the larger (perhaps enclosed) structure that is here called *the temple of the Lord.*

The golden lampstand was replenished with oil every morning, for it was against the regulations of the law of Moses to allow the light to go out at night (Exodus 27:20, 21; 30:7, 8). That the incident recorded in our text is said to have occurred before *the lamp of God* went out indicates that it took place in the early morning hours, before all the oil was consumed.

B. The Call (vv. 4-10)

⁴Then the Lord called Samuel. Samuel answered, "Here I am."

In the darkness *Samuel* heard his name *called.* The voice probably awakened him from his sleep. Promptly he responded so that whoever had spoken would know that his words had been heard.

⁵And he ran to Eli and said, "Here I am; you called me."
But Eli said, "I did not call; go back and lie down." So he went and lay down.

Naturally the boy thought that the person speaking was Eli. What else could he think? But Eli *did not call,* nor had he heard anyone speak. Probably supposing that Samuel had been dreaming, Eli sent him back to bed.

*⁶Again the L*ORD *called, "Samuel!" And Samuel got up and went to Eli and said, "Here I am; you called me."*

"My son," Eli said, "I did not call; go back and lie down."

Again came the call, too plain to ignore. Samuel could only respond as he had done before, and Eli could only send him *back* to bed again.

*⁷Now Samuel did not yet know the L*ORD: *The word of the L*ORD *had not yet been revealed to him.*

Of course, Samuel had been taught about *the Lord.* He must have known that his mother had dedicated him to the Lord's service; he must have known that Eli was training him for that service. But he was not yet personally acquainted with the Lord; that is, the Lord had never spoken to him before. He must have been puzzled by the repeated sound of his name, but he had no reason to think that the Lord was speaking.

*⁸The L*ORD *called Samuel a third time, and Samuel got up and went to Eli and said, "Here I am; you called me."*

*Then Eli realized that the L*ORD *was calling the boy.*

At last Eli *realized* the truth. It was not that his young helper was dreaming; it was that *the Lord was calling the boy.*

*⁹So Eli told Samuel, "Go and lie down, and if he calls you, say, 'Speak, L*ORD, *for your servant is listening.'" So Samuel went and lay down in his place.*

In certain respects, Eli does not appear to possess the spiritual perception that one might expect from a high priest. Previously he had watched Hannah pray and concluded that she was drunk (1 Samuel 1:12-14). His failure to discipline his sons brought the rebuke of an unnamed man of God (1 Samuel 2:27-36) and the judgment of God that would be announced, ironically, by the one whom he was now advising to listen to what the Lord had to say.

*¹⁰The L*ORD *came and stood there, calling as at the other times, "Samuel! Samuel!"*

Then Samuel said, "Speak, for your servant is listening."

The words *the Lord came and stood there* are not used of the Lord's other encounters with Samuel. A figure of some kind is implied, but we are not told whether or not Samuel saw anything. He did answer according to Eli's instructions—almost. Eli had told him to say, "Speak, Lord, for your servant is listening." Perhaps the boy was afraid to utter the sacred name. He said, *"Speak, for your servant is listening."*

The Lord then told Samuel that he would carry out his judgment against Eli and his family because Eli had failed to restrain the reckless wickedness of his sons (vv. 11-14). As stated earlier, Eli had heard that before from another prophet. Hearing it again from Samuel confirmed that the Lord had indeed spoken to him. The old man accepted his punishment with resignation (1 Samuel 3:15-18).

II. The Lord Speaks Through Samuel (1 Samuel 3:19-21)
A. Samuel's Reputation Grows (vv. 19, 20)

¹⁹The Lᴏʀᴅ was with Samuel as he grew up, and he let none of his words fall to the ground.

As Samuel *grew up,* he continued in the service of God to which his mother had dedicated him. *The Lord was with Samuel,* guiding his speech so that *none of his words* could *fall to the ground;* that is, nothing he said was false or mistaken. What he said about the past or present was true; what he said about the future came true in the proper time.

²⁰And all Israel from Dan to Beersheba recognized that Samuel was attested as a prophet of the Lᴏʀᴅ.

Samuel's reputation spread *from Dan* in the far northern part of Israel *to Beersheba* in the far south. (See the map on page 78.) The truth of his teaching and the accuracy of his predictions convinced *all Israel* that he was *a prophet of the Lord.*

B. God's Revelation Continues (v. 21)

²¹The Lᴏʀᴅ continued to appear at Shiloh, and there he revealed himself to Samuel through his word.

The Lord appeared not just once to Samuel; he *continued to appear* to him *at Shiloh.* The last part of the verse explains that the Lord did not appear in a visible form to be seen by Samuel or anyone else; *he revealed himself to Samuel through his word.* Such a word was desperately needed in all Israel, for, as the beginning of this chapter stated, "the word of the Lord was rare" (1 Samuel 3:1). As a result of God's calling Samuel, this tragic situation was reversed: "Samuel's word came to all Israel" (1 Samuel 4:1). Thus Samuel was not only the answer to Hannah's physical barrenness, he was also the answer to Israel's spiritual barrenness.

How to Say It

AMMONITES. *Am*-un-ites.

BEERSHEBA. Beer-*she*-buh.

BETHLEHEM. *Beth*-lih-hem.

BOAZ. Bo-az.

CANAAN. *Kay*-nun.

CHEMOSH. *Kee*-mosh.

ELIMELECH. Ee-*lim*-eh-leck.

ELKANAH. *El*-kuh-nuh or El-*kay*-nuh.

ELOHIM (*Hebrew***).** El-o-*heem*.

HANNAH. *Han*-uh.

JERUSALEM. Juh-*roo*-suh-lem.

JESSE. *Jess*-ee.

JOSEPHUS. Jo-*see*-fus.

KILION. *Kil*-ee-on.

MACHPELAH. Mack-*pea*-luh.

MAHLON. *Mah*-lon.

MAMRE. *Mam*-reh.

MARA. *Mah*-ruh.

MESSIAH. Meh-*sigh*-uh.

MOABITES. *Mo*-ub-ites.

MOABITESS. *Mo*-ub-*ite*-ess (strong accent on *Mo*).

NAOMI. Nay-*oh*-me.

NAZIRITE. *Naz*-ih-rite.

OBED. *O*-bed.

ORPAH. *Or*-pah.

PENINNAH. Peh-*nin*-uh.

SAMSON. *Sam*-sun.

SAMUEL. *Sam*-you-el.

SHILOH. *Shy*-low.

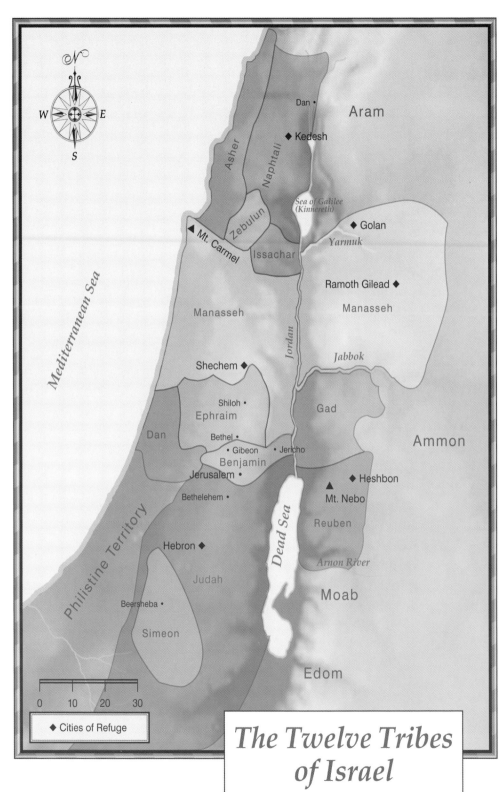

The Twelve Tribes
of Israel

Chapter 4

Beginnings of the Monarchy in Israel
1 Samuel 8:1-9, 19-22; 10:17-26; 13:5-14; 15:10-16, 22, 23

ISRAEL DEMANDS A KING (1 SAMUEL 8:1-9, 19-22)

Establishing the Groundwork

One of the problems confronting Israel in the time of the judges was the lack of central leadership. The judges seem to have been more local leaders than national, with the ministry of one judge often overlapping that of another. (Note the overlapping dates on the chart on page 38.)

This overlap makes sorting out the chronology difficult, but sometimes there are clues to help us. It is noteworthy that during Samuel's ministry in Israel, the Philistines posed a threat similar to that which they posed during Samson's judgeship. This has led many Bible students to conclude that their ministries were contemporary. In introducing the account of Samson, the inspired writer says the Philistines oppressed Israel for 40 years (Judges 13:1), but Samson judged Israel only 20 (Judges 16:31). It is likely that the Philistine oppression began some time before Samson began his work. One suggestion is that the oppression began midway through the judgeship of Eli (1 Samuel 4:18). In fact, it was probably the same oppression mentioned in Judges 10:7, 8, and at first included the Ammonites. Eighteen years into that oppression, Jephthah defeated the Ammonites (Judges 10:17–11:33). Two years later, the Philistines (who were not defeated by Jephthah) were still a problem and even captured the ark of the covenant from the Israelites. Eli died when he heard the news of the ark's capture (1 Samuel 4:17, 18).

But that was the beginning of the Philistines' undoing. God troubled them in their own cities for seven months (1 Samuel 5:1–6:1), and Samson troubled them for 20 years (Judges 15:20). Shortly after Samson's death, Samuel led the nation in a great revival at Mizpah (1 Samuel 7:5, 6), at which time the Philistines made one last attack but were routed by the Israelites with the Lord's help (1 Samuel 7:10-13). "The Philistines did not invade Israelite territory again" until years later, while Saul was king. They were kept under control "throughout Samuel's lifetime" (1 Samuel 7:13).

With peace restored, Samuel proceeded to encourage the people to remain loyal to the Lord. He became a kind of "circuit judge," traveling from place to place so that people could more easily come to him for guidance in deciding cases according to God's law (1 Samuel 7:15-17).

In previous studies, we have seen the steps taken by Moses and Joshua to prepare for the time when they would no longer be around to provide guidance for God's people. As Samuel grew older, he too faced this same crossroads. However, Samuel's idea of how this should be handled differed from the people's thinking. The turn of events that resulted ushered in a new chapter in the history of God's people.

Examining the Text

I. A Change Demanded (1 Samuel 8:1-5)
A. Disappointing Sons (vv. 1-3)

¹When Samuel grew old, he appointed his sons as judges for Israel.

Perhaps Samuel's already heavy caseload was growing heavier, while he himself was losing energy as he *grew old*. It seemed reasonable to get some help, which Samuel found by appointing *his sons as judges*.

²The name of his firstborn was Joel and the name of his second was Abijah, and they served at Beersheba.

Samuel's circuit (1 Samuel 7:16, 17) was in central Israel. *Beersheba*, on the other hand, was approximately 50 miles away to the south. It was much more convenient for people in that part of the country to have a court closer to where they lived.

³But his sons did not walk in his ways. They turned aside after dishonest gain and accepted bribes and perverted justice.

Samuel had managed the nation admirably, but he had not done so well with *his sons*. They had become selfish and greedy for *dishonest gain*. They did not care for law or *justice*; they saw their judgeship only as an opportunity to enrich themselves. They *accepted bribes*, selling each decision they made to the highest bidder. Ironically, Samuel was repeating the mistakes of his mentor Eli, who also had two sons, both of whom *did not walk* in *ways* that pleased the Lord.

B. Demand for a King (vv. 4, 5)

⁴So all the elders of Israel gathered together and came to Samuel at Ramah.

The corruption of Joel and Abijah was too evident to be hidden. News of it spread all over the country. *Elders* in the towns of Israel had supported

Samuel and his exemplary leadership, but now they were alarmed, as they should have been, at the prospect of his sons being in leadership roles. Their proposed solution, however, was not as admirable as their concern over the improper behavior of Samuel's sons. In fact, it betrayed some impropriety in their own motives.

5They said to him, "You are old, and your sons do not walk in your ways; now appoint a king to lead us, such as all the other nations have."

Both of the elders' statements would have been difficult for Samuel to hear. No one likes to be reminded that he is getting *old*; however, that is something over which one has no control. For Samuel to hear that *your sons do not walk in your ways* was something over which he did have control. He probably realized upon hearing the accusation that he had not been as diligent in pursuing his fatherly duties as he had been in leading the nation.

Samuel had been known as a just judge for a long time, but he had been known even longer as a prophet of God (1 Samuel 3:20). With the help of the Lord, perhaps he would provide Israel with a *king* who would be as capable a leader as Samuel himself. With such a man in charge, peace and prosperity would continue. Besides, *all the other nations* around Israel had kings, and they seemed to be getting along quite well. If Israel were given a king who was better than any other, would it not become a nation more prosperous and respected than any other?

II. A Change Discussed (1 Samuel 8:6-9)
A. Samuel's Prayer (v. 6)

6But when they said, "Give us a king to lead us," this displeased Samuel; so he prayed to the LORD.

The elders' request *displeased Samuel.* Probably he took the request personally. He felt that he was being rejected, as the Lord's words to him in verse 7 indicate. After all Samuel had done for Israel, it may have seemed to him most ungrateful for the people to disregard the plan for leadership that he had proposed. (Perhaps, deep down, he was also displeased with himself and with his failure to do a better job with his sons.)

Additionally, Samuel knew enough about national affairs to know that a *king* would not solve Israel's problem. Having a king would be no better than having a judge, unless the king were a better man.

Despite the hurt he felt, Samuel reacted to the request in the right way. Instead of criticizing or denouncing the elders' appeal, he *prayed to the Lord.* Samuel preferred to give the elders no answer until he could give them God's answer.

B. God's Perspective (vv. 7-9)

⁷And the LORD told him: "Listen to all that the people are saying to you; it is not you they have rejected, but they have rejected me as their king.

Here we see the real problem with the elders' request: It was a rejection of God and his rule over Israel. The problem was not so much the request—God had provided in the law for a time when *the people* would desire a king (Deuteronomy 17:14-20)—as the reason for the request. God had called Israel to be his own "treasured possession" (Exodus 19:5), distinct from all other nations. Now the elders were abandoning that call and asking to be like "all the other nations." They had forgotten that God was their real King.

⁸"As they have done from the day I brought them up out of Egypt until this day, forsaking me and serving other gods, so they are doing to you.

Rejecting God was not something new for the Israelites. These people had been doing it ever since they had left *Egypt* to begin their national life. They had built and worshiped a golden calf at Mount Sinai. They had balked at their first opportunity to conquer the promised land. And after they entered that land, they had sunk into sin again and again. Their present rejection of God and of Samuel was part of a tragic pattern—and the Israelites are not the only ones who have followed such a pattern.

⁹"Now listen to them; but warn them solemnly and let them know what the king who will reign over them will do."

Both in verse 7 and here in verse 9, we see that God told Samuel to *listen* to the elders and do as they asked. Why allow them to do something that was not the best choice for them to make? As your own child grew toward adulthood, didn't you sometimes decide that it was best to let him go his own mistaken way and learn from his error? So God let the people have their way, and later generations learned the disadvantages of having another *king* besides the Lord.

If you have ever decided to let your child go his own mistaken way, perhaps you also explained why you thought that way was mistaken. Likewise the Lord told Samuel to *warn* the people *solemnly* that having a king was not best for them, and to explain why. This protest is recorded in verses 10-18. A king, said Samuel, would become an expensive item for God's people to maintain. (Note the repeated use of the word *take* in Samuel's warning.) In time the people would cry to the Lord because of oppression by their king, just as they had cried because of oppression by enemies; but this time the Lord would not be as quick to respond.

III. A Change Determined (1 Samuel 8:19-22)

No doubt the elders had discussed their concerns at length before they approached Samuel. They thought the solution they proposed was the best possible one. Perhaps they felt so sure that they hardly heard Samuel's warning about what a king would cost the nation. At least we know they were not convinced by it. They repeated their request more emphatically, this time with additional support from the people.

A. Demand Repeated (vv. 19, 20)

¹⁹But the people refused to listen to Samuel. "No!" they said. "We want a king over us.

Usually *the people* had gratefully accepted Samuel's leadership, but this time they resisted. Their desire was stated as a demand more than a request: *We want a king over us.*

²⁰"Then we will be like all the other nations, with a king to lead us and to go out before us and fight our battles."

The people repeated the desire to *be like all the other nations.* But Israel had been set apart to be different from all the nations, to be the one nation in all the world that was governed by God's law, and to be a living demonstration that the way of obedience to God is the best way there is. To be like all the nations would be to forsake the very purpose for which the nation of Israel had been created.

Another reason given for the demand was that our *king* may *lead us.* The word for *lead* here (as also in v. 5) is the same one usually translated "judge." The people wanted the king to be responsible for enforcing the law and administering justice. They wanted a king to do what judges had done previously—what Samuel had done (1 Samuel 7:6, 15-17). No wonder Samuel took the request as a rejection (v. 7). We wonder whether the elders in particular also hoped that a king would relieve them of their own leadership responsibilities. Obviously he would not. Even if Israel had a king, each of the elders would still be responsible for obeying the law and guiding the younger generation to obey it.

Finally, the people desired that the king *go out before us and fight our battles.* They wanted the king to be responsible for Israel's national defense. But had they forgotten that there was a better protection already available to them—the protection of the Lord God Almighty? He would keep them safe if they would obey his law. He had proved that again and again. Was the desire for a king an attempt by the people to gain that security without the condition—to bypass their responsibility to obey God? If so, they were badly mistaken. No king (no matter how capable he might be) could take the responsibility of obedience from God's people.

B. Demand Granted (vv. 21, 22)

²¹When Samuel heard all that the people said, he repeated it before the Lord.

When the discussion was over, Samuel again went to *the Lord* in prayer. The decision in this matter would affect the nation for centuries to come. Samuel wanted it to be the Lord's decision, not his.

²²The Lord answered, "Listen to them and give them a king."
Then Samuel said to the men of Israel, "Everyone go back to his town."

Again the Lord told Samuel to *listen to* the people, to let them have their own way and thus learn their own lesson. Samuel then told the assembled elders to go home and wait for God to make known his choice of a man to be king. Chapters 9 and 10 tell how this was done, resulting in the selection of Saul as Israel's first king.

SAUL PRESENTED AS ISRAEL'S FIRST KING (1 SAMUEL 10:17-26)

Establishing the Groundwork

Having granted the Israelites' request for a king, God proceeded to guide Samuel to the man whom he had chosen as Israel's first king and to guide that man toward Samuel. First Samuel 9 introduces us to a man from the tribe of Benjamin, whose name was Saul. His father Kish is described as "a man of standing" (1 Samuel 9:1). Saul himself is described as "an impressive young man without equal among the Israelites—a head taller than any of the others" (v. 2).

On one occasion, some donkeys belonging to Kish were lost; and Saul was told to take one of the servants and search for them. When the two men were unable to find the donkeys, the servant suggested that they consult a man of God in the area and see if he could help them. That man of God was Samuel, to whom God had spoken the following on the day before he met Saul: "About this time tomorrow I will send you a man from the land of Benjamin. Anoint him leader over my people Israel; he will deliver my people from the hand of the Philistines" (1 Samuel 9:16). In a private ceremony, Samuel anointed Saul and gave him a series of signs that would signify God's special presence with him (1 Samuel 10:1-9). The public selection of this young man to become king of Israel took place not long afterward.

I. Summarizing the Past (1 Samuel 10:17-19)
A. God's Faithfulness (vv. 17, 18)

17Samuel summoned the people of Israel to the LORD at Mizpah

Mizpah was located in the territory of the tribe of Benjamin, a few miles north of Jerusalem. It was probably chosen as a meeting place because it was centrally located in Israel, and because it had an ample water supply and a level area for a large gathering such as this one would likely be. It may also have been chosen for its historical significance. Years earlier, Israel had met at Mizpah at Samuel's direction for a ceremony of rededication to the Lord. It was on that same occasion that God had given the people a decisive victory over the Philistines (1 Samuel 7:5-14).

18 . . . and said to them, "This is what the Lord, the God of Israel, says: 'I brought Israel up out of Egypt, and I delivered you from the power of Egypt and all the kingdoms that oppressed you.'

In these few words spoken by Samuel, God reminded the people of all the blessings and help he had given them in the past. He had rescued them from their bitter bondage under *the power of Egypt*. He had *delivered* them from *all the kingdoms* that had opposed their march toward the promised land (Numbers 21:21-35). Once the people had taken possession of the promised land, the Lord had rescued them from all who had *oppressed* them.

B. Israel's Unfaithfulness (v. 19)

19"But you have now rejected your God, who saves you out of all your calamities and distresses. And you have said, 'No, set a king over us.' So now present yourselves before the Lord by your tribes and clans."

Yes, *God* had been faithful to his people, rescuing them from every difficulty. But they had not been faithful to him. In demanding a *king*, they were forgetting that God himself was their real King. He had saved them *out of all* their *calamities and distresses*. He had always been able to deliver them from any enemy.

Now, however, the people were asking for a king, desiring that he do for them exactly what the Lord had done for them all along—to fight their battles (1 Samuel 8:20). It is true that the deliverance God had given was dependent upon the people's walking in his ways. Could it be that they believed that an earthly king would not be so demanding? Or that he would give them national independence through military might, not requiring too much of them? What the people failed to discern was that, if they had fulfilled their own responsibility by obeying the law, no battles would have been needed! The Lord would have given them victory over every foe.

The people, however, had made their choice. Disregarding the warnings of God and Samuel, they had persisted in demanding a king. Therefore, said Samuel, they should prepare to *present* themselves *before the Lord* so he could designate the one from among them who should be their king. They should present themselves first by *tribes* and then by the smaller groups *of clans*.

II. Selecting a King (1 Samuel 10:20-26)

Though the people had rejected God in their demand for a king, Samuel wanted their first king to be God's choice; and he wanted the people to understand that God was making this choice.

A. Identifying the Tribe (v. 20)

²⁰When Samuel brought all the tribes of Israel near, the tribe of Benjamin was chosen.

We need not suppose that entire *tribes* came before Samuel and the Lord. Perhaps one man was called forward to represent each tribe. We are not told exactly how *the tribe of Benjamin was chosen* from the rest. Possibly the Urim and Thummim, which the high priest was to use in making important decisions (Exodus 28:30; Numbers 27:21), were used to help make this choice (though we do not know exactly what the Urim and Thummim were or what using them involved).

Another suggestion is that a "casting of lots" of some kind was used and that God was asked to guide the result. For example, a white pebble might be placed in a jar with eleven dark ones. A man of each tribe would reach into the jar without looking and take a pebble. The tribe whose representative drew out the white pebble would be taken as the chosen tribe. Or, each tribe might mark a small stone with the name or symbol of that tribe. The stones would be put in a jar. Samuel, as God's prophet, would then select one of the stones without looking, and the tribe indicated by that stone would be the chosen tribe. Whatever the procedure, Benjamin was revealed to be the chosen tribe.

B. Identifying the Person (v. 21)

²¹ᵃThen he brought forward the tribe of Benjamin, clan by clan, and Matri's clan was chosen. Finally Saul son of Kish was chosen.

Perhaps by the same procedure previously used, *Matri's clan was chosen* from all the families of the tribe of *Benjamin*. By a final step, *Saul son of Kish was chosen* from all the men of Matri's family.

²¹ᵇ**But when they looked for him, he was not to be found.**

Saul's absence here tells us that a man could be included among the candidates without even being present. Perhaps an elder of Matri's family wrote the names of the men of that family on separate stones, and Samuel or someone else randomly selected the stone with Saul's name on it. Whatever the process was, it is clear that all Israel was convinced, and rightly so, that God was making this choice.

When Saul's name was announced, naturally everyone began looking for him. But *he was not to be found.*

C. Introducing the Person (vv. 22-24)

²²**So they inquired further of the Lord, "Has the man come here yet?" And the Lord said, "Yes, he has hidden himself among the baggage."**

Saul was not in the crowd. Was it possible that he had not arrived at Mizpah yet? That question was put to the Lord, and he answered it plainly: Saul was hiding *among the baggage.* The Hebrew word rendered *baggage* seems to describe supplies of some kind. People who walked two or three days to get to Mizpah would have brought a lot of such items, including clothing, blankets, food, and cooking utensils. Perhaps a particular area (possibly a large tent) had been designated as a place to keep such items—a "baggage depot" of sorts. There Saul had *hidden himself.*

The question of Saul's whereabouts was not so easily answered by a procedure such as "casting lots." That is one reason for putting a "perhaps" with the above suggestions of the procedure used to select who would be Israel's first king. We do not really know how the selection was made, and likewise we do not know how the Lord responded to this question. Somehow God *said* where Saul was, which suggests a clear and direct verbal communication. Most likely he inspired his prophet Samuel with the answer. One might think it reasonable, then, to believe he had done the same thing with choosing the tribe, clan, and man before. At the same time, a procedure like the one described above would prove Samuel was not manipulating the results. Once the man had been selected, there was no need for such assurance. Finding the man where Samuel said he could be found was proof enough that God had spoken to the prophet. At any rate, by some clear and unmistakable means, God revealed the truth to Samuel and the Israelites.

We need to remember that Saul knew in advance that he would be chosen as Israel's king. (See 1 Samuel 9:1–10:16.) Why, then, was he hiding? Was he bashful, afraid to face the stares of the crowd? Was he modest, shrinking from the praise that would be heaped upon him? Was he frightened by the responsibility he was being given? One must keep in mind that this was something new for both him and the nation: Saul had never been a king, and Israel had never had a king.

23They ran and brought him out, and as he stood among the people he was a head taller than any of the others.

Eager men *ran* to where the baggage was and escorted the reluctant king to the throng of his waiting *people*. Instantly everyone noticed that he was *a head taller than any of them*. He looked like a king!

24Samuel said to all the people, "Do you see the man the Lord has chosen? There is no one like him among all the people."
Then the people shouted, "Long live the king!"

Samuel made two observations. First, *the Lord* had *chosen* this man to be their king. *All the people* had seen that no man or group of men had made the choice. If it was made by casting lots, they had asked God to determine the outcome; and they believed that he had done so.

Second, Saul's appearance seemed to verify the choice. Like a royal figure, he towered above the common people. Saul's fellow Israelites responded to Samuel's words with a roar of approval: *"Long live the king!"*

D. Instructing the People (vv. 25, 26)

25Samuel explained to the people the regulations of the kingship. He wrote them down on a scroll and deposited it before the Lord. Then Samuel dismissed the people, each to his own home.

While *the people* were assembled, Samuel *explained* to them *the regulations of the kingship*. The people had asked for a king in order to be "like all the other nations" (1 Samuel 8:5, 19, 20); but even with a king in place, Israel still was to be different from all the nations. Israel's was to be a limited kingship. The law God had given was still the law of the land. No king had the authority to change that. In fact, the king was bound by that law just as much as the "common people" were.

Centuries earlier, when the law was given through Moses, God anticipated the request for a king and gave some guidelines for him. These are found in Deuteronomy 17:14-20. The king must be a man of Israel, never a foreigner. He was not to make an alliance with Egypt in order to strengthen his military forces with horses and chariots. He was not to have a harem full of wives, nor was he to fill his treasury with great quantities of silver and gold. In addition, the king was to have his own copy of God's law. He was to read from it every day and be careful to obey it completely. All this and more may have been included in the *regulations* that Samuel presented to the people on this day.

After giving these instructions to the assembled people, Samuel sent them *home*. He also *wrote* his words concerning the kingdom *on a scroll* (probably at a later time) and *deposited it before the Lord*. This may mean that a copy of these regulations was kept in the tabernacle. There it would be available for future reference as needed.

²⁶Saul also went to his home in Gibeah, accompanied by valiant men whose hearts God had touched.

What does a new king do in a country that never had a king before? This one simply *went back home*, as other people did. (*Gibeah* was located about four miles southeast of Mizpah.) Still, Saul's life was not quite the same, for he went *accompanied by valiant men whose hearts God had touched*. Perhaps he touched their hearts with sincere concern for the king and the kingdom. As a result they volunteered to assist the new king in any way they could.

The record adds that Saul wisely ignored the dissidents who sneered at him (v. 27); and when a national emergency arose, this new king knew what a king must do. In fact, he did it so well that the people enthusiastically reaffirmed their allegiance to him (1 Samuel 11:1-15).

SAUL DISOBEYS GOD (1 SAMUEL 13:5-14)

Establishing the Groundwork

After Saul had defeated the Ammonites and rescued the town of Jabesh Gilead from their threat (1 Samuel 11:1-11), Samuel called the people to meet in Gilgal to celebrate the victory, reaffirm the kingship, and give thanks to the Lord (vv. 12-15). There "all the Israelites held a great celebration" (v. 15). Samuel also used this occasion to present a kind of "farewell address," preparing the nation for the transition to life under a king. Samuel reviewed his own life of service to the people, perhaps to provide an example to Saul of the kind of leadership he should demonstrate to God's people. Samuel also related the history of the nation to this point, calling attention to "what an evil thing you did in the eyes of the Lord when you asked for a king" (1 Samuel 12:17). Yet all was not hopeless; Samuel encouraged the people to remain true to the Lord and emphasized that he would still be engaged in a ministry of prayer and teaching (v. 23). He concluded with a warning that having a king could never be considered a substitute for the people's faithfulness toward God: "Yet if you persist in doing evil, both you and your king will be swept away" (v. 25).

Of the men who had accompanied Saul in his battle with the Ammonites (330,000, according to 1 Samuel 11:8), it appears that he selected 3,000 of them to form a standing army. On one occasion he deployed 2,000 of them at Micmash (located within the tribe of Benjamin about eight miles northeast of Jerusalem) and in the hill country of Bethel. The remaining thousand were under the command of Saul's son Jonathan at Gibeah, Saul's hometown (1 Samuel 13:2). A Philistine outpost at Geba (v. 3) would have been located between these detachments of Israelites. (See the map on page 102.)

It was Jonathan who began hostilities with the Philistines, who by this time had re-established their oppression of the Israelites (1 Samuel 13:16-22). With his 1,000 men, Jonathan "attacked the Philistine outpost at Geba" (v. 3). Apparently news of this soon reached other Philistine outposts. Saul realized that the Philistines would soon be out in force to avenge Jonathan's actions (v. 4). Saul issued a call throughout the land, and the Israelites (including most likely the men he had recently dismissed) began to assemble for battle at Gilgal, down in the Jordan Valley (v. 4).

It is important to note, in reading the biblical record of Saul, that we are not given a complete biography (this is true of any Bible person, including Jesus). Thus it is difficult to know how much time has passed between the events in 1 Samuel 12 and those in chapter 13. That some years have elapsed is clear from the mention of Saul's son Jonathan, who appears for the first time in the Bible in chapter 13 and is old enough to lead troops into battle. Regarding any individual, the Bible provides what the Spirit of God knew would be necessary for our spiritual instruction; and he guided the various writers of Scripture to include those details (2 Peter 1:21).

Examining the Text

I. Approaching Danger (1 Samuel 13:5-7)
A. Philistines' Preparation (v. 5)

⁵The Philistines assembled to fight Israel, with three thousand chariots, six thousand charioteers, and soldiers as numerous as the sand on the seashore. They went up and camped at Micmash, east of Beth Aven.

No doubt the *Philistines* hoped to spread panic among the Israelites by amassing such a large force of *chariots, charioteers,* and *soldiers* as described here. They also hoped to attack Saul and his smaller force before additional Israelites could arrive to provide support.

Micmash (also spelled *Michmash)* was situated on elevated terrain overlooking a deep ravine that separated it from Geba (mentioned in verse 3). Saul and his men had been at Micmash not long before (v. 2), but they had withdrawn to Gilgal in the Jordan Valley to await the arrival of the remainder of their army (v. 4).

B. Israelites' Panic (vv. 6, 7)

⁶When the men of Israel saw that their situation was critical and that their army was hard pressed, they hid in caves and thickets, among the rocks, and in pits and cisterns.

Saul had previously won a great victory over the Ammonites, as recorded in 1 Samuel 11, but that had been a foe far inferior to the Philistines. The sheer size of the Philistine army was frightening. In addition, the Philistines possessed a clear superiority in weaponry due to the absence of blacksmiths in Israel, as noted in 1 Samuel 13:19-22. This passage also records that at this time in Israel's history, "not a soldier with Saul and Jonathan had a sword or spear in his hand; only Saul and his son Jonathan had them" (v. 22). Israelites living near the invasion route of the Philistines *hid* in any available spot, leaving their homes and farms to be pillaged.

⁷Some Hebrews even crossed the Jordan to the land of Gad and Gilead. Saul remained at Gilgal, and all the troops with him were quaking with fear.

Instead of hiding near their homes, *some Hebrews* looked for safety farther away. Hoping the war would be confined to the west side of the Jordan River, they *crossed the Jordan* to the east side, where the tribe of *Gad* had settled. (See the map on page 78.) *Gilead* was even farther away, to the north and east of Gad. Even those who *remained* with Saul at *Gilgal* were *quaking with fear* at the daunting challenge before them.

II. Anxiety of Saul (1 Samuel 13:8, 9)

During a time of battle, waiting may be harder than fighting, especially if those who are waiting are in a state of panic. So it was with Saul and his soldiers at Gilgal. It is not difficult to imagine that these men were too nervous to sleep well, their appetites failed, and their fear grew more intense with every passing day.

A. Intimidated Men (v. 8)

⁸He waited seven days, the time set by Samuel; but Samuel did not come to Gilgal, and Saul's men began to scatter.

Earlier, when Samuel had first discussed the kingship with Saul, he had given Saul the following instructions: "Once these signs [those described by Samuel] are fulfilled, do whatever your hand finds to do, for God is with you. Go down ahead of me to Gilgal. I will surely come down to you to sacrifice burnt offerings and fellowship offerings, but you must wait seven days until I come to you and tell you what you are to do" (1 Samuel 10:7, 8). But the record immediately after that includes no mention of a trip to Gilgal a week ahead of Samuel. Saul returned home to Gibeah (v. 10) and later assembled with the rest of the nation at Mizpah, where he was made king (vv. 17-26). Thus some have concluded Samuel's words expressed a general policy for Saul's reign, not instructions for a single event. When Saul was sure of what to do, he was to act promptly and decisively. In other situations of a critical nature, when it was not entirely clear what Saul was to do, he was to go to Gilgal and wait for Samuel to come and advise him. Such an arrangement highlighted the fact that the king in Israel was not to act independently at all times; rather, he must remain accountable to the prophet.

With certain situations, Saul had acted quickly, following the command to "do whatever your hand finds to do." Such was the case when the Ammonites threatened the town of Jabesh Gilead (1 Samuel 11:1-8). We have no record of times before the one recorded here when Saul waited at Gilgal seven days for the prophet's counsel; perhaps the need had never before arisen.

While Saul was at Micmash, Samuel may have reminded him of his earlier instructions. With or without such a reminder, Saul remembered and proceeded on to Gilgal (1 Samuel 13:4). Hard as it must have been under the circumstances, *he waited seven days, the time set by Samuel.* But the seventh day came, and still Samuel had not arrived. By now Saul's situation had become desperate. Whatever *men* had remained with him *began to scatter.* Saul felt that he could wait for the prophet no longer.

B. Ill-advised Sacrifice (v. 9)

⁹So he said, "Bring me the burnt offering and the fellowship offerings." And Saul offered up the burnt offering.

On the face of it, this verse appears to say that *Saul* himself may have *offered up the burnt offering.* Perhaps he did, but we need not suppose that this was the case. (Saul was not condemned for usurping the priestly function, as a later king of Judah was—2 Chronicles 26:16-21; he was censured for not waiting for Samuel.) There was at least one priest in Saul's camp, who had custody of the ark of the covenant (1 Samuel 14:2, 3, 18). Perhaps this priest conducted the sacrifice according to the regulations given in the law of Moses. But the king had been told to wait for Samuel's arrival. That was the Lord's command given through his prophet, and Saul had chosen to disobey it. The *fellowship offerings* were those that were eaten by the worshiper. Such offerings would be meaningless, however, if presented as part of an act of defiance of God's authority.

III. Arrival of Samuel (1 Samuel 13:10-14)
A. Samuel's Confrontation (vv. 10, 11a)

10Just as he finished making the offering, Samuel arrived, and Saul went out to greet him.

Some Bible students believe it is unfair to condemn Saul for his action. They claim that he waited seven days according to Samuel's instructions. They say that Samuel broke his promise by failing to come in seven days, and therefore Saul was no longer bound to obey the prophet's command. Others think that Saul did not wait until the seven days had ended, but only until the seventh day began. They suggest that Saul made his offering on the seventh day, and Samuel came on that day as he had promised.

In any case, the command to Saul was not only to wait seven days, but also to wait for the arrival of Samuel. This he clearly failed to do.

11a"What have you done?" asked Samuel.

The question of Samuel implies a rebuke. Saul had been given specific instructions, but his fear was greater than his faith.

B. Saul's Claim (vv. 11b, 12)

11bSaul replied, "When I saw that the men were scattering, and that you did not come at the set time, and that the Philistines were assembling at Micmash,

Saul did not answer Samuel's question by telling what he had done. Like a guilty child caught in the act, the king began to try to explain why he had done it. He gave three excuses:

1. His troops were *scattering.* Every passing day had made his army less prepared for battle.

2. Samuel had *not come at the set time.*

3. *The Philistines were assembling at Micmash* and poised to strike. They could attack any day.

If Saul had walked more by faith than by sight, he could easily have seen the fallacy in his reasoning.

1. It would be better to lose his whole army than to lose the Lord's help by disobeying him.

2. Samuel's delay called for more trust in God, not for disobedience.

3. The gathering of the Philistines in large numbers provided a perfect opportunity for the Lord to defeat them and to demonstrate his mighty power. Did Saul not know what the Lord had done with Gideon's 300 against the Midianite hordes?

> ¹² ". . . I thought, 'Now the Philistines will come down against me at Gilgal, and I have not sought the LORD's favor.' So I felt compelled to offer the burnt offering."

It appears that a terrific struggle went on within the heart of the king, occasioned by the fact that he knew he ought not to proceed contrary to the prophet's instructions. But circumstances were such that he *felt compelled to offer the burnt offering.* "I didn't want to, but I had no choice," Saul was saying. The imminent danger demanded immediate action. The Philistines might attack at any time, and it was unthinkable to go into battle without asking for the Lord's help.

Here Saul displayed a mixture of both good and bad thinking. Yes, it is wise to seek God's help in any crisis; but it is foolish to think his help can be gained by disobeying him.

C. Samuel's Chastisement (vv. 13, 14)

We may feel inclined to sympathize with Saul. The man was in a critical situation, and it was getting worse. After all, he did wait a week, and then sought the Lord's help. What's wrong with that? But Samuel pronounced the sentence of the Lord, and his word is more reliable than our feelings.

> ¹³"You acted foolishly," Samuel said. "You have not kept the command the LORD your God gave you; if you had, he would have established your kingdom over Israel for all time.

Samuel told Saul that he had *acted foolishly* by disobeying *the command the Lord* had given him. No matter how desperate the circumstance, no matter how urgent the need, no matter how rational the excuses may seem, it is foolish to disobey the Lord. Had Saul followed the instructions given him by Samuel, the Lord would have *established* his *kingdom over Israel for all time.* In other words, Saul's descendants would have been rulers in Israel throughout the coming generations; and the Messiah would have come from his line. But now that would never happen, and Saul could blame no one but himself.

> *¹⁴"But now your kingdom will not endure; the LORD has sought out a man after his own heart and appointed him leader of his people, because you have not kept the LORD's command."*

Again, Samuel emphasized to Saul that *your kingdom will not endure*. This does not mean that Saul was finished ruling Israel as of that moment. It simply repeats the message of the previous verse: Saul would have no dynasty. To head such a lasting line of kings, the Lord had chosen someone else, *a man after his own heart*. We know that man was David, but most likely only God knew his identity at this point. Samuel himself did not know who Saul's successor would be until he was later told to go to the house of Jesse and anoint the man chosen by God (1 Samuel 16:1-13).

As for Saul, God still had work for him to do. The Lord used him and Jonathan to win a victory over the Philistines at Micmash (1 Samuel 14:1-23). He used Saul to defeat other enemies of Israel as well (1 Samuel 14:47, 48). A later act of disobedience resulted in the Lord's rejection of him as king (see the next study), but even then Saul continued to rule for several years. In the meantime, David was being prepared to become the next king of Israel.

SAUL IS REJECTED AS KING (1 SAMUEL 15:10-16, 22, 23)

Establishing the Groundwork

First Samuel 15 begins with a command from Samuel to Saul to "totally destroy" the Amalekites. Samuel prefaced this command with a reminder to Saul that Samuel was the one sent by the Lord to anoint Saul as king over Israel. Thus it was important that he listen to the message from the Lord that Samuel was about to give him. It seems as though Saul was being given a "second chance" to demonstrate his willingness to obey God and to show a different spirit from that shown in 1 Samuel 13:5-14 when he had failed to follow the Lord's instructions.

The Amalekites were a nomadic people descended from Esau (Genesis 36:12, 15, 16). They usually resided in the Negev and Sinai regions south of the promised land. When Samuel commanded Saul to destroy them, he referred to "what they did to Israel when they waylaid them as they came up from Egypt" (v. 2). This is recorded in Exodus 17:8-16. At that time God had said that he would "completely blot out the memory of Amalek from under heaven" (Exodus 17:14). Now Saul was being given the responsibility of administering the Lord's judgment against this wicked people.

The purpose of these actions against the Amalekites was not conquest. No spoils were to be taken by the Israelites (1 Samuel 15:3). Saul summoned the men of Israel and led them out to complete the task he had been given. However, Saul spared Agag, the Amalekite king, along with "the best of the sheep and cattle, the fat calves and lambs—everything that was good" (v. 9).

The victory over the Amalekites was complete; and the people were in possession of the best of the livestock, some of which Saul would eventually claim that he had spared in order to offer them as a sacrifice. Saul was quite happy with himself and, given his later reaction to Samuel's arrival (v. 13), seems to have believed that the prophet would be pleased with his actions.

Examining the Text

I. God's Message to Samuel (1 Samuel 15:10, 11)
A. God's Sorrow (vv. 10, 11a)

10, 11aThen the word of the LORD came to Samuel: "I am grieved that I have made Saul king, because he has turned away from me and has not carried out my instructions."

For God to be *grieved* at something he had done does not mean that he had made a mistake in that action. (See the discussion of this term in the comments on Genesis 6:6 in chapter 2 of volume 1.) Any change in God's attitude or action occurs because those with whom God is dealing have changed. God acts consistently toward obedience and disobedience throughout Scripture. He is changeless in that sense—a point that Samuel made later to Saul (1 Samuel 15:29). God had chosen Saul to be the first king of Israel and had given him every opportunity and blessing. By his disloyalty Saul proved himself to be unfit to serve as the leader of God's people. In the case of the Amalekites, Saul had done only part of what God commanded; therefore he had not *carried out* the Lord's *instructions*, though he would later claim to Samuel that he had (v. 13). Saul's "obedience" was nothing more than the exercise of his self-will.

B. Samuel's Supplication (v. 11b)

11bSamuel was troubled, and he cried out to the LORD all that night.

The Hebrew word rendered *troubled* is used elsewhere in the Old Testament to indicate anger. That Samuel's anger was directed against Saul might seem natural, but he may also have been thinking about the impact of Saul's disobedience on the nation. No doubt Saul's actions while serving as the leader of God's people would have serious consequences for their spiritual well-being. Later we are told that Samuel "mourned" for Saul (v. 35). While he had warned the people about what life under a king would involve (1 Samuel 8:10-18), his response to Saul's disobedience was not an "I-told-you-so" attitude. He was genuinely concerned for Saul and for the nation.

II. Samuel's Message to Saul (1 Samuel 15:12-16, 22, 23)
A. Disobedience Exhibited (v. 12)

12Early in the morning Samuel got up and went to meet Saul, but he was told, "Saul has gone to Carmel. There he has set up a monument in his own honor and has turned and gone on down to Gilgal."

Though Samuel had experienced a rather sleepless night, he still arose *early in the morning* to carry out his responsibility of confronting Saul. However, Saul had *gone to Carmel*, a town in the hill country of Judah. *There* he had *set up a monument in his own honor*, apparently to commemorate his victory over the Amalekites. So proud was he of his accomplishments that he did not even seem aware that he had not fully obeyed the commands given him by the Lord through Samuel. He was more interested in promoting himself than in obeying the Lord.

From Carmel Saul had *gone on down to Gilgal*. Here Samuel had assembled the people and reaffirmed Saul's kingship following Saul's victory over the Ammonites (1 Samuel 11:14). Gilgal was also the place where Saul had earlier ignored Samuel's counsel and was told that none of his descendants would follow him as king (1 Samuel 13:8-14). Was Saul planning to continue his victory celebration at the very location where he had earlier been reprimanded by Samuel for his disobedience? This was hardly a time for celebration, as Saul would soon discover.

B. Disobedience Exposed (vv. 13-16)

13When Samuel reached him, Saul said, "The LORD bless you! I have carried out the LORD's instructions."

It seems incredible that Saul would greet Samuel in such an enthusiastic manner and would actually claim before the Lord's prophet that he had *carried out the Lord's instructions*. But this he did, and the tragedy is that apparently he actually believed in his loyalty to the Lord. We today can be equally guilty of such spiritual "blind spots" and should guard ourselves against such self-deception. We need to remind ourselves constantly that partial obedience amounts to disobedience in God's eyes.

14But Samuel said, "What then is this bleating of sheep in my ears? What is this lowing of cattle that I hear?"

Samuel may have been old (1 Samuel 8:1, 5), but he was not deaf! God had told Saul to destroy everything belonging to the Amalekites. The war against these people was primarily to carry out God's judgment against them; it was not to be used as an opportunity for Israel to accumulate spoils. Yet even as Saul was proclaiming to Samuel his obedience to God, there was the *bleating of sheep* and the *lowing of cattle*, drowning out the words of Saul and clearly proving that his claim was a lie.

15Saul answered, "The soldiers brought them from the Amalekites; they spared the best of the sheep and cattle to sacrifice to the Lord your God, but we totally destroyed the rest."

It is sad to observe Saul's attempt to divert any blame from himself by calling attention to what *the soldiers* did. Yet according to verse 9, "Saul and the army" *spared* those whom the Lord had commanded to be destroyed. Saul claimed that *the best* of the livestock had been spared in order *to sacrifice* them *to the Lord*. We may question whether this was the real reason for sparing these animals. But even if we give Saul the benefit of the doubt and assume that his actions were done for the Lord, this does not excuse his actions. To clothe self-will with religious language does not make it any less presumptuous or proud.

Saul also added, *we totally destroyed the rest*. Thus when it came to acting in obedience to God's command, Saul included himself among the number. Any disobedient actions were attributed to the soldiers. Many students have also noted Saul's use of the words *your God* in referring to the Lord. One might have expected "my God" or "our God." Possibly Saul was sensing a distance between himself and God (and Samuel as well), even though he was professing obedience to God. However, we do not want to read too much into the expression. As noted in comments on Genesis 27:20 in volume 1, the expression is used quite innocently in the Scripture. (See 2 Kings 19:4; 1 Chronicles 22:11.)

16"Stop!" Samuel said to Saul. "Let me tell you what the Lord said to me last night."
"Tell me," Saul replied.

It was during the *night* that the boy Samuel had received a message from God about the judgment that God would bring upon the priest Eli and his family (1 Samuel 3:11-14). Now Samuel was about to declare similar words of judgment upon a king. But as a prophet of God, his responsibility was to speak *what the Lord said*, regardless of who would be affected.

C. Obedience Expected (vv. 22, 23)

According to verses 17-21, Samuel reviewed how God had taken Saul, when he was "small in [his] own eyes," and anointed him as king over Israel. Samuel then challenged Saul's actions concerning the Amalekites, to which Saul responded with yet another attempt to defend his conduct. Once again he called attention to the actions of the soldiers (rather than his own) and claimed that any livestock that had been spared were spared for the purposes of providing sacrifices to the Lord. It was clear that Saul did not grasp the seriousness of his behavior and was not at all sensitive to what God demanded of him.

²²But Samuel replied:
"Does the Lord delight in burnt offerings and sacrifices
*   as much as in obeying the voice of the Lord?*
To obey is better than sacrifice,
*   and to heed is better than the fat of rams.*

Burnt offerings and sacrifices were a part of the requirements in the law given by God through Moses. But they were never meant to be an end in themselves, as if bringing those offerings was all God required of his people. Such acts of worship are designed to aid and to promote our obedience to God's will and his way. When they are made substitutes for daily obedience, they can be only offensive to God. Obedience, not simply the outward show of religion through acts of public worship, demonstrates the true condition of the heart in one's relationship with God. And that is as true for us today as it was for Saul in his day.

²³"For rebellion is like the sin of divination,
*   and arrogance like the evil of idolatry.*
Because you have rejected the word of the Lord,
*   he has rejected you as king."*

The one who rejects *the word of the Lord* as his standard for guidance must look for guidance from another source. That source may be *divination* (the use of the occult and related practices to receive direction) or *idolatry* (which was a temptation to God's people through much of Old Testament history). Saul had not sunk to the level of either of these practices, though he would, near the end of his life, consult a witch for guidance (1 Samuel 28). But at this point, he had substituted his own will in place of God's clear word through the prophet Samuel. He had chosen what he wanted to do, not what God said he must do. This was *rebellion*, and it was really no better than putting a witch or an idol in the place of God. Saul's *arrogance* had elevated his own ego above God, thus it was the same as idolatry.

In response to Samuel's solemn words of judgment, Saul finally uttered the words "I have sinned" (v. 24), which he should have spoken long before this. Once more Samuel told Saul that the kingdom would be given to "one of your neighbors—to one better than you" (v. 28). Again this individual is not named; but with Saul's rejection now certain, one may assume that the selection of the next king will take place before long. That selection process will be the topic of the first passage covered in the next chapter of studies.

How to Say It

ABIJAH. Uh-*bye*-juh.

AGAG. *Ay*-gag.

AMALEKITES. *Am*-uh-leh-kites or Uh-*mal*-ih-kites.

AMMONITES. *Am*-un-ites.

BEERSHEBA. Beer-*she*-buh.

BENJAMIN. *Ben*-juh-mun.

BETH AVEN. *Beth Ay*-ven (strong accent on *ay*).

BETHEL. *Beth*-ul.

CARMEL. *Car*-mul.

ESAU. *Ee*-saw.

GEBA. *Gee*-buh (*G* as in *get*).

GIBEAH. *Gib*-ee-uh (*G* as in *get*).

GILGAL. *Gil*-gal (*G* as in *get*).

JABESH GILEAD. *Jay*-besh *Gil*-ee-ud (strong accent on *Gil*).

JERUSALEM. Juh-*roo*-suh-lem.

MATRI. *May*-try.

MICMASH. *Mik*-mash.

MIZPAH. *Miz*-pah.

NEGEV. *Neg*-ev.

PHILISTINES. Fuh-*liss*-teens or *Fill*-us-teens.

RAMAH. *Ray*-muh.

SINAI. *Sigh*-nye or *Sigh*-nay-eye.

THUMMIM. *Thum*-im (*th* as in *thin*).

URIM. *You*-rim.

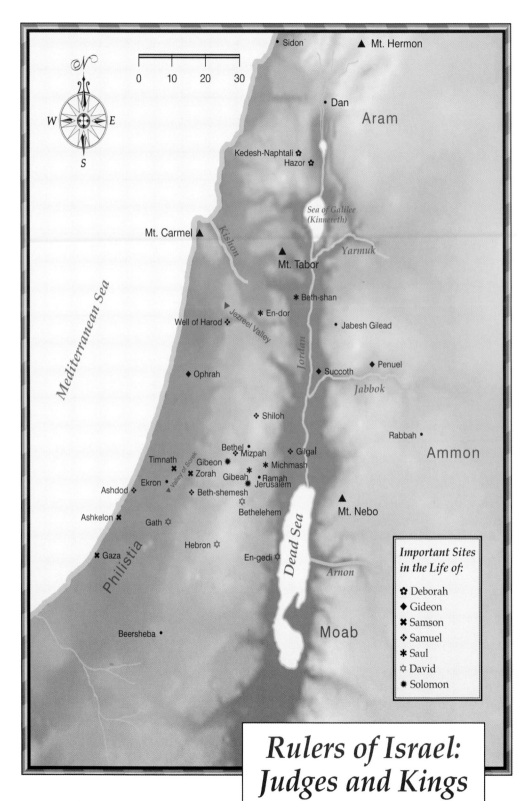

Rulers of Israel:
Judges and Kings

Chapter 5

Prelude to the Reign of David

1 Samuel 16:1-13; 18:1-16; 2 Samuel 1:17-27; 5:1-5

DAVID ANOINTED AS KING (1 SAMUEL 16:1-13)

Establishing the Groundwork

After Samuel's confrontation of Saul, both men went to their respective homes: Samuel to Ramah, and Saul to Gibeah (1 Samuel 15:34). Verse 35 states, "Until the day Samuel died, he did not go to see Saul again, though Samuel mourned for him." Though Samuel's love and concern for Saul never lessened, the prophet sought no more contact with Saul since the Lord had rejected him as king. Saul did come to Samuel on one occasion during his quest to find David (1 Samuel 19:22), and, as noted earlier, he visited a witch in order to consult Samuel after his death. Samuel, however, was to turn his attention to a replacement for Saul.

Examining the Text

I. Conversing with God (1 Samuel 16:1-3)

A. Command to Samuel (v. 1)

¹The LORD said to Samuel, "How long will you mourn for Saul, since I have rejected him as king over Israel? Fill your horn with oil and be on your way; I am sending you to Jesse of Bethlehem. I have chosen one of his sons to be king."

The time to *mourn for Saul* was over. The Lord's prophet had to be about the Lord's business: to anoint a man to replace Saul as *king*. This did not mean that the new king would take office immediately. Saul himself had been anointed in private, when no one but he and Samuel knew about it (1 Samuel 9:27–10:1). This new king's anointing would be known to only a few; Saul would remain king for several years to come. Samuel did not yet know whom he was to anoint, but it would be one of the *sons* of *Jesse*, a citizen of *Bethlehem*.

B. Concern by Samuel (v. 2)

²But Samuel said, "How can I go? Saul will hear about it and kill me."
The LORD said, "Take a heifer with you and say, 'I have come to sacrifice to
the LORD.'

Modest Saul had been tolerant of those who had opposed his kingship
at the beginning of his reign (1 Samuel 10:27; 11:12, 13). But Saul was no
longer modest and no longer tolerant. He had shown himself arrogant
enough to go his own way in defiance of God's order. Now God was telling
Samuel to anoint another man to replace Saul. If Saul heard about that, he
would call it treason. It is likely that Samuel would be punished by death.
But the Lord had a ready answer for Samuel's dilemma. Saul need not know
about the anointing. Samuel could take a *heifer* (young cow) to Bethlehem and
offer a *sacrifice* there. It was not necessary that Saul be informed about the
other purpose of the trip.

C. Commission for Samuel (v. 3)

³"Invite Jesse to the sacrifice, and I will show you what to do. You are to
anoint for me the one I indicate."

Samuel was to *invite Jesse to the sacrifice.* Later verses indicate that he was
to invite Jesse's sons as well. In many sacrifices, only a small part of the
sacrificed animal was actually burned on the altar. In this case, probably a
part of the meat of the sacrificed heifer would provide a feast for the guests.

By this time, Samuel had been known as a judge of Israel for many years.
It was not likely that any of the Israelites would have declined an invitation
from him to attend a sacrifice. Once those invited were assembled, God
would give Samuel further instructions. Most important, he would tell him
whom to *anoint.*

II. Congregating at Bethlehem (1 Samuel 16:4, 5)
A. Concern of the Elders (v. 4)

⁴Samuel did what the LORD said. When he arrived at Bethlehem, the elders of
the town trembled when they met him. They asked, "Do you come in peace?"

The elders of the town trembled at Samuel's arrival. Perhaps they had heard
of Samuel's recent execution of the king of the Amalekites (1 Samuel 15:33).
Had he come to *Bethlehem* to accuse the elders or certain citizens of the town
of having committed some terrible wrong? Or had he *come in peace?* The
elders were frightened.

B. Consecration of the People (v. 5)

⁵Samuel replied, "Yes, in peace; I have come to sacrifice to the LORD. Consecrate yourselves and come to the sacrifice with me." Then he consecrated Jesse and his sons and invited them to the sacrifice.

Samuel reassured the elders: he had come *in peace.* His purpose was *to sacrifice to the Lord.* The text seems to indicate that he invited the elders to be present as well as Jesse and his sons, but in the following verses only Jesse and his sons are mentioned. Possibly the events recorded from verse 6 on involved a private meeting of only Samuel and Jesse and his sons, at some time during the proceedings.

In the days before running water was common in the homes of rural America, it was customary for farmers to bathe only on Saturday night. Then on Sunday morning they put on clean clothes to go to church. In a somewhat similar manner, the ancient Israelites *consecrated* themselves before meeting the Lord in a special way. Exodus 19:10-14 tells of an occasion when such ceremonial cleansing included putting on clean clothes. *Jesse and his sons* received special treatment as they were prepared by Samuel himself.

III. Considering Jesse's Sons (1 Samuel 16:6-13)
A. Contrasting Standards (vv. 6, 7)

⁶When they arrived, Samuel saw Eliab and thought, "Surely the LORD's anointed stands here before the LORD."

Jesse and his sons met with Samuel at the place of sacrifice. Samuel first *saw Eliab,* probably because he was the oldest of Jesse's sons (1 Samuel 17:28); and Samuel liked what he saw. *Surely* this fine-looking young man was to be Israel's next king!

⁷But the LORD said to Samuel, "Do not consider his appearance or his height, for I have rejected him. The LORD does not look at the things man looks at. Man looks at the outward appearance, but the LORD looks at the heart."

People like to have a leader who looks the part—one who is tall and handsome and stands out from his peers. But other qualifications are more important. Samuel thought that no one could be a more capable king than Eliab, but the Lord knew better. He was looking for a man after his own *heart* (1 Samuel 13:14).

B. Continuing Review (vv. 8-10)

⁸Then Jesse called Abinadab and had him pass in front of Samuel. But Samuel said, "The LORD has not chosen this one either."

Apparently Samuel had made known to Jesse his purpose to appoint a king as well as to offer a sacrifice. Jesse was presenting his sons one by one, probably in order of their ages. The Lord rejected the second as he had rejected the first.

> *⁹Jesse then had Shammah pass by, but Samuel said, "Nor has the Lord chosen this one."*

The third son likewise was rejected. It seems that the Lord, without words, made his will known to Samuel's mind, and Samuel conveyed that message to Jesse. From Samuel's youth he had thus been revealing the will of God, so that "all Israel from Dan to Beersheba recognized that Samuel was attested as a prophet of the Lord" (1 Samuel 3:20).

> *¹⁰Jesse had seven of his sons pass before Samuel, but Samuel said to him, "The Lord has not chosen these."*

No longer naming the *sons* one by one, the record adds that four more of them were presented *before Samuel*. Most likely they were presented one by one, and one by one the Lord rejected them.

C. Calling for David (vv. 11, 12)

> *¹¹So he asked Jesse, "Are these all the sons you have?"*
> *"There is still the youngest," Jesse answered, "but he is tending the sheep."*
> *Samuel said, "Send for him; we will not sit down until he arrives."*

Did *Jesse* have any other sons? That was Samuel's first question. Yes, said Jesse, but only one—*the youngest*. It had not seemed necessary to have him present. Surely *he* would not be chosen to rule his older brothers and the entire nation of Israel. Someone was needed to take care of the *sheep*, and naturally that duty had fallen to the "kid brother." But now all the other brothers had been rejected. There was nothing to do but send for the one who remained.

Note that the sacrifice that Samuel had come to offer has not been mentioned since verse 5. Perhaps at that point (when Jesse and his seven sons "arrived," verse 6) the sacrifice was offered. The meat for the family feast would then have been cooking while Samuel was searching for the chosen king. Perhaps Samuel now said, *We will not sit down* (to the feast) *until he arrives*. Or possibly *we will not sit down* merely means that we will not rest—we will not end the search for God's chosen king—until the youngest son has been included.

> *¹²So he sent and had him brought in. He was ruddy, with a fine appearance and handsome features.*
> *Then the Lord said, "Rise and anoint him; he is the one."*

We can only guess how far away the young man was with the sheep, or how long it took for him to join the family. But when he came, Samuel noticed his *fine appearance and handsome features*. Perhaps he looked as good as the oldest son who had impressed Samuel at the beginning of his search (v. 6). Some students take *ruddy* to mean that the young man had a healthy outdoor complexion; others take it to indicate that he had red hair. But it was neither his complexion nor his hair that the Lord focused on. He saw the young man's heart, and he gave Samuel a quick and clear message: *Rise and anoint him; he is the one.*

D. Confirming God's Chosen (v. 13)

¹³So Samuel took the horn of oil and anointed him in the presence of his brothers, and from that day on the Spirit of the LORD came upon David in power. Samuel then went to Ramah.

On an earlier occasion, Samuel had anointed Saul in private (1 Samuel 9:27–10:1). Only Samuel and Saul knew about this until the time came to reveal the choice and let all Israel know that God had made it (1 Samuel 10:17-24). In the same way, the anointing of Israel's new king was known only to his family (unless the elders of Bethlehem were also there). Undoubtedly any who were present were warned not to tell anyone what had happened. If arrogant King Saul heard about it, surely he would want to kill both Samuel and the son of Jesse who was *anointed*. And he would probably pour out his wrath on any others who were witnesses, treating them as coconspirators.

The Spirit of the Lord came upon David. Now at last we are given the name of this youngest son of Jesse, who was anointed to be king. He was *David*. After becoming king, he would subdue enemy nations and build Israel into an empire. He would also become known as "Israel's singer of songs" (2 Samuel 23:1), writing many of the songs we treasure in the book of Psalms. The evidence for the presence of God's Spirit on David is not recorded, as it was when the Spirit *came upon* Saul *in power* (1 Samuel 10:6, 10, 11). Instead, the mention of the Spirit's presence on David seems to be given to contrast the fact that "the Spirit of the Lord had departed from Saul" (v. 14).

Samuel then went to Ramah, which was his home (1 Samuel 7:17). For a long time the anointing of David seemed to make no difference—either to David or to the nation. In fact, David went back to herding sheep (1 Samuel 16:19) and did not become king until several years later, after Saul was dead. In the meantime he served King Saul in several ways. His music subdued an evil spirit that troubled Saul (1 Samuel 16:14-23). He killed the giant Goliath, and the invading Philistines fled (1 Samuel 17:49-51). He led Saul's troops in battle so successfully that the king became jealous of his popularity (1 Samuel 18:5-9). When Saul determined to murder him, David fled instead of fighting (1 Samuel 19:8-18). Not until Saul was dead did David become king of Judah (2 Samuel 2:1-4), and then seven and a half more years passed before he became king of all Israel (2 Samuel 5:4, 5).

JONATHAN'S LOVE FOR DAVID; SAUL'S FEAR OF DAVID (1 SAMUEL 18:1-16)

Establishing the Groundwork

The previous passage that was examined ended with a reference to the Spirit's coming upon David in power (1 Samuel 16:13). We may assume that the Spirit guided David's hand on the harp strings that banished an evil spirit from Saul (1 Samuel 16:14-23), guided the same hand as it hurled a stone at Goliath (1 Samuel 17:49), guided David's mind in his military strategy (1 Samuel 18:5) and the administration of justice (2 Samuel 8:15), and inspired the many psalms of David (2 Samuel 23:1, 2). When the ceremony of anointing was over, Samuel went back home and David continued with his work as a shepherd. But that work was interrupted in interesting ways.

Saul was troubled by an evil spirit, evidently one who could be driven away only by the music of David's harp, which, as noted above, likely reflected the influence of the Spirit of God. David was called to play for the king whenever the evil spirit manifested its influence, and the evil spirit fled. David could then return to his father's sheep until Saul needed him again (1 Samuel 17:15).

During these events, the Philistines remained a constant threat to the Israelites. Three of David's brothers were in the army recruited to fight the Philistines, and on one occasion David went to their camp to take them some food from home. He arrived at a time when a Philistine giant named Goliath was challenging any man of Israel to meet him in single combat. No one in the army seemed inclined to accept the challenge, so David did. He felled the giant with one stone from his sling, then used the giant's own sword to cut off his head. The Israelites proceeded to win a decisive victory over the Philistines that day (1 Samuel 17:1-54).

David's courageous action ended his work as a shepherd. He was kept in the service of the king, and soon became a general of the army. Our next passage notes how David's popularity with all of Israel increased dramatically and how he and Saul's son Jonathan became especially close friends. Only one person in the entire nation seemed to hold a negative attitude toward David—and that was King Saul himself.

I. Jonathan's Love for David (1 Samuel 18:1-4)

Let us note that Jonathan took the initiative in establishing this friendship. His doing so says much about the character of this son of Saul and reveals how different his attitude toward David was from his father's.

A. Stated in Words (vv. 1, 2)

¹After David had finished talking with Saul, Jonathan became one in spirit with David, and he loved him as himself.

Some individuals in Jonathan's position might have been jealous of David, but not he. A valiant warrior himself, Jonathan had received the same kind of admiration from the people as was now being showered upon this newcomer. Yet far from being envious, Jonathan was filled with admiration for David. Instead of seeing David's accomplishments as the basis for hostility, Jonathan saw them as the basis for friendship; and he *became one in spirit with David*. One quality of a person who would be a friend and have a friend is the capacity of seeing and appreciating in another that which is noble and admirable. This Jonathan possessed to a marked degree. As Saul's son, he could be considered the rightful successor to his father's throne; yet he did not hesitate to offer his love and friendship to David, even when it was clear that David would be Saul's successor.

Some have given considerable attention to the use of the word *loved* here and in verse 3, proposing that the relationship between David and Jonathan was homosexual in nature. But the Bible gives absolutely no indication of this. The Hebrew word that is here translated "loved" is also used of Saul's initial affinity for David (1 Samuel 16:21, where it is rendered "liked him very much" in the *New International Version*) and of Hiram King of Tyre's friendly relations with David (1 Kings 5:1, where it is translated "had always been on friendly terms with" in the *New International Version*). Thus the word can have political or diplomatic overtones.

²From that day Saul kept David with him and did not let him return to his father's house.

According to 1 Samuel 17:15, David's contact with Saul was at first intermittent. He was called upon whenever Saul was troubled by an evil spirit, and his playing of the harp resulted in the spirit's leaving Saul (1 Samuel 16:23). But once David had demonstrated his prowess on the battlefield with Goliath, his shepherding days were over.

B. Shown by Actions (vv. 3, 4)

³And Jonathan made a covenant with David because he loved him as himself.

Jonathan demonstrated the sincerity of his love for David by making a *covenant* with him. Again, Jonathan took the initiative in further cementing this bond of friendship. It would not have been appropriate for David, a commoner at this point, to propose a friendship pact between himself and the king's son. But the king's son could do so.

⁴Jonathan took off the robe he was wearing and gave it to David, along with his tunic, and even his sword, his bow and his belt.

As a means of what might be considered "ratifying" the covenant he was making with David, Jonathan gave to David certain articles of clothing and some of his weaponry. To receive any part of the clothing that had been worn by a ruler or by his oldest son and heir was considered in the ancient Near East the highest honor that could be conferred on a subject. It is possible that in giving David these items, Jonathan was recognizing that David was the appointed successor to Saul.

Specifically, *Jonathan took off the robe he was wearing*—most likely the piece of clothing that designated rank or royalty (perhaps similar to Joseph's "richly ornamented robe" in Genesis 37:3). He also gave David *his tunic*, a term that designated the military garments that were worn over the robe. In addition, Jonathan gave up *his sword, his bow and his belt*. All of these were part of his military gear; in fact, David referred especially to Jonathan's bow in the lament he composed after Jonathan's and Saul's deaths (2 Samuel 1:22).

II. David's Success in Battle (1 Samuel 18:5-7)
A. Appreciated by All (v. 5)

⁵Whatever Saul sent him to do, David did it so successfully that Saul gave him a high rank in the army. This pleased all the people, and Saul's officers as well.

These initial expeditions in which David took part were probably not on a large scale, since David had little actual military experience. But as his abilities on the battlefield became evident, he was eventually given *a high rank in the army*. He soon became a national hero and was even highly respected by *Saul's officers*. Thus even those most loyal to Saul found nothing objectionable in David's conduct and did not react with jealousy to his rapid promotion and his rising popularity.

This entire verse is likely a summary of David's exploits, which may have occupied some length of time. The next verse, however, goes back and resumes the account from the time of the defeat of the Philistines following the death of Goliath.

B. Acclaimed by the Women (vv. 6, 7)

⁶When the men were returning home after David had killed the Philistine, the women came out from all the towns of Israel to meet King Saul with singing and dancing, with joyful songs and with tambourines and lutes.

As the Israelites *were returning home* following their victory over the Philistines, which had been the direct result of David's killing of *the Philistine* (Goliath), various Israelite *women came out . . . to meet King Saul* since he was leading the victory procession. It was customary in Old Testament times for women to thus welcome their men returning from triumph. There was much *singing and dancing*, accompanied by *tambourines and lutes*. The Hebrew word translated *lutes* comes from the word for "three" and may describe a three-stringed instrument or a triangular-shaped instrument.

⁷As they danced, they sang:
"Saul has slain his thousands,
*   and David his tens of thousands."*

The words *they sang* are literally "they answered" in the Hebrew text, indicating perhaps some kind of antiphonal singing in which a part of the women sang *Saul has slain his thousands* and another part responded with *and David his tens of thousands*. The terms *thousands* and *tens of thousands* were probably not intended to be taken literally; each represented a large number. (See the similar expression in Psalm 91:7 and Micah 6:7.) The refrain became quite popular and came to be known even among the Philistines (1 Samuel 21:10, 11; 29:5).

III. Saul's Jealousy of David (1 Samuel 18:8-12)

A. Evil Thoughts (v. 8)

⁸Saul was very angry; this refrain galled him. "They have credited David with tens of thousands," he thought, "but me with only thousands. What more can he get but the kingdom?"

Saul took the words of the women's *refrain* literally and became *very angry* at the idea that David was being *credited* with accomplishing more than he had. Gone was the humility that he had shown when, years earlier, Samuel had first intimated that he was to become Israel's first king (1 Samuel 9:21). Now his pride was hurt and he was upset. It is easy for someone in that frame of mind to try to "read" certain situations and make accusations about people that may not be warranted. In this case, Saul began to speculate that the adoration being directed toward David might result in losing his *kingdom* to this young "upstart."

One should note that Samuel had already told Saul that because of his disobedience, he was to be replaced by someone else "better" than he was (1 Samuel 13:13, 14; 15:27, 28). This must have been in the back of Saul's mind as he witnessed the rising tide of David's popularity.

B. Evil Eye (v. 9)

⁹And from that time on Saul kept a jealous eye on David.

The *jealous eye* that *Saul kept* on David blinded him to the excellence of character that this young man possessed. As time passed and David's popularity showed no signs of declining, the king became increasingly frustrated and desperate.

C. Evil Actions (vv. 10-12)

¹⁰The next day an evil spirit from God came forcefully upon Saul. He was prophesying in his house, while David was playing the harp, as he usually did. Saul had a spear in his hand

The *evil spirit from God* is first mentioned in 1 Samuel 16:14-23, following the anointing of David by Samuel to become Israel's next king. Some may question how an evil spirit could come from God. God has complete control over all spirits, both good and evil, but we should not forget that God exercises his sovereignty through a permissive will as well as a positive and active will. God permits human beings to do evil if that is their choice. He did not make Saul do wrong by deliberately overpowering his will through sending an evil spirit. This is contrary to much clear teaching of both Testaments. God is a God of holiness and truth. He seeks to lead individuals to righteousness, not wrongdoing. Saul had had numerous opportunities to accept such leading from God. God had sent the prophet Samuel to reveal his will to Saul.

Instead Saul had chosen to disobey God and to ignore his commands, as studies in the previous chapter from 1 Samuel 13 and 1 Samuel 15 have indicated. Saul had placed himself, through his own foolish choices, in a position in which God's judgment was administered through the sending of an evil spirit. The process may be similar to that described by Paul in Romans 1:21-28, where the statement "God gave them over" is used of people who have chosen to follow "the sinful desires of their hearts" (v. 24) rather than the path of righteousness.

On the occasion mentioned in this verse, Saul *was prophesying in his house.* The Hebrew form of this verb is used both of prophesying that originates with God and prophesying that has evil as its source. The emphasis of the word seems to be more on the emotional fervor of the one prophesying, which can be either an attitude of praise or one of ranting or raving, as it clearly was in Saul's case. (Another example of this kind of erratic conduct is seen in the behavior of the prophets of Baal on Mount Carmel, according to 1 Kings 18:27-29.) Saul acted like one possessed, but he was not possessed by the Spirit of God.

It is also noted that on this occasion, *David was playing the harp, as he usually did.* Previously David's harp playing had had a soothing effect on Saul (1 Samuel 16:23). Now, however, David was more than a harp player; he had become Saul's rival to the throne. David came to represent all the greatness and goodness that Saul had failed to attain as a leader in Israel.

Why Saul *had a spear in his hand* at this moment is not known. He may have been looking over some new weaponry, or he may have become very fearful and suspicious as part of his rising jealousy toward David. Perhaps he felt more secure with a weapon near him.

[11] . . . and he hurled it, saying to himself, "I'll pin David to the wall." But David eluded him twice.

Saul's brooding hostility toward David suddenly erupted into an overt act. He tried to kill David while David was engaged in trying to help him. That *David eluded him twice* may refer to two separate occasions rather than two attempts on his life at this moment. Some believe the second attempt was the one recorded in 1 Samuel 19:9, 10. Others believe that the attempt recorded there was actually a third attempt. Either way, it required great courage for David to place himself in a position where a second or third attempt on his life could be made. It is apparent that he harbored no ill will against Saul, yet Saul wanted to reward David's loyalty and service by killing him.

[12]Saul was afraid of David, because the Lord was with David but had left Saul.

One would think that David would have been afraid of Saul, who was king and who had tried to kill him. Yet it was Saul who *was afraid of David,* because he realized that David's resources in the Lord were more than he possessed, even as king. God was *with David,* as he had been with Joseph in Pharaoh's prison and as he was later to be with Daniel in the lions' den. The trust in God that was honed through such experiences as these is often reflected in David's psalms.

IV. The Lord's Presence with David (1 Samuel 18:13-16)
A. David's Continued Success (vv. 13, 14)

¹³So he sent David away from him and gave him command over a thousand men, and David led the troops in their campaigns.

Since Saul could no longer feel at ease around David, he removed David from his immediate presence by assigning him duties on the battlefield. Specifically, he *gave* David *command over a thousand men.* Verses 17-25 of this chapter indicate that part of Saul's motive for doing this was the hope that David would be killed in battle.

¹⁴In everything he did he had great success, because the Lord was with him.

The *success* that David had experienced previously (v. 5) continued, *because the Lord was with him.* The contrast between David and Saul throughout this passage is striking. The Lord was with David because David was willing to trust the Lord. If Saul had not been disobedient, selfish, and stubborn, God would have continued to be with him too, and his kingship would have been blessed.

B. Saul's Continued Fear (v. 15)

¹⁵When Saul saw how successful he was, he was afraid of him.

David's continued success only served to increase Saul's fear of him. Much of the remainder of the account of Saul in 1 Samuel focuses on his quest to do away with David. Eventually David was forced to leave the court of Saul (and the friendship of Jonathan), becoming a fugitive whom Saul spent much time and effort trying to find.

The conclusion of Saul's life was indeed tragic. No trace of the humility or the heroic spirit of his early days remained, no turning to God in confidence as he had when he rescued Jabesh Gilead from the Ammonites (1 Samuel 11:13). Before what would be his final battle with the Philistines, Saul sought counsel from a witch (1 Samuel 28:4-25) so that he might be able to speak with Samuel, who had died earlier (1 Samuel 25:1). But the prophet had nothing encouraging to say to Saul; his words were alarming and ominous: "The Lord will hand over both Israel and you to the Philistines, and tomorrow you and your sons will be with me" (1 Samuel 28:19). After hearing from Samuel, Saul "fell full length on the ground, filled with fear because of Samuel's words" (v. 20). During the ensuing battle on Mount Gilboa, Saul was badly wounded and, to avoid further abuse from the Philistines, fell on his own sword (1 Samuel 31:1-6).

C. The People's Continued Adoration (v. 16)

16But all Israel and Judah loved David, because he led them in their campaigns.

The verb forms in this verse, in Hebrew, are all participles, indicating a continuance of the attitude or action expressed. *All Israel and Judah* continued to love and admire David, because of his conduct and his valor as *he led them in their campaigns.* Later his military prowess will be cited as one reason for him to become king over all Israel (2 Samuel 5:1, 2).

The reference here to both Israel and Judah, years before the division of the kingdom occurred, is not so odd. (See also 1 Samuel 11:8.) It likely bears testimony to the existence of a certain separateness that later became a definite rift.

DAVID'S LAMENT FOR SAUL AND JONATHAN (2 SAMUEL 1:17-27)

Establishing the Groundwork

As noted toward the end of the previous study, so intense was Saul's hostility toward David that David was forced to leave Saul's court and go into hiding in the Judean hill country south of Bethlehem. Saul continued to pursue David, and at least twice David had the opportunity to kill Saul; but he spared him because Saul was "the Lord's anointed" (1 Samuel 24:1-6, 10; 26:1-11, 23).

During David's flight from Saul, about 400 men who were dissatisfied with Saul as king had gathered around David, apparently looking to him for leadership (1 Samuel 22:1, 2). Before long, this group became a formidable fighting force, eventually growing in number to 600. For a time they came and lived among Achish, king of the Philistines, because David believed that such an action would cause Saul to cease his pursuit of David (1 Samuel 27:1, 2). When Achish decided to launch a campaign against Saul, he sought to enlist David and his men in the effort. Some of the Philistine rulers did not trust David, however, so Achish sent him to Ziklag, a town located on the border between Philistia and Israel that Achish had given David as a base of operations (1 Samuel 27:5, 6).

While David was at Ziklag, he received news of the death of Saul. The messenger who brought the news, an Amalekite, claimed to have killed Saul (2 Samuel 1:1-10), expecting David to reward him for his actions. (Apparently the Amalekite knew something of the hostility between Saul and David.) But the messenger was lying, for Saul had taken his own life (1 Samuel 31:4). His lie cost him his life; David had the Amalekite put to death for claiming to have killed the Lord's anointed (2 Samuel 1:13-16).

"Israel's singer of songs" (2 Samuel 23:1) then proceeded to compose a very touching lament in honor of both Saul and Jonathan.

Examining the Text

I. Lament for Saul (2 Samuel 1:17-21)

Poets sometimes puzzle us with their figurative language. Sometimes they abandon the ordinary practices of grammar for the sake of meter and rhyme. For the same reason, they sometimes find and use words we never heard of before; or they use them in ways with which we are unfamiliar. We have to guess at the meaning or use a dictionary. In other cases they include a word that has more than one meaning, and again we have to guess at which meaning the poet is using.

The Hebrew poetry found in the Old Testament exhibits these same qualities. In addition, the poets sometimes abbreviate; and a translator has to add certain words to make sense in English. However, not all translators add the same words. Thus, if we read David's lament in two or more versions, we may find some puzzling differences. But regardless of the version used, the message of this text is unmistakably clear: David is expressing heartfelt grief at the deaths of Saul and Jonathan.

A. Prelude (vv. 17, 18)

¹⁷David took up this lament concerning Saul and his son Jonathan,

We can understand why David felt grief for *Jonathan*, the dear friend who had actually turned against his own father and had risked his own life to save David from death (1 Samuel 20:27-34). More surprising may be David's grief over *Saul*, the vindictive king who had pursued David relentlessly in order to kill him. But David's grief for Saul was real, too. Saul was God's anointed ruler, and for a time he had served God's people well. David loved and respected him for that. If David were a lesser man with personal ambitions, he would have found the death of Saul and his three sons a reason to celebrate; for it presented him the opportunity to become king. David, however, was a man of integrity; and he held the office of the king in high regard. There was no way he was going to cheapen that office by using Saul's death to further his own agenda.

¹⁸ . . . and ordered that the men of Judah be taught this lament of the bow (it is written in the Book of Jashar):

Here is a good example of the problems one can encounter in working with Hebrew poetry. Translating the Hebrew words as literally as possible, we read, "And he said to teach the sons of Judah bow." The translators of the *New International Version* took this reference to the bow to indicate that the lament that follows was known as *lament of the bow* (which perhaps eventually became its title), because it praises the bow of Jonathan (v. 22). Apparently David wanted his own tribe (the tribe of *Judah*) to learn the lament and thus commemorate the loss of Saul (even though Saul was of the tribe of Benjamin, not Judah). The *New American Standard Bible* reads, "the song of the bow" instead of "the lament of the bow." This may have the same meaning, but some students believe it means that the following lament is to be sung to the tune of another song called "the Song of the Bow."

Whatever meaning we give to the first part of verse 18, the latter part tells us that the following lament, or else another song sung to the same tune, *is written in the Book of Jashar.* The Hebrew word *Jashar* means straight, upright, or righteous. The book is also mentioned in Joshua 10:13, where it is said to contain the account of how the sun stood still to allow the Israelites to win an important battle during the time of Joshua. Apparently the book was a record of some of the significant people and events in Israel's history. At some point it was lost or destroyed.

B. Israel's Distress (v. 19)

¹⁹*"Your glory, O Israel, lies slain on your heights.*
   How the mighty have fallen!

What does the phrase *your glory, O Israel* describe? It may refer to King Saul or to both Saul and Jonathan, who are the primary subjects of the lament. Or, it may refer to all the men of Israel *slain* in the battle with the Philistines—praising them as the finest men in Israel's army. Possibly a combination of these concepts is meant. The term *heights* apparently describes Mount Gilboa and the highlands around it.

C. Enemies' Delight (v. 20)

²⁰*"Tell it not in Gath,*
   proclaim it not in the streets of Ashkelon,
lest the daughters of the Philistines be glad,
   lest the daughters of the uncircumcised rejoice.

Gath and *Ashkelon* were two of the Philistines' chief cities. (See the map on page 102.) David was wishing that the news of Saul's death could never be told there. His wish was in vain, of course. First Samuel 31:9, 10 tells how the news was heralded in every Philistine town. According to 1 Samuel 18:6, 7, the women of Israel celebrated the triumph of their men in battle; here the Philistine women *rejoice* in the victory achieved by their soldiers.

D. Mountains' Drought (v. 21)

²¹*"O mountains of Gilboa,*
may you have neither dew nor rain,
nor fields that yield offerings [of grain].
For there the shield of the mighty was defiled,
the shield of Saul—no longer rubbed with oil."

The phrase *mountains of Gilboa* describes the highlands running southeast and south of the valley of Jezreel. These were verdant in spring. The steeper slopes were usually covered with woodlands, while on the level places one could produce fields of *grain*, some of which would be used as *offerings* to the Lord. (The brackets that appear with the words *of grain* indicate words supplied by the translator that are not in the original Hebrew text. They have been added to assist in understanding the meaning of the passage.) In David's grief he longed for all that region to be desolate—a waterless desert—because of the tragedy that had taken place there. *There the shield of the mighty* King Saul was disgraced by defeat, soiled by blood and by the dirt of the ground, and abandoned on the battlefield of defeat.

The final part of the verse presents another puzzle to the translator. Rendered word for word, it says, "the shield of Saul, not anointed with oil." *The New International Version* says that *the shield of Saul* was *no longer rubbed with oil.* Many students think that a warrior's shield was rubbed with oil to make it bright and shining. Others believe that the oil was meant to serve as a kind of lubricant, making arrows and spears glance off the shield more readily. But after the tragic battle on Mount Gilboa, Saul's shield was neither bright nor lubricated; it was *defiled* with blood and dirt—and because of that David mourned.

II. Praise for Saul and Jonathan (2 Samuel 1:22-24)

From a wail of grief, David's song now turns to a eulogy for the dead. Though three of Saul's sons had been killed in the horrible battle (1 Samuel 31:2), the eulogy centers on Saul and just one son, Jonathan. Of course, Jonathan had been David's closest friend.

A. Their Courage (v. 22)

22"From the blood of the slain,
from the flesh of the mighty,
the bow of Jonathan did not turn back,
the sword of Saul did not return unsatisfied.

Jonathan and *Saul* had been both valiant and victorious in battle. Jonathan seems to have possessed particular skill with the *bow* (1 Samuel 20:20, 36, 37). Saul, on the other hand, is associated with the *sword*. His size would have given him a definite advantage in combat with that weapon. The ancients sometimes spoke of the arrow as drinking the *blood* of its victim, while the sword was pictured as eating his *flesh*. David's association of these two weapons with Jonathan and Saul indicates that they were a formidable combat team. Individually, each man had made his mark on the battlefield as well. Saul had left the family farm to raise an army and win a dramatic victory for the people of Jabesh Gilead (1 Samuel 11:1-11). Jonathan, with only one companion, had attacked a Philistine garrison and put it to flight (1 Samuel 14:1-23). Saul and Jonathan truly had been successful before the battle in which they died, and even in that fatal fight their courage had not weakened.

B. Their Character (v. 23)

23"Saul and Jonathan—
in life they were loved and gracious,
and in death they were not parted.
They were swifter than eagles,
they were stronger than lions.

Perhaps when we think of Saul we remember the insane jealousy that moved him to try to kill David, who had done him nothing but good. David, however, remembered how *loved and gracious* Saul had been before that. Saul had received a shepherd boy into the royal court and had promoted him to a place of command over many older men.

Meanwhile, David and Jonathan had become the best of friends (1 Samuel 18:1-5). Jonathan disagreed vocally with his father's treatment of David (1 Samuel 20:32) and even helped David escape Saul's wrath (vv. 35-42). Yet he continued to serve faithfully in Israel's army under the command of his father. Together they died bravely on the field of battle.

Eagles are renowned for swiftness; *lions* are famous for their strength. In eulogizing these qualities of Saul and Jonathan, David was using appropriate standards of comparison.

C. Saul's Concern for Israel (v. 24)

²⁴"O daughters of Israel,
*   weep for Saul,*
who clothed you in scarlet and finery,
*   who adorned your garments with ornaments of gold."*

Here David called the women of *Israel* to join him in mourning for Saul. Israel's first king had done much for them. They were able to wear fine clothing and golden jewelry because the nation had prospered during his administration. Some of these costly clothes and jewels were likely among the spoils of Saul's successful wars (1 Samuel 14:47, 48).

III. Lament for Jonathan (2 Samuel 1:25-27)

The last stanza of David's lament expresses his grief over the loss of Jonathan, his dearest friend.

A. Jonathan's Death (v. 25)

²⁵"How the mighty have fallen in battle!
*   Jonathan lies slain on your heights.*

How the mighty have fallen! This cry of grief introduced the lament for Saul (v. 19); now it introduces the lament for Jonathan. But the Hebrew word for *mighty* is plural. The mourning is for both Saul and Jonathan, yes, and perhaps includes the warriors of Israel who died in the battle with the Philistines. However, the latter line of the verse centers attention on *Jonathan*. Along with the other heroes of Israel, he was *slain* in that fierce battle on the *heights* of his homeland—the elevated terrain on and around Mount Gilboa.

B. David's Grief (v. 26)

²⁶"I grieve for you, Jonathan my brother;
*   you were very dear to me.*
Your love for me was wonderful,
*   more wonderful than that of women.*

The Hebrew verb translated *grieve* means to be narrow or confining. David felt pressed and burdened by an overwhelming sense of grief over the death of his dearest friend. Many of us know that feeling, for we too have lost loved ones. Added to the crushing weight of sorrow is the feeling of utter helplessness. The dear one is dead. Nothing can be done about that. David's dear one was so close that he was more than a friend. David calls him *Jonathan my brother.*

As mentioned earlier in the comments on 1 Samuel 18:1, there is no suggestion in the Bible of a homosexual relationship between David and Jonathan; and no indication of this is to be seen in the closing line of the verse before us. David was simply stating that the strength of the bond between him and Jonathan was not one commonly found among men.

C. Closing Words of Sorrow (v. 27)

27 "How the mighty have fallen!
*   The weapons of war have perished!"*

How the mighty have fallen! This cry was the introduction of the lament for Saul (v. 19) and the lament for Jonathan (v. 25). Now it becomes the sorrowful conclusion of the entire elegy. How great and how sad is the contrast between mighty and fallen!

Obviously *the weapons of war* could not perish as the warriors themselves did, but the Hebrew word for *perished* can sometimes mean lost. (It is thus translated in 1 Samuel 9:3 and Ezekiel 34:16, for examples.) Perhaps the weapons left on the battlefield were gathered up by the Philistines who came back to steal the clothing and armor of the dead (1 Samuel 31:8-10). Thus the dead warriors and their weapons were both lost to Israel. Some Bible students believe the term *the weapons of war* refers not to literal weapons but to Saul and Jonathan. The phrase would thus be similar in meaning to the word "glory" in verse 19 at the beginning of this moving tribute.

DAVID BECOMES KING OF ALL ISRAEL (2 SAMUEL 5:1-5)

Establishing the Groundwork

Not all of Saul's sons died in the battle on Mount Gilboa. Another son, Ish-Bosheth, was supported as king by all the tribes of Israel except Judah, whose people made David their king. That Judah favored David as king is not surprising, given that David was from Bethlehem of Judah and had spent much of his time as a fugitive from Saul in the Judean countryside. David established his capital at Hebron, 19 miles southwest of Jerusalem.

A time of civil war and treacherous intrigue is recorded in 2 Samuel 2–4. As a result, "David grew stronger and stronger, while the house of Saul grew weaker and weaker" (2 Samuel 3:1). When a bitter disagreement occurred between Ish-Bosheth and his general, Abner (who had been Saul's general), Abner decided to abandon Ish-Bosheth and throw his support to David (2 Samuel 3:6-21).

David's general, Joab, was not pleased with this turn of events. He likely suspected that any deal with Abner might result in Abner's replacing Joab as general. Besides, Abner had killed Joab's brother during the aforementioned civil conflict. So Joab killed Abner, thus avenging his brother's death and also securing his own position as commander of David's army (2 Samuel 3:22-30).

Later two officers of Ish-Bosheth's army took it upon themselves to kill Ish-Bosheth. They carried his head to David, expecting to gain his favor for having killed the rival king and making it easier for David to assume power over all Israel. But David had the assassins executed (2 Samuel 4:1-12), much as he had had the Amalekite killed who claimed to have put Saul to death.

With both Ish-Bosheth, whom the tribes other than Judah had made their king, and Abner his general dead, these tribes had no leader. Abner, however, had already persuaded the elders of the entire nation to endorse David as king (2 Samuel 3:17, 18). Thus the stage was set for the events recorded in the next passage to be examined.

Examining the Text

I. The People's Choice of David (2 Samuel 5:1, 2)
A. A Fellow Israelite (v. 1)

¹All the tribes of Israel came to David at Hebron and said, "We are your own flesh and blood.

All the tribes of Israel likely describes the elders (v. 3) representing all the tribes who had made Saul's son Ish-Bosheth king following Saul's death. All of the tribes, including Judah, were David's kinsmen; all were one family; all were descended from Jacob, whose other name was *Israel.* Therefore it was fitting for *David* to be king over all of them.

B. Proven Ability (v. 2a)

²ᵃ"In the past, while Saul was king over us, you were the one who led Israel on their military campaigns.

A second reason for supporting David as king was that he had proved competent when he was a general in Saul's army and *led Israel on their military campaigns.* His outstanding ability on the battlefield was known to all.

C. The Lord's Desire (v. 2b)

²ᵇ"And the LORD said to you, 'You will shepherd my people Israel, and you will become their ruler.'"

Many years earlier, the Lord had chosen David to succeed Saul as king and had sent Samuel to anoint him. The young man who had been watching his father's sheep when Samuel came to Jesse's house was set apart to become *shepherd* of God's *people*. That had not been announced to the entire nation, of course; at that point, Saul would have regarded such an act as treason (1 Samuel 16:1, 2). It was known only to a few people in Bethlehem. But now there was no longer any reason to keep the matter a secret. All Israel knew David was the Lord's choice.

II. David's Covenant with the Elders (2 Samuel 5:3-5)
A. Set Apart as King (v. 3)

³When all the elders of Israel had come to King David at Hebron, the king made a compact with them at Hebron before the LORD, and they anointed David king over Israel.

The reasons listed in verses 1 and 2 were compelling (of course, at this point there was no other candidate for the throne). Gladly *David . . . made a* covenant (the Hebrew word for *compact* is usually translated "covenant") with *all the elders of Israel*, thus ending the strife among the tribes. Specific terms of this agreement are not mentioned. Perhaps David promised not to punish those who had been fighting against him during the civil war between the tribes. Whatever agreements were made, both David and the elders made their promises solemnly *before the Lord*.

The elders then *anointed David king over Israel*. This was the third time David had been anointed. The first anointing meant that God had chosen him to be king (1 Samuel 16:1-13). The second one meant that the tribe of Judah had chosen him to be its king (2 Samuel 2:4). This third anointing meant that all Israel was making God's choice their choice.

B. Summary of Reign (vv. 4, 5)

⁴, ⁵David was thirty years old when he became king, and he reigned forty years. In Hebron he reigned over Judah seven years and six months, and in Jerusalem he reigned over all Israel and Judah thirty-three years.

David was king of *Judah seven years and six months* before becoming king *over all Israel*. Not long after he began to reign over the entire nation, David and his men marched to *Jerusalem* and took the city from the Jebusites who had resided there and who boasted that David would never be able to take the city from them (2 Samuel 5:6-9). Jerusalem then replaced *Hebron* as David's capital city.

How to Say It

ABINADAB. Uh-*bin*-uh-dab.

ACHISH. *Ay*-kish.

AMALEKITE. *Am*-uh-leh-kites or Uh-*mal*-ih-kite.

ASHKELON. *Ash*-ke-lon or *As*-ke-lon.

BEERSHEBA. Beer-*she*-buh.

BETHLEHEM. *Beth*-lih-hem.

ELIAB. Ee-*lye*-ab.

GIBEAH. *Gib*-ee-uh (G as in *get*).

GILBOA. Gil-*bo*-uh (G as in *get*).

GOLIATH. Go-*lye*-uth.

HEBRON. *Hee*-brun or *Heb*-run.

ISH-BOSHETH. Ish-*bo*-sheth.

JABESH-GILEAD. *Jay*-besh-*gil*-ee-ud (strong accent on *gil*).

JASHAR. *Jay*-sher.

JEBUSITES. *Jeb*-yuh-sites.

JERUSALEM. Juh-*roo*-suh-lem.

JESSE. *Jess*-ee.

JEZREEL. *Jez*-ree-el or *Jez*-reel.

JOAB. *Jo*-ab.

JOSHUA. *Josh*-yew-uh.

JUDEAN. Joo-*dee*-un.

PHILISTIA. Fuh-*liss*-tee-uh.

PHILISTINE. Fuh-*liss*-teens or*Fill*-us-teen.

RAMAH. *Ray*-muh.

SHAMMAH. *Sham*-muh.

ZIKLAG. *Zik*-lag.

Chapter 6

The Reign of David

2 Samuel 7:1-16; 11:2-5, 14-18, 26, 27; 12:10, 13-15;
1 Chronicles 28:5-10, 20, 21

GOD'S SPECIAL PROMISE TO DAVID (2 SAMUEL 7:1-16)

Establishing the Groundwork

It was noted in the previous chapter that one of King David's first acts was to capture Jerusalem and make it his capital city. That city had been captured and burned long before by members of the tribe of Judah during the conquest under Joshua (Judges 1:8); however, Joshua 15:63 notes that they were unable to drive out the Jebusites who were inhabiting the city.

Jerusalem's location made it a better choice for David's capital than Hebron, where he had reigned as king of Judah (2 Samuel 5:5). It was on a hill, so defending the city would be much easier. And it was located near the border of Judah and Benjamin; thus David did not appear to be favoring either Judah or the remainder of his kingdom to the north.

Another noteworthy achievement in the early stages of David's reign was not of his choosing; it was forced on him. The Philistines, who had defeated King Saul, gathered their forces in order to let the new king know that they were still the dominant people of the region. But David twice defeated them, and for a time they gave Israel no more trouble (2 Samuel 5:17-25).

Once David had gained firm control of his kingdom, he began to think about the ark of the covenant. For many years it had been separated from its original home in the tabernacle. The Philistines had captured it and taken it away (1 Samuel 4:1-11). But their possession of the ark had brought only trouble to them, so they returned it to Israel. There it was kept in a private home in Kiriath Jearim (1 Samuel 5:1–7:2). Apparently it was sometimes carried into battle by the army (see (1 Samuel 14:18), but it must have been returned to its place at Kiriath Jearim after each campaign.

After becoming king, David wanted to bring the ark to Jerusalem. The first attempt ended in disaster because the ark was not carried properly (2 Samuel 6:1-11; 1 Chronicles 13; 15:12, 13), but a second attempt was successful. The ark was then placed inside a tent that David provided for it (2 Samuel 6:12-19; 1 Chronicles 15:1–16:1).

There was great rejoicing when Israel brought the ark to Jerusalem. David himself "danced before the Lord with all his might" (2 Samuel 6:14, 15) on this occasion. But soon the king began to have second thoughts—not about having brought the ark into his capital city, but about the meager housing he had provided for it. A portable tabernacle had been an appropriate place for the ark when Israel was traveling in the desert. It had been God's tent in the midst of the tents of his people. But now his people were living in houses. David himself was residing comfortably in a new palace in Jerusalem (2 Samuel 5:11). Shouldn't God's house be superior to David's?

Examining the Text

I. Plans for God's House (2 Samuel 7:1-7)
A. David's Thoughts (vv. 1-3)

¹After the king was settled in his palace and the Lord had given him rest from all his enemies around him,

With God's help, David had become *king* of all Israel. He had defeated, not only the Philistines, but any other *enemies* that had threatened the nation. Many of those victories are described in 2 Samuel 8:1-14. Thus the events described in the passage before us may have occurred after those described in chapter 8. The arrangement of this material may be topical more than chronological; since chapter 6 records the bringing of the ark of the covenant to Jerusalem, chapter 7 appropriately follows with the account of David's desire to build a fitting house for the ark.

² . . . he said to Nathan the prophet, "Here I am, living in a palace of cedar, while the ark of God remains in a tent."

David's palace was probably of stone on the outside, but on the inside it was covered with *cedar* brought from faraway Lebanon with the help of King Hiram of Tyre (2 Samuel 5:11). No doubt David's house was among the finest in Jerusalem, yet God's house in the same city was only a *tent!*

³Nathan replied to the king, "Whatever you have in mind, go ahead and do it, for the Lord is with you."

Nathan could tell what was in the king's *mind*. It was apparent from David's words that he wanted to build a house for the Lord—a house finer than the king's to serve as a fitting place for the ark of God. That sounded reasonable, so Nathan said, *Go ahead and do it.*

B. God's Thoughts (vv. 4-7)

⁴That night the word of the LORD came to Nathan, saying:

Without waiting to be asked, Nathan had given an uninspired opinion to David. Without waiting to be asked, the Lord now gave his own *word* to Nathan.

⁵"Go and tell my servant David, 'This is what the LORD says: Are you the one to build me a house to dwell in?

The Lord spoke to Nathan, but the message was for *David*. It was couched in the form of a question: *Are you the one to build me a house to dwell in?* The question implies a negative answer. David was not criticized for wanting to build a house for the ark, and so we gather that his motives were sincere. But David had "shed much blood" and had "fought many wars" (1 Chronicles 22:7, 8); and so God did not permit him to build the temple, even though he did allow David to make extensive preparations for it before his death (1 Chronicles 22:5).

⁶"I have not dwelt in a house from the day I brought the Israelites up out of Egypt to this day. I have been moving from place to place with a tent as my dwelling.

Approximately four and a half centuries had passed since the Lord had *brought the Israelites up out of Egypt*. Those centuries had been characterized by some trying times for God's people. During the most recent of these, the period of the judges, the society was unstable and at times completely chaotic. Throughout those days, the people lacked either the inclination or the resources to build a fitting house for the ark. A more or less permanent place for the ark and for the tabernacle had been established at Shiloh during the time of Joshua (Joshua 18:1).

On one occasion, the sons of Eli had taken the ark into battle to insure victory over the Philistines. But the Israelites were soundly defeated, the two sons of Eli were killed, and the ark was captured by the Philistines (1 Samuel 4:1-11). To celebrate their victory, the Philistines had carried the ark with them back to one of their chief cities, Ashdod, and placed it beside the idol of Dagon in his temple. But the results were disastrous for the Philistines; the hand of the Lord "was heavy upon the people," sending painful physical afflictions upon them. The ark was then moved to other Philistine cities, with similar results (1 Samuel 5:6-12). Realizing the source of their difficulty, the Philistines then sent the ark back to the Israelites (1 Samuel 6). It remained in the town of Kiriath Jearim until David brought it to Jerusalem. During the first attempt to carry the ark, Uzzah was put to death because the ark was not being carried properly, according to the law of Moses (1 Chronicles 13:5-11). For three months, the ark was kept in the possession of Obed-Edom until the ark was brought into Jerusalem in the way prescribed by God (1 Chronicles 13:14; 15:11-15; 16:1).

> *7"Wherever I have moved with all the Israelites, did I ever say to any of their rulers whom I commanded to shepherd my people Israel, "Why have you not built me a house of cedar?"'"*

Wherever . . . the Israelites went in their travels, the Lord had never *commanded* anyone in *Israel* to build a *house of cedar* for him. A house of cedar was usually one built of stone and paneled with wood from the cedars of Lebanon. God had never desired that building such a structure be a high priority for those who led his *people Israel*; he was more concerned that they fulfill their task as his people's shepherds.

II. Plans for David's House
A. God's Provisions for David (vv. 8, 9)

Often, when asking his people to obey him, God first reminded them that they were indebted to him for benefits many and great. In this case he spoke of benefits to David personally as well as those to the nation of Israel as a whole.

> *8"Now then, tell my servant David, 'This is what the LORD Almighty says: I took you from the pasture and from following the flock to be ruler over my people Israel.*

David's rise from shepherd to king was not his own accomplishment; it was God's doing.

> *9"'I have been with you wherever you have gone, and I have cut off all your enemies from before you. Now I will make your name great, like the names of the greatest men of the earth.*

God's blessings to David did not end with his being made king. God had *been with* him through the years of struggle and exile until he could actually claim the throne. Now his *enemies*, both inside and outside the nation, had been defeated. Because of those many conquests, David's *name* had become *great* in the eyes of the nations surrounding Israel. God's promise *I will make your name great* is reminiscent of his promise to Abraham (Genesis 12:2).

B. God's Provisions for Israel (vv. 10, 11a)

> *10a"'And I will provide a place for my people Israel and will plant them so that they can have a home of their own and no longer be disturbed.*

This also brings to mind another promise God had given long before, beginning with Abraham (Genesis 17:8). He would give his *people* a land of their own; he would establish them securely in that land; he would protect them from their pagan neighbors. Of course, this abbreviated form of the promise did not cancel the conditions that were attached to it. The people of Israel were to have the promised land and its abundant blessings as long as they obeyed God. If they disobeyed, they would forfeit those blessings and would lose possession of the land. This is stated at length in Deuteronomy 28:15-68.

10b, 11a **"Wicked people will not oppress them anymore, as they did at the beginning and have done ever since the time I appointed leaders over my people Israel. I will also give you rest from all your enemies.**

Wicked people had tried to harm God's people ever since the beginning of their existence as a nation. The Amalekites had attacked them not long after the exodus (Exodus 17:8-14). Then there were the pagan peoples that surrounded Israel and oppressed them during the period of the judges. The term may also describe corrupt individuals who arose from among the Israelites, such as Hophni and Phinehas, the two wicked sons of Eli. All of those problems were in the past; better times were in store for the people, thanks to David and the *rest* from Israel's *enemies* that God had provided through him (v. 1). This peaceful rest would continue if both the king and the people obeyed God's law.

C. God's Provisions for David's House (vv. 11b-16)

David was thinking about building for the Lord a house—a magnificent temple that would stand through centuries of time. The Lord was steering David away from that plan because he had a better plan. The Lord promised to build a house for David—not a building of stone and wood, but a household, a family, a dynasty that would rule forever!

11b **"'The LORD declares to you that the LORD himself will establish a house for you:**

David should give up the idea of building a house for the *Lord;* instead, he should consider the different kind of *house* the Lord was going to build for him. Any house the Lord would build for David would be far superior to whatever house David might build for the Lord.

12 **"'When your days are over and you rest with your fathers, I will raise up your offspring to succeed you, who will come from your own body, and I will establish his kingdom.**

When David's life on earth was over, his son would take his place as king; and God would *establish his kingdom* as he had David's. Thus David's house, or family, would continue to rule.

13"'He is the one who will build a house for my Name, and I will establish the throne of his kingdom forever.'"

This verse makes it clear that God did not forbid the building of a temple, but he wanted it to be done by David's son. As previously noted, David was a "warrior" who had "shed blood" (1 Chronicles 28:2, 3). This is not to say that David's activity in those battles was wrong. God approved David's wars and gave him victory in them, but still he preferred to have his temple built by Solomon, a man of peace, whose reign was characterized by very little conflict with enemies. (The name *Solomon* means "peaceful.")

This leads us to consider a practical reason for postponing the temple building until the reign of Solomon. Senior citizens in Europe and America can remember the troubled years of World War II. Hardly anything was built unless it was needed in the war effort. Most available material and manpower were directed to that cause. So it was during the years of David's wars, and for that reason the building of the temple was left for a man of peace to undertake during a time of peace. At that point, Israel's men could be released from any military duty; and Solomon could assemble an army of workers to help with the temple (1 Kings 5:13-16).

David accepted God's decision without complaint. As previously noted, he later received plans for the temple from the Lord, and then passed them on to Solomon to use in carrying out the task (1 Chronicles 22:2-5; 28:11-19).

Then the Lord added, *I will establish the throne of his kingdom forever*, thus adding *forever* to the promise of verse 12. Certainly Solomon would not last forever, but the throne of his kingdom would. Because of the sins of the people, there were times when that promise seemed uncertain. At one point the people of Israel were captives in Babylon, having no king of their own. Then they were ruled by the Persians and later by the Romans.

"But when the time had fully come" (Galatians 4:4), Jesus was born. He was a son of David, but, more importantly, he was the Son of God. He rules a kingdom "not of this world" (John 18:36), "that will never be destroyed, . . . but . . . will itself endure forever" (Daniel 2:44). Thus these words of God to David looked beyond his earthly kingdom to a greater fulfillment in Christ. As Paul writes in Romans 1:3, 4, Jesus "as to his human nature was a descendant of David, and . . . through the Spirit of holiness was declared with power to be the Son of God by his resurrection from the dead: Jesus Christ our Lord." Of Jesus, the angel Gabriel had told Mary prior to his birth, "The Lord God will give him the throne of his father David, and he will reign over the house of Jacob forever; his kingdom will never end" (Luke 1:32, 33).

14"'I will be his father, and he will be my son. When he does wrong, I will punish him with the rod of men, with floggings inflicted by men.

God had previously promised David that he would raise up one of his offspring to succeed him (v. 12). Now God himself promised to be a *father* to that *son*. This suggests a relationship that would be both warm and intimate. At the same time, it also suggests a relationship in which the father on occasion may have to discipline the son. When this was necessary, the Lord would use *the rod of men* to *punish* the wayward son. Several times, with later kings who were descendants of David, God did use some of the neighboring pagan nations to carry out his discipline. For example, Manasseh, who was one of the most wicked kings in the history of God's people, was taken captive to Babylon for a time before humbling himself before God (2 Chronicles 33:10-13).

Previously the suggestion was made that these words of God to David also included a fulfillment in Jesus. How would the promise of the verse before us apply to him, since he was sinless and did nothing *wrong*? The answer lies in the suffering he took upon himself for sinners; as Isaiah prophesied, "The Lord has laid on him the iniquity of us all" (Isaiah 53:6). "God made him who had no sin to be sin for us" (2 Corinthians 5:21). In the process of experiencing that suffering, Jesus also was punished with the rod of men.

15"'But my love will never be taken away from him, as I took it away from Saul, whom I removed from before you.

In the early portion of the reign of *Saul*, God had provided him with special favor and help. God had withdrawn these, however, when Saul ceased to obey and became proud and rebellious. In fact, God had withdrawn his Spirit from Saul (1 Samuel 16:14) following his rejection of Saul as Israel's king and the anointing of David to be the next king (1 Samuel 15:26; 1 Samuel 16:13).

Now God was ready to give favor and help to David's son Solomon, and he was promising not to take away that support as he had *taken* it *away from* Saul. He would arrange for Solomon to be punished for his disobedience (v. 14), but would not take the kingdom away from him entirely. In time he would take a large part of it from Solomon's son, but that did not occur in Solomon's lifetime (1 Kings 11:9-13).

In the case of Jesus, God's favor was not withdrawn. Jesus suffered immeasurable pain and agony and was put to death on the cross. At one point he even sensed that his Father had forsaken him (Matthew 27:46). But God did not abandon him; he raised him to life and then "exalted him to the highest place and gave him the name that is above every name" (Philippians 2:9).

16"'Your house and your kingdom will endure forever before me; your throne will be established forever.'"

This final section of the words of Nathan lays out the three primary elements of God's covenant with David. David is to have an eternal *house*, an eternal *kingdom*, and an eternal *throne*. It is noteworthy that kings of David's line continued to rule in Jerusalem (even during the time when Jerusalem was part of the southern kingdom of Judah after the nation divided) until the Babylonian captivity. In contrast, the rival northern kingdom was characterized by frequent chaos and turmoil; and there were several revolutions that brought in new dynasties.

Ultimately the threefold promise of an eternal house, kingdom, and throne is completely fulfilled only in David's descendant Jesus. He is the King of kings, who conquered death and later ascended to Heaven to take his throne at the right hand of God (see Romans 8:34; Ephesians 1:18-20; Hebrews 1:3).

DAVID'S SIN WITH BATHSHEBA
(2 SAMUEL 11:2-5, 14-18, 26, 27; 12:10, 13-15)

Establishing the Groundwork

Chapters 8-10 in 2 Samuel reveal David to be both a highly capable military leader and a compassionate individual willing to help someone who had no means of repaying him for any help given. Following the record of David's victories in chapter 8 is the statement, "The Lord gave David victory wherever he went" (v. 14). The next verse notes that he did "what was just and right for all his people." That sense of justice and righteousness moved David to inquire whether there remained any individuals from the family of Saul to whom he could show kindness out of respect for an oath he had made to his dear friend Jonathan (1 Samuel 20:12-17). David was informed about a son of Jonathan named Mephibosheth, who was crippled in both feet (2 Samuel 9:3). Mephibosheth was brought to David's house and given a place of honor at the king's table (vv. 9-13).

Second Samuel 10 resumes the account of David's military achievements. After the Ammonites (who resided to the east of Israel) had disgraced some of David's soldiers, they realized that they needed to prepare for battle with the Israelites. The Ammonites enlisted the help of Arameans from the north to fight against Israel, but David's forces routed both Ammonites and Arameans until "the Arameans were afraid to help the Ammonites anymore" (2 Samuel 10:19).

The war with the Ammonites was put on hold through the winter months (as battles often were), but resumed in the spring. This time David stayed in Jerusalem, putting Joab in command of the army. Again Joab defeated the Ammonites, who took refuge in their chief city, Rabbah, where Joab initiated a siege (2 Samuel 11:1).

Examining the Text

I. Adultery (2 Samuel 11:2-5)

During this time David lived at ease in his palace in Jerusalem. It is certainly worth observing that in the past David had gone to battle with his men, as noted above. Now, however, he was relaxing in Jerusalem "at the time when kings go off to war" (2 Samuel 11:1). If we were reading this account for the first time, we would probably question David's behavior; for we have been so accustomed to seeing him on the battlefield. It is almost as if we are being prepared for something out of character for David, because he is not acting "like himself." And this is true: had David been where he was supposed to be, and had he been doing what he was supposed to be doing, perhaps the following sorry incident never would have occurred.

A. Temptation (v. 2)

²One evening David got up from his bed and walked around on the roof of the palace. From the roof he saw a woman bathing. The woman was very beautiful,

In the crowded city of Jerusalem, every house, including the king's *palace*, had a flat *roof* that could be used as we use a porch or patio—as a pleasant place to relax in the open air. Perhaps David had just awakened from a nap. As he *walked* across the *roof*, he caught sight of a *beautiful* neighbor taking her bath. She may have been in an enclosed courtyard of the house where she lived, with walls around her but no roof overhead. David found the sight very attractive.

B. Inquiry (v. 3)

³ . . . and David sent someone to find out about her. The man said, "Isn't this Bathsheba, the daughter of Eliam and the wife of Uriah the Hittite?"

Who was that lovely lady next door? David *sent someone to find out about her.* The investigator came back with the lady's name, her father's name, and her husband's name. Perhaps he also brought the information that her husband, *Uriah the Hittite*, was miles away east of the Jordan, serving in the army that was besieging Rabbah.

C. Sin (v. 4)

⁴Then David sent messengers to get her. She came to him, and he slept with her. (She had purified herself from her uncleanness.) Then she went back home.

This time *David sent* more than one messenger. If the woman seemed reluctant to come, they could bring her anyway. The text gives no hints about her willingness or reluctance. Some students suppose that she was a virtuous woman who objected vigorously, though she was too dignified to be dragged kicking and screaming to the king. Others believe that she staged her bath with the deliberate purpose of seducing the king. Either explanation is mere speculation, however. The text focuses on David, and as for him, the record is clear. While for most of his life he did what was right in God's eyes, what he did on this occasion was wrong. "The thing David had done displeased the Lord" (v. 27).

We are told that before committing this act, *Bathsheba purified herself from her uncleanness*. This indicates that she had just become ceremonially clean, according to the law of Moses, following the time of uncleanness associated with the menstrual cycle (Leviticus 15:19-30). This also makes it clear that she was not already pregnant by Uriah when David *slept with her*.

D. Consequence (v. 5)

⁵The woman conceived and sent word to David, saying, "I am pregnant."

Bad news! Bathsheba was *pregnant*. Her adultery could not be denied. According to the law of Moses, both she and David should be put to death for this act (Leviticus 20:10). She simply relayed the news to the king without further comment. Now the matter was his to deal with. What would he do?

II. Murder (2 Samuel 11:14-18, 26, 27)

David's first thought was to make it appear that Bathsheba's baby belonged to her husband, Uriah. So he sent for Uriah and encouraged him to go home to his wife. If he spent a night with her, everyone would assume that he was the father of Bathsheba's child.

But Uriah was a loyal soldier. (In fact, according to 2 Samuel 23:24, 39, he was one of David's most dependable soldiers.) He thought it was not right for him to enjoy a night with his wife while his comrades were risking their lives on the field of battle. He spent two nights with David's men in Jerusalem, then returned to the siege (2 Samuel 11:6-13). So David was still left with his dilemma.

A. Planned (vv. 14, 15)

14In the morning David wrote a letter to Joab and sent it with Uriah.

This was the *morning* after Uriah's second night with the king's men. He was now going back to take his place with the troops besieging Rabbah. David gave him *a letter* to carry *to Joab*, commander of those troops.

15In it he wrote, "Put Uriah in the front line where the fighting is fiercest. Then withdraw from him so he will be struck down and die."

It was murder that David ordered—murder disguised to look like death in battle, but still murder. Both David and his commander Joab were battle-hardened veterans. The loss of a few soldiers seemed a small matter. It happened in every conflict; it was the price of victory. Now it was to be the price of hiding the king's adultery. *Uriah,* who had shown such devotion to the king, was to be assigned to a place of intense *fighting* and then abandoned during the fighting to increase the likelihood of his death.

B. Accomplished (vv. 16, 17)

16So while Joab had the city under siege, he put Uriah at a place where he knew the strongest defenders were.

Joab had *had the city under siege* long enough to know that the *strongest defenders* were posted in a certain place, probably to guard an important gate leading into the city. Israel's troops were all around the city so that no one could go out or come in; but they were too far away to be reached by arrows from the wall. Now Joab sent *Uriah* and some other men nearer the wall at the point where those defenders were stationed. We are not told what the mission of the little group was supposed to be. Possibly they were to draw the defenders out from the city so that the other troops could swarm in and overpower them. If so, we have no report that the ploy was successful.

17When the men of the city came out and fought against Joab, some of the men in David's army fell; moreover, Uriah the Hittite died.

Those *men of the city* whom Joab knew about did venture out to fight with the small detachment of his troops that had approached the wall. During the fighting *some of the men* of Israel were killed. *Uriah* was one of them. Whatever the small group's mission was, Joab's—and David's—mission was a success.

C. Reported (v. 18)

¹⁸Joab sent David a full account of the battle.

Joab promptly s*ent David a full account of the battle.* He thought the king would be angry when he learned that some men had been killed because they had recklessly ventured near the wall, but he knew what would soothe that anger. The messenger must report, "Also, your servant Uriah the Hittite is dead." That, after all, was the king's objective. So King David sent back to Joab a message of assurance, telling him not to feel badly about the loss (vv. 19-25).

D. Hidden (vv. 26, 27)

²⁶When Uriah's wife heard that her husband was dead, she mourned for him.

Bathsheba's mourning could not have been very long (we may wonder how sincere it was), but she did go through the motions.

²⁷After the time of mourning was over, David had her brought to his house, and she became his wife and bore him a son. But the thing David had done displeased the LORD.

David's scheme seemed to have succeeded: he had a beautiful *wife* to add to those he already had (2 Samuel 3:1-5), and soon she *bore him a son.* In fact, Bathsheba seems to have become David's favorite wife. He even bequeathed his kingdom to one of her sons (not the one mentioned here). Was she really the true love of his life? Or did he feel obligated to favor her because he had killed her husband? We do not know.

But the thing David had done displeased the Lord. Thus David's scheme yielded a greater harvest of grief than of joy. It is noteworthy that the only time the Lord is mentioned in this sad chapter is in this final verse.

III. Punishment and Pardon (2 Samuel 12:10, 13-15)

Interestingly, the word *send* or *sent* appears frequently in the account of David's adultery with Bathsheba (2 Samuel 11:2-6, 14). As if to respond to what David had done, "The Lord *sent* Nathan" the prophet to rebuke David's sin (2 Samuel 12:1). The prophet went with a parable. He told of a rich man who had plenty of lambs in his flock, but stole the one pet lamb of a poor man to prepare for dinner. When David angrily declared that such a man ought to be put to death, Nathan turned that judgment back on the king himself: "You are the man!" David had wives enough of his own, yet he had stolen the one wife of poor Uriah. To make matters worse, he had murdered Uriah himself. King though he was, David would not escape punishment.

A. Condemnation (v. 10)

10 "'Now, therefore, the sword will never depart from your house, because you despised me and took the wife of Uriah the Hittite to be your own.'"

Often in Scripture the punishment that God announces to a guilty party matches in some manner the sin or crime that has been committed (see, for examples, Numbers 14:34 and Jeremiah 8:1, 2). Here God's judgment declared that since David had used "the sword of the Ammonites" to kill Uriah (v. 9), the *sword* would *never depart from your house.*

Later chapters of 2 Samuel reveal how this prophecy of Nathan came painfully true for David. Conscious of his own adultery and murder, David failed to deal sternly with his sons when they committed similar sins. Partly because of this failure, such wrongdoing multiplied.

No sooner do we leave this message of judgment in 2 Samuel 12 that we come to the incident in which David's son Amnon raped his half sister, Tamar. David was angry, but apparently did not punish Amnon. Two years later, David's son Absalom, the full brother of Tamar, had Amnon killed in an act of revenge. Absalom then fled the country, but after a while he was allowed to return. Perhaps encouraged by David's leniency, Absalom began to gather followers and eventually staged a revolt to take his father's throne for himself. David had to flee from Jerusalem, after which Absalom took his father's concubines for his own, thus fulfilling the words Nathan spoke to David in verses 11 and 12 of 2 Samuel 12. David soon gathered his forces and put down the revolt, but Absalom was killed along with many others in the ensuing conflict. The record of these instances of discord is found in 2 Samuel 13–18.

During David's final years, his son Adonijah also plotted to take the throne. This time the plot was thwarted before it became too widespread; but soon after David's death, Adonijah was executed for his continuing ambition to be king (1 Kings 1:5-53; 2:13-25). Thus, to the end of David's life and beyond, the sword truly did not depart from his house. Some have observed that the fourfold restoration that David had proposed for the villain in Nathan's parable (2 Samuel 12:6) was required of David, in that four of his sons (the child born out of wedlock, Amnon, Absalom, and Adonijah) all died untimely deaths.

B. Confession and Pardon (v. 13)

13 Then David said to Nathan, "I have sinned against the LORD."
Nathan replied, "The LORD has taken away your sin. You are not going to die.

An evil king might have had Nathan beheaded for daring to expose the king's wrongdoing, but David was a good king who had done an evil deed. When the fact of David's sin was plainly set before him, he humbly confessed it. Nathan then gave the welcome news: *The Lord has taken away your sin*. What that meant is explained in the next statement: *You are not going to die*; that is, David was not to be put to death immediately, as he himself had said he ought to be (v. 5). In fact, according to the Mosaic law, David had committed two sins (adultery and murder) that were worthy of death.

David had been living his masquerade for fairly close to a year at this point, since the child conceived out of wedlock had already been born. Psalm 51 was composed by David to express the confession of his wrongdoing to God.

B. Punishment Promised (v. 14)

14 "But because by doing this you have made the enemies of the Lord show utter contempt, the son born to you will die."

God's forgiveness does not remove all the evil consequences of an evil deed. David would not die immediately, but *the son* of his adultery would. The reason for this is given: *because by doing this you have made the enemies of the Lord show utter contempt*. David had tried to hide his sin, but in time it would become known. The Lord's people would grieve (as we do upon reading of this incident) because the good king had done such a terrible deed. But the Lord's enemies would sneer. They would say, "What kind of a god is your God, that he blesses a king who does such a wicked thing?" However, when the child died, everyone would realize that the Lord was not blessing David's adultery. Thus the blasphemy of the enemies would be stopped.

C. Punishment Given (v. 15)

15 After Nathan had gone home, the Lord struck the child that Uriah's wife had borne to David, and he became ill.

Verse 18 adds that *the child* died after a week of sickness. Of course, that was not the end of David's punishment. The dire prediction of verses 11 and 12 remained to be fulfilled.

Throughout the Bible, David is honored as a hero and as a man after God's own heart. Yet no effort is made to hide his sin. His wicked acts and their consequences are exposed in all their horror. And yet such a sinner as David was not beyond the reach of God's grace and forgiveness. Neither is any of us.

DAVID PREPARES FOR BUILDING THE TEMPLE (1 CHRONICLES 28:5-10, 20, 21)

Establishing the Groundwork

With this study, we come to our first passage taken from the books of Chronicles. Perhaps a consideration of the purpose for these two books is in order before examining the relevant passage.

At first glance the books of 1 and 2 Chronicles may seem to be unnecessary additions to the Old Testament. After all, don't they cover the same period of history as 1 and 2 Samuel and 1 and 2 Kings? And why the extensive genealogies that take up the first nine chapters of 1 Chronicles? (Those aren't exactly the most thrilling portions of the Bible to read!)

Most students of the Bible believe that the books of Chronicles were written after the Babylonian captivity and after God's people had returned home to rebuild their temple in Jerusalem. It is worth noting that the final two verses of 2 Chronicles and the first three verses of the book of Ezra are virtually the same. Because of this, some have proposed that Ezra may have been the author of the books of Chronicles as well as the book that bears his name. Certainly Ezra was well qualified for such a task (see Ezra 7:6, 10).

Why would Ezra (assuming him to be the author) compose such a record as that found in the books of Chronicles? Consider the following hypothetical situation: A congregation experiences an especially trying set of circumstances, such as a fire that destroys its sanctuary, a split of some kind, or a crisis within the leadership. The result would likely be a keen sense of loss of purpose and direction within the congregation. Questions would surface, such as, "Where do we go from here?" and "What is God's will for us now?" How would a church in such a situation get the people back on track and restore a sense of direction and purpose?

One answer might be to call attention to the history of the congregation and review God's faithfulness over the years in preserving the people through other difficult times. By considering such examples from the congregation's history, the people may be encouraged to continue to "fight the good fight." They would do what was necessary to see themselves through the current series of events.

God's people faced a similar scenario after the Babylonian captivity and the return to their homeland. They too must have wondered, "Where do we go from here? Does God still have a purpose for us?" For God's covenant people, there were other burning issues as well: "Is God's covenant still intact? Are the promises made to Abraham and David still binding?"

The material found in 1 and 2 Chronicles seems especially intended (through the guidance of the Holy Spirit) to address these and other crucial issues in the minds of those who were part of the rebuilding effort in Judah. The genealogies in 1 Chronicles 1–9 would not have been dull or boring to the original readers; they would have given the postexilic generation a sense of identity with their past. They would have been encouraged by realizing that the link with the individuals and tribes mentioned in these chapters had not been severed by the captivity and exile.

There is a special emphasis in 1 and 2 Chronicles on the reigns of David and Solomon and all their achievements, especially where matters pertaining to worship, such as the temple, are concerned. This let the postexilic community know that all of this was still a part of their history and their identity. God was not finished with them yet!

An earlier study from 2 Samuel 7 included God's promise to David that "your offspring to succeed you" would build a house for the Lord (vv. 12, 13). Even though David wanted to build the temple and had collected materials for it, God forbade him because he had been a man of war and because he had shed much blood (1 Chronicles 28:3). However, David was allowed to assist his son in making preparations for this structure. The following passage includes words of counsel and challenge from a king to "all the officials of Israel" (1 Chronicles 28:1), but also from a father to his son (vv. 9, 10, 20, 21).

I. Recalling the Past (1 Chronicles 28:5-7)
A. God's Plan for Solomon (vv. 5, 6)

5"Of all my sons—and the LORD has given me many—he has chosen my son Solomon to sit on the throne of the kingdom of the LORD over Israel.

David had six *sons* born from six different wives during his seven and one-half years in Hebron (2 Samuel 3:2-5; 1 Chronicles 3:1-4). When David made Jerusalem his capital, he took more concubines and wives; and more children were born (2 Samuel 5:13-16; 1 Chronicles 3:5-9; 14:3-7). Indeed, God had *given* David *many* sons. And even though *Solomon* was not David's firstborn, it is he who was chosen to sit on David's *throne*.

6"He said to me: 'Solomon your son is the one who will build my house and my courts, for I have chosen him to be my son, and I will be his father.

It was by divine direction that David announced Solomon as his successor (1 Chronicles 22:5-13) and the future builder of the temple that David himself had so much wanted to build (1 Chronicles 22:7, 8). The words *chosen him to be my son, and I will be his father* are similar to those found in 2 Samuel 7:13, 14.

B. God's Promise to Solomon (v. 7)

⁷"*"I will establish his kingdom forever if he is unswerving in carrying out my commands and laws, as is being done at this time."*"

Again, these words echo the Lord's promise found in 2 Samuel 7:13-15. The author of Chronicles does not mention the potential punishment of 2 Samuel 7:14b: "When he does wrong, I will punish him with the rod of men." Even without this, however, the conditional nature of Solomon's reign is clear because of the little word *if. If* Solomon would obey God's commands, then *his kingdom* (dynasty) would last *forever.*

At the time Chronicles was written (likely more than five centuries after Solomon), there was no Davidic king on a throne in Jerusalem. By that time the remnant in Jerusalem knew the conditional nature of the Davidic dynasty because of the destruction by the Babylonians in 586 BC. Eventually the people began to entertain the hope that God would restore Israel's fortunes by raising up an anointed one like David and bringing about a return to the golden age of David.

It is important to keep in mind how Jesus fulfilled the "forever" part of the promise to David. Many of David's descendants who ruled God's people were hardly individuals "after God's own heart." But their sinfulness did not negate God's promise to David that one of his descendants would be given an eternal kingdom, house, and dynasty (2 Samuel 7:16). Jesus was that descendant.

II. Regarding the Present (1 Chronicles 28:8-10)
A. Charge to the People (v. 8)

⁸"*So now I charge you in the sight of all Israel and of the assembly of the Lᴏʀᴅ, and in the hearing of our God: Be careful to follow all the commands of the Lᴏʀᴅ your God, that you may possess this good land and pass it on as an inheritance to your descendants forever.*"

Those whom David addressed on this occasion are listed in 1 Chronicles 28:1. In short, they were Israel's leaders and bravest warriors. David concluded his address to them by presenting two witnesses to his words: *all Israel and . . . the assembly of the Lord.* These people were charged to obey the Lord's *commands* in order to *possess this good land and pass it on as an inheritance to* their *descendants forever.* The word *forever,* as noted in previous studies, can carry the meaning in some passages of "for a long time" or "into the distant future." (See the comments on Genesis 17:7 in chapter 4 of the volume of studies covering the Pentateuch.)

As mentioned in the "Groundwork" section of this study, by the time Chronicles was written, Judah had lost her territory once; and only a remnant populated the land. The people had to learn the hard way that disobedience meant the loss of land, just as God had predicted (see Deuteronomy 31:14-18). For the ancient Israelites, keeping the land was always conditioned on obedience.

B. Charge to Solomon (vv. 9, 10)

⁹*"And you, my son Solomon, acknowledge the God of your father, and serve him with wholehearted devotion and with a willing mind, for the Lᴏʀᴅ searches every heart and understands every motive behind the thoughts. If you seek him, he will be found by you; but if you forsake him, he will reject you forever.*

David charged *Solomon* to *acknowledge the God of your father.* To know or acknowledge God is an important covenant concept, whether one is speaking in Old Testament or New Testament terms (see Jeremiah 22:16; Hosea 6:6; Philippians 3:8-10). To know God is to *serve him* faithfully in covenant relationship. Solomon was to do this *with wholehearted devotion and with a willing mind.* Such a challenge brings to mind the command, "Love the Lord your God with all your heart and with all your soul and with all your strength" (Deuteronomy 6:5).

The final statement in this charge to Solomon applies to anyone's relationship with God: *If you seek him, he will be found by you; but if you forsake him, he will reject you forever.* The prophet Isaiah offered a similar challenge two centuries after Solomon's time: "Seek the Lord while he may be found; call on him while he is near" (Isaiah 55:6).

¹⁰*"Consider now, for the Lᴏʀᴅ has chosen you to build a temple as a sanctuary. Be strong and do the work."*

God was the one who had *chosen* Solomon *to build a temple.* This would be a major undertaking for Solomon to accomplish, so David charged his son to *be strong and do the work.* The exhortation *be strong* is reminiscent of Moses' (and the Lord's) words to Joshua regarding the undertaking of leading God's people into the promised land (Deuteronomy 31:7, 23; Joshua 1:6-9). Joshua carried out this task, which Moses had desired to do, just as Solomon completed a task (building the temple) that David had desired to do.

III. Further Exhortations to Solomon (1 Chronicles 28:20, 21)
A. Strength From the Lord (v. 20)

²⁰David also said to Solomon his son, "Be strong and courageous, and do the work. Do not be afraid or discouraged, for the Lord God, my God, is with you. He will not fail you or forsake you until all the work for the service of the temple of the Lord is finished.

Solomon had previously heard the words *Be strong and courageous* from his father David in a private setting (1 Chronicles 22:13). Now this exhortation was given, along with other charges, to Solomon in public. This procedure is similar to that which characterized the appointments of both Saul and David to the kingship in Israel. With each, there was a private anointing (by Samuel) then a public recognition of the individual.

David reminded Solomon of God's presence *with* him to empower him in carrying out the *work* that lay ahead. David had done much to prepare his son for this task, but soon David would no longer be with Solomon and would not witness the completion of the project. God, however, would see the task to its completion and beyond.

B. Support From Others (v. 21)

²¹"The divisions of the priests and Levites are ready for all the work on the temple of God, and every willing man skilled in any craft will help you in all the work. The officials and all the people will obey your every command."

First Chronicles 23–26 lists all those who were to participate in the building and maintenance of the new *temple*. The *priests and Levites* were especially important in this regard.

Organizationally, the Levites were divided into three groups corresponding to the sons of Levi: Gershon, Kohath, and Merari (1 Chronicles 23:6-23). They were to be in charge of the service of the temple of the Lord upon its completion (1 Chronicles 23:24-32). Duties in the temple included singing (1 Chronicles 15:16, 17; 25:1-8), gatekeeping (26:1-19), oversight of the treasuries (26:20-28), and various other responsibilities (26:29-32).

We should recall that while all priests were Levites, not all Levites were priests. Priests were descendants of Aaron's sons Eleazar and Ithamar (Numbers 3:2-4). David had organized the priests into twenty-four divisions for purposes of serving in the temple (1 Chronicles 24:1-19).

Just as God had provided and empowered men to build the tabernacle (Exodus 31:1-11), so he now provided *every willing man skilled in any craft* to build the temple. And just as God had shown Moses the plans for building the tabernacle (Exodus 25–30), so now David had revealed to Solomon the plans for building the temple—plans inspired by the Spirit of God (1 Chronicles 28:19). In addition, not only those with specialized duties, but also *all the people* were to be at the disposal of Solomon. The young king could begin the work given him, assured that he had been supplied with adequate resources, both divine and human.

How to Say It

ABRAHAM. *Ay*-bruh-ham.

ABSALOM. *Ab*-suh-lum.

ADONIJAH. Ad-o-*nye*-juh.

AMALEKITES. *Am*-uh-leh-kites or Uh-*mal*-ih-kites.

AMMONITES. *Am*-un-ites.

AMNON. *Am*-nun.

ARAMEANS. *Ar*-uh-*me*-uns (strong accent on *me*).

ASHDOD. *Ash*-dod.

BABYLON. *Bab*-uh-lun.

BABYLONIAN. Bab-ih-*low*-nee-un.

BATHSHEBA. Bath-*she*-buh.

ELEAZAR. El-ih-*a*-zar or E-lih-*a*-zar.

ELIAM. Ih-*lye*-am.

GABRIEL. *Gay*-bree-ul.

HIRAM. *High*-rum.

HITTITES. *Hit*-ites or *Hit*-tites.

HOPHNI. *Hoff*-nye.

ITHAMAR. *Ith*-uh-mar.

JEBUSITES. *Jeb*-yuh-sites.

JERUSALEM. Juh-*roo*-suh-lem.

KIRIATH JEARIM. *Kir*-yuth *Jee*-uh-rim.

LEBANON. *Leb*-uh-nun.

MANASSEH. Muh-*nass*-uh.

MEPHIBOSHETH. Meh-*fib*-o-sheth.

MOSAIC. Mo-*zay*-ik.

NATHAN. *Nay*-thun (*th* as in *thin*).

OBED-EDOM. O-bed-*ee*-dum (strong accent on *ee*).

PERSIANS. *Per*-zhunz.

PHILISTINES. Fuh-*liss*-teenz or *Fill*-us-teenz.

PHINEHAS. *Fin*-ee-us.

RABBAH. *Rab*-buh.

SHILOH. *Shy*-low.

SOLOMON. *Sol*-o-mun.

TAMAR. *Tay*-mer.

TYRE. Tire.

URIAH. Yu-*rye*-uh.

UZZAH. *Uz*-zuh.

Chapter 7

The Reign of Solomon

1 Kings 3:3-14; 2 Chronicles 5:7-14;
1 Kings 8:22, 23, 27-30; 9:1-5; 11:1-13

SOLOMON ASKS GOD FOR WISDOM (1 KINGS 3:3-14)

Establishing the Groundwork

Although they were father and son, David and Solomon were two very different men whose reigns formed a striking contrast. David had been reared in the Judean countryside, watching and protecting sheep. He was a tough, aggressive man of action (as Goliath discovered!). Later he was forced to survive as a fugitive from Saul. As king of Israel, David put these rigorous experiences to good use, becoming an outstanding military commander and a highly respected leader.

On the other hand, Solomon had grown up surrounded by the luxuries of royalty and palace life. He was given a stable kingdom to rule. He was able to remain at home (rarely did he go out to fight a battle) and to concentrate on maintaining and enhancing what his father had bequeathed to him.

As different as these two men were, the key to being a successful king was exactly the same for both: an unwavering devotion to the God of Israel and his timeless commandments. The greatest legacy David left to his son was not his building plans or his highly organized administration. It is found in these words: "Be strong, show yourself a man, and observe what the Lord your God requires" (1 Kings 2:2, 3).

Examining the Text

I. Solomon's Devotion to God (1 Kings 3:3, 4)

According to David's words in 1 Chronicles 22:6-10, God had designated Solomon as David's successor even before Solomon was born. However, not everyone in David's family was pleased with that choice. An older son, Absalom, gathered followers enough to stage a powerful revolt in an attempt to make himself king. But the revolt failed, and Absalom died during the conflict (2 Samuel 15–18).

Then a man named Sheba led another revolt. Sheba was from the tribe of Benjamin and may have been acting out of loyalty to King Saul's memory, for Saul was also from the tribe of Benjamin. Sheba, however, failed to gather enough followers to start a war. When Joab led his troops out to capture him, he took refuge in a walled city. Far from providing a refuge for him, the people of the city cut off his head and threw it over the wall to Joab (2 Samuel 20:1-22).

When David was feeble with age, there was yet another attempt to take the throne by force. It was led by Adonijah, another son older than Solomon. He even enlisted the help of Joab, longtime general of David's army. They staged a celebration and announced that Adonijah was king. But David, though old, was not too feeble to respond to this challenge. Before Adonijah's celebration was over, David's supporters staged a similar celebration and announced that Solomon was king. Adonijah's supporters then deserted him. (Perhaps they remembered what had happened to Absalom's revolt!) So Adonijah's effort failed, and Solomon became king while David was still living (1 Kings 1:5-53).

The opening verses of 1 Kings 2 record David's final counsel to Solomon and David's death (vv. 1-12). The remaining verses then recount the vigorous way in which Solomon secured his kingship, noting in particular the executions of the treasonous Adonijah and of Joab. Chapter 3 highlights Solomon's attitude as he began his reign over God's people.

A. His Obedience (v. 3)

³Solomon showed his love for the Lord by walking according to the statutes of his father David, except that he offered sacrifices and burned incense on the high places.

At this point the young king's heart was committed to obeying and serving God. The one exception noted to his living *according to the statutes* given him by *his father David* was *that he offered sacrifices and burned incense on the high places.* God's law was given before Israel reached the promised land, but it prescribed that any sacrifices and incense offered in the promised land should be offered in the place where God would "choose . . . to put his Name there" (Deuteronomy 12:5-7). The *high places* were places of worship scattered throughout the country and were associated in some cases with pagan practices (as in Numbers 33:51, 52). This one exception to Solomon's devotion is a foreshadowing of the more grievous errors that would mar his later reign (1 Kings 11:7, 8).

At this time the ark of the covenant (the special symbol of God's presence) was in Jerusalem, while the tabernacle, with the altar on which God had prescribed that all sacrifices be made, was located at Gibeon (about seven miles northwest of Jerusalem). The lack of a central place of worship seems to have left some question in the minds of the Israelites about the proper place for offering sacrifices (1 Kings 3:2). Even Samuel offered sacrifices at a high place (1 Samuel 9:11-14, 19, 25). It appears that the use of these high places was tolerated by God as long as such locations had no ties to pagan worship.

After Solomon built the temple in Jerusalem, God clearly designated it as the central place of worship (1 Kings 9:1-3). From that time on, worship at the high places was no longer to be tolerated. Even so, however, the practice persisted. Several of the later kings of Judah are noted as faithful except for their failure to remove the high places (e.g., Joash, 2 Kings 12:2, 3; Amaziah, 2 Kings 14:1-4; Azariah, 2 Kings 15:1-4; and Jotham, 2 Kings 15:32-35).

B. His Offerings (v. 4)

4The king went to Gibeon to offer sacrifices, for that was the most important high place, and Solomon offered a thousand burnt offerings on that altar.

Probably the *high place* at *Gibeon* was considered *most important* because the tabernacle that Moses had made was there (2 Chronicles 1:3). The proper procedure for making *burnt offerings* is described in Leviticus 1. Such an offering might be a bull, a sheep, or a goat. Presenting *a thousand* of them was generous—even for a *king*. Possibly these offerings were made during a celebration that lasted several days. Such a large number reflected Solomon's desire to have God's blessing on his reign.

II. Solomon's Request of God (1 Kings 3:5-9)

A. Appearance of God (v. 5)

5At Gibeon the LORD appeared to Solomon during the night in a dream, and God said, "Ask for whatever you want me to give you."

Fiction abounds in stories of a fairy, genie, or other imaginary creature who offers to grant a wish—or even three wishes—to some fortunate mortal. But we are reading factual history, and it records that *the Lord appeared to Solomon . . . in a dream* and told him to make one request.

B. Acknowledgment of Blessings (v. 6)

6Solomon answered, "You have shown great kindness to your servant, my father David, because he was faithful to you and righteous and upright in heart. You have continued this great kindness to him and have given him a son to sit on his throne this very day.

Before voicing any request, Solomon expressed his appreciation for what God had done for *David* his *father.* With rare exceptions, David had been *faithful . . . and righteous and upright in heart.* Because of this, God had *shown* to him *great kindness.* The word rendered *great kindness* here is a rich Hebrew word, sometimes translated as *mercy, loving-kindness, goodness,* or *favor.* Each of these words is an apt description of what God had shown toward David.

God's own summary of what he had done for David is found in 2 Samuel 7:8, 9: God had raised David from a shepherd to a king; God had been with him continually; God had given him victory over his enemies; and God had made him famous. Furthermore, God had promised that David's descendants would rule after him and that David's house and his kingdom would be established forever (2 Samuel 7:12, 16). Here Solomon acknowledged that God was beginning to keep that promise by giving the *throne* to him, David's *son.*

C. Awareness of Need (vv. 7-9)

7"Now, O Lord my God, you have made your servant king in place of my father David. But I am only a little child and do not know how to carry out my duties.

The phrase *a little child* reflects Solomon's awareness of his inadequacy to rule Israel. At the same time, he came to the throne well prepared: undoubtedly his natural talent was great, and the teaching David had given him was no small thing. It included general instruction about doing right (Proverbs 4:3-9), and it provided practical advice for dealing with specific cases (1 Kings 2:1-9). Still, Solomon was right in recognizing that his ability was not enough to *carry out* the formidable challenge before him.

8"Your servant is here among the people you have chosen, a great people, too numerous to count or number.

Some students estimate that there were more than six million *people* in Israel at this time. How could a new king know the needs of all of them, much less their wants? There were twelve tribes, every one of them motivated to some degree by tribal pride and jealousy. How could a king mold them into one nation under God? Solomon was wise enough to know that he was facing a fearsome task.

9"So give your servant a discerning heart to govern your people and to distinguish between right and wrong. For who is able to govern this great people of yours?"

A discerning heart! Living in the royal palace, Solomon needed heartfelt sympathy to appreciate the concerns of the millions of Israelites who lived in ordinary houses and toiled at ordinary tasks. He needed wisdom enough to understand the many regulations written in the law. He needed the practical good sense to apply those regulations fairly in all circumstances.

Who is able to govern this great people of yours? No one is able to do that; it is too much for any human being. Desperately the king needed wisdom from above, and it was to his credit that he realized what he needed.

III. God's Promises to Solomon (1 Kings 3:10-14)
A. Acceptable Request (v. 10)

10The Lord was pleased that Solomon had asked for this.

The Lord was pleased with Solomon's request and gave him that for which he *had asked*: Solomon's wisdom became the wonder of the world and of the ages. There had never been, and never would be, anyone like him.

B. Abundant Provisions (vv. 11, 12)

11So God said to him, "Since you have asked for this and not for long life or wealth for yourself, nor have asked for the death of your enemies but for discernment in administering justice,

Solomon could have made any number of selfish requests, asking for a *long life* or for *wealth* or for *the death of* his *enemies*. Instead, and above anything else, Solomon asked for *discernment in administering justice*. The word *administering* is based on the Hebrew word for "to hear." It has the implication of one who listens judiciously, evaluating carefully all factors in a given situation. Solomon asked for God's help in this task, for centuries of history had proved that the welfare of his nation depended on obeying God faithfully.

12". . . I will do what you have asked. I will give you a wise and discerning heart, so that there will never have been anyone like you, nor will there ever be.

Solomon's request was within the will of God and was readily granted. God would *give* Solomon *a wise and discerning heart*. Tragically, Solomon would not do what was necessary to maintain such a heart; because of the influence of his many foreign wives, "his heart was not fully devoted to the Lord his God, as the heart of David his father had been" (1 Kings 11:4).

C. Additional Blessings (vv. 13, 14)

13"Moreover, I will give you what you have not asked for—both riches and honor—so that in your lifetime you will have no equal among kings.

Paul wrote that God "is able to do immeasurably more than all we ask or imagine" (Ephesians 3:20). Solomon learned that through God's response to his request. Since the young king had chosen unselfishly in response to God's offer, God granted him the additional blessings of *riches and honor*. In both of these areas, Solomon had *no equal among kings*. See the description in 1 Kings 10:14-29, which summarizes Solomon's vast wealth and also states, "The whole world sought audience with Solomon to hear the wisdom God had put in his heart" (v. 24).

14"And if you walk in my ways and obey my statutes and commands as David your father did, I will give you a long life."

While God would give Solomon unparalleled riches and honor, the blessing of *long life* was conditional. It was contingent on Solomon's obedience to God's *statutes and commands*—an obedience that had been demonstrated in the life of *David*, Solomon's *father*. Certainly David's obedience had not been perfect. But the general pattern of his life had been one of obedience. Sadly, that would not be the case with Solomon. Both he and the nation of Israel would pay dearly for his failure later in his life to *walk in* God's *ways*.

DEDICATION OF SOLOMON'S TEMPLE
(2 CHRONICLES 5:7-14; 1 KINGS 8:22, 23, 27-30; 9:1-5)

Establishing the Groundwork

One of Solomon's most noteworthy accomplishments was the building of the temple in Jerusalem, thus fulfilling a promise that God had made to David (2 Samuel 7:12, 13). The temple that Solomon built is described in chapter 6 of 1 Kings. God himself was its architect. He revealed his plans to David, and David passed them on to Solomon (1 Chronicles 28:11, 12). The heart of the temple had the same sacred rooms as the tabernacle: the Holy Place and the Most Holy Place. The latter, which housed the ark of the covenant, was a cube—30 feet long and wide and high. The Holy Place next to it was the same in width but was twice as long.

The height of the structure was notable—45 feet, rising like a tower above the court around it. Thus there must have been a large space under the roof of the temple and above the ceiling of the Most Holy Place. Across the front of the temple was a porch 15 feet wide. Inside the temple the stone walls were covered with cedar, which was intricately carved and then overlaid with gold. Against the outside of the walls, three stories of side rooms were built. Above these side rooms, the temple walls had narrow windows that allowed some light to enter. According to 1 Kings 6:38, the entire structure took seven years to build. It must have been an impressive sight!

First Kings 7:1-12 describes other buildings in the vicinity of the temple. The structure known as "the Palace of the Forest of Lebanon" probably had that name because its many pillars were made of cedar wood from Lebanon. No doubt they stood as majestically as the trunks of a forest. The purpose of this house is not stated. Perhaps it served as a guest house and reception area, for Solomon was visited by some of the great men and women of his time (1 Kings 10:24). The queen of Sheba is perhaps the most famous example (1 Kings 10:1-13).

First Kings 7:13-22 records that Solomon commissioned an expert metal worker from Tyre to make two massive pillars of brass for the porch of the temple. The rest of that chapter describes the furnishings of the temple, and chapter 8 records the installation of the ark of the covenant and the temple dedication. The Scriptures to be covered in this next section are taken from both the account in 1 Kings and the record in 2 Chronicles, which specifically records how the ark of the covenant was brought into this magnificent structure amidst great celebration. (For a discussion of the relationship between the books of Chronicles and the books of Samuel and Kings, see "Establishing the Groundwork" under the study of 1 Chronicles 28:5-10, 20, 21, in the previous chapter.)

Examining the Text

I. The Ark in the Temple (2 Chronicles 5:7-10)
A. Carrying the Ark (vv. 7-9)

⁷The priests then brought the ark of the Lord's covenant to its place in the inner sanctuary of the temple, the Most Holy Place, and put it beneath the wings of the cherubim.

On this sacred occasion, the Levitical *priests* were responsible for bringing *the ark of the Lord's covenant to its place in the inner sanctuary of the temple*, also called *the Most Holy Place* or the Holy of Holies. Verses 4 and 5 note that the Levites (those who were not priests but who had been given the responsibility to care for any sacred items) had also assisted in carrying the ark and the sacred furnishings from Zion, where the ark had been kept until this time (2 Chronicles 1:4). "Zion" was the location in the lower city where David had put the tent that he had erected to house the ark when he had returned it from Kiriath Jearim. Failure to convey the ark properly had resulted in the sudden death of Uzzah during David's reign (1 Chronicles 15:11-15).

Mention of the "Tent of Meeting" here is a little surprising, however. The last mention of it was in 2 Chronicles 1. There Solomon "went to the high place at Gibeon, for God's Tent of Meeting was there, which Moses the Lord's servant had made in the desert" (v. 3). No mention has since been made of this tent's being moved, but here in chapter 5 "they brought up the ark and the Tent of Meeting and all the sacred furnishings in it" (v. 5) from Zion. Some students assume the Tent of Meeting, with all its sacred furnishings, was at some point moved from Gibeon to Zion and reunited with the ark. Others assume the "Tent of Meeting" in chapter 5 refers to the tent that David had erected for the ark (2 Chronicles 1:4) and that the "sacred furnishings" mentioned here are the ones Solomon made for the temple in chapter 4. It's impossible to say with certainty which answer is correct. Either way, it is difficult to believe that the high place at Gibeon would have continued to function as a place of sacrifice once the temple had been completed and furnished.

The ark of the Lord's covenant was a box in which the Israelites kept the stone tablets on which God had inscribed the Ten Commandments (v. 10). Made of wood and covered with gold, it measured about 45 inches long by 27 inches wide and 27 inches deep (Exodus 25:10-16). The ark was more than a storage chest, however. Upon its cover were two *cherubim* (heavenly beings, discussed more fully in the comments below on verse 8) elaborately made of gold, and between the cherubim was the special place of God's presence. From that place he spoke to his servant Moses (Exodus 25:17-22).

This does not mean that God was confined to the place above the ark of the covenant. Solomon, in his prayer at the dedication of the temple, acknowledged that his temple could never confine God any more than "even the highest heavens" could (2 Chronicles 6:18). God could speak from other places besides this place *in the inner sanctuary of the temple*, but this place was to have a special significance for God's people, as Solomon would later note in his eloquent prayer (1 Kings 8:22-53).

⁸The cherubim spread their wings over the place of the ark and covered the ark and its carrying poles.

The shape of the *cherubim* has been much discussed. Some students have suggested that they were winged bulls with human heads, such as are often seen in the religious art of ancient Mesopotamia. We should think twice, however, before accepting the notion that inspired men of Israel copied their designs from pagan neighbors. Of course, there is no reason to think that the cherubim were chubby babies with wings, such as those painted by medieval artists. The first-century Jewish historian Josephus wrote, "Nobody can tell, or even conjecture, what was the shape of these cherubim." Perhaps he is right.

> [9]*These poles were so long that their ends, extending from the ark, could be seen from in front of the inner sanctuary, but not from outside the Holy Place; and they are still there today.*

The *poles* to be used in carrying the *ark* were inserted into four gold rings that were attached to the ark (two on each side). The poles were never to be removed from the rings, so that human hands would never need to touch the ark (Exodus 25:10-15). The poles *were so long* that one could see the ends of them from within *the Holy Place*, which was adjacent to the Most Holy Place.

The author of 2 Chronicles notes that the poles *are still there today*. As noted previously, 1 and 2 Chronicles were most likely written after the Babylonian captivity. (See the background material on these books in the "Groundwork" section on 1 Chronicles 28:5-10, 20, 21, in chapter 6 of this volume.) When the Babylonians destroyed the Jerusalem temple in 586 BC, King Nebuchadnezzar "carried to Babylon all the articles from the temple of God, both large and small" (2 Chronicles 36:18). Those items were later returned to Jerusalem to be placed in a second temple, as commanded by Cyrus king of Persia (Ezra 1:5-8). While the ark of the covenant is not specifically mentioned among these items, it is possible that it was taken to Babylon then returned later with those who traveled to Jerusalem to rebuild the temple. Thus when the author of 1 and 2 Chronicles (possibly Ezra) wrote that the poles used to carry the ark *are still there today*, this may reflect that the ark, with carrying poles still in place, had been restored to its rightful place among God's people. Today much speculation exists as to the whereabouts of the ark, but in reality we do not know with certainty where it is or even whether or not it still exists.

Some students think the reference to the poles' still being present "today" comes not from the author of 2 Chronicles, but to a source the author used in compiling his record. The events of 1 and 2 Chronicles span a time too long for one author to have had firsthand knowledge of all of them. Thus, it's not unreasonable to believe that Ezra, or some other scribe, compiled the facts from historical sources available to him after the exile. That some kind of historical records were available and were being searched is clear from Ezra 2:62. God's inspiration can guide a scribe to compile a factual report from ancient records just as easily as it can guide him to write a trustworthy original report. Still, one wonders why the inspired scribe would include such a note if it were not in some sense true in his own time.

B. Contents of the Ark (v. 10)

¹⁰There was nothing in the ark except the two tablets that Moses had placed in it at Horeb, where the LORD made a covenant with the Israelites after they came out of Egypt.

The *two tablets* in the *ark* were the tablets of stone on which God had inscribed the Ten Commandments at Mount Horeb, also known as Mount Sinai (Exodus 3:1, 12; 19:16-18). At one time the ark had also held a container of manna and Aaron's rod that had budded miraculously as evidence that Aaron was God's chosen leader (Exodus 16:32-34; Numbers 17:1-11; Hebrews 9:4). Apparently the manna and Aaron's rod had been lost at some point, possibly during the seven months when the ark was in the possession of the Philistines (1 Samuel 5:1; 6:1).

II. Praise in the Temple (2 Chronicles 5:11-13a)

Everything that Solomon did regarding the temple was done on a grand scale. The ceremony at the dedication of the temple was something to be remembered.

A. Priests (v. 11)

¹¹The priests then withdrew from the Holy Place. All the priests who were there had consecrated themselves, regardless of their divisions.

The *priests* had carried the ark to its place in the temple (v. 7). Now they withdrew from there to join in the ceremony of dedication. David had divided the priests into 24 groups, or *divisions* (1 Chronicles 24:1-19). Each division served in the temple for one month, and then did not serve again until the other 23 divisions had taken their turns. For this great occasion, however, *all the priests had consecrated themselves* and were prepared to serve at the same time. And they were all needed to officiate at the enormous number of sacrifices that were presented. Second Chronicles 5:6 describes sacrifices too numerous to be counted. So many were offered that additional space was set aside for that purpose (2 Chronicles 7:7). No doubt all 24 divisions of priests were kept busy.

B. Levites (v. 12)

12All the Levites who were musicians—Asaph, Heman, Jeduthun and their sons and relatives—stood on the east side of the altar, dressed in fine linen and playing cymbals, harps and lyres. They were accompanied by 120 priests sounding trumpets.

All the Levites who were musicians were also present to take part in this celebration. Of the tribe of Levi, only the family of Aaron could serve as priests. The other Levitical families helped in various ways with the temple activities and ceremonies. David, who had organized the priests into divisions as noted in comments on the preceding verse, did the same for the musicians, according to 1 Chronicles 25:1-31. There it is stated that he "set apart some of the sons of Asaph, Heman and Jeduthun for the ministry of prophesying, accompanied by harps, lyres and cymbals" (v. 1). Thus not only are the same men mentioned in the verse before us, but the same instruments are as well. First Chronicles 23:5 says that David had set aside 4,000 of the Levites to praise God through the use of musical instruments. The combination of such an orchestra with *120 priests sounding trumpets* would have been a thrill to hear!

C. Song (v. 13a)

13aThe trumpeters and singers joined in unison, as with one voice, to give praise and thanks to the LORD. Accompanied by trumpets, cymbals and other instruments, they raised their voices in praise to the LORD and sang:
"He is good;
his love endures forever."

It is almost impossible to imagine the stirring harmony as the instrumentalists accompanied thousands of voices singing the praises of God's abundant and everlasting goodness and love. The words *He is good; his love endures forever* are found in the opening verse of Psalm 136, and *his love endures forever* forms the refrain in the second part of each succeeding verse. Perhaps this was the psalm used by the worshipers as *they raised their voices in praise to the Lord.*

III. God in the Temple (2 Chronicles 5:13b, 14)
A. The Cloud (vv. 13b, 14a)

13b, 14aThen the temple of the LORD was filled with a cloud, and the priests could not perform their service because of the cloud,

Just as a *cloud* "covered the Tent of Meeting" when the tabernacle had been erected (Exodus 40:34), here *the temple of the Lord was filled with a cloud.*

And as Moses "could not enter the Tent of Meeting because the cloud had settled upon it" (Exodus 40:35), here *the priests could not perform their service because of the cloud.* Such a cloud seemed designed to veil the presence of God, yet at the same time it showed that he is with his people.

B. The Glory (v. 14b)

14b . . . for the glory of the Lord filled the temple of God.

The glory of the Lord had filled the tabernacle (Exodus 40:34, 35), and now it *filled the temple of God.* Solomon responded to this demonstration of God's presence with one of the most moving prayers recorded in the Bible.

IV. Prayer for the Temple (1 Kings 8:22, 23, 27-30)
A. Praise to the Lord (vv. 22, 23, 27)

22 Then Solomon stood before the altar of the Lord in front of the whole assembly of Israel, spread out his hands toward heaven

Solomon had spoken to the *assembly* gathered on this occasion, following the glory of the Lord's filling the temple (vv. 14-21). Now his upraised arms made it plain that he was speaking in prayer to God.

23 . . . and said: "O Lord, God of Israel, there is no God like you in heaven above or on earth below—you who keep your covenant of love with your servants who continue wholeheartedly in your way.

The *Lord* stands alone as the one and only *God.* In all creation there is none to be compared with him. Evidence of that is seen in the way he kept the *covenant* he had made at Sinai when his people had come out of Egypt. He had promised to bless his people with prosperity and happiness if they would *wholeheartedly* obey his law. God's promise had been kept faultlessly for nearly five centuries (1 Kings 6:1). The same covenant had promised disaster to the people if they did not obey, and that promise had also been kept.

Solomon then noted how faithful God had been in keeping his promise to Solomon's father David, and he prayed that God would keep his promise that David's descendants would continue to rule (vv. 24-26). With verse 27, he returned to the recognition of God's uniqueness and superiority.

27 "But will God really dwell on earth? The heavens, even the highest heaven, cannot contain you. How much less this temple I have built!

God is great beyond our comprehension. All of outer space is too small to *contain* him. How absurd it would be to think that he could be found only in that tiny *temple* that Solomon had just completed!

B. Plea for Mercy (vv. 28-30)

28"Yet give attention to your servant's prayer and his plea for mercy, O LORD my God. Hear the cry and the prayer that your servant is praying in your presence this day.

Understanding that God was not confined to the temple, Solomon nevertheless pleaded that God would *give attention* to the *prayer* that he was about to speak as that temple was being dedicated.

29"May your eyes be open toward this temple night and day, this place of which you said, 'My Name shall be there,' so that you will hear the prayer your servant prays toward this place.

Though God lived in the distant Heaven, Solomon prayed that he would give special attention to the *temple night and day.* Before Israel reached the promised land, God had promised that he would put his name at a specific *place* in that land. That place was to be a special place of contact with God: the people of Israel were to present their offerings there (Deuteronomy 12:10, 11). Then God had promised David that Solomon would build a place for God's name (2 Samuel 7:13). Now Solomon had completed the temple and placed in it the ark of the covenant, the visible symbol of God's presence. God had signaled his acceptance of the temple by filling it with his glory. Surely this was the place of which God could say, *My Name shall be there.*

True, God could not be confined to the temple; yet in a special sense he was there, as he had demonstrated by filling that place with his glory. Solomon asked for God's special attention, not only to the *prayer* he was making before the temple that day, but also to whatever prayer he later would make *toward this place.*

30"Hear the supplication of your servant and of your people Israel when they pray toward this place. Hear from heaven, your dwelling place, and when you hear, forgive."

Now Solomon pleaded that the Lord would hear not only his prayers, but the prayers that all *Israel* would *pray toward* this special *place* of God's presence—especially prayers for pardon. Read on in verses 31-40 to see this verified. Solomon foresaw the time when the people of Israel would fall into idolatry and other sins, as they had often done before. God would punish their sinning with national disaster, as he had often done before. In misery they would repent of their sins and plead for forgiveness, as they had often done before. Solomon prayed that God would be merciful and *forgive* them yet again.

Second Chronicles 5:3 (see also 1 Kings 8:2) indicates that the occasion during which the dedication of the temple took place was "the festival in the seventh month." This would have been the Feast of Tabernacles. For 14 days (7 days for celebrating the dedication of the temple and 7 more for observing the Feast of Tabernacles), the people rejoiced and then returned to their homes "joyful and glad in heart for all the good things the Lord had done for his servant David and his people Israel" (1 Kings 8:65, 66). It is noteworthy that David was not forgotten on this occasion. He had danced with joy before the ark as it was brought to Jerusalem and placed in the tent he had prepared for it (2 Samuel 6:12-15). He had longed to build a temple for his God, but he had not been permitted to do so. Would not his heart have overflowed with joy, had he been privileged to share in the dedication of this magnificent temple built by his son?

V. Warning Concerning the Temple (1 Kings 9:1-5)

Solomon's prayer, recorded in 1 Kings 8, was followed by an appearance of the Lord to him, recorded at the beginning of chapter 9.

A. The Lord's Appearance (vv. 1, 2)

¹When Solomon had finished building the temple of the Lord and the royal palace, and had achieved all he had desired to do

We are now looking at a time not only after Solomon completed the *temple*, but also after he completed many other great buildings such as the *royal palace* and the Palace of the Forest of Lebanon (1 Kings 7:1, 2). In fact, *all* that Solomon *had desired to do* he *had achieved*. Some have suggested that this was a kind of crossroads in Solomon's reign and that God was appearing to him to remind him of his responsibility to be faithful as David his father had been.

². . . the Lord appeared to him a second time, as he had appeared to him at Gibeon.

Pride can often follow the accomplishment of great things, even when those things have been done for God. Since Solomon had reached a point where he could be tempted to rest on his laurels, it was both appropriate and necessary that the Lord appear to him and remind him not to lose sight of the true priorities of his kingship.

At Gibeon the Lord had *appeared* to Solomon in a dream by night and had said, "Ask for whatever you want me to give you" (1 Kings 3:5). Now he appeared again in a similar way.

B. The Lord's Acceptance (v. 3)

³The Lord said to him:

"I have heard the prayer and plea you have made before me; I have consecrated this temple, which you have built, by putting my Name there forever. My eyes and my heart will always be there.

The Lord had *heard* Solomon's *prayer*, and in response he had *consecrated* the new *temple*: he had made it holy, set it apart, dedicated it as the place foretold in Deuteronomy 12:10, 11. It was to be the national worship center of Israel—the place where sacrifices and offerings would be made. God's *eyes* and *heart* would *be there:* he would be watching and cherishing that temple *always.*

C. Solomon's Accountability (v. 4)

⁴"As for you, if you walk before me in integrity of heart and uprightness, as David your father did, and do all I command and observe my decrees and laws,

With only a few exceptions, *David* had obeyed God with wholehearted devotion and upright living. If Solomon would do the same, he could be sure that God would keep the promise found in the next verse.

D. The Lord's Assurance (v. 5)

⁵". . . I will establish your royal throne over Israel forever, as I promised David your father when I said, 'You shall never fail to have a man on the throne of Israel.'"

God had promised that David's *royal throne* would last *forever*, and that one of David's descendants would always be king (2 Samuel 7:11-16). Now the Lord made the same promise to Solomon, under the condition stated in the previous verse. This same condition is emphasized strongly in the succeeding verses (vv. 6-9). If Israel turned to idolatry and wickedness, it would lose the promised land; and Solomon's magnificent temple would be destroyed. Sadly, this is eventually what happened (2 Kings 24:10-13; 25:8, 9, 13-17).

SOLOMON TURNS AWAY FROM GOD (1 KINGS 11:1-13)

Establishing the Groundwork

"One thing I do," wrote Paul in Philippians 3:13. His words reflect the single-minded, unshakable devotion to God that gave the apostle an abiding peace and freedom, even when confined to prison in Rome. Such a perspective stands in glaring contrast to that which came to characterize King Solomon. Solomon sought to maintain a plurality in two areas where God had clearly commanded that there be only one: gods and wives. When Solomon multiplied these, he also multiplied his troubles.

Solomon's reign would have been far more positive and productive if he had lived his life as a man of one God and one woman. He seems to have realized this later in life, as the writings of Ecclesiastes, focusing on one God (Ecclesiastes 12:13, 14), and the Song of Songs, focusing on the relationship between one man and one woman, indicate.

Some question how Solomon, who possessed such unparalleled wisdom, could have acted as foolishly as he did. Like any gift (and Solomon's wisdom was a gift from the Lord), wisdom must be "opened" and used properly. If one's heart is not in tune with God and his purposes, then any of God's gifts is vulnerable to being misused or ignored altogether. One of the key emphases in the next passage to be examined is the condition of Solomon's heart and how it was "turned" from God (1 Kings 11:2, 4, 9). Thus this man, so renowned for his wisdom, failed to apply his own counsel as recorded in Proverbs 4:23: "Above all else, guard your heart, for it is the wellspring of life."

Examining the Text

I. Solomon's Women (1 Kings 11:1-3)
A. Foreign Women (v. 1)

¹King Solomon, however, loved many foreign women besides Pharaoh's daughter—Moabites, Ammonites, Edomites, Sidonians and Hittites.

Early in his reign Solomon had made an alliance with Pharaoh, king of Egypt, and strengthened the bond by taking that ruler's *daughter* as his wife (1 Kings 3:1). But as Solomon's fame spread, his contacts with other peoples increased. The *foreign women* whom Solomon *loved* included *many . . . besides Pharaoh's daughter*. The *Moabites* lived east of the Dead Sea. The *Ammonites* lived east of Israel and north of Moab. The *Edomites* lived south of the Dead Sea. The *Sidonians* took their name from Sidon, a city of Phoenicia north of Israel on the Mediterranean coast. The *Hittites* were prominent in Syria and Palestine for centuries. At this time they probably were strongest in the territory east of Phoenicia.

David had subdued these smaller nations and made them part of his empire, which was now ruled by Solomon. Each nation managed its own affairs but paid tribute to Israel. Since Solomon was respected and admired throughout the known world, there was a certain prestige in being associated with him. A foreign ruler might consider it a privilege to be a father-in-law to such a man. Also, if one of the subject kings ever thought of rebelling and refusing to pay tribute to Israel, he might be restrained by remembering that his daughter was in Jerusalem. She easily could be made a prisoner or a slave instead of a wife.

B. Forbidden Women (vv. 2, 3)

²They were from nations about which the Lᴏʀᴅ had told the Israelites, "You must not intermarry with them, because they will surely turn your hearts after their gods." Nevertheless, Solomon held fast to them in love.

God *had told the Israelites* to destroy the pagan *nations* that inhabited the promised land. His people were not to associate with them; specifically, they were not to marry pagans (Deuteronomy 7:1-5). The reason was very simple: *they will surely turn your hearts after their gods.*

Solomon, however, became engrossed in preserving the stability of his empire. For political expediency he ignored God's law. He spoke affectionately to pagan kings; he took their daughters into his harem. The love for God, which should have consumed Solomon's heart, was replaced by *love* for his wives.

³He had seven hundred wives of royal birth and three hundred concubines, and his wives led him astray.

It seems hard to believe that Solomon could have accumulated *seven hundred* princesses from the five small nations that were named in verse 1. As mentioned earlier, we know he made an alliance with Egypt and cemented that treaty by marrying the Egyptian king's daughter. Perhaps he did the same with countries west and south of Egypt, and with the kingdoms in Arabia, in Asia Minor north of the Mediterranean, and even in Mesopotamia. Even so, it appears that a smaller country must have had several of its princesses in Solomon's harem. Solomon was the greatest and most feared king on earth. It was an honor to be allied with him—and it was politically prudent as well.

It should be noted that nowhere does the Old Testament give its approval to polygamy. Since God made only one woman for Adam, monogamy is implied from the beginning (Genesis 2:24). But neither does the Old Testament forbid a plurality of wives. Such was the custom among the neighbors of Israel, and it seems that God permitted man to discover for himself the evils that were a part of this practice.

God did forbid his people from intermarrying with pagans (as noted previously in verse 2), and he specifically issued this warning to any king who would rule in Israel, "He must not take many wives, or his heart will be led astray" (Deuteronomy 17:17). Having a large harem was considered a status symbol for kings in the ancient world, but God wanted a king in Israel to understand that his security was to be found in faithfulness to God's standards, not those of the surrounding peoples.

Concubines have been described as "second-class wives." They had no royal fathers; they were not chosen for political purposes, and so their status was inferior. We wonder, then, why they were chosen. When Solomon saw an extremely beautiful woman, did he simply take her home to keep for his own? We wonder if these *three hundred* were the prettiest, the most vivacious, the most interesting, and the best loved of the thousand. We have no way to be certain. The record simply notes that the king had three hundred concubines.

Our tabloid-infested society would love to know all the intimate details of life in such a household as this. The Scriptures provide only the most significant detail of all: *his wives led him astray*. God's earlier warning in Deuteronomy 17:17 proved to be well founded.

II. Solomon's Idolatry (1 Kings 11:4-8)

God had said, "You shall have no other gods before me" (Exodus 20:3). Perhaps Solomon had no intention of breaking that law when he began his reign. But he married an Egyptian bride and built her a palace (1 Kings 7:8). Perhaps he allowed her to worship her pagan gods in that palace—where no one else could see. That set a precedent for allowing his other wives to practice their religions. As the number of wives grew, keeping their religious practices private grew more and more difficult. Solomon's tolerance of false religion led to support, and his support eventually resulted in actual worship.

A. His Wandering Heart (v. 4)

4As Solomon grew old, his wives turned his heart after other gods, and his heart was not fully devoted to the LORD his God, as the heart of David his father had been.

Perhaps during the early years of his reign, when the words of *David his father* were still fresh in his mind, Solomon made an effort to distance himself from the pagan idols and practices of his many wives. But as he *grew old*, his will to resist seems to have weakened. In time, *his wives turned his heart after other gods*.

B. His False Gods (vv. 5-8)

⁵He followed Ashtoreth the goddess of the Sidonians, and Molech the detestable god of the Ammonites.

Ashtoreth was a *goddess* worshiped by many pagans along the Mediterranean coast. She was portrayed in somewhat different ways in the various towns and territories. Solomon followed the Sidonian version, probably because a wife from Sidon brought this goddess to Jerusalem.

As noted earlier, the *Ammonites* lived east of Israel. Groups of them worshiped differing versions of their so-called god, *Molech*. The name is derived from a word that means *king*. This deity was especially *detestable* because some of his worshipers burned their children in sacrifice to him, which Israelites were forbidden to do (Leviticus 18:21). Solomon did not go that far, but one of his descendants (approximately two centuries later) did (2 Kings 16:1-3).

⁶So Solomon did evil in the eyes of the Lord; he did not follow the Lord completely, as David his father had done.

Any involvement with false gods was *evil*. Solomon knew that, but for the sake of his wives he drifted into idolatry of various kinds. The description of *David* as "fully devoted" (v. 4) and as following the Lord *completely* is not meant to ignore the grievous sins he committed. David was repentant when confronted with his wrongdoing (2 Samuel 12:13), and the overall thrust of his life was that of being a man after God's own heart (Acts 13:22). Also, David was never guilty of idolatry.

⁷On a hill east of Jerusalem, Solomon built a high place for Chemosh the detestable god of Moab, and for Molech the detestable god of the Ammonites.

A high place describes a place of worship. They were called high places because many of them were located on hilltops, but the name came to be given even to shrines that were set up in the valleys. The sites mentioned here most likely were situated on the Mount of Olives, which is a *hill east of Jerusalem*.

To the south of the Ammonites lived the people of Moab, and it seems that the Moabite god *Chemosh* was similar to the false deity the Ammonites called *Molech*. Second Kings 3:26, 27 records that the king of Moab offered his son as a burnt offering, and a Moabite record (known as the Moabite Stone) adds that he made the offering to Chemosh.

Solomon's support of the high places helps us understand why God's plan was for Israel to worship him at the one place that he would choose (Deuteronomy 12:10, 11). While worship at the high places was tolerated (1 Samuel 9:25), God knew that it also had the potential to open the door to the actual worship of false gods. This is exactly what happened in the case of Solomon.

⁸He did the same for all his foreign wives, who burned incense and offered sacrifices to their gods.

We should not imply from this statement that Solomon made seven hundred worship places for his seven hundred *wives*. Perhaps dozens of wives worshiped at each place he built. Still, there must have been a bewildering number of shrines in and near Jerusalem. Probably none of them was as big as the temple of the Lord, and none was as richly adorned with gold and silver; but a visitor in the area would not conclude that the Lord was the one and only God worshiped in Jerusalem.

III. Solomon's Punishment (1 Kings 11:9-13)
A. Punishment Promised (vv. 9-11)

⁹The Lord became angry with Solomon because his heart had turned away from the Lord, the God of Israel, who had appeared to him twice.

The Lord is rightly *angry* with wrongdoing, and Solomon's conduct was clearly wrong. With his great wisdom, he should have managed his own *heart* better; he should have kept it faithful to the Lord. His turning away was the more inexcusable because the Lord *had appeared to him twice*. The first time he had granted Solomon's request for wisdom and had added a bonus of riches and honor (1 Kings 3:5-14). The second time he had promised continued success to Solomon if Solomon remained faithful to him and disaster if Solomon did not (1 Kings 9:2-9). With that promise as plain as words could make it, how could Solomon turn from God? But he did.

¹⁰Although he had forbidden Solomon to follow other gods, Solomon did not keep the Lord's command.

The law forbade idolatry (as clearly stated in the first two of the Ten Commandments). The Lord had appeared to Solomon and *had forbidden* him *to follow other gods* (1 Kings 9:6, 7). But Solomon had disobeyed.

¹¹So the Lord said to Solomon, "Since this is your attitude and you have not kept my covenant and my decrees, which I commanded you, I will most certainly tear the kingdom away from you and give it to one of your subordinates.

With all his wisdom Solomon must have known that Israel had turned away from God time after time and that disaster had followed every instance of turning away. How could Solomon think that he could turn to idols without escaping punishment? Most likely he simply stopped thinking about pleasing God and thought only of pleasing his wives.

The punishment prescribed by God must have hurt Solomon deeply. The *kingdom* that David his father had left him to rule and had prepared him to rule, and that represented Israel at the height of its glory was to be taken from Solomon and given to one of his *subordinates*. That individual was Jeroboam, who received a special prophetic message recorded later in this chapter (vv. 27-33).

B. Punishment Postponed (v. 12)

12 "Nevertheless, for the sake of David your father, I will not do it during your lifetime. I will tear it out of the hand of your son.

Solomon certainly deserved punishment, but it was postponed—not for his *sake,* but for David's. *David* had served God heroically many years. God would not let his empire collapse so quickly. That would happen after Solomon's *son* came to power. At that time, the kingdom divided and the "subordinate" mentioned in verse 11 (Jeroboam) became king of the northern part (1 Kings 11:26-31; 12:20).

Did this mean that Solomon himself would escape punishment? No. God had promised long life to Solomon if he would be obedient to him (1 Kings 3:14). But disobedient Solomon died rather young, probably no more than 60 years of age. And Solomon must have felt a great measure of regret, knowing that he would pass on to his son only a fraction of what his *father* David had provided for him.

C. Punishment Pared (v. 13)

13 "Yet I will not tear the whole kingdom from him, but will give him one tribe for the sake of David my servant and for the sake of Jerusalem, which I have chosen."

In addition to declaring that Solomon's punishment would be postponed, God also modified the punishment by stating that Solomon's son, Rehoboam, would not lose *the whole kingdom*. He would continue to rule the *one tribe* of Judah (1 Kings 12:17, 20), though some from the tribe of Benjamin also chose to support Rehoboam (1 Kings 12:21). God had a great plan for David's kingdom, and his plan would not be frustrated by Solomon's sin.

How to Say It

AARON. *Air*-un.

ABSALOM. *Ab*-suh-lum.

ADONIJAH. Ad-o-*nye*-juh.

AMAZIAH. Am-uh-*zye*-uh.

AMMONITES. *Am*-un-ites.

ASAPH. *Ay*-saff.

ASHTORETH. *Ash*-toe-reth.

AZARIAH. Az-uh-*rye*-uh.

BABYLONIAN. Bab-ih-*low*-nee-un.

CHEMOSH. *Kee*-mosh.

CHERUBIM. *chair*-uh-bim.

EDOMITES. *Ee*-dum-ites.

GIBEON. *Gib*-e-un (G as in *get*).

GOLIATH. Go-*lye*-uth.

HITTITES. *Hit*-ites or *Hit*-tites.

HOREB. *Ho*-reb.

JEDUTHUN. Jeh-*doo*-thun.

JEROBOAM. Jair-uh-*boe*-um.

JOAB. *Jo*-ab.

JOASH. *Jo*-ash.

JOSEPHUS. Jo-*see*-fus.

JOTHAM. *Jo*-thum.

LEVITES. *Lee*-vites.

LEVITICAL. Leh-*vit*-ih-kul.

MEDITERRANEAN. *Med*-uh-tuh-*ray*-nee-un (strong accent on *ray*).

MESOPOTAMIA. *Mes*-uh-puh-*tay*-me-uh (strong accent on *tay*).

MOABITES. *Mo*-ub-ites.

MOLECH. *Mo*-lek.

PHARAOH. *Fair*-o or *Fay*-roe.

PHOENICIA. Fuh-*nish*-uh.

REHOBOAM. Ree-huh-*boe*-um.

SHEBA. *She*-buh.

SIDONIANS. Sigh-*doe*-nee-unz.

SINAI. *Sigh*-nye or *Sigh*-nay-eye.

SOLOMON. *Sol*-o-mun.

TYRE. Tire.

Chapter 8

The Division of the Kingdom and the Early Ministry of Elijah

1 Kings 12:1-20, 25-33; 17:1-16; 18:20-24, 30-35, 38, 39

THE NATION DIVIDES (1 KINGS 12:1-20)

Establishing the Groundwork

The previous chapter of this volume concluded with the sad record of God's judgment on Solomon: "The Lord became angry with Solomon because his heart had turned away from the Lord, the God of Israel, who had appeared to him twice" (1 Kings 11:9). God then sent the prophet Ahijah to seek out Jeroboam, whom Solomon had made a leader of one of the groups of laborers that Solomon commissioned from the tribes of Israel (1 Kings 5:13, 14; 11:28). Ahijah dramatized his message by taking a cloak and tearing it into 12 pieces. These pieces symbolized the 12 tribes of Israel. Ten of these pieces the prophet gave to Jeroboam, signifying that he would become the leader of 10 of the tribes (1 Kings 11:29-31).

First Kings 11:26 notes that at some point Jeroboam "rebelled against the king" (Solomon). Some students suggest that Jeroboam "jumped the gun," initiating some kind of rebellion against Solomon in an attempt to force the fulfillment of Ahijah's prophecy. Possibly the prophecy became known to Solomon, and he attempted to eliminate the threat posed by Jeroboam. Whatever the circumstances of the rebellion, through some means Solomon apparently learned of it and sought to kill Jeroboam. Jeroboam fled to Egypt, where he remained until Solomon's death (1 Kings 11:40). When Solomon's son Rehoboam ascended the throne, he journeyed to Shechem for the coronation service, which is where we resume our studies.

Examining the Text

I. The People's Appeal (1 Kings 12:1-5)
A. Assembling in Shechem (vv. 1, 2)

¹Rehoboam went to Shechem, for all the Israelites had gone there to make him king.

The city of *Shechem* was located about 30 miles north of Jerusalem in a valley between Mount Gerizim and Mount Ebal. It was a city with great historical significance for the nation of Israel. Abraham had built an altar there (Genesis 12:6, 7). Later Jacob purchased a plot of ground in that vicinity, where he pitched his tent and erected an altar (Genesis 33:18-20). "Jacob's well," which guides in the Holy Land still show to modern tourists, was also located in this territory (John 4:5, 6). Joshua's farewell address, during which he urged the Israelites to be faithful to God's covenant with them, was delivered at Shechem (Joshua 24:1).

With so much history associated with it, one can see why Shechem might be selected as the place for the coronation of Israel's next king. It might be selected if, for example, the country did not already have a capital with a kingly palace. But Israel did have such a capital—Jerusalem. Why, then, did *Rehoboam* go to Shechem rather than having the people come to Jerusalem *to make him king?* This may suggest that the dissension among the people that is apparent in their complaint (v. 4) was already threatening to tear the country apart. Perhaps the northern tribes in particular, burdened by Solomon's building campaigns, were also growing weary of having to travel to Jerusalem for special occasions. They would assemble for the coronation, but at a more central location. Apparently Rehoboam believed that he did not possess enough clout to challenge the people's desire, so he traveled to Shechem.

²When Jeroboam son of Nebat heard this (he was still in Egypt, where he had fled from King Solomon), he returned from Egypt.

Another ominous piece of information is provided here: *Jeroboam*, who had been in *Egypt*, suddenly *returned from* there upon hearing of Rehoboam's upcoming coronation in Shechem. Jeroboam had gone to Egypt to escape from *King Solomon*, as previously noted in the "Groundwork" section.

B. Approaching Rehoboam (vv. 3, 4)

³So they sent for Jeroboam, and he and the whole assembly of Israel went to Rehoboam and said to him:

Still another piece of evidence that trouble was brewing was that the Israelites *sent for Jeroboam* when they became aware of his return from Egypt. Although Jeroboam had been in exile, he was apparently so well respected that the people wanted him to serve as their spokesman when they met with Rehoboam. If Rehoboam was aware of his father's suspicions toward Jeroboam (1 Kings 11:40), the latter's return at this particular time surely must have been unsettling to Rehoboam. *The whole assembly of Israel* probably refs to a group of selected representatives of all the tribes. Jeroboam and these delegates approached Rehoboam to present a united appeal.

> *⁴"Your father put a heavy yoke on us, but now lighten the harsh labor and the heavy yoke he put on us, and we will serve you."*

Years earlier, when the nation of Israel first wanted a king, Samuel had warned the people that having a king would carry certain negative consequences (1 Samuel 8:10-18). His dire predictions that a king would levy a heavy tax burden upon them and conscript their sons and daughters for his service had come to pass during the reign of Solomon (1 Kings 5:13, 14; 9:15, 22). Now the people wanted relief. They were not asking for the complete abolition of all taxes or other burdens laid upon them by Solomon. All they were asking was that Rehoboam would *lighten* their *heavy yoke,* and then they would *serve* him.

Certainly this was not an unreasonable request of a new king. The people's statement left open the question of what they would do if Rehoboam denied their request, though one may imply from their words that they would not be willing to serve Rehoboam if he refused to comply with their request.

C. Asking for Time (v. 5)

> *⁵Rehoboam answered, "Go away for three days and then come back to me." So the people went away.*

Growing up in Solomon's palace, Rehoboam may well have been isolated from *the people* and their hardships. Thus it was reasonable for him to take some time to examine the facts and evaluate the situation before he made a decision. And if he did decide to do something to address the concerns voiced by the people, he would need time to work out the details of any proposals he would submit to them. On the other hand, Rehoboam may simply have been stalling for time—like many politicians do today when they are confronted with hard decisions. Regardless of his motives, the people were willing to give him time to consider the matter.

II. Rehoboam's Advisers (1 Kings 12:6-11)
A. Older Men (vv. 6, 7)

> *⁶Then King Rehoboam consulted the elders who had served his father Solomon during his lifetime. "How would you advise me to answer these people?" he asked.*

The first step Rehoboam took in determining how to *answer these people* was a wise one. He *consulted the elders* who had counseled *his father Solomon.* They had observed the mistakes that had ruined Solomon's once-promising reign. They saw how his growing extravagance had placed an increasingly heavy burden on the people by demanding that they furnish both the manpower and the taxes necessary to complete and maintain his many projects and enterprises. No doubt, these men had heard some of the complaints that the people had made.

> **⁷They replied, "If today you will be a servant to these people and serve them and give them a favorable answer, they will always be your servants."**

These senior counselors advised Rehoboam to become *a servant to these people*. This was quite different from the usual demeanor of ancient monarchs, who were notorious for their arrogant and haughty behavior. These wise elders, however, were declaring a great truth: a ruler who is willing to *serve* the people will soon have subjects who are willing to serve him. Jesus was a perfect model of this kind of servant leadership (Matthew 20:25-28). And while many pay lip service to it, few leaders in politics, business, or even the church have truly understood this principle.

B. Younger Men (vv. 8-11)

> **⁸But Rehoboam rejected the advice the elders gave him and consulted the young men who had grown up with him and were serving him.**

We can only guess at Rehoboam's motives for rejecting *the advice the elders gave him*. Perhaps he had turned to them first simply out of courtesy, knowing ahead of time that he would not take their advice. Or he may have resented the fact that their words, in effect, criticized the actions of his father. Perhaps Rehoboam also realized that if he followed their counsel, he would have to do without some of the privileges that Solomon had enjoyed. Rehoboam was like many of us: when someone gives us advice we don't like, we turn to someone else who we think will give advice more to our liking.

In Rehoboam's case, this meant consulting some *young men*. This was a group of his peers—men whom he knew better, for they had *grown up with him*. We usually feel more comfortable among people we have grown up with or have known for a long time. Apparently these younger men had been Rehoboam's companions or servants in the palace, since they *were serving him*. They knew how he thought and knew the answers that he wanted to hear.

> **⁹He asked them, "What is your advice? How should we answer these people who say to me, 'Lighten the yoke your father put on us'?"**

In speaking to these younger men, Rehoboam posed his question differently from the way he consulted the older counselors. In speaking to the older men he asked, "How would you advise me to answer these people?"

(v. 6). But to the young men he asked, *How should we answer these people?* Quite obviously Rehoboam identified with, and felt at ease with, the younger men more than the older men.

> *¹⁰The young men who had grown up with him replied, "Tell these people who have said to you, 'Your father put a heavy yoke on us, but make our yoke lighter'—tell them, 'My little finger is thicker than my father's waist.*

In sharp contrast to the response of the older counselors, the answer of these *young men* showed utter contempt for *the people*. As companions of Rehoboam, these men had probably lived lives of ease and comfort. Such a lifestyle had left them with little understanding of the plight of the general populace, who were burdened by a heavy tax load. Thus, these men had little or no sympathy for the people's suffering. No doubt, this was one reason Jeroboam was considered a fitting representative for the people (vv. 2, 3): he had worked among them (1 Kings 11:28) and was aware of their grievances.

The arrogance of these young advisers is almost beyond belief. They acknowledged that Solomon had placed a *heavy* burden on the people, but they urged Rehoboam to increase that burden rather than grant relief. They even told Rehoboam the words he should use: *My little finger is thicker than my father's waist.* The meaning of this proverbial expression was quite clear: Rehoboam's weakest actions would be more severe than his father's strongest actions.

> *¹¹" 'My father laid on you a heavy yoke; I will make it even heavier. My father scourged you with whips; I will scourge you with scorpions.'"*

While the reference to *whips* and *scorpions* could have been figurative, on occasion Solomon's overseers may have used actual whips on their workers. Some students have suggested that *scorpions* describes an especially painful whip in which pieces of metal or bone were embedded to cause lacerations in the flesh of the victim.

III. Rehoboam's Answer (1 Kings 12:12-15)
A. Harsh Reply (vv. 12-14)

> *¹²Three days later Jeroboam and all the people returned to Rehoboam, as the king had said, "Come back to me in three days."*

When the *three days* that *Rehoboam* had requested had passed, *all the people*, led by *Jeroboam*, again assembled to hear the king's response to their petition. Most likely they had used this time to discuss possible replies he might make. Had he responded favorably to their petition, they probably would have been willing to return home, supportive of Rehoboam. But they also must have considered the possibility that Rehoboam would reject their request.

13, 14The king answered the people harshly. Rejecting the advice given him by the elders, he followed the advice of the young men and said, "My father made your yoke heavy; I will make it even heavier. My father scourged you with whips; I will scourge you with scorpions."

Rehoboam proceeded to use the very words suggested by the *young men* whom he had consulted (vv. 10, 11). His answer to the people reflected utter contempt for God's standards for kingship in Israel, as given earlier through Moses (Deuteronomy 17:14-20).

B. Higher Purpose (v. 15)

15So the king did not listen to the people, for this turn of events was from the LORD, to fulfill the word the LORD had spoken to Jeroboam son of Nebat through Ahijah the Shilonite.

By such a statement as this, the writer of the record in 1 Kings is not excusing the foolish actions of Rehoboam or the rebellion of the northern tribes. Through these *events*, however, the larger purposes of *the Lord* were being accomplished. These events occurred to bring about the punishment that the Lord had declared would come upon the nation because of Solomon's departure from God's ways (1 Kings 11:9-13). Specifically, *the Lord had spoken to Jeroboam . . . through* the prophet *Ahijah* concerning the ten tribes of Israel over which he would rule (vv. 29-39). God used the actions of a tactless *king* to accomplish his plan, just as he used the actions of Joseph's brothers to accomplish a higher purpose (Genesis 50:19, 20).

IV. The People's Anger (1 Kings 12:16-20)
A. Animosity of the Northern Tribes (v. 16)

16When all Israel saw that the king refused to listen to them, they answered the king:

> ***"What share do we have in David,***
> ***what part in Jesse's son?***
> ***To your tents, O Israel!***
> ***Look after your own house, O David!"***

So the Israelites went home.

Rehoboam's brash rejection of the people's request broke open wounds that actually had been festering for many years. During the time of the judges, tensions manifested themselves on at least three occasions (Judges 8:1-3; 12:1-6; 20:1-48). Later, after King Saul's death, only Judah crowned David as king, while the northern tribes remained loyal to Saul's house, crowning his son

Ish-Bosheth king (2 Samuel 2:8-10). In addition, following Absalom's revolt and David's return to power, the northern tribes briefly supported a rebel from the tribe of Benjamin named Sheba (2 Samuel 19:41–20:22). In fact, the words spoken here to Rehoboam are strikingly reminiscent of those that initiated Sheba's revolt against David (2 Samuel 20:1).

To your tents, O Israel. Some students interpret this as a call to arms. It is a reasonable assumption, but not required. It may have been simply a call for the people to leave the meeting with the king and to depart to their homes. Regardless of the immediate intent, however, the eventual result of this response is clear. Negotiations between Rehoboam and the northern tribes were angrily terminated. The northern tribes voiced their allegiance to Jeroboam as king, and Ahijah's prophecy of the kingdom's division came to pass.

B. Actions of Rehoboam (vv. 17-19)

17But as for the Israelites who were living in the towns of Judah, Rehoboam still ruled over them.

Ahijah had told Jeroboam that one tribe would be given to Solomon's son for David's sake (1 Kings 11:34-36). However, the word *Israelites* may also refer to the members of other tribes who were *living in the towns* within the territory of *Judah.*

18King Rehoboam sent out Adoniram, who was in charge of forced labor, but all Israel stoned him to death. King Rehoboam, however, managed to get into his chariot and escape to Jerusalem.

Apparently Rehoboam had remained at Shechem for a time and had *sent out Adoniram, who was in charge of forced labor,* from there. But the system of forced labor that had been instituted under Solomon (1 Kings 5:13, 14) was likely part of the "heavy yoke" that the people wanted Rehoboam to lighten (1 Kings 12:3, 4). Dispatching Adnoiram was another foolish gesture on Rehoboam's part and may indicate that he did not yet realize the seriousness of the northern tribes' rebellion. When the people *stoned* Adoniram *to death,* Rehoboam quickly understood that a state of war actually existed. He also recognized that he himself was in danger, so he hastily returned to the safety of *Jerusalem.*

19So Israel has been in rebellion against the house of David to this day.

Through the folly of Rehoboam, the threatened revolt became a reality. The expression *to this day* seems to indicate a perspective before the fall of the northern kingdom to the Assyrians in 722 BC. That may surprise the reader since 1 and 2 Kings (originally one book) were clearly written later.

Second Kings closes with the fall of Jerusalem (586 BC) and the beginning of the exile. It is possible that the expression came from a source used by the author of 1 and 2 Kings and does not reflect statements of the author himself, who may have compiled 1 and 2 Kings some time after the fall of Jerusalem. (The record in 1 and 2 Kings gives no indication of a specific time when the record was compiled or who the author was.) But why would an inspired writer include a detail that was no longer true in his own day? If the original record was written by an inspired prophet, the compiler probably felt compelled to leave it unchanged, even in such "minor" details.

The split of the kingdom occurred in the year 931 BC (some suggest 930). After the split, the term *Israel* came to designate the northern kingdom, which fell to the Assyrians in 722 BC. The term *Judah* designated the southern kingdom. The expression *to this day* may have reflected a hope that the two kingdoms would ultimately be reunited.

C. Acceptance of Jeroboam (v. 20)

²⁰*When all the Israelites heard that Jeroboam had returned, they sent and called him to the assembly and made him king over all Israel. Only the tribe of Judah remained loyal to the house of David.*

Given the meaning of "Israel" in the preceding verse, the phrase *all the Israelites* would designate the residents of the ten northern tribes. With the crowning of Jeroboam as the *king* of these tribes, the division was now final. Of all those who had assembled earlier to crown Rehoboam king, *only the tribe of Judah remained loyal to the house of David*. Verse 21 notes that the tribe of Benjamin also sided with Judah. This was likely because the city of Jerusalem was located within the tribe of Benjamin (Joshua 18:21, 28), near the border between Judah and Benjamin (see the map on page 78); and Benjamin wanted to maintain its allegiance to the house of David.

The "ten tribes" that Jeroboam was told he would rule (1 Kings 11:35) thus included all the tribes except for Judah and Benjamin. A question may be raised concerning the tribe of Simeon, which had been given territory within Judah following the conquest under Joshua (Joshua 19:1-9). Why was this tribe not included within the southern kingdom? Some have suggested an apparent movement of many (perhaps most) Simeonites, some time prior to the division, to the northern kingdom. In both 2 Chronicles 15:9 and 34:6, Simeon is mentioned along with the tribes of Ephraim and Manasseh in such a manner as to suggest that all three tribes were by that time in some way linked together.

Immediately upon his return to Jerusalem, Rehoboam assembled his army and made preparations for war against the other tribes (v. 21). However, God sent the prophet Shemaiah to forbid such action; and Rehoboam heeded his message (vv. 22-24).

JEROBOAM'S COUNTERFEIT WORSHIP (1 KINGS 12:25-33)

Establishing the Groundwork

Jeroboam had scarcely begun his reign before he began to fear that the loyalties of his subjects would not last. He was wise enough to realize that there are forces in the world stronger than military power. The people had become accustomed to making regular trips to Jerusalem to worship. Such habits could not be uprooted overnight. And the ties to the house of David could not be easily severed. Perhaps, not long after those who had disavowed their loyalty to David (1 Kings 12:16) returned home, they began to entertain doubts about the soundness of their decision.

Jeroboam realized that the two kingdoms would not long remain separate if they both recognized one central place of worship and one priesthood. If the people in the northern tribes began to rethink their allegiance to him and determined that they had acted too hastily and needed to reaffirm their loyalties to the house of David, Jeroboam would likely be branded as a traitor. He would probably suffer the same fate as Adoniram, the man in charge of forced labor who had been stoned to death (1 Kings 12:18). But Jeroboam was a shrewd leader. He recognized that it was much easier to corrupt a religion than to wipe it out.

Examining the Text

I. New Places for Worship (1 Kings 12:25-30)
A. Jeroboam's Dilemma (vv. 25-27)

25Then Jeroboam fortified Shechem in the hill country of Ephraim and lived there. From there he went out and built up Peniel.

Shechem was where Rehoboam came to be crowned king and from which he fled when the revolt broke out (1 Kings 12:1, 18). Now Jeroboam made it his capital and residence. For this reason he gave special attention to it and *fortified* its defenses.

Peniel was roughly parallel with Shechem on the eastern side of the Jordan, on the brook Jabbok. (This name, meaning "face of God," was given by Jacob after he wrestled with an angel, according to Genesis 32:30.) It was so located that it commanded the road that ran to the east from the Jordan Valley. By fortifying this place as well, Jeroboam protected his new capital from an assault from the east.

26Jeroboam thought to himself, "The kingdom will now likely revert to the house of David.

Despite his efforts to establish his authority and fortify his defenses, *Jeroboam* was still unsure of how firmly he was in control. He began to think of the unpleasant scenario described in the "Groundwork" section above. The people in the north might *revert* to Jerusalem to be ruled by Rehoboam, the king who belonged *to the house of David*. David was still recognized as a great national hero—the builder of Israel's empire. The people had rebelled without hesitation against his grandson when he had refused to lighten their financial burdens. Would they go back just as quickly if Rehoboam agreed to do what they asked? If they did, Jeroboam would likely have to flee again—assuming he could get away before being arrested and executed for treason.

27"If these people go up to offer sacrifices at the temple of the Lord in Jerusalem, they will again give their allegiance to their lord, Rehoboam king of Judah. They will kill me and return to King Rehoboam."

According to the law of Moses, the men of Israel were required to assemble three times each year for the religious festivals of Passover, Pentecost, and Tabernacles (Exodus 23:14-17). Though given before Israel reached the promised land, these requirements looked forward to a central place of worship in that land (Deuteronomy 12:5-7). For years that place had been the magnificent *temple* that Solomon had built in *Jerusalem*; but Jeroboam realized that continuing that practice constituted a threat to his newly gained power. Jeroboam made plans to prevent this from happening.

B. Jeroboam's Solution (vv. 28-30)

28After seeking advice, the king made two golden calves. He said to the people, "It is too much for you to go up to Jerusalem. Here are your gods, O Israel, who brought you up out of Egypt."

After seeking advice, Jeroboam devised a plan to keep the people of the north from going to Jerusalem. He *made two golden calves*. He then told the people, *It is too much for you to go up to Jerusalem*. They had asked for lighter burdens (v. 4); now Jeroboam was offering to remove the burden of a long trip to Jerusalem three times a year. That trip was *too much*; they could worship just as well much closer to home.

Jeroboam's new religion consisted of a dangerous blend of truth and falsehood. He linked his religion with the act that led to Israel's establishment as a nation: their deliverance from slavery in *Egypt*. However, he credited this deliverance to the *gods* that were represented by the golden calves. Many Bible students note that pagan peoples often represented their gods as standing on the backs of bulls or calves. Apparently Jeroboam did not attempt to portray a deity; he simply erected the calves with no gods on their backs. The word rendered *gods* in this verse is the Hebrew *Elohim* and is normally translated as *God*. In such instances, whatever verb, adjective, or pronoun is used with *Elohim* is, appropriately, singular. Here, however, the verb *brought . . . up* is plural. Jeroboam was not thinking of the one God. His act was a blatant violation of both the first and the second Commandments. It also opened the door for the entry of idolatry into the northern kingdom. As verse 30 notes, "This thing became a sin."

²⁹One he set up in Bethel, and the other in Dan.

Bethel was located at the southern end of Jeroboam's kingdom, just ten miles north of Jerusalem; *Dan* was situated at the northern end, north of the Sea of Galilee. A family could travel to the place that was more convenient. (See the map on page 192.)

³⁰And this thing became a sin; the people went even as far as Dan to worship the one there.

This thing (Jeroboam's counterfeit religion) *became a sin*. It explicitly violated the second Commandment: "You shall not make for yourself an idol . . . you shall not bow down to them or worship them" (Exodus 20:4, 5). Jeroboam's actions came to receive their own stigma in the biblical record, as both kings and the people of Israel in general were said to continue in "the sins of Jeroboam" (1 Kings 16:31; 2 Kings 3:3; 10:29, 31; 13:6; 14:24; 17:22). Because of these sins, God determined to destroy the house of Jeroboam "from the face of the earth" (1 Kings 13:34; 14:14-16; 15:29, 30).

That *the people went even as far as Dan to worship* the golden calf placed there does not mean that the people worshiped only at Dan and not at Bethel, for the following verses repeatedly mention worship at Bethel. Perhaps we should understand the statement to indicate the zeal with which the people accepted the new religion. Observe the irony: it was "too much" for the people to go to Jerusalem, yet they were willing to journey to distant Dan in the north to participate in the sinful practices encouraged by Jeroboam.

II. New Practices of Worship (1 Kings 12:31-33)
A. Places and Priests (v. 31)

31Jeroboam built shrines on high places and appointed priests from all sorts of people, even though they were not Levites.

The Hebrew text literally reads, "*Jeroboam* made a house of *high places*." Perhaps Jeroboam made a house, or a temple of some sort, for each of his golden calves. Such an act represented yet another attempt by Jeroboam to lure people in the northern kingdom from worship in the Jerusalem temple by providing a convenient substitute.

The phrase may also mean that Jeroboam *built shrines on* other *high places*, perhaps in addition to the main shrines at Bethel and Dan. This may indicate that he attempted to use already-existing shrines as places to worship the gods represented by the golden calves. That such additional sites existed throughout the northern kingdom is clear from 1 Kings 13:32, 33. Bethel, however, remained the most prominent place of worship, and the one at which the king himself made offerings (1 Kings 13:1).

As another ingredient of his counterfeit religion, Jeroboam *appointed priests from all sorts of people, even though they were not Levites*. First Kings 13:33 elaborates on this: "Anyone who wanted to become a priest he consecrated for the high places." The Lord had appointed Aaron and his descendants to be priests, and they were members of the tribe of Levi (Hebrews 7:5). Now, however, Jeroboam chose priests from other tribes. Second Chronicles 11:13, 14 tells us that legitimate priests and Levites from "all their districts throughout Israel" came to Judah, for Jeroboam would not allow them to carry out their appointed tasks. Perhaps he did this because the priests and Levites in his kingdom refused to take part in his idolatry, but this is not stated in the Bible.

B. Festival (vv. 32, 33)

32He instituted a festival on the fifteenth day of the eighth month, like the festival held in Judah, and offered sacrifices on the altar. This he did in Bethel, sacrificing to the calves he had made. And at Bethel he also installed priests at the high places he had made.

In Judah the Feast of Tabernacles began on the fifteenth day of the seventh month (Leviticus 23:33-36). In yet another effort to lure people away from the worship in Jerusalem, Jeroboam instituted a similar feast in his domain and set its observance a month later than the Feast of Tabernacles. It has been noted that the change to the *eighth month* made this feast more convenient for farmers in the northern kingdom, where the harvest was approximately one month later than in Judah. *He also offered sacrifices on the altar*, perhaps similar to those prescribed for the Feast of Tabernacles (Numbers 29:12-39). Likely the *priests' duties in Bethel* resembled those of the priests in Jerusalem.

Thus Bethel housed a center of worship similar to the one in Jerusalem. No doubt it was smaller and less ornate than the one that Solomon had taken seven years to build in Jerusalem (1 Kings 6:37, 38), but it had all the proper religious ingredients, including priests, an altar, and sacrifices. The differences, however, were critical. The temple was not in the place God had chosen. The feast was not in the month God had appointed. The priests did not belong to the priestly tribe. The sacrifices were offered *to the calves* Jeroboam *had made*. The entire system was counterfeit!

> ³³*On the fifteenth day of the eighth month, a month of his own choosing, he offered sacrifices on the altar he had built at Bethel. So he instituted the festival for the Israelites and went up to the altar to make offerings.*

Here the counterfeit ceremonies are summarized. Sacrifices were offered and a festival was established in imitation of the ceremonies at Jerusalem. Yet none of it was commanded by the Lord; it was all of Jeroboam's *own choosing*. It was *instituted* by his own mouth, not by the mouth of the Lord. Thus it was doomed to fail.

BEGINNING OF ELIJAH'S MINISTRY (1 KINGS 17:1-16)

Establishing the Groundwork

For approximately the next 350 years after the kingdom was split, the history of God's people comprised the history of two separate kingdoms—the northern kingdom (Israel) and the southern kingdom (Judah). During that time, relations between the two ranged from cooperation in the face of a common enemy to bitter conflict. The Bible notes that, following the division of the kingdom, "there was continual warfare between Rehoboam and Jeroboam" (1 Kings 14:30). Tensions continued during the reigns of later kings (1 Kings 15:16).

The northern kingdom never experienced any degree of stability until the reign of Omri, who came to power in approximately 885 BC (almost 50 years after the division). Although Omri brought prosperity to the northern kingdom, he "did evil in the eyes of the Lord and sinned more than all those [kings] before him" (1 Kings 16:25). Perhaps his most grievous evil was allowing the influence of his pagan neighbors to the north, who worshiped many false gods, to infiltrate his kingdom. This is indicated by the fact that Omri's son Ahab, who ascended the throne in 874 BC, married Jezebel, "daughter of Ethbaal king of the Sidonians" (1 Kings 16:31). Most likely this was a marriage designed to seal an alliance between Israel and the Phoenicians to the north. Jezebel, however, was a strong-willed woman and a fervent worshiper of Baal who never missed an opportunity to promote his worship. Thus this marriage, though arranged for political reasons, wrought spiritual disaster in Israel; for it allowed Baal worship to gain a foothold.

It was at this crucial time in the northern kingdom's history, when pagan worship was making serious inroads among God's people, that God called Elijah (in approximately 860 BC) to confront a powerful but corrupt couple and to counter their influence on behalf of the true God.

Examining the Text

I. Elijah's Ministry Begins (1 Kings 17:1-7)
A. Elijah's Courage (v. 1)

¹Now Elijah the Tishbite, from Tishbe in Gilead, said to Ahab, "As the Lord, the God of Israel, lives, whom I serve, there will be neither dew nor rain in the next few years except at my word."

The name *Elijah* means "The Lord is God." The Scriptures tell us nothing about Elijah's family; he appears suddenly, without any introduction. Even what we learn from this verse is not entirely clear. *Gilead* was the territory east of the Jordan River, extending from the northern end of the Dead Sea northward to the Yarmuk River, south of the Sea of Galilee. The exact location of *Tishbe* is not certain.

Ahab reigned over Israel 22 years. During that time he "did more evil in the eyes of the Lord than any of those before him." He worshiped Baal and even "set up an altar for Baal" in Samaria (the capital of Israel). He "did more to provoke the Lord, the God of Israel, to anger than did all the kings of Israel before him" (1 Kings 16:29-33). Elijah was called of God to confront Ahab with his sins and to remind him of Israel's real King, to whom Ahab was accountable.

The ministry of Elijah began with a sobering announcement of God's judgment. The prophet's first words authenticated his message: *As the Lord, the God of Israel, lives, whom I serve.* The Lord, not Baal, was still in charge of Israel, in spite of Jezebel's aggressive efforts on behalf of Baal. The judgment was that there would *be neither dew nor rain in the next few years.* (There are two

New Testament references to this incident, Luke 4:25 and James 5:17, both indicating that *the next few years* amounted to three and a half years.) Elijah's words constituted a direct challenge to Baal on behalf of Israel's true God, for Baal was believed by his followers to be the god of fertility—in human beings and in all of nature. As such, he supposedly controlled the rain.

B. God's Care (vv. 2-7)

2, 3Then the word of the LORD came to Elijah: "Leave here, turn eastward and hide in the Kerith Ravine, east of the Jordan.

Once Elijah had delivered his message, God ordered him to *hide*. During the time of famine, God's messenger and word would be withdrawn from his people. Most likely Elijah's personal safety was also a factor. Since Palestine has a dry season that generally lasts from May to October, some time may have elapsed before it became obvious that Elijah's prophecy was being fulfilled. When that became apparent, Ahab would probably try to kill him.

God instructed Elijah to go *eastward* and take refuge *in the Kerith Ravine*. While there is some disagreement about its location, this was probably a small stream *east of the Jordan* River, emptying into the Jordan or one of its tributaries.

4"You will drink from the brook, and I have ordered the ravens to feed you there."

God not only supplied a hiding place for Elijah, but he also provided water and food. The *brook*, which was probably fed by springs, would supply water for a time; and the food would be brought by *ravens*. Obviously such behavior would have been most unusual for ravens, but the God who created them had no difficulty in commanding them to act in this manner.

5So he did what the LORD had told him. He went to the Kerith Ravine, east of the Jordan, and stayed there.

We wonder why Ahab did not seize Elijah immediately and either imprison him or kill him. Perhaps he did not believe that the prophet, or his God, could harm him. Most likely Elijah did not tarry long in Ahab's presence to give the king time to act. He seems to have set out at once for the hiding place God had provided for him.

6The ravens brought him bread and meat in the morning and bread and meat in the evening, and he drank from the brook.

The *brook* Kerith was isolated enough to provide both security and solitude for Elijah.

7Some time later the brook dried up because there had been no rain in the land.

Although this *brook* was probably fed by springs, a prolonged drought would have *dried up* even these springs. God was signaling to Elijah that it was time for him to begin a new phase in his ministry.

II. Elijah's Ministry Broadens (1 Kings 17:8-16)
A. God's Plan (vv. 8, 9)

8, 9Then the word of the LORD came to him: "Go at once to Zarephath of Sidon and stay there. I have commanded a widow in that place to supply you with food."

The new phase took Elijah to *Zarephath*. This town was located on the Mediterranean Sea about halfway between the two Phoenician cities of Tyre and *Sidon*. At this point in history, the town was under the control of Sidon.

Sending Elijah to Phoenicia, the very center of Baal worship, and telling him that he would find sustenance from a *widow* (often the poorest of the poor in the ancient world) may seem like another unusual way to provide for him. For now, however, God's hand of judgment (expressed through the famine) remained on the nation of Israel. His blessing was about to be experienced by a non-Israelite. Jesus later used this incident to rebuke those in the Nazareth synagogue for their scornful attitudes and to emphasize God's concern for others outside the "chosen people" (Luke 4:23-26).

B. Elijah's Petition (vv. 10, 11)

10So he went to Zarephath. When he came to the town gate, a widow was there gathering sticks. He called to her and asked, "Would you bring me a little water in a jar so I may have a drink?"

In making his way from his hiding place by the brook Kerith, it is likely that Elijah traveled along the east side of the Jordan River as far north as its headwaters at Dan. From there he would have traveled westward to *Zarephath*. By taking such a route, he would have been able to avoid Ahab, who had begun a search all over the kingdom for him (1 Kings 18:8-10).

When Elijah approached *the town gate*, he saw a *widow* who was *gathering sticks* to build a fire for cooking. At that point he apparently did not know that this was the woman who would feed him. Thirsty from his long travels, he asked for *a little water in a jar*. To provide a drink of water to strangers was considered a common courtesy in this part of the ancient world. Even though the drought had reached into Phoenicia, the springs there were fed from the peaks of the Lebanon Mountains and thus would still contain water when most other sources had dried up.

Judging from the widow's words to Elijah in verse 12, it is difficult to know whether she was a follower of the true God or was simply acknowledging the Lord as Elijah's God (note her reference to "*your* God"). Perhaps the woman was a refugee from Israel or had in some other way learned of the true God.

11As she was going to get it, he called, "And bring me, please, a piece of bread."

The widow's response to Elijah's request for a drink may have been the clue indicating to him that this was the woman whom God had mentioned earlier. So he added the request that she *bring* him *a piece of bread*—which would have been more available than any other food.

C. Widow's Plight (v. 12)

12"As surely as the LORD your God lives," she replied, "I don't have any bread—only a handful of flour in a jar and a little oil in a jug. I am gathering a few sticks to take home and make a meal for myself and my son, that we may eat it—and die."

The widow was not immediately able to comply with the prophet's request. She did not have *any bread*. While this area of Phoenicia did have water available for drinking, it had not been able to escape other consequences of the drought. The widow had just enough *flour* and *oil* to provide something for her and her *son* to *eat*. After that they faced starvation.

D. Elijah's Promise (vv. 13, 14)

13Elijah said to her, "Don't be afraid. Go home and do as you have said. But first make a small cake of bread for me from what you have and bring it to me, and then make something for yourself and your son.

The words *Don't be afraid* are found on several occasions in the Scriptures when a person was confronted with an overwhelming or frightening situation. This woman certainly needed such reassurance because she knew that she had barely enough flour and oil to prepare food for herself and her son. Yet this stranger was asking to be fed *first!*

14"For this is what the LORD, the God of Israel, says: 'The jar of flour will not be used up and the jug of oil will not run dry until the day the LORD gives rain on the land.'"

This is what the Lord, the God of Israel, says. By this expression Elijah stated the authority for his reassuring words to the woman. As is so often the case, when God gives he gives bountifully. He would provide the woman with *flour* and *oil* until the drought was over.

E. God's Provision (vv. 15, 16)

15, 16She went away and did as Elijah had told her. So there was food every day for Elijah and for the woman and her family. For the jar of flour was not used up and the jug of oil did not run dry, in keeping with the word of the Lord spoken by Elijah.

Encouraged by the prophet's words, the woman proceeded to do as *Elijah* had asked. And God did indeed miraculously provide for her, her son, and Elijah. *There was food every day* for all three of them—during not only the time that Elijah stayed with the woman, but during the time that passed until the rains returned. Later, during Elijah's stay with the widow and her son, God provided another miracle through Elijah by raising the widow's son from the dead (vv. 17-24).

THE CONTEST ON MOUNT CARMEL
(1 KINGS 18:20-24, 30-35, 38, 39)

Establishing the Groundwork

In the third year of the drought that Elijah had announced, the Lord told Elijah to "Go, and present yourself to Ahab, and I will send rain on the land" (1 Kings 18:1). Elijah sent a message to Ahab through Obadiah, an official of Ahab's who was also a devout follower of the Lord.

When prophet and king met, Elijah issued a challenge to Ahab to summon all Israel to assemble at Mount Carmel. Ahab was also to gather the 450 prophets of Baal and the 400 prophets of Asherah (1 Kings 18:19). The goddess Asherah was believed to be Baal's consort.

At this point, Elijah did not specify what he planned to do at Mount Carmel. The next passage to be examined begins by describing Ahab's compliance with Elijah's challenge.

Examining the Text

I. People Addressed (1 Kings 18:20-24)
A. The Place (v. 20)

20So Ahab sent word throughout all Israel and assembled the prophets on Mount Carmel.

Ahab did as Elijah said and *sent word throughout all Israel* and gathered *the prophets on Mount Carmel.* Later Elijah observed that the 450 prophets of Baal were present (v. 22), but he said nothing about the 400 prophets of Asherah.

For some unknown reason, Jezebel apparently forbade her prophets to come to Mount Carmel. Probably her failure to comply with Elijah's challenge was simply an act of defiance. Maybe Ahab was willing to do what Elijah said, but Jezebel was not about to!

One may ask why Mount Carmel served as the place for this assembly. Mount Carmel is actually a mountain ridge some 12 miles in length. Near the summit of the ridge is a plateau where a contest such as this one can take place. A spring of water is close at hand. It flows even during extremely dry seasons. This explains how Elijah could have 12 containers of water poured on his sacrifice (as verses 33 and 34 will show), even though this incident occurred during drought conditions. (See the map on page 192.) It also commanded a view of the Mediterranean Sea, over which approaching rain clouds could be seen easily (vv. 42-45).

B. The Plea (v. 21)

²¹Elijah went before the people and said, "How long will you waver between two opinions? If the Lᴏʀᴅ is God, follow him; but if Baal is God, follow him." But the people said nothing.

Elijah began his address to the Israelites with a question: *How long will you waver between two opinions?* The issue facing the people on this occasion was remarkably simple. Two options confronted them: the way of the Lord and the way of *Baal*. In today's pluralistic religious climate, Elijah's statement is still timely. We may choose a narrow road to salvation or a wide road to destruction (Matthew 7:13, 14).

Observe the audience's passive, apathetic response: *the people said nothing.* Perhaps they were cowering in fear, knowing that to answer in favor of Baal would displease Elijah, while answering in favor of the Lord would ignite the rage of Jezebel. Perhaps their silence reflected their lack of passion for or interest in anything having to do with spiritual matters. It is also possible that Elijah's uncompromising words made all too clear their failure to obey the Lord; thus their silence may have indicated a sense of shame or embarrassment. In any case, the safe response (from a worldly point of view) was to keep quiet.

C. The Plan (vv. 22-24)

²²Then Elijah said to them, "I am the only one of the Lᴏʀᴅ's prophets left, but Baal has four hundred and fifty prophets.

Elijah observed that he was *the only one of the Lord's prophets left.* Yet we know from an earlier statement in 1 Kings 18:4 that Obadiah, one of Ahab's officials, had hidden 100 prophets of the Lord from Jezebel's murderous fury. In addition there were prophets such as Micaiah (22:8) and several unnamed men who were part of the group known as the "sons of the prophets" (20:35).

Elijah may have been unaware of these others at this point, assuming that during his three-and-a-half-year absence the others had been killed. He would later complain to the Lord that the Israelites had "put [the Lord's] prophets to death with the sword" and that he was "the only one left" (1 Kings 19:14). On the other hand, some students take Elijah's later complaint to be hyperbole and believe that his point here was that he was the only one of the Lord's prophets who was present for this confrontation.

Elijah's emphasis on the contrast between *one* and *four hundred and fifty* highlights a key principle: truth is not determined by the number of people who embrace a certain position. Truth is truth, no matter how many or how few hold to it at any given time.

> **23, 24 "Get two bulls for us. Let them choose one for themselves, and let them cut it into pieces and put it on the wood but not set fire to it. I will prepare the other bull and put it on the wood but not set fire to it. Then you call on the name of your god, and I will call on the name of the LORD. The god who answers by fire—he is God."**
>
> **Then all the people said, "What you say is good."**

The rules of the contest were simple. Each side was to prepare a bull in the same manner: they would *cut it into pieces,* and lay it *on the wood.* Then each side was to *call on the name* of its deity. The God who responded *by fire* would prove himself to be the true God.

The fire that Elijah mentioned may refer to lightning. Remember that the issue at hand was which deity is in control of the rains. Lightning would serve as a signal of the coming of the drought-ending rains. That would demonstrate decisively to those gathered on Mount Carmel which God is in control of the forces of nature.

Perhaps the prophets of Baal relished the opportunity to go first. Should Baal respond to their cries, the contest essentially would be over. However, their going first only set the stage for what Elijah was going to do, because it would highlight how powerless Baal really was. Verses 25-29 record the futile efforts of the pagan prophets. The threefold emphasis at the conclusion of verse 29 provides a solemn closure to their failure and the pathetic plight it left them in: "There was no response, no one answered, no one paid attention." Then Elijah stepped to center stage—a stage that had been set for a dramatic display of divine power.

II. Preparation Accomplished (1 Kings 18:30-35)
A. Setting Up the Altar (vv. 30-32)

³⁰Then Elijah said to all the people, "Come here to me." They came to him, and he repaired the altar of the LORD, which was in ruins.

While nothing is said specifically about the altar used by the prophets of Baal, it is noted that Elijah *repaired the altar of the Lord, which was in ruins.* This altar may have been a victim of the apathy and neglect of the people toward the worship of the true God, or it may have been destroyed as a result of the promotion of Baal worship during Ahab's reign.

³¹Elijah took twelve stones, one for each of the tribes descended from Jacob, to whom the word of the LORD had come, saying, "Your name shall be Israel."

The use of *twelve stones* by Elijah is noteworthy in light of the fact that the nation of Israel had been divided for several decades by this time. Yet Elijah recognized through this action that God's original intention was that the Israelites be twelve *tribes*—yet one nation—under him.

³²With the stones he built an altar in the name of the LORD, and he dug a trench around it large enough to hold two seahs of seed.

The act described earlier in verse 30 as repairing the altar of the Lord is now described in another way: Elijah *built an altar in the name of the Lord.* Elijah was building an altar under the authority of and in reverence for the true God. God's name had lost none of its power, in spite of Ahab and Jezebel's attempts to stamp it out.

This verse also notes that Elijah made a *trench* about the altar, *large enough to hold two seahs of seed.* This is equivalent to about 13 quarts. If such an act seemed odd to the onlookers, it did not compare with what Elijah would do after he had positioned the sacrifice on the wood.

B. Soaking the Sacrifice (vv. 33-35)

³³, ³⁴He arranged the wood, cut the bull into pieces and laid it on the wood. Then he said to them, "Fill four large jars with water and pour it on the offering and on the wood."
"Do it again," he said, and they did it again.
"Do it a third time," he ordered, and they did it the third time.

Elijah proceeded to prepare the sacrifice according to the rules established earlier. But then he did something else quite unexpected: he commanded that *four* barrels of *water* be poured *on the offering* three times. As noted earlier, water may have been available from the streams that flowed at higher elevations, such as that of Mount Carmel, despite the severe drought that was now in its fourth year (Luke 4:25; James 5:17).

35The water ran down around the altar and even filled the trench.

By soaking completely the sacrifice and *the altar,* Elijah set the stage for an even more impressive demonstration of the power of the true God. At the same time, Elijah was also putting his own reputation as the Lord's prophet on the line. He would look utterly foolish if God failed to answer.

Elijah's actions also indicated to the audience that he was not engaging in any kind of trickery to ignite his sacrifice. If the sacrifice is ignited, the only possible explanation will be that God has done it.

The prayer of Elijah, recorded in verses 36 and 37, was a simple, earnest plea to the Lord, quite different from the frenzied madness of the prophets of Baal. And whereas there was no response of any kind to the prophets of Baal, such was not the case when Elijah prayed.

III. Prayer Answered (1 Kings 18:38, 39)
A. The Lord's Response (v. 38)

38Then the fire of the Lord fell and burned up the sacrifice, the wood, the stones and the soil, and also licked up the water in the trench.

In a spectacular display of unmistakably divine power, *the fire of the Lord* consumed everything that was part of the preparation for *the sacrifice.* Even the *water in the trench* was *licked up* by the fire.

B. The People's Reaction (v. 39)

39When all the people saw this, they fell prostrate and cried, "The Lord—he is God! The Lord—he is God!"

All the people, who were silent earlier when confronted by Elijah (v. 21), did not hesitate to express their reaction after what they had just witnessed. What else could they conclude? *The Lord—he is God!*

The aftermath of the contest on Mount Carmel included the slaughter of the prophets of Baal. That was in accordance with the law of Moses concerning false prophets: "a prophet who speaks in the name of other gods must be put to death" (Deuteronomy 18:20). In addition, the long-awaited rains soon came. The drought had ended, and, more importantly, the Lord, his prophet, and his word had been vindicated.

How to Say It

ADONIRAM. Uh-*don*-uh-ram.

AHIJAH. Uh-*high*-juh.

ASHERAH. Uh-*she*-ruh.

BAAL. *Bay*-ul.

EBAL. *Ee*-bull.

ELIJAH. Ee-*lye*-juh.

ELOHIM (*Hebrew*). El-o-*heem*.

EPHRAIM. *Ee*-fray-im.

ETHBAAL. Eth-*bay*-ul.

GALILEE. *Gal*-uh-lee.

GERIZIM. *Gair*-ih-zeem or Guh-*rye*-zim.

GILEAD. *Gil*-ee-ud (G as in *get*).

JABBOK. *Jab*-uck.

JEROBOAM. Jair-uh-*boe*-um.

JEZEBEL. *Jez*-uh-bel.

KERITH. *Key*-rith.

MANASSEH. Muh-*nass*-uh.

MICAIAH. My-*kay*-uh.

NAZARETH. *Naz*-uh-reth.

NEBAT. *Nee*-bat.

OBADIAH. O-buh-*dye*-uh.

OMRI. *Ahm*-rye.

PENIEL. Peh-*nye*-el.

PHOENICIANS. Fuh-*nish*-unz.

REHOBOAM. Ree-huh-*boe*-um.

SAMARIA. Suh-*mare*-ee-uh.

SHECHEM. *Shee*-kem or *Shek*-em.

SHEMAIAH. She-*may*-yuh or Shee-*my*-uh.

SHILONITE. *Shy*-lo-nite.

SIDONIANS. Sigh-*doe*-nee-unz.

SOLOMON. *Sol*-o-mun.

SYNAGOGUE. *sin*-uh-gog.

TISHBE. *Tish*-be.

ZAREPHATH. *Zair*-uh-fath.

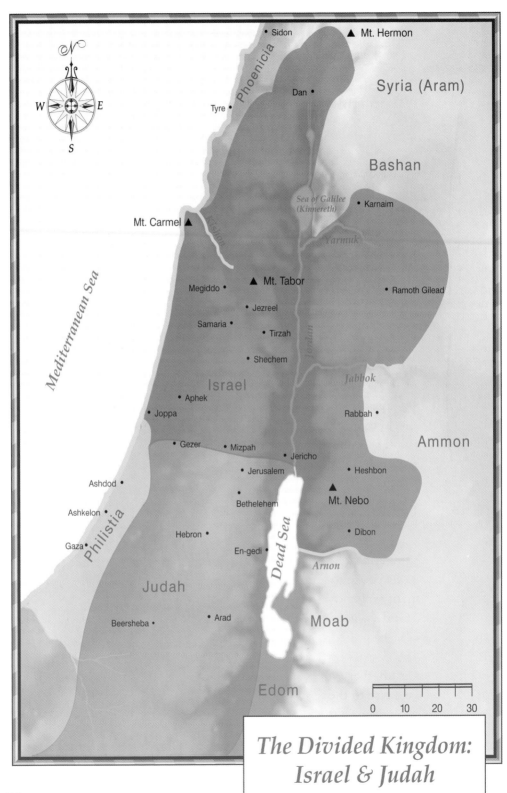

The Divided Kingdom:
Israel & Judah

Chapter 9

The Divided Monarchy
in the Times of Elijah and Elisha

1 Kings 21:1-11, 15-20; 22:13-28; 2 Kings 5:1-14; 7:1-9

NABOTH'S VINEYARD (1 KINGS 21:1-11, 15-20)

Establishing the Groundwork

The previous chapter concluded with a study of Elijah's contest with the prophets of Baal on Mount Carmel, as described in 1 Kings 18. That "mountaintop experience" for the prophet Elijah was followed—as is so often the case after a mountaintop experience—by a drastic descent into the valley of despair and discouragement.

First Kings 19 tells us that as soon as wicked Jezebel heard about what had happened on Mount Carmel, she vowed to even the score by killing Elijah. When Elijah learned of her intentions, he ran for his life; and he did not stop until he reached the Judean wilderness south of Beersheba—well over a hundred miles even if he could have taken a straight-line course! Fearful, disappointed, and exhausted, the prophet cried out for God to let him die; but God was not through with his servant just yet.

After Elijah had eaten and rested, he proceeded farther southward into the Sinai Peninsula and came to Mount Horeb (also called Mount Sinai, the place where Moses had received God's law). There God spoke to Elijah. He instructed his prophet to stand on the mountain while God passed by. Subsequently there was a series of natural phenomena: "a great and powerful wind," an earthquake, and a fire (1 Kings 19:11). But God was in none of these. Instead, he spoke to Elijah by means of a "gentle whisper" (v. 12), a phrase that many will know by the *King James Version*'s rendering of "a still small voice." God assigned Elijah a series of tasks to carry out, including the anointing of Elisha to be his successor as a prophet of the Lord (1 Kings 19:15, 16). God also assured Elijah that he was not alone in standing for the Lord and his truth; there still remained "seven thousand in Israel" who had not sworn allegiance to the false god Baal (v. 18).

Elijah next appears in the biblical record when God sent him to Naboth's vineyard to confront King Ahab. Ahab had gone there to take possession of it, having obtained it through the deceitful, murderous tactics of his wife Jezebel.

I. Disappointed King (1 Kings 21:1-4)
A. Ahab's Offer (vv. 1, 2)

¹*Some time later there was an incident involving a vineyard belonging to Naboth the Jezreelite. The vineyard was in Jezreel, close to the palace of Ahab king of Samaria.*

The phrase *some time later* refers to a period of time after a series of events recorded in 1 Kings 20. Ben-Hadad, king of Aram (or Syria), located to the northeast of Israel, invaded Israel and besieged *Samaria*, the capital city. With God's help, King Ahab and his forces were able to defeat the Aramean forces and withstand the siege. In a later conflict, God enabled Ahab's outnumbered army to shatter completely Ben-Hadad's forces, causing the Aramean king to plead for mercy. Because Ahab made a treaty with Ben-Hadad and agreed to spare him in spite of the fact that God had determined that the man should die, Ahab came under God's judgment. An unnamed prophet brought this message of condemnation to Ahab: "Therefore it is your life for his life, your people for his people" (1 Kings 20:42). Ahab then returned to Samaria "sullen and angry" (v. 43). Perhaps he sought Naboth's *vineyard* as a diversion from the somber news of his coming death.

Samaria had become the capital of the northern kingdom through the efforts of Ahab's father Omri (1 Kings 16:23, 24). *Jezreel,* where Naboth's vineyard was said to be *close to* Ahab's *palace,* was some 20 miles north and east of Samaria (see the map on page 192). What seems to be a contradiction is quickly resolved when one realizes that Ahab maintained a residence in Jezreel (2 Kings 9:30) in addition to his official palace in Samaria. The residence in Jezreel may have been to Ahab what Camp David is to U.S. presidents today.

²*Ahab said to Naboth, "Let me have your vineyard to use for a vegetable garden, since it is close to my palace. In exchange I will give you a better vineyard or, if you prefer, I will pay you whatever it is worth."*

We are not told how large the plot of ground was on which Naboth's *vineyard* grew, but if it was within the walls of the city it could not have been large. Ahab wanted the plot *for a vegetable garden*, perhaps where certain items could be grown for the royal table. His request was not, on the surface, an unreasonable one; and his offer may seem fair enough. The right of ownership and cultivation of private property was recognized even by this selfish ruler.

B. Naboth's Refusal (v. 3)

3But Naboth replied, "The LORD forbid that I should give you the inheritance of my fathers."

Naboth was a man of both courage and integrity. He had the courage to refuse to comply with an offer from the king, and the courage to confess his faith in *the Lord* before King Ahab, who worshiped Baal (1 Kings 16:30-32). His integrity is seen in his adherence to the laws God had given his people to govern the sale and transfer of land. Those laws bound property to a family (Leviticus 25:23; Numbers 36:7, 9). They were a part of God's desire to encourage his people to understand that the promised land was his gift to them and had to be accepted and used on his terms. Naboth refused to sell his property to the king because he acknowledged his obedience to Israel's real King. He did not even call his possession a vineyard; he referred to it as *the inheritance of my fathers.*

C. Ahab's Reaction (v. 4)

4So Ahab went home, sullen and angry because Naboth the Jezreelite had said, "I will not give you the inheritance of my fathers." He lay on his bed sulking and refused to eat.

Even though Ahab had strayed far from the Lord and his laws, he still possessed some degree of respect for those laws. He did not want to use brute force to take Naboth's vineyard from him. At the same time, Ahab was upset at Naboth's refusal to accept his offer. He *went home, sullen and angry* (the same two words were used in 1 Kings 20:43 to describe his reaction to the message of judgment from the unnamed prophet). Like a spoiled child who does not get his own way, the king of Israel went to his room to pout: *He lay on his bed sulking and refused to eat.*

II. Devious Queen (vv. 5-11)
A. Speaking to Ahab (vv. 5, 6)

5His wife Jezebel came in and asked him, "Why are you so sullen? Why won't you eat?"

Like the mother of a spoiled child, *Jezebel came* to ask what was wrong with her husband. (Perhaps she had seen him act like this before.)

6He answered her, "Because I said to Naboth the Jezreelite, 'Sell me your vineyard; or if you prefer, I will give you another vineyard in its place.' But he said, 'I will not give you my vineyard.'"

The king explained why he was so "sullen," and he still sounded like a spoiled child. As he told it, he had made a more-than-fair offer to Naboth and had been turned down. It may be noteworthy that Ahab did not refer to the "inheritance," as Naboth had in his refusal (v. 3); he spoke of the *vineyard*, ignoring the larger issue of what God's law said about selling property.

B. Acting Against Naboth (vv. 7-11)

⁷Jezebel his wife said, "Is this how you act as king over Israel? Get up and eat! Cheer up. I'll get you the vineyard of Naboth the Jezreelite."

Jezebel's words might be paraphrased, "Are you the king, or aren't you?" As she saw it, a king ought to take what he wanted, regardless of what the Lord's (or anyone's) law said. Having been raised in the pagan territory of Sidon (1 Kings 16:30, 31), she had no respect whatsoever for the God of Israel and his ways. The restrictions on kingship (as stated by Moses in Deuteronomy 17:14-20) meant nothing to her. She would *get the vineyard* that Ahab wanted.

⁸So she wrote letters in Ahab's name, placed his seal on them, and sent them to the elders and nobles who lived in Naboth's city with him.

Brazenly Jezebel *wrote letters*, giving orders to the *elders and nobles*, the men who governed Jezreel, *Naboth's city* of residence. She used *Ahab's name* and *placed his seal on them* (an impression made in wax or clay with a name or insignia on it) to give them royal authority. Did Ahab know what his wife was doing? That is not clear, but it is clear that the head of the nation was not the head of his own house.

⁹In those letters she wrote:
"Proclaim a day of fasting and seat Naboth in a prominent place among the people.

To *proclaim a day of fasting* was usually done because of a terrible sin or crime that threatened to bring God's judgment on the people. The fast would demonstrate the people's repentance. In addition, the person or persons guilty of the sin or crime would be punished; and thus the city would not be punished. Naboth was seated *in a prominent place* so that he could be highlighted as the accused man when the proper time came to do so. Again, Jezebel's arrogance and her contempt for the Lord are shown by her perversion of a spiritually beneficial practice in order to use it to accomplish her wicked aims.

¹⁰"But seat two scoundrels opposite him and have them testify that he has cursed both God and the king. Then take him out and stone him to death."

Jezebel was ordering a murder, but she wanted to make it appear legal—from the standpoint of both God's law and man's law. There had to be *two* witnesses to any capital offense (Numbers 35:30; Deuteronomy 17:2-6). *Death* by stoning was the legal penalty for blasphemy against God. The guilty party was to be taken "outside the camp" (or in this case the city) where punishment was administered (Leviticus 24:16).

11So the elders and nobles who lived in Naboth's city did as Jezebel directed in the letters she had written to them.

The elders and nobles in Jezreel likely knew of Naboth's reputation as a man of integrity and godly character. Sadly, however, they apparently feared Jezebel more than they feared God. They did exactly as she *directed* (vv. 12-14). So a man who did fear God and his law died as a criminal, and his property was left to be confiscated by the state. Triumphant (and no doubt quite proud of herself), Jezebel told her husband to go and take possession of Naboth's vineyard (vv. 15, 16). For a time it looked as if her "might makes right" policy had worked.

III. Daring Prophet (1 Kings 21:17-20)
A. Elijah's Mission (vv. 17, 18)

17Then the word of the Lord came to Elijah the Tishbite:

As previously noted, *Elijah* is first introduced in the biblical record in 1 Kings 17, where he is also described as a *Tishbite,* "from Tishbe in Gilead," and as someone through whom *the word of the Lord came* (vv. 1, 2). At that time Elijah spoke the Lord's message to Ahab (v. 1); now he was speaking it again in order to confront Ahab and hold him accountable for a hideous act.

18"Go down to meet Ahab king of Israel, who rules in Samaria. He is now in Naboth's vineyard, where he has gone to take possession of it.

Though Ahab ruled as *king of Israel* from his capital in *Samaria,* he had by this time gone to *Naboth's vineyard,* which he expected to be his before long.

B. Elijah's Message (vv. 19, 20)

19Say to him, 'This is what the Lord says: Have you not murdered a man and seized his property?' Then say to him, 'This is what the Lord says: In the place where dogs licked up Naboth's blood, dogs will lick up your blood—yes, yours!'"

The opening words of Elijah's message would tell Ahab immediately that the Lord knew what had happened and held Ahab responsible. That may indicate that Ahab knew about the queen's plot and consented to it. But even if he did not know, he was guilty. He knew how ruthless Jezebel was. She had ordered the murder of the Lord's prophets (1 Kings 18:13) and had threatened to kill Elijah (1 Kings 19:1, 2).

The punishment that God declared through Elijah fit the crime of Ahab. *Dogs* would lick up his *blood* just as they had *licked up* the blood of Naboth. Eventually the prophet's words came to pass, after Ahab was mortally wounded in battle against the Arameans. His blood flowed out into his chariot; and when the chariot was washed, the blood of Ahab was indeed licked up by dogs (1 Kings 22:34-38).

> *²⁰Ahab said to Elijah, "So you have found me, my enemy!"*
>
> *"I have found you," he answered, "because you have sold yourself to do evil in the eyes of the LORD."*

Just as Ahab was about to begin enjoying his newly gained possession, there was the prophet! Ahab did not need to ask why Elijah had come; he knew! On a previous occasion, Ahab had referred to Elijah as the "troubler of Israel" (1 Kings 18:16, 17). Here he again refused to acknowledge the prophet as God's spokesman; he called him *my enemy*. His response to the prophet's arrival was to blame him for the problems that were the consequences of Ahab's own wrongdoing.

The verses that follow record the remainder of Elijah's words of divine judgment, which had a profound impact on Ahab. He "tore his clothes, put on sackcloth and fasted. He lay in sackcloth and went around meekly" (v. 27). This clearly was not just a public display that Ahab put on to impress those about him. It is obvious that his repentance was sincere, for God delayed part of the announced punishment. The house of Ahab would fall, but not in Ahab's days; it would fall in the days of his son (vv. 28, 29). Yet as sincere as his repentance was, it still did not lead to complete devotion to the Lord. Ahab would continue to resist the Lord's direction and his prophets, as the next incident well illustrates.

MICAIAH'S COURAGE (1 KINGS 22:13-28)

Establishing the Groundwork

The comments on 1 Kings 21:1 (see p. 194) referred to two battles between the Israelites and the Arameans that are mentioned in 1 Kings 20. On both occasions Ahab defeated the Aramean forces in fulfillment of a promise given by a prophet of the Lord. After the second battle, Ahab made a treaty with Ben-Hadad (against the will of the Lord, as indicated in 1 Kings 20:32-43). This treaty involved the return of certain cities to Israel that the Arameans had captured (1 Kings 20:34). One of these was Ramoth in Gilead (called Ramoth Gilead in the passage examined below). (For the location of Gilead, see the comments on 1 Kings 17:1, page 182. Ramoth was located in the eastern part of this territory. See also the map on page 192.)

The Arameans, however, had not honored Ahab's treaty. (Their possession of Ramoth gave them easier access to Israelite territory.) After three years had passed (1 Kings 22:1), Ahab decided to attack the Arameans and recapture what was rightfully his.

By this time, Ahab was on good terms with Jehoshaphat, the king of Judah. So when Jehoshaphat came to visit Ahab in Samaria, Ahab asked for his assistance in recapturing the city of Ramoth Gilead. Jehoshaphat was willing to ally himself with Ahab in such a venture, but he wanted to be sure that the campaign carried the blessings of the Lord. To reassure him, Ahab brought in 400 men, apparently a group of court prophets who were essentially nothing more than the king's "yes-men," and asked them whether or not he should go into battle at Ramoth Gilead. To a man they agreed (1 Kings 22:6). But Jehoshaphat was suspicious of their response. Somehow he was not convinced that they spoke for Yahweh—the Lord. "Is there not a prophet of the Lord here whom we can inquire of?" he asked (v. 7).

Ahab admitted that there was such a prophet, Micaiah, but apparently he was in prison. "I hate him," said Ahab, "because he never prophesies anything good about me, but always bad" (v. 8). Ahab seemed unwilling to accept the simple truth that the reason prophets such as Micaiah always said bad things about him was that he tended to do bad things. But Jehoshaphat insisted that he wanted to hear Micaiah, so Ahab reluctantly sent for him. Micaiah's conduct in these circumstances and his refusal to back down before a king who had nothing but contempt for him remains a stirring example of the courage that God's people are sometimes called upon to demonstrate.

Examining the Text

I. Determined Attitude (1 Kings 22:13, 14)
A. Messenger's Suggestion (v. 13)

¹³The messenger who had gone to summon Micaiah said to him, "Look, as one man the other prophets are predicting success for the king. Let your word agree with theirs, and speak favorably."

The messenger who had gone to summon Micaiah in obedience to Ahab's command (v. 9) offered some friendly advice. All the other prophets who had come before Ahab and Jehoshaphat had promised victory to Ahab. It seemed that the sensible thing for Micaiah to do was to *agree* with them. Why should he anger Ahab by giving an unwelcome message? That would probably mean only more time in prison.

B. Micaiah's Stand (v. 14)

¹⁴But Micaiah said, "As surely as the L*ORD*** lives, I can tell him only what the L***ORD*** tells me."**

Micaiah's response is one that any true prophet of the Lord could have voiced. A real prophet does not choose what he will say; he says *only what the Lord tells* him to say. And it does not matter whether the person hearing the message is a king or a beggar; God's truth must be spoken regardless of the audience.

II. Disastrous Prediction (1 Kings 22:15-18)
A. Micaiah's Sarcasm (v. 15)

¹⁵When he arrived, the king asked him, "Micaiah, shall we go to war against Ramoth Gilead, or shall I refrain?"

"Attack and be victorious," he answered, "for the L*ORD*** will give it into the king's hand."**

Micaiah began by delivering the same message as the other prophets (v. 12). But he must have spoken in such a way that everyone knew his words were not to be taken seriously. Perhaps he spoke in a mocking, sarcastic tone. Perhaps he mimicked the manner of the false prophets, indicating that he was impersonating one of them instead of giving his own answer.

B. Ahab's Response (v. 16)

¹⁶The king said to him, "How many times must I make you swear to tell me nothing but the truth in the name of the L*ORD***?"**

Angered by Micaiah's reply, Ahab demanded that the prophet *tell . . . nothing but the truth in the name of the Lord*. But Ahab did not really want to hear the Lord's truth. This entire procedure was nothing more than a show for the benefit of Jehoshaphat. What Ahab really wanted Micaiah to say were words that would encourage Judah's king to accompany him in the campaign to take Ramoth Gilead from the Arameans.

C. Micaiah's Message (v. 17)

17Then Micaiah answered, "I saw all Israel scattered on the hills like sheep without a shepherd, and the Lord said, 'These people have no master. Let each one go home in peace.'"

Micaiah related two visions that revealed the true word of the Lord to Ahab. First, he described the nation of *Israel* as *sheep* that were *scattered* because there was no longer a *shepherd* to lead them.

D. Ahab's Disgust (v. 18)

18The king of Israel said to Jehoshaphat, "Didn't I tell you that he never prophesies anything good about me, but only bad?"

Ahab did not need an interpreter to help him understand the meaning of Micaiah's words. He quickly realized that the prophet was predicting Ahab's removal from office. The people in Micaiah's vision had no "master," or leader, because Ahab would no longer be present to lead them.

But instead of heeding Micaiah's warning, Ahab used it to prove his earlier charge (v. 8) that the prophet carried a grudge against him and was out to get him. This is a time-honored method of avoiding having to face painful truth: blame the messenger and seek to discredit him.

III. Distressing Vision (1 Kings 22:19-23)
A. The Lord on His Throne (v. 19)

19Micaiah continued, "Therefore hear the word of the Lord: I saw the Lord sitting on his throne with all the host of heaven standing around him on his right and on his left.

Micaiah was not easily intimidated. Though he realized that he could be endangering his life if he said any more, he refused to remain silent. He told of another vision in which he *saw the Lord* in the position of an ancient ruler: *sitting on his throne.* And, just as a ruler was often surrounded by his advisers, the Lord was surrounded by *all the host of heaven.* From the succeeding verses we know that the host in this vision also included evil spirits—perhaps in the same way that Satan presented himself before the Lord in Job 1:6 and 2:1.

B. A Lying Spirit on a Mission (vv. 20-23)

20And the Lord said, 'Who will entice Ahab into attacking Ramoth Gilead and going to his death there?'
"One suggested this, and another that.

Micaiah's vision continued with a description of how the Lord asked the members of the host of Heaven *who* would *entice Ahab* to go to his downfall at *Ramoth Gilead*. The issue was not just who would go, but what means would be employed to achieve it. Thus, *one suggested this, and another that*. Again, this was similar to the way in which an earthly ruler would ask his advisers for help in solving a specific problem.

> 21-23 *"Finally, a spirit came forward, stood before the Lord and said, 'I will entice him.'*
>
> *"'By what means?' the Lord asked.*
>
> *"'I will go out and be a lying spirit in the mouths of all his prophets,' he said.*
>
> *"'You will succeed in enticing him,' said the Lord. 'Go and do it.'*
>
> *"So now the Lord has put a lying spirit in the mouths of all these prophets of yours. The Lord has decreed disaster for you."*

These verses (and the entire scene described in Micaiah's vision) have created no little controversy among Bible students. We are told clearly in Scripture that God does not lie (Titus 1:2). Yet in this passage he appears to be encouraging, if not causing, lying. Two ways to understand Micaiah's vision have been suggested.

Some believe that the vision is not to be taken literally; that is, it should not be understood as a description of actual events occurring in Heaven. They point out that God does not need the "advice" of the host of Heaven; he possesses all wisdom and knowledge. They also claim that the false prophets surrounding Ahab did not need an evil spirit to make them say what they did. They were guided primarily by their own selfish interests. In this view the *lying spirit* was a personification of the attitude that governed the false *prophets*, and the vision was a symbolic way of saying that God allowed the prophets to speak falsely and lure Ahab to his death. A second view takes the vision more literally. It holds that the lying spirit was a demon, or perhaps the devil himself. (Some suggest that one of God's spirits, or angels, could have assumed the role of a lying spirit in order to carry out God's judgment against Ahab.)

Whether we take this heavenly scene literally or figuratively, we must keep in mind that God's actions did not violate Ahab's freedom of choice in this matter. God allowed the lying spirit to work among him and the false prophets; but these men, by their own defiance of God and his truth, had opened their lives to such an influence. Ahab, because of his unparalleled wickedness (1 Kings 21:25, 26), had placed himself under God's judgment. He had rejected the path of life and chosen the path of death (Deuteronomy 30:19).

IV. Disturbing Announcement (1 Kings 22:24-28)
A. Zedekiah's Anger (v. 24)

24Then Zedekiah son of Kenaanah went up and slapped Micaiah in the face. "Which way did the spirit from the Lord go when he went from me to speak to you?" he asked.

Zedekiah was mentioned earlier in 1 Kings 22 as one of the prophets who predicted victory for Ahab and even used a visual aid to reinforce his "prophecy" (v. 11). He seems to have been the spokesman for the court prophets. He was so incensed by Micaiah's words that he *slapped* him *in the face.*

Zedekiah asked Micaiah, *"Which way did the spirit from the Lord go when he went from me to speak to you?"* The meaning of *spirit* here is different from that in verses 21-23. Zedekiah was asserting that he, not Micaiah, had the spirit of prophecy sent by God. (Quite possibly the word *spirit* should be capitalized to indicate the Holy Spirit; the *New International Version* suggests this in a footnote.) Zedekiah's sarcastic question asked, "How did God's Spirit leave me and go to you?"

B. Micaiah's Reply (v. 25)

25Micaiah replied, "You will find out on the day you go to hide in an inner room."

Micaiah's reply stated an important truth: the real test of any prophecy is whether or not it is fulfilled in the way it was stated (Deuteronomy 18:21, 22). Micaiah was quite willing to have his and the court prophets' conflicting prophecies tested in this manner. Would Ahab go into battle and meet disaster as Micaiah had predicted? Or would he go into battle and triumph as the court prophets had predicted? The answer would come, declared Micaiah, when Zedekiah would have to go into hiding from those who were angry that his advice had led to Ahab's death. At that point he would no longer be able to maintain the pretense that he really spoke for God. The fact that he had lied would be undeniable.

C. Ahab's Anger (vv. 26, 27)

26The king of Israel then ordered, "Take Micaiah and send him back to Amon the ruler of the city and to Joash the king's son

Ahab was furious with Micaiah and his message. The king's immediate concern was that it might upset Jehoshaphat so much that he would return to Judah and not accompany him on his campaign against the Arameans. Thus he ordered *Amon the ruler* (perhaps we would use the term *mayor*) of *the city* of Samaria to put Micaiah *back* in prison (implying that he had been there previously). *Joash* may have been Amon's assistant or involved in some other way in administering the prison. He is called *the king's son*, which some commentators think may be a title for an important official rather than a description of Joash's relationship to Ahab.

> ²⁷" . . . and say, 'This is what the king says: Put this fellow in prison and give him nothing but bread and water until I return safely.'"

Ahab not only sent Micaiah back to *prison* but placed him on a very sparse diet as further punishment. The king's words *until I return safely* had an ominous ring to them. Ahab meant that when he returned from battle, he would administer a more severe punishment to Micaiah, perhaps even death. But these words were ominous only for Ahab. He was being presumptuous to assume that he would return at all, as the next verse indicates.

D. Micaiah's Promise (v. 28)

> ²⁸Micaiah declared, "If you ever return safely, the Lord has not spoken through me." Then he added, "Mark my words, all you people!"

Micaiah refused to be intimidated by Ahab or the court prophets. Instead of going back quietly to his cell, he made one further pronouncement. If Ahab *ever* did *return safely*, it would be clear evidence that Micaiah had *not spoken* the truth. Micaiah was willing to submit his prophecy to the test suggested in Deuteronomy 18:21, 22. By these words he signed his own death warrant, in effect; for if Ahab did return, he almost certainly would execute the prophet.

Mark my words, all you people! Micaiah's final words before being taken to prison were not limited to those around him. He wanted as many as possible to be aware of what had just transpired, so that all of them could later recognize who really spoke for God.

The concluding verses of 1 Kings 22 record the events that followed Micaiah's confrontation with Ahab. Ahab chose to ignore Micaiah's warning and was able to persuade Jehoshaphat to accompany him on the campaign to retake Ramoth Gilead. However, to provide some additional "insurance" that Micaiah's prediction would not come true, Ahab disguised himself but somehow convinced Jehoshaphat to go into the battle wearing full royal regalia.

Predictably, the results were nearly disastrous for the king of Judah. The king of Aram had ordered his troops to concentrate on capturing or killing Ahab. Seeing someone dressed as a king, they attacked Jehoshaphat's chariot and might have seized him had he not cried out.

Elsewhere on the battlefield Ahab apparently was feeling quite secure in his disguise. Suddenly an arrow shot at random found a chink in the king's armor, and Ahab bled to death in his chariot. Without a leader the soldiers of Israel abandoned the battlefield and scattered to their homes (v. 36), thus fulfilling Micaiah's prophecy (v. 17). Ahab's body was carried back to Samaria and buried. Later his chariot was washed out, and the dogs licked up his blood, fulfilling the prophecy given earlier by Elijah in Naboth's vineyard (1 Kings 21:17-19).

The Scriptures are silent about what happened to Micaiah. With Ahab dead, he may have been released from prison. On the other hand, Jezebel remained the real power behind Ahab's two sons and successors, Ahaziah and Jehoram. She may have had the prophet executed. If so, Micaiah died, knowing that he had not compromised the Lord or his message. A far more horrendous death awaited wicked Jezebel (2 Kings 9:30-37).

NAAMAN'S LEPROSY (2 KINGS 5:1-14)

Establishing the Groundwork

The story of Naaman occurred during the ministry of the prophet Elisha. The Lord had designated Elisha to be Elijah's successor while Elijah was at Mount Horeb, having fled from Jezebel's threat (1 Kings 19:1-3, 8, 15, 16). At this point in the history of God's people, the twelve tribes had been divided into two separate nations for a little less than a hundred years. Elisha continued Elijah's ministry to the northern kingdom (usually referred to as Israel), where Baal worship had made serious inroads because of the influence of King Ahab and his pagan wife Jezebel.

Previous studies have noted the intermittent war between Israel and Aram that occurred during the ministry of Elijah. This conflict continued during the ministry of Elisha. It provides the background for the account of Naaman—an incident that involved both countries in a most unusual set of circumstances.

The following text from 2 Kings refers to the king of Israel and the king of Aram, though it does not mention either by name. Most likely the king of Israel was a son of Ahab named Joram or Jehoram (but usually spelled as Joram in most English Bibles to distinguish him from the Jehoram who was king of Judah at about the same time; see 2 Kings 1:17). The king of Aram was Ben-Hadad, the same king with whom the Israelites under King Ahab had done battle in 1 Kings 20.

Examining the Text

I. Syrian's Plight (2 Kings 5:1-4)
A. Naaman's Situation (v. 1)

¹Now Naaman was commander of the army of the king of Aram. He was a great man in the sight of his master and highly regarded, because through him the LORD had given victory to Aram. He was a valiant soldier, but he had leprosy.

Naaman is introduced to us as *commander of the army of the king of Aram*. This means that he was a high-ranking officer in the army of that country. (He is called Naaman the Syrian by Jesus in Luke 4:27; the terms *Syrian* and *Aramean* are interchangeable.) He had distinguished himself in this capacity, as indicated by the descriptions that *he was a great man, highly regarded*, and *a valiant soldier*. But while Naaman was unquestionably a capable leader in his own right, he was in truth an instrument in the greater, more honorable, and mightier hands of the Lord. It was *through* Naaman that *the Lord had given victory to Aram*.

When we study Old Testament history, we usually think of God's activity in delivering his people from their oppressors (as in the exodus or in the days of the judges). But God is the Lord of all nations (Isaiah 14:26, 27). He is as capable of aiding them as he is of aiding the Israelites. In this case, his deliverance of Aram may refer to a victory that that nation achieved over the Assyrians around the middle of the ninth century BC, the time in which the events in today's lesson take place.

One might think that the fact that Naaman *had leprosy* would have prevented him from carrying out any kind of military activity. However, the Hebrew word often translated "leprosy" in our Bibles does not always indicate the severe, debilitating affliction (known technically as "Hansen's disease") that we often associate with that term. It can also describe less serious skin conditions, such as psoriasis or eczema.

Naaman's condition, whatever it may be, was most likely in its earliest stages. Note Naaman's reference to "the spot" in verse 11, as if there was a specific place on his skin that was particularly troublesome.

B. Possible Solution (vv. 2-4)

², ³Now bands from Aram had gone out and had taken captive a young girl from Israel, and she served Naaman's wife. She said to her mistress, "If only my master would see the prophet who is in Samaria! He would cure him of his leprosy."

The strategy of the Arameans against Israel at this particular time involved dispatching a series of smaller *bands* of troops that engaged the Israelites in brief skirmishes at certain key locations. Often both captives and goods were seized in the process.

During one such excursion, the Arameans *had taken captive a young girl.* Many of the captives exhibited bitterness or hatred toward their captors. This Israelite girl, however, apparently developed a great respect for Naaman, whose *wife* she *served.* (This may say something about how Naaman and his wife treated this girl.)

One day the girl voiced her concern for her *master* (Naaman) to Naaman's wife. The girl was convinced that if only Naaman could consult *the prophet* (Elisha) *who* was *in Samaria* (the capital of the northern kingdom), then *he would cure him of his leprosy.*

⁴Naaman went to his master and told him what the girl from Israel had said.

Naaman told *his master* about the Israelite girl's suggestion. That the term *master* refers to the king of Aram is clear from the fact that it is the Aramean king who responded to Namaan in the next verse.

II. King's Panic (2 Kings 5:5-7)
A. Letter Sent (v. 5)

⁵"By all means, go," the king of Aram replied. "I will send a letter to the king of Israel." So Naaman left, taking with him ten talents of silver, six thousand shekels of gold and ten sets of clothing.

The king's words conveyed a sense of urgency. In speaking them, *the king of Aram* indicated his concern for Naaman's health. The king, too, respected this "valiant soldier" (v. 1) and valued his skill on the battlefield.

The fact that the king of Aram could *send a letter to the king of Israel* may reflect more cordial relations than could be indicated by the skirmishes that were taking place during this time. However, a treaty was agreed to by the Israelites and the Arameans during the reign of King Ahab (1 Kings 20:34). The existence of this treaty seems to have been recognized during King Joram's reign as well, in spite of the occasional Aramean raids into Israel.

In the ancient Near East, it was common to provide some kind of payment whenever certain services were requested of a prophet. Thus Balak offered a huge reward for Balaam's prophecy (Numbers 22:15-17) and Saul even felt a need to pay Samuel for information about his lost donkeys (1 Samuel 9:6-10). This was characteristic of pagan prophets more than it was of the Lord's prophets, as illustrated by Elisha's later refusal to accept any such offer from Naaman (2 Kings 5:15, 16). But Naaman, coming from a pagan background, believed that such a payment was part of the "protocol" when dealing with a prophet.

Naaman's gift was impressive indeed: *ten talents of silver, six thousand shekels of gold and ten sets of clothing.* Ten sets of clothes would be quite an addition to anyone's wardrobe, even today. But what were the gold and silver worth? A shekel weighed just a bit over four-tenths of an ounce. Using a more contemporary standard of $750 per Troy ounce, this amount of gold equated to over $1,600,000! Similarly, strict conversion of the silver's weight and comparing it with modern silver prices yields a value of some $140,000. But these calculations do not give us the complete picture. To get an idea of the value of ten talents of silver, note that it is five times the price King Omri of Israel paid to buy the hill on which he built the city of Samaria (1 Kings 16:24). What does six acres of undeveloped commercial real estate sell for in your town?

B. Letter Read (vv. 6, 7)

6The letter that he took to the king of Israel read: "With this letter I am sending my servant Naaman to you so that you may cure him of his leprosy."

The contents of this letter may provide another illustration of the pagan mindset of the Arameans. Apparently the king of Aram assumed that the prophet in Samaria was under the control of the king (as prophets usually were in pagan countries). So the Aramean king directed his request for Naaman's healing directly to Joram, *the king of Israel.* Another possibility is that the king of Aram assumed that Joram knew of Elisha and would convey the message of the letter to him.

7As soon as the king of Israel read the letter, he tore his robes and said, "Am I God? Can I kill and bring back to life? Why does this fellow send someone to me to be cured of his leprosy? See how he is trying to pick a quarrel with me!"

The king of Aram probably was not aware of the tension that existed between the prophet Elisha and the spiritually weak King Joram (see 2 Kings 6:30-32, where Joram is most likely the king described in the text). When Joram read the letter, he did not think of Elisha at all. He viewed the letter as nothing more than a political ploy devised by the king of Aram to start a conflict with Israel. He *tore his robes,* which was the customary way of expressing shock, dismay, or grief.

III. Prophet's Proposal (2 Kings 5:8-14)

Verse 7 probably records what Joram said to his advisers, while Naaman remained in a separate room and did not hear it. Perhaps Naaman was kept waiting for some time while the king and his counselors discussed how they could answer the king of Aram. Meanwhile, word of the impossible demand leaked out, along with word of the king's fear. Swiftly the news spread throughout the city. There must have been a feeling of alarm everywhere, for no one wanted to resume the war with Aram. But Elisha was not alarmed. He knew that he could address Joram's concerns and grant the king of Aram's request.

A. Elisha's Command (vv. 8-10)

⁸When Elisha the man of God heard that the king of Israel had torn his robes, he sent him this message: "Why have you torn your robes? Have the man come to me and he will know that there is a prophet in Israel."

When the prophet *Elisha . . . heard* of the king's reaction, he chided the king for such a faithless response. This issue was nothing to tear one's *robes* over. *"Have the man come to me and he will know that there is a prophet in Israel"* (even if King Joram didn't).

Joram had asked the question, "Am I God?" (v. 7). Certainly he was not, nor was Elisha; but Elisha was a *man of God* who would address the concerns expressed by the king of Aram. The real King in Israel was still the Lord.

⁹So Naaman went with his horses and chariots and stopped at the door of Elisha's house.

Elisha's message was passed on to Naaman, who proceeded to the prophet's house. The text mentions Naaman's *horses and chariots*, perhaps to highlight the fact that Naaman had brought his typical military entourage. Naaman probably hoped to impress Elisha with just how worthy he was of the prophet's attention. So he stood *at the door of Elisha's house*, waiting (perhaps somewhat impatiently) for the prophet to come out.

¹⁰Elisha sent a messenger to say to him, "Go, wash yourself seven times in the Jordan, and your flesh will be restored and you will be cleansed."

In most pagan environments, a prophet showed great respect for the king and for other important leaders (such as someone of Naaman's reputation). Perhaps Naaman expected Elisha to emerge from his house and express his admiration that such a renowned individual would seek his assistance. If so, how surprised and offended Naaman must have been that Elisha himself did not even bother to appear! Instead, the prophet merely *sent a messenger*, whose word was simple: Naaman must *wash* in the *Jordan* River *seven times*, then his leprosy would be cured. To Naaman, however, things were not as simple as they may have seemed to Elisha!

B. Naaman's Pride (vv. 11, 12)

[11]But Naaman went away angry and said, "I thought that he would surely come out to me and stand and call on the name of the LORD his God, wave his hand over the spot and cure me of my leprosy.

Naaman was *angry*, both at the prophet's refusal to *come out* to see him and even more by such a seemingly ridiculous "prescription" to treat the general's leprosy. Again, perhaps Naaman's more pagan-oriented thinking contributed to his reaction. He expected a much more elaborate, flamboyant display of power—something appropriate for a man of his standing. To be told he must go to the Jordan River, probably about 20 miles away, was an insult.

[12]"Are not Abana and Pharpar, the rivers of Damascus, better than any of the waters of Israel? Couldn't I wash in them and be cleansed?" So he turned and went off in a rage.

From the standpoint of sheer logic, Naaman's response to the prophet's suggested cure seems to make sense. If a river were a necessary part of the remedy for his leprosy, why did it have to be the Jordan, which was often sluggish and muddy? There were rivers in Aram and its capital *Damascus* that were just as good, if not better.

Clearly, Naaman's ego had taken a beating. He had come to Elisha with a certain set of expectations, and none of them had been met. *So he turned* and left *in a rage*.

C. Servants' Counsel (v. 13)

[13]Naaman's servants went to him and said, "My father, if the prophet had told you to do some great thing, would you not have done it? How much more, then, when he tells you, 'Wash and be cleansed'!"

Naaman was blessed to have some very discerning (not to mention courageous!) *servants*, who took it upon themselves to approach the frustrated Aramean. They brought their own brand of logic to the situation. They began by addressing Naaman as *father*, another indication of the high respect in which Naaman was held by all who knew him.

They then pointed out that if Elisha had told Naaman to perform *some great* feat of strength or endurance to prove his worth, Naaman would have accepted the challenge. He ought therefore to accept the very simple request of the *prophet*, even though it seemed absurd. The issue came down to this: how badly did Naaman want to rid himself of his leprosy?

D. Naaman's Compliance (v. 14)

14So he went down and dipped himself in the Jordan seven times, as the man of God had told him, and his flesh was restored and became clean like that of a young boy.

It is never easy to confront and try to reason with an angry person. Naaman's servants are to be commended for their willingness to do so. Their gentle but persuasive and firm logic convinced Naaman that his immediate reaction was wrong.

So Naaman proceeded to go to the *Jordan* River and dip himself *seven times*. And as *the man of God* had promised, Naaman's flesh *became clean like that of a young boy*. It should be noted that Naaman's heart had become like that of a child as well, for he had humbled himself before the Lord and his messenger Elisha. When he returned to thank Elisha, the prophet did come out and speak to the humbled and grateful general, and sent him on his way in peace (vv. 15-19).

A DAY OF GOOD NEWS (2 KINGS 7:1-9)

Establishing the Groundwork

The setting for the next passage under consideration is, once again, the conflict between the Israelites and the Arameans during the time of Elisha's ministry. The Arameans under Ben-Hadad had besieged Samaria, the capital of the northern kingdom. This siege had reduced the people to starvation, causing some of them even to resort to cannibalism (2 Kings 6:24-29). Learning of this, Joram, the king of Israel, tore his garments and donned sackcloth to indicate his distress over the city's plight. That was an appropriate response. But blaming Elisha for the horrible conditions that existed was not appropriate. The king furthered his error when he ordered the execution of the prophet and sent one of his court officers to Elisha's house to carry it out. With prophetic insight, Elisha knew the messenger was coming and told the elders who were present with him to hold the door against the messenger. Apparently the king himself followed not far behind (2 Kings 6:30-32); perhaps he had rethought his decision to have Elisha killed and wanted to stop the messenger from doing so.

When the king arrived, he asked Elisha, "Why should I wait for the Lord any longer?" (v. 33). This may imply that Elisha had previously urged the king to wait for divine intervention. But with the city growing increasingly desperate because of the Arameans' siege, the king wondered why he should wait any longer. Why not just surrender to the Arameans? The answer came through a divinely guided series of events.

Examining the Text

I. Elisha's Declarations (2 Kings 7:1, 2)
A. Prophecy Spoken (v. 1)

¹Elisha said, "Hear the word of the Lord. This is what the Lord says: About this time tomorrow, a seah of flour will sell for a shekel and two seahs of barley for a shekel at the gate of Samaria."

Even as Elisha was speaking, his life hung in the balance. The prophet's fate depended on how the king would respond to his words. Elisha began by making it clear that his message was *the word of the Lord*—and it was a message of hope for the despairing king and his people. *About this time tomorrow*, said the prophet, food would be available for the starving city. The measure of a *seah* was approximately seven quarts. At this time, a *shekel* was not a coin but a measure of weight, probably of silver. The exact value of it is difficult to determine. Most commentators indicate that a shekel was a rather high price to pay for the measure of flour indicated here, but it would be much less than the prices current during the famine created by the siege (2 Kings 6:25).

The meaning of Elisha's words was clear: the siege of the city would soon be lifted, and the famine would end. The transactions he had described would take place *at the gate of Samaria*, which was the usual place for business to be conducted in a city.

B. Prophecy Spurned (v. 2a)

²ᵃThe officer on whose arm the king was leaning said to the man of God, "Look, even if the Lord should open the floodgates of the heavens, could this happen?"

The officer on whose arm the king was leaning describes a military officer who accompanied the king. Apparently the king himself did not respond to Elisha's words, so the officer spoke up. His words expressed his disbelief in Elisha's message and thus in the power of *the Lord* to bring about what Elisha had predicted.

C. Further Prophecy (v. 2b)

²ᵇ"You will see it with your own eyes," answered Elisha, "but you will not eat any of it!"

Elisha's prophecy of the coming availability of food was precise. His prediction about what would befall this officer, however, was more vague, perhaps deliberately so. Verses 17-20 of this chapter tell us of the fulfillment of Elisha's words. After it was discovered that the Arameans had fled their camp, the king appointed the officer to be in charge of the city gate. Upon hearing the news that there was food to be found outside the walls of the city, the starving people inside the city stampeded through the gate and trampled the officer to death.

II. Four Lepers' Decision (2 Kings 7:3, 4)
A. Pondering the Future (v. 3)

³Now there were four men with leprosy at the entrance of the city gate. They said to each other, "Why stay here until we die?

The law of Moses prohibited people *with leprosy* from living inside a city (Leviticus 13:45, 46; Numbers 5:1-4). Often these individuals would gather near *the city gate*, where, presumably, their friends inside the city would bring food for them. Because of the siege of Samaria and the accompanying famine, the plight of these *four* lepers was worse than usual.

B. Preparing to Act (v. 4)

⁴"If we say, 'We'll go into the city'—the famine is there, and we will die. And if we stay here, we will die. So let's go over to the camp of the Arameans and surrender. If they spare us, we live; if they kill us, then we die."

The lepers' choices were limited. Even if they could sneak into Samaria, what good would it do? The famine was there, no less than outside the *city*. Whether they went into the city or remained where they were, they would *die* from starvation.

Their third option, and the one they chose, was to leave the city gate and *surrender* to the *Arameans*, who were besieging the city. They probably figured that the Arameans would *kill* them. If that happened, at least they would not suffer a long, lingering death. Perhaps they entertained a glimmer of hope that the Arameans would *spare* them. If these Arameans had heard about the healing of Naaman (an Aramean commander) from leprosy through the intervention of an Israelite prophet, possibly they would remember it and extend mercy to these lepers.

III. Four Lepers' Discovery (2 Kings 7:5-9)
A. Empty Camp (v. 5)

⁵At dusk they got up and went to the camp of the Arameans. When they reached the edge of the camp, not a man was there,

The lepers may have waited until *dusk* to carry out their plan to avoid being seen as deserting to the enemy and consequently being shot by archers on the walls of Samaria. Imagine the shock of the lepers when they *reached the edge of* the Arameans' *camp* and found it abandoned!

B. Explanation (vv. 6, 7)

⁶ . . . for the Lord had caused the Arameans to hear the sound of chariots and horses and a great army, so that they said to one another, "Look, the king of Israel has hired the Hittite and Egyptian kings to attack us!"

The reason the Arameans' camp was deserted was that a miracle had occurred! As dusk had fallen (v. 5), *the Lord had caused* the *sound* of a mighty, advancing *army* to fall on the ears of the Aramean forces—an army they did not want to meet in combat. The Arameans' first thought was that *the king of Israel* had somehow got a messenger past their besieging army and was able to hire *Hittite and Egyptian* mercenaries to come to his rescue. The Hittites were located north of Aram. Both the Hittites and the Egyptians had centuries of experience in chariot warfare and were considered skilled in the use of this weapon.

⁷So they got up and fled in the dusk and abandoned their tents and their horses and donkeys. They left the camp as it was and ran for their lives.

This chaotic departure of the Aramean army occurred also at *dusk*. It seems, therefore, that not long before the lepers entered the outskirts of the camp from Samaria, the Arameans had fled, going in the opposite direction. In their haste the Arameans left their animals tethered where they were (v. 10). The animals would not have had saddles or bridles on, and to equip them for riding would have taken more time than the frightened men dared take. *They left the camp as it was and ran for their lives.*

C. Excitement (vv. 8, 9)

⁸The men who had leprosy reached the edge of the camp and entered one of the tents. They ate and drank, and carried away silver, gold and clothes, and went off and hid them. They returned and entered another tent and took some things from it and hid them also.

When the four lepers entered the Aramean *camp*, the only sign of life they saw in the gathering darkness was the tethered animals; they neither saw nor heard any soldiers. When it became obvious that the Arameans had abandoned the camp, the lepers satisfied their immediate need—food. After they had eaten their fill, they began to look over the wealth that had been left behind. Since they could not carry all of it with them, they *hid* it, probably in the ground. Their plan, no doubt, was to come back later and retrieve it.

> ⁹**Then they said to each other, "We're not doing right. This is a day of good news and we are keeping it to ourselves. If we wait until daylight, punishment will overtake us. Let's go at once and report this to the royal palace."**

It may be that the lepers' consciences were pricked when they stopped to realize that they were *keeping* this *good news* to themselves, while all the people inside Samaria were starving to death. It also appears that they were thinking about what would happen to them if they did not share their discovery. They were concerned lest *punishment* should *overtake* them. This suggests that the lepers began to think that if they kept quiet about their discovery and spent the entire night gratifying only themselves, they would be found out when morning came and would be punished for what they had done.

Many have called attention to the application of this passage to Christians. We who are Christians are like these lepers. We have come upon a vast treasure—the wonderful news of salvation in Jesus Christ. We should, of course, rejoice in that fact. At the same time, however, we have a moral obligation to share this news with others. More than that, we have a divine mandate to do so. The lepers knew they would be punished if they did not do what was right. Dare we neglect our Lord's mandate?

Once the lepers recognized their obligation to share their good news, they returned to Samaria with word of their find. At first the king was skeptical, fearing that the Arameans had set an ambush for him and his people. So he sent out scouts, who, when they returned, confirmed the lepers' report. Word quickly swept through the city, and the people rushed out to gather the food and wealth that the Arameans had left behind. In the process two of Elisha's prophecies were fulfilled. A seah of flour did sell for a shekel, and two seahs of barley sold for a shekel (v. 16). In addition, the officer who had ridiculed Elisha's prophecy was trampled to death by the people as they rushed out of Samaria (vv. 19, 20).

How to Say It

ABANA. *Ab*-uh-nuh or Uh-*ban*-uh.

AHAB. *Ay*-hab.

AHAZIAH. Ay-huh-*zye*-uh.

AMON. *Ay*-mun.

ARAM. *Air*-um.

ARAMEAN. *Ar*-uh-*me*-un (strong accent on *me*).

ASSYRIANS. Uh-*sear*-e-unz.

BEERSHEBA. Beer-*she*-buh.

BEN-HADAD. Ben-*hay*-dad.

CARMEL. *Car*-mul..

DAMASCUS. Duh-*mass*-kus.

ELIJAH. Ee-*lye*-juh.

ELISHA. E-*lye*-shuh.

GILEAD. *Gil*-ee-ud (G as in *get*).

HITTITE. *Hit*-ites or *Hit*-tite.

HOREB. *Ho*-reb.

JEHORAM. Jeh-*ho*-rum.

JEHOSHAPHAT. Jeh-*hosh*-uh-fat.

JEZEBEL. *Jez*-uh-bel.

JEZREEL. *Jez*-ree-el or *Jez*-reel.

JEZREELITE. *Jez*-ree-el-ite.

JOASH. *Jo*-ash.

JORAM. *Jo*-ram.

JORDAN. *Jor*-dun.

JUDEAN. Joo-*dee*-un.

KENAANAH. Keh-*nay*-uh-nuh.

MICAIAH. My-*kay*-uh.

NAAMAN. *Nay*-uh-mun.

NABOTH. *Nay*-bawth.

PHARPAR. *Far*-par.

RAMOTH. *Ray*-muth.

SAMARIA. Suh-*mare*-ee-uh.

SIDON. *Sigh*-dun.

SINAI. *Sigh*-nye or *Sigh*-nay-eye.

TISHBE. *Tish*-be.

TISHBITE. *Tish*-bite.

ZEDEKIAH. Zed-uh-*kye*-uh.

Chapter 10

The Divided Monarchy from Jehu to the Fall of the Northern Kingdom

2 Kings 9:1-12; 11:4, 9-12, 17-20; 17:6-18

JEHU IS ANOINTED AS KING OF ISRAEL (2 KINGS 9:1-12)

Establishing the Groundwork

One of the more noteworthy (and also tragic) circumstances surrounding the history of the divided monarchy is the way in which the ruling families of the northern kingdom (Israel) and the southern kingdom (Judah) became interrelated. The two kingdoms had developed closer relations during the reigns of Ahab in Israel and Jehoshaphat in Judah. The incident involving the prophet Micaiah occurred as a result of the desire of Ahab to secure the cooperation of Jehoshaphat in retaking Ramoth Gilead from the Arameans. Jehoshaphat also entered into an agreement with Ahab's son, Ahaziah, involving a fleet of trading ships (2 Chronicles 20:35-37).

Relationships between Israel and Judah were further cemented during the reign of Jehoshaphat's son, Jehoram, who married Athaliah, the daughter of Ahab and Jezebel (2 Kings 8:16-18). (Note that this Jehoram, a king of Judah, is a different king from the Jehoram—or Joram—a king of Israel, who was mentioned in the previous chapter.) This marriage resulted in the introduction of Baal worship into Judah; apparently Athaliah's influence on Jehoram was similar to that of Jezebel on Ahab. Jehoram had a son, Ahaziah, who succeeded him as king. Again, this king of Judah is not to be confused with the son of Ahab of the same name. That Ahaziah succeeded his father and preceded Joram as king of Israel. (See the chart on page 234.)

At one point, Joram, the king of Israel and a son of Ahab, continued his father's battle with the Arameans at Ramoth Gilead. (Second Kings 9:14 indicates that this was a battle to keep Ramoth Gilead from being taken by the Arameans.) As his father had done, Joram enlisted the king of Judah's help (in this case Ahaziah, son of Jehoram and grandson of Jehoshaphat). And like his father, Joram was wounded during the battle. He went back to Jezreel, where the king of Israel had a residence, to recover from his wounds. King Ahaziah of Judah came to visit him there (2 Kings 8:28, 29). During this visit, the Lord brought about a significant change in power in Israel that also had consequences for Judah.

Examining the Text

I. A Prophet's Assignment (2 Kings 9:1-10)
A. Task Given (vv. 1-3)

¹The prophet Elisha summoned a man from the company of the prophets and said to him, "Tuck your cloak into your belt, take this flask of oil with you and go to Ramoth Gilead.

The company of the prophets (literally "sons of the prophets" in the Hebrew text) seems to have been comprised of young men who gathered about Elijah and Elisha, probably to be instructed in the way of the Lord. Possibly they could be considered as "student prophets." Elisha in particular had frequent contact with this group, as this and several other accounts in 2 Kings illustrate (2 Kings 2:1-18; 4:1-7, 38-41; 6:1-7). The group was also especially active during the time of Samuel (1 Samuel 10:5; 19:19, 20). Since both of these periods of Old Testament history (Samuel's and Elijah and Elisha's) were times of spiritual laxity among God's people, the "sons of the prophets" may have served to provide a setting in which those who needed fellowship and spiritual encouragement could find it.

Although the *man* from the company of the prophets mentioned in this verse appears to be nothing more than a messenger at this point, later it will be clear that he is acting as a prophet with a message from the Lord (vv. 3, 4). For now he was given a specific task to carry out: *take* a *flask of oil* and *go to Ramoth Gilead.*

²"When you get there, look for Jehu son of Jehoshaphat, the son of Nimshi. Go to him, get him away from his companions and take him into an inner room.

The messenger's assignment was not to be carried out in a public setting or even shared with some select group. He was to convey his message in strict secrecy to one man: *Jehu,* a veteran officer in Israel's army who had served under King Ahab years earlier (vv. 25, 26). To assist in identifying the man, his father and grandfather also were named. (The *Jehoshaphat* mentioned here is a different man from the king of Judah of the same name.) The messenger was to find Jehu and give his message to no one else.

³"Then take the flask and pour the oil on his head and declare, 'This is what the LORD says: I anoint you king over Israel.' Then open the door and run; don't delay!"

The messenger sent by Elisha was in fact speaking *what the Lord* had to say. The messenger's hand was to *pour the oil on* Jehu's *head*, and the messenger's voice was to speak; but the message was the Lord's: *I anoint you king over Israel.* Such a declaration would have startled any officer in the Israelite army. It called him to treason against his king, to initiate a revolution! The message also included specific instructions for Jehu to follow.

Perhaps Jehu would have preferred time to think about his response to such an announcement, but the messenger did not stay. He was not to prove his credentials, nor try to prove that the Lord had sent him. He was not even to mention the prophet Elisha, whose influence in national affairs was well known by this time. He was simply to convey the Lord's message, then to *open the door and run* without *delay.*

B. Task Carried Out (vv. 4-10)

⁴So the young man, the prophet, went to Ramoth Gilead.

We are not told where this *young man* started his trip or how far he traveled; he simply obeyed Elisha's command.

⁵When he arrived, he found the army officers sitting together. "I have a message for you, commander," he said.
"For which of us?" asked Jehu.
"For you, commander," he replied.

Upon his arrival at Ramoth Gilead, the messenger found his way to army headquarters, where *the army officers* were *sitting together.* The messenger approached the group, perhaps ushered in by a soldier who was on guard at the entrance to the city. *"I have a message for you, commander,"* he explained. The word *commander* was vague enough that it could have applied to any of the men sitting before the messenger. Jehu therefore asked *which* officer the messenger meant. The fact that Jehu asked the question suggests that he was the highest ranking officer present. The messenger did not have to ask, "Which one of you is Jehu?" Apparently he knew Jehu by sight. This leads us to wonder whether Jehu also knew him and knew that he was a member of the company of the prophets. As a veteran officer in the Israelite army, Jehu likely knew how much Elisha had helped the Israelites' cause against the Arameans (2 Kings 6:8-23).

⁶Jehu got up and went into the house. Then the prophet poured the oil on Jehu's head and declared, "This is what the LORD, the God of Israel, says: 'I anoint you king over the LORD's people Israel.

One might surmise that the officers of the army had taken the best house in Ramoth Gilead for their headquarters. Perhaps they were sitting in the open air of the courtyard. Upon hearing that the messenger's words were for him personally, Jehu *got up and went into the house.* The *prophet* then lost no time. Opening up his flask, he *poured the oil on Jehu's head* and spoke the words that Elisha had told him to say. God was making this man *king* of *Israel!* But Israel had a king at this point, Joram, and he did not intend to abdicate. He would have to be removed by force if there was to be another king.

> **⁷"You are to destroy the house of Ahab your master, and I will avenge the blood of my servants the prophets and the blood of all the Lord's servants shed by Jezebel.**

Ahab was already dead by this time (his death is recorded in 1 Kings 22:29-40), but the punishment of his *house,* or family, was not yet complete. Disaster to his family had been prophesied by Elijah after the murder of Naboth; but when Ahab humbled himself before the Lord, the disaster was postponed (1 Kings 21:17-29). Now the time had come for Elijah's words to be fulfilled. As noted earlier, Jehu had heard these words when Elijah first spoke them (2 Kings 9:24-26).

In addition, the Lord planned to *avenge the blood* of his *prophets* and other *servants* who had been put to death through the actions of Ahab's wife Jezebel. First Kings 18:4 mentions Jezebel's murder of the Lord's prophets, but it also tells how Obadiah, an official in Ahab's palace, took action to rescue some of the prophets from Jezebel's intentions.

> **⁸"The whole house of Ahab will perish. I will cut off from Ahab every last male in Israel—slave or free.**

Here the punishment to be carried out on the house of Ahab is specified: it will involve *every last male in Israel—slave or free.* It was not necessary that all the women be put to death, as most of them had no political influence and no guilt in participating in the sins of the family. Of course, murderous Jezebel was an exception; her punishment had already been announced. The phrase *slave or free* may be a way of saying, "men of all classes."

> **⁹"I will make the house of Ahab like the house of Jeroboam son of Nebat and like the house of Baasha son of Ahijah.**

The evils of *Jeroboam,* the first king of the northern kingdom after the split of the kingdom occurred, have already been noted in chapter 8 (see the comments on 1 Kings 12:25-33). Because of those evils, his house was cut off so that there were no descendants left (1 Kings 15:27-30). *Baasha,* who carried out this punishment, became the third king of the northern kingdom. He too "did evil in the eyes of the Lord, walking in the ways of Jeroboam and in his sin" (1 Kings 15:33, 34). A later king of Israel, Zimri, put Baasha's family to death, in fulfillment of a message given (ironically) by a prophet named Jehu (1 Kings 16:9-13). The *Ahijah* who was the father of Baasha is probably a different man from Ahijah the prophet.

> *¹⁰"As for Jezebel, dogs will devour her on the plot of ground at Jezreel, and no one will bury her."' Then he opened the door and ran.*

Now the specific punishment that *Jezebel* would receive was described, and it was repulsive indeed. She would not have the dignity of a queen's burial; *dogs* would *devour her* body before it could be buried.

Once the prophet had spoken what Elisha had commanded him to say, he then proceeded to do what Elisha had told him to do upon completion of his mission. Without waiting for a response from Jehu; *he opened the door and ran.*

II. Jehu's Announcement (2 Kings 9:11, 12)
A. Officer's Question (v. 11)

> *¹¹When Jehu went out to his fellow officers, one of them asked him, "Is everything all right? Why did this madman come to you?"*
> *"You know the man and the sort of things he says," Jehu replied.*

While the messenger left the house in haste, Jehu probably emerged more slowly and thoughtfully. It is hard to imagine the expression on his face. Did he appear startled, shaken, upset, awestruck, skeptical? We are not told, but the questions raised by one of *his fellow officers* suggest that there was something strange in his appearance. *"Is everything all right? Why did this madman come to you?"* To the officer, it seemed odd for a messenger to arrive on an urgent secret errand and then leave running when no one was pursuing him.

Jehu's reply to the officer's questions is also a bit odd: *"You know the man and the sort of things he says."* Jehu seems to have thought that the men gathered with him knew the messenger. Did Jehu suspect that his fellow officers had sent the man and told him what to say? Perhaps Jehu and these officers already had been talking about a revolution against the current king. Probably there were many in the northern kingdom who resented the Baal worship that Jezebel promoted and were tired of her influence, which had not diminished since her husband Ahab's death. Perhaps other wrongs of the current king (Joram) were resented as well. Most likely Jehu by this point was a popular and respected commander in the army, and probably the cream of Israel's army was under his command. He was in a perfect position to lead a coup and overthrow the government. If some semi-serious plotting had been taking place prior to this point, Jehu might suspect that the officers were trying to hurry the process along by hiring someone from the company of the prophets to give the Lord's approval.

The above scenario is speculation, of course. The biblical record says nothing of any plot before the messenger came. But if no one had considered a revolution before this time, why did Jehu think his companions knew the messenger and his message?

B. Jehu's Answer (v. 12)

12"That's not true!" they said. "Tell us."
Jehu said, "Here is what he told me: 'This is what the Lord says: I anoint you king over Israel.'"

The other officers denied that they knew the messenger and his message; they urged Jehu to *tell* them what he said. Apparently Jehu believed them and proceeded to repeat what the messenger had spoken as the word of the Lord.

The response of the other officers was swift and enthusiastic. With an impromptu ceremony they heralded Jehu as king, and the revolution began (v. 13). Such quick action suggests once again that the officers had been thinking about this matter prior to this time, and so does the rapid efficiency of the revolution. With almost no resistance, Jehu and his supporters wiped out the family of Ahab, solidifying Jehu's position as king and fulfilling the prophecy spoken by Elijah in Naboth's vineyard (1 Kings 21:20-22). The details of Jehu's actions are found in the remainder of 2 Kings 9 and in chapter 10. Second Kings 10:28 states, "So Jehu destroyed Baal worship in Israel." The record then adds that Jehu did not turn away from the sins of Jeroboam but continued to promote the worship of the golden calves that Jeroboam had set up in Dan and Bethel (v. 29).

For the good that Jehu did accomplish in destroying Baal worship, the Lord promised him a "mini-dynasty" of four generations (v. 30). This was certainly not the kind of dynasty that was promised to someone like David; but, given the pattern of chaos and revolution that often characterized the history of the northern kingdom, it was something of an achievement.

ATHALIAH'S WICKED REIGN IN JUDAH (2 KINGS 11:4, 9-12, 17-19)

Establishing the Groundwork

The previous study noted that after being anointed as king of Israel by one of the company of the prophets, Jehu carried out the Lord's judgment against the family of Ahab. That began with putting to death the current king of Israel—Joram, who was a son of Ahab. As noted earlier, Joram had gone to Jezreel, where the king of Israel had a residence, to recover from wounds suffered while fighting the Arameans. King Ahaziah of Judah (who was Joram's nephew) had come to visit him there (2 Kings 8:28, 29). When Joram learned from a lookout that Jehu was approaching (according to 2 Kings 9:20, the fact that Jehu drove "like a madman" identified him), Joram and Ahaziah went out to meet him. The place of meeting offered a foretaste of the disaster that was about to occur: it was "at the plot of ground that had belonged to Naboth the Jezreelite" (v. 21). There, in fulfillment of the Lord's word spoken through Elijah (1 Kings 21:19, 28, 29), Joram was put to death. Ahaziah was wounded, and died later at Megiddo. His body was taken to Jerusalem for burial (2 Kings 9:27-29).

While this turn of events meant that Israel had a king (Jehu), the southern kingdom of Judah was left with a sudden vacancy in its leadership. Second Chronicles 22:9 notes, "So there was no one in the house of Ahaziah powerful enough to retain the kingdom." Ahaziah's mother, Athaliah (the daughter of Ahab and Jezebel), chose this moment to seize power in Judah and then (in a very Jezebel-like act) "proceeded to destroy the whole royal family" (2 Kings 11:1). She would have succeeded had it not been for a sister of Ahaziah who took one of Ahaziah's sons, an infant named Joash, and hid him and his nurse so that he was not slaughtered along with other members of the royal family. Athaliah was the only woman to rule either Israel or Judah (though certainly her mother Jezebel had a significant and negative influence on Ahab).

The next six years were no doubt some of the darkest for Judah during the period of the divided monarchy. Meanwhile, young Joash, unknown to his wicked grandmother, "remained hidden with his nurse at the temple of the Lord" (2 Kings 11:3). Since Athaliah held to the Baal worship that her mother sought to promote in the northern kingdom, the temple of the Lord was probably a safe place for Joash to be kept. Athaliah's presence there would be highly unlikely.

Examining the Text

I. Special Preparation (2 Kings 11:4)

A. Meeting with People (v. 4a)

4a. In the seventh year Jehoiada sent for the commanders of units of a hundred, the Carites and the guards and had them brought to him at the temple of the LORD.

The seventh year refers to the seventh year after Joash had been hidden by his aunt for six years (v. 3). This would also signify the seventh year of Joash's life, since 2 Kings 11:21 indicates he was seven years old when he began to reign following the action about to be spearheaded by *Jehoiada*. Jehoiada was a priest (v. 9) and a godly man who was no doubt greatly disturbed over Athaliah's seizing of power, but even more over the fact that someone from the family of David was not in power. Why he waited until the seventh year to carry out his plan is not known. Jehoiada may have simply bided his time until he was sure his plan to rid the land of Athaliah would work. As a priest, he was probably not accustomed to acting in the political and military arenas; but the circumstances before him were such that it could not be avoided.

Even so, Jehoiada had to have exercised great caution throughout this effort. The slightest slip would have cost the lives of all who were involved. We may be certain that Athaliah was not without her faithful henchmen, ready at a moment's notice to do her bidding. So Jehoiada made certain he had sufficient support. He *sent for the commanders of units of a hundred*. Second Chronicles 23:1 lists the names of these commanders; there were five of them. These men "went throughout Judah and gathered the Levites and the heads of Israelite families from all the towns" (2 Chronicles 23:2). The *Carites* were apparently mercenary soldiers from Caria, which was located in what today would be southwestern Turkey. Some have suggested that they may be the same group as the Kerethites mentioned in 2 Samuel 8:18 and 1 Kings 1:38. These and other *guards* were assembled *at the temple of the Lord*.

B. Making a Covenant (v. 4b)

4b. He made a covenant with them and put them under oath at the temple of the Lord. Then he showed them the king's son.

At the temple, Jehoiada *made a covenant with* those present and *put them under oath*. He wanted them to understand the seriousness of what they were about to do and did not want them to renege on any promise of support they would make. By doing this at the temple, the significance of making their promise before the Lord would be especially clear.

Imagine the reaction of those gathered when Jehoiada *showed them the king's son!* Most likely they were not aware that any of the royal family had survived Athaliah's murderous purge. We are not told how they knew that the boy standing before them was indeed Ahaziah's son; perhaps his aunt and nurse were present for this occasion as well and spoke on his behalf.

II. Sweeping Action (2 Kings 11:9-12)

A. Providing for the King's Defense (vv. 9-11)

⁹The commanders of units of a hundred did just as Jehoiada the priest ordered. Each one took his men—those who were going on duty on the Sabbath and those who were going off duty—and came to Jehoiada the priest.

Verses 5-8 show that the plan of Jehoiada was to use all the guards, both those who were *on duty* each *Sabbath* at various times and those who were *off duty*, in such a way that the temple area could be controlled and the young king crowned. Some of the guards were to be used to protect the king himself, and some were to be held in reserve to crush any armed support of Athaliah that might arise. All of this was carefully organized by Jehoiada.

¹⁰Then he gave the commanders the spears and shields that had belonged to King David and that were in the temple of the LORD.

King David had taken gold *shields* as plunder in one of his battles and had dedicated them to the Lord (2 Samuel 8:7, 11). Apparently other spoils included weaponry such as *spears*. Later Solomon had placed these in the temple he built. The temple had been plundered during the reign of Solomon's son Rehoboam (1 Kings 14:25, 26), but apparently the items belonging to David had been hidden and were not taken. Now, with a descendant of David about to be made king of Judah, it was most fitting that the restoration of the rule of the Davidic house be accompanied by the use of weapons that had belonged to David himself.

¹¹The guards, each with his weapon in his hand, stationed themselves around the king—near the altar and the temple, from the south side to the north side of the temple.

A cordon was drawn up with each *weapon* in clear view and ready for use, in a line of protection and fierce defiance. Whatever might happen, these troops were ready to give their lives that the rightful monarchy might reign in Judah. Jehoiada had prepared fully for the overthrow of wicked Athaliah. The entire operation proceeded like clockwork.

B. Presenting the King (v. 12)

¹²Jehoiada brought out the king's son and put the crown on him; he presented him with a copy of the covenant and proclaimed him king. They anointed him, and the people clapped their hands and shouted, "Long live the king!"

Here the formal induction of *the king's son* into office was accomplished. A *crown* was placed on Joash's head, and he was given *a copy of the covenant.*

This may have been a copy of the covenant that the Lord had established with his people at Mount Sinai (the "Book of the Covenant"; Exodus 24:7), a copy of Deuteronomy ("this law"; Deuteronomy 17:18), or a part of that book dealing especially with a king's duties (Deuteronomy 17:14-20). Joash was then *anointed*, and this was followed by the enthusiastic approval of the *people* who were present. The cry *"Long live the king!"* followed Saul's public presentation as Israel's first king (1 Samuel 10:24).

The noise of this ceremony with its cheering and clapping brought Athaliah to the temple area. She cried out, "Treason! Treason!" when she realized what was happening, but there was no one to stand up for her. She was hurried away from the temple grounds and executed (vv. 13-16).

III. Solemn Covenant (2 Kings 11:17-20)
A. Declared in Words (v. 17)

17Jehoiada then made a covenant between the Lord and the king and the people that they would be the Lord's people. He also made a covenant between the king and the people.

With evil Athaliah no longer in power, Jehoiada looked to the future of God's people under the new leadership of a king from the house of David. He *made a covenant between the Lord and the king and the people that they would be the Lord's people.* After years of spiritual chaos, it must have been encouraging to all present to take part in this public acknowledgment of an obligation to serve the Lord alone. Jehoiada also *made* a mutual *covenant between the king and the people.* Since Joash was only seven years old, perhaps the people would be tempted to think that their obligations to him were minimal. Possibly they would be more vulnerable to suggestions of rebellion against a boy. Jehoiada wanted to secure the full devotion of the people to their new king.

B. Demonstrated by Actions (vv. 18-20)

18aAll the people of the land went to the temple of Baal and tore it down. They smashed the altars and idols to pieces and killed Mattan the priest of Baal in front of the altars.

The ceremony of covenant-making was followed by a firm commitment to action. The *temple of Baal*, which no doubt had been supported and promoted through the efforts of Athaliah, was torn down. The *altars and idols* used in Baal worship were smashed, and *the priest of Baal* was put to death. However, the reformation in Judah did not go so far as to destroy all the high places that competed with the authorized worship of the Lord in his temple (2 Kings 12:3).

18b, 19Then Jehoiada the priest posted guards at the temple of the LORD. He took with him the commanders of hundreds, the Carites, the guards and all the people of the land, and together they brought the king down from the temple of the LORD and went into the palace, entering by way of the gate of the guards. The king then took his place on the royal throne,

Even though Athaliah was dead, Jehoiada did not want to risk any harm coming to young Joash from any of the queen's supporters who still remained. He provided protection for the new king *from the temple of the Lord* to the *place* where he was seated *on the royal throne*, using the same groups that he had used previously to protect the king (v. 4).

20 . . . and all the people of the land rejoiced. And the city was quiet, because Athaliah had been slain with the sword at the palace.

With Athaliah's death and Joash's establishment as king of Judah, rejoicing occurred throughout *the land*; and at last *the city was quiet*. The words of Proverbs 11:10 come to mind: "When the righteous prosper, the city rejoices; when the wicked perish, there are shouts of joy."

One should pause and reflect on how close the Davidic line came to being extinguished through the efforts of wicked Athaliah. God used many individuals, such as the godly priest Jehoiada, to preserve that line and maintain the lineage through which the Messiah, Jesus Christ, would come.

FALL OF THE NORTHERN KINGDOM (2 KINGS 17:6-18)

Establishing the Groundwork

With this study we move into the eighth century BC—a century that began on a positive note for both Israel and Judah but ended with the northern kingdom having fallen to the Assyrians as the consequence of God's judgment on it. A visitor to Israel and Judah during the first half of this century would have found both nations prospering and enjoying peace with their neighbors. At the time, both nations were being ruled by strong kings—Jeroboam II in Israel and Uzziah in Judah. In part, the good times had come because Assyria, the primary power to the northeast, was in a temporary period of decline. But the good times would not last much longer. The external prosperity of Israel in particular masked serious spiritual and moral problems. These problems could not be masked from God, nor from his prophets (such as Hosea and Amos), who warned of imminent judgment.

In 745 BC Tiglath-Pileser III came to power in Assyria. He gave immediate attention to reviving its prominence on the world stage. He soon turned his attention westward to Syria and Israel. These two nations had been bitter enemies at one time, but, fearing Assyria's might, they had formed a coalition against Tiglath-Pileser and tried to force Judah to join them. (This is recorded in 2 Kings 16:5-9 and Isaiah 7:1-4.) But none of Israel's efforts, no matter how valiant, could save her from the might of Assyria—for Assyria was God's instrument of judgment against his people.

Examining the Text

I. A Horrible Tragedy (2 Kings 17:6)
A. Samaria Destroyed (v. 6a)

6aIn the ninth year of Hoshea, the king of Assyria captured Samaria

The death of Jeroboam II brought a period of turmoil to Israel. Five men occupied the throne in less than 20 years. Sometime around 738 BC the Assyrians, under Tiglath-Pileser III, seized portions of the land and took captives to Assyria (2 Kings 15:29). The king, Pekah, was later assassinated as the result of a conspiracy led by Hoshea, who then replaced him on the throne. (In Assyrian records Tiglath-Pileser III claims responsibility for placing Hoshea on the throne. He may have backed Hoshea in order to gain a more cooperative king to be his vassal.)

However, after about six years, Hoshea rebelled against Assyria (2 Kings 17:4). As a result Shalmaneser V, who had replaced Tiglath-Pileser III as king of Assyria, marched against Israel. In 725 BC the Assyrians laid siege to Samaria, the capital of Israel. Samaria had been strongly fortified and was able to withstand the siege for three years, finally falling in 722 BC.

B. Captives Taken (v. 6b)

6b . . . and deported the Israelites to Assyria. He settled them in Halah, in Gozan on the Habor River and in the towns of the Medes.

According to the records of Sargon II (who succeeded Shalmaneser V), the Assyrians *deported* 27,290 people from Samaria. Deportation served two purposes: it provided slaves for the Assyrians, and, by deporting the nation's leaders, it decreased the likelihood of another revolt. As an additional defense against further insurrection, the Assyrians settled in Israel conquered people from other parts of their empire.

The exact location of *Halah* is unknown, but some scholars place it north and east of Nineveh, Assyria's capital. The *Habor River* emptied into the Euphrates River, and *Gozan* was a city situated on the Habor. The *Medes* occupied an area east of the Tigris River in what is modern Iran.

II. A History of Sin (2 Kings 17:7-12)
A. Fearing Other Gods (v. 7)

⁷All this took place because the Israelites had sinned against the Lᴏʀᴅ their God, who had brought them up out of Egypt from under the power of Pharaoh king of Egypt. They worshiped other gods

The first six verses of this chapter give an explanation of some of the international maneuvering for power that was taking place during the nine years of Hoshea's reign. These verses seem to place the blame for Israel's fall on Hoshea's flawed political schemes. The verse before us, however, makes it clear that Hoshea was not the only one responsible for the punishment that God administered to the nation. *The Israelites had sinned*; the people, along with the king, were guilty.

They had *worshiped other gods* in spite of the many centuries during which the true God had blessed them and watched over them. They had forgotten all that he had done for them, including the event that had made them a nation: when he *brought them up out of Egypt*. One should recall that when Jeroboam set up his golden calves in Dan and Bethel, he declared that these were the "gods, O Israel, who brought you up out of Egypt" (1 Kings 12:28). The northern kingdom was suffering the consequences of Jeroboam's denial of the foundational redemptive event in Israel's history.

This verse should not be taken to imply that everyone in Israel had turned away from the Lord. Just as in Elijah's day, there were certainly many who had remained faithful to God (1 Kings 19:18). One of the great tragedies of sin is that in a time of national disaster, the faithful and innocent often have to suffer along with the wicked.

B. Living as the Pagans (v. 8)

⁸ . . . and followed the practices of the nations the Lᴏʀᴅ had driven out before them, as well as the practices that the kings of Israel had introduced.

When the Israelites entered the land of Canaan, the pagan inhabitants of the land engaged in such sinful *practices* as cult prostitution and child sacrifice. God ordered the Israelites to destroy totally these sinful people (Deuteronomy 7:1-5), but this command was never completely carried out. (See Joshua 13:13; 17:13; Judges 1:27-35; 2:1-3.) Later, godless *kings of Israel* such as Jeroboam and Ahab (spurred on by his wife Jezebel) invented pagan gods or imported them from foreign lands and encouraged the people to follow statutes made by men, not ordained by God (1 Kings 12:26-33; 16:30-33; 21:25, 26).

C. Building Idols (vv. 9-12)

⁹*The Israelites secretly did things against the L*ORD *their God that were not right. From watchtower to fortified city they built themselves high places in all their towns.*

This verse and those that follow mention specific ways in which the people *did things against the Lord their God*—things *that were not right.*

The sins of the people included practices done *secretly* and others that were carried out publicly, at the various *high places.* Earlier in Israel's history, some of these places were used in worshiping the Lord (1 Samuel 9:11-14; 1 Kings 3:2). Once the temple was completed, the people were supposed to worship there—the place where the Lord had put his name (1 Kings 9:3). By the time described in our text, the high places were devoted mainly to pagan worship.

The phrase *from watchtower to fortified city* means "throughout the whole land," from the most isolated vineyard (where a tower was built in order to watch for thieves or animals) to the most well-defended city. The corruption of the people was a national disgrace.

¹⁰*They set up sacred stones and Asherah poles on every high hill and under every spreading tree.*

These *sacred stones* or obelisks were monuments that were set up as objects of worship. The making of such images was strictly forbidden by the Second Commandment (Exodus 20:4). The term *Asherah poles* refers to trunks of trees or posts set up as places of worship for the Canaanite fertility goddess Asherah. As noted in a previous study, Asherah was considered the consort or lover of Baal. The "worship" of Baal and Asherah often included illicit sex acts performed in order to induce them to grant fertility to humans, livestock, and crops.

¹¹, ¹²*At every high place they burned incense, as the nations whom the L*ORD *had driven out before them had done. They did wicked things that provoked the L*ORD *to anger. They worshiped idols, though the L*ORD *had said, "You shall not do this."*

Incense was recognized as a symbol of prayer (Psalm 141:2). In this case, the incense was a symbol of prayers offered to pagan gods, not to the Lord. The phrase *whom the Lord had driven out before them* hinted at the punishment the Israelites were to suffer. God had given his people clear warning of this when he first issued his law. If the Israelites failed to obey the Lord, they would be treated as those whom the Lord had driven out of the land (Leviticus 18:26-28).

III. A History of Warnings (2 Kings 17:13-18)
A. Prophets Sent (v. 13)

13The Lord warned Israel and Judah through all his prophets and seers: "Turn from your evil ways. Observe my commands and decrees, in accordance with the entire Law that I commanded your fathers to obey and that I delivered to you through my servants the prophets."

God gave the Israelites his *Law* in order to show them how to live as his people. But that was not all he did. Again and again he had raised up judges to deliver them from their oppressors in the promised land. He permitted them to have kings, though he recognized that such a request was really not in the people's best interests. In addition the Lord sent *prophets and seers* who *warned* the people to *turn from* their *evil ways*. While the term *prophets* describes the office these messengers held, *seers* calls attention to the means by which they often received their messages from God— through dreams and visions.

B. Warnings Rejected (vv. 14-17)

14But they would not listen and were as stiff-necked as their fathers, who did not trust in the Lord their God.

In spite of God's efforts to turn them back, his wayward people continued in their sinful ways. They stiffened their necks like stubborn animals that refuse to obey the person who holds the reins.

15They rejected his decrees and the covenant he had made with their fathers and the warnings he had given them. They followed worthless idols and themselves became worthless. They imitated the nations around them although the Lord had ordered them, "Do not do as they do," and they did the things the Lord had forbidden them to do.

They rejected his decrees and the covenant that God *had made with their fathers* at Mount Sinai. Instead of God's law becoming a testimony to the people's faithfulness toward him, it testified against them. Instead of building their faith on the many clear evidences of God's guidance, they preferred following the emptiness of the false gods that were really no gods at all. Thus they *became worthless* to God—that is, they failed to fulfill the purpose for which he had called them out of Egypt to be a nation.

16They forsook all the commands of the Lord their God and made for themselves two idols cast in the shape of calves, and an Asherah pole. They bowed down to all the starry hosts, and they worshiped Baal.

The *idols* mentioned here were made by melting precious metal and pouring it into a *cast* or mold. Specifically noted were the *two* golden *calves* that Jeroboam had set up at Dan and at Bethel after the kingdom had divided (1 Kings 12:26-30). As noted under verse 10, the word *Asherah pole* describes a trunk or pole set up for the worship of the pagan goddess Asherah.

> *¹⁷They sacrificed their sons and daughters in the fire. They practiced divination and sorcery and sold themselves to do evil in the eyes of the Lᴏʀᴅ, provoking him to anger.*

Child sacrifice was common to the worship of the pagan god Molech. The Israelites had substituted the God of love with a god of brutality. Is it any wonder that God was provoked to *anger?* Will God be any less angry with our society, which has sacrificed countless unborn babies through abortion?

Divination is the practice of attempting to learn the future through means forbidden by God. Sometimes this was accomplished through trances or dreams. In other cases the entrails of sacrificed animals were "interpreted," or lots were cast to provide such information. God condemned such practices (Deuteronomy 18:9-14).

The word *sorcery* describes the efforts of magicians to invoke the aid of evil spirits to influence human affairs. These activities were also condemned by God. When people turn away from serving God, they often turn to strange and bizarre practices. We see many in our time who have departed from God and his revealed truth to embrace the so-called "New Age" philosophy or some other deceptive cult—or even the occult.

C. Judgment Carried Out (v. 18)

> *¹⁸So the Lᴏʀᴅ was very angry with Israel and removed them from his presence. Only the tribe of Judah was left.*

Secular historians might attribute Israel's decline and fall solely to political or military factors. But the divinely inspired historian saw something else. He saw the hand of God's judgment using pagan powers to execute his judgment. *The Lord was very angry with Israel*—and with good reason. For centuries he had watched over Israel, guiding her, protecting her, and sending prophets to warn her when she departed from God's ways. Time and again she had rejected these warnings. And so God *removed them from his presence,* and *only the tribe of Judah* survived. But Judah did not learn from Israel's experience, and it also felt God's anger about 135 years later. The enemy was different (Babylon), but the reason Judah fell was the same reason Israel did—disobedience.

How to Say It

AHAZIAH. Ay-huh-*zye*-uh.

AHIJAH. Uh-*high*-juh.

ARAMEANS. *Ar*-uh-*me*-uns (strong accent on *me*).

ASHERAH. Uh-*she*-ruh.

ATHALIAH. Ath-uh-*lye*-uh.

BAAL. *Bay*-ul.

BAASHA. *Bay*-uh-shuh.

CANAANITE. *Kay*-nun-ite.

CARIA. *Care*-ee-uh.

CARITES. *Care*-ites.

ELIJAH. Ee-*lye*-juh.

ELISHA. E-*lye*-shuh.

GILEAD. *Gil*-ee-ud (G as in *get*).

GOZAN. *Go*-zan.

HABOR. *Hay*-bor.

HALAH. *Hay*-luh.

HOSHEA. Ho-*shay*-uh.

JEHOIADA. Jee-*hoy*-uh-duh.

JEHORAM. Jeh-*ho*-rum.

JEHOSHAPHAT. Jeh-*hosh*-uh-fat.

JEHU. *Jay*-hew.

JEROBOAM. Jair-uh-*boe*-um.

JEZREEL. *Jez*-ree-el or *Jez*-reel.

JORAM. *Jo*-ram.

KERETHITES. *Ker*-uh-thites.

MATTAN. *Mat*-an.

MEGIDDO. Muh-*gid*-doe.

MICAIAH. My-*kay*-uh.

MOLECH. *Mo*-lek.

NABOTH. *Nay*-bawth.

NEBAT. *Nee*-bat.

NIMSHI. *Nim*-shy.

PEKAH. *Peek*-uh.

RAMOTH. *Ray*-muth.

SHALMANESER. Shal-mun-*ee*-zer.

TIGLATH-PILESER. *Tig*-lath-pih-*lee*-zer.

ZIMRI. *Zim*-rye.

The Kings of Israel and Judah

Rule	Kings of Israel	Years B.C.	Kings of Judah	Rule
22	Jeroboam I	931	Rehoboam	17
		913	Abijah or Abijam	3
		911	Asa	41
2	Nadab	910		
24	Baasha	909		
2	Elah	886		
7 days	Zimri	885		
12	Omri	885		
22	Ahab	874		
		873	Jehoshaphat	25+++
2	Ahaziah	853		
		853	Jehoram	8*
12	Joram or Jehoram	852		
		841	Ahaziah	
28	Jehu	841	Athaliah	6
		835	Joash or Jehoash	40
17	Jehoahaz	814		
16	Jehoash	798		
		796	Amaziah	29++
		790	Uzziah or Azariah	52+++
41+	Jeroboam II	782		
6 mo.	Zechariah	752		
1 mo.	Shallum	752		
10	Menahem	752		
		750	Jotham	16+
		743	Ahaz	16+
2	Pekahiah	742		
20**	Pekah	740		
9	Hoshea	732		
		727	Hezekiah	29+
FALL OF SAMARIA (End of Divided Kingdom)		722		
		695	Manasseh	55+
		642	Amon	2
		640	Josiah	31
		609	Jehoahaz	3 mo.
		609	Jehoiakim	11
		598	Jehoiachin	3 mo.
		597	Zedekiah	11
		586	FALL OF JERUSALEM	

*Does not include co-regency.
+Includes co-regency with his father.
++Includes co-regency with his son.
+++Includes co-regency with his father and with his son.
**Includes years as rival with preceding dynasty.

Chapter 11

The Kingdom of Judah from Hezekiah to the Fall of Jerusalem

2 Chronicles 30:1-12; 2 Kings 19:14-20, 32-34; 22:8-13;
23:21-23; 25:1-7; 2 Chronicles 36:15-21

HEZEKIAH OBSERVES THE PASSOVER (2 CHRONICLES 30:1-12)

Establishing the Groundwork

It was noted before that Judah (the southern kingdom) lasted approximately 135 years longer than the northern kingdom of Israel did. Certainly one of the reasons for this must be the presence of godly kings in Judah. In contrast, Israel did not have even one king who was considered righteous in God's sight. In addition, the northern kingdom began in a highly suspect manner, tainted by the counterfeit religious practices instituted by Jeroboam. His actions opened the door for Baal worship to gain a foothold in Israel, which it eventually did through the efforts of Ahab and Jezebel.

The next section of study highlights one of the most outstanding kings to rule over Judah. His name was Hezekiah, and he led Judah during one of the most unsettling periods of Old Testament history. There is considerable discussion among Bible students as to the exact dates of Hezekiah's reign (apparently a co-regency with his father was involved), but it seems most likely that he began his sole reign as king after Israel fell to the Assyrians in 722 BC. His father was Ahaz, ironically one of the worst kings to rule Judah. (To add to the irony, Hezekiah's son Manasseh would be even more wicked than Ahaz and would bring Judah to a point where God determined that his judgment must be administered.)

The beginning of the record of Hezekiah's reign according to 2 Kings 18 calls attention to some of his noteworthy achievements. First, it is noted that he "did what was right in the eyes of the Lord, just as his father David had done" (v. 3). Second, the record cites his desire to rid the land of pagan worship practices, including the "high places" (v. 4). These places of worship became a problem, especially after Solomon's temple had been completed and the Lord had promised to bless it with his presence (1 Kings 9:3). Hezekiah even smashed to pieces the bronze snake that Moses had constructed for the Israelites (Numbers 21:4-9), because it had become nothing more than an idol to God's people (2 Kings 18:4).

Finally, Hezekiah is given this remarkable accolade: "There was no one like him among all the kings of Judah, either before him or after him" (2 Kings 18:5). A later king of Judah, Josiah, would receive a similar tribute (2 Kings 23:25), leading some to wonder how both statements could be true. In each of these two verses, however, a particular strength of each king is highlighted: with Hezekiah, his trust in the Lord is especially noteworthy; with Josiah, the issue setting him apart is his obedience to the law of Moses.

Our study of Hezekiah focuses on two incidents that illustrate how "he held fast to the Lord and did not cease to follow him" (2 Kings 18:6).

Examining the Text

I. Passover Renewed (2 Chronicles 30:1-4)

The Passover marked the anniversary of the Israelites' release from slavery in Egypt. It had been ignored during the sixteen-year reign of Hezekiah's father Ahaz because of that king's rejection of the Lord and his devotion to the gods of the pagans. Hezekiah intended to restore the Passover to its proper place in the life of the nation.

A. Passover Declared (v. 1)

¹Hezekiah sent word to all Israel and Judah and also wrote letters to Ephraim and Manasseh, inviting them to come to the temple of the LORD in Jerusalem and celebrate the Passover to the LORD, the God of Israel.

Slightly more than 200 years had passed since 10 of Israel's 12 tribes had stopped coming to *Jerusalem* to worship because of the practices that Jeroboam had instituted in the northern kingdom (1 Kings 12:26-33). As previously noted, the northern kingdom had most likely fallen by the time Hezekiah's reign as sole ruler of Judah began. The Assyrians had taken captives from Israel and settled them in various Assyrian towns (2 Kings 17:6), and they had brought in residents of foreign locales to live in the towns of Israel (v. 24). Northern tribes including *Ephraim and Manasseh* were in a state of disarray. Hezekiah longed to see reform take place and to see old hostilities forgotten by inviting all of God's people to come and *celebrate the Passover*—the feast that marked the beginning of Israel as a nation set free from bondage in Egypt by *the Lord, the God of Israel.*

B. Passover Delayed (vv. 2-4)

²The king and his officials and the whole assembly in Jerusalem decided to celebrate the Passover in the second month.

Hezekiah showed a great deal of prudence with his plan. In consulting *his officials and the whole assembly in Jerusalem* (at least the heads of the families in that city), *the king* acted neither hastily nor unilaterally. His consultations undoubtedly revealed that the regular, appointed time of the Passover was to be the fourteenth day of "the first month" (late March or early April to us) and that it ushered in the weeklong Feast of Unleavened Bread (Leviticus 23:5, 6). The law further provided for an alternative date *in the second month*. If anyone was "unclean" at Passover time, or had journeyed to a distant location, that person could celebrate the Passover in the second month instead of the first (Numbers 9:9-11).

³, ⁴They had not been able to celebrate it at the regular time because not enough priests had consecrated themselves and the people had not assembled in Jerusalem. The plan seemed right both to the king and to the whole assembly.

This verse gives two reasons for delaying the celebration of the Passover by one month. First, *not enough priests had consecrated themselves.* Hezekiah had spent the first month of the first year of his reign purifying the temple and removing all the unclean, forbidden items from it (2 Chronicles 29:3-11, 15-19). When the cleansed temple was rededicated, there were not enough consecrated priests to offer the sacrifices (2 Chronicles 29:34). Hezekiah's respect for the holiness of God was such that it *seemed* best to postpone the Passover until the priests were properly consecrated. After the reign of Hezekiah's predecessor, his wicked father Ahaz, most of the people as well as many of the priests were undoubtedly unclean in some way; and time was required for them to sanctify themselves.

Second, the Passover could not be celebrated at the regular time because *the people had not assembled in Jerusalem.* The decision *to celebrate* this feast must have been made while the temple was being cleansed in the first month of the first year of Hezekiah's reign (2 Chronicles 29:3-5). At that time, it was too late for invitations to be sent to all Israel and for the people to assemble at Jerusalem for a Passover in the first month. Delaying the Passover until the second month provided time to "get the message out" regarding this important event.

II. People Invited (2 Chronicles 30:5-9)

As noted above, the Passover celebration was part of the Feast of Unleavened Bread. According to the law of Moses, all adult male Israelites must be present (Exodus 23:14-17; Deuteronomy 16:16). The godly Hezekiah made sure this happened.

A. Extent of the Invitation (v. 5)

5They decided to send a proclamation throughout Israel, from Beersheba to Dan, calling the people to come to Jerusalem and celebrate the Passover to the Lord, the God of Israel. It had not been celebrated in large numbers according to what was written.

Beersheba in the south and *Dan* in the north—about 150 miles apart—marked the limits of all *Israel* before the division of the kingdom. The expression "from Dan to Beersheba" became familiar as a designation for the entire Israelite people (1 Samuel 3:20; 2 Samuel 3:9, 10; 17:11; 24:1, 2). The invitation was to be sent *throughout* all of that territory. That the Passover *had not been celebrated in large numbers* indicates only sporadic (at best) Passover observances over the past 200 years since the division of the kingdom. We wonder how much of any part of *what was written* in the law had been taught to the people during that period. Certainly little teaching had occurred during the reign of Ahaz.

B. Speed of the Invitation (v. 6a)

6a. At the king's command, couriers went throughout Israel and Judah with letters from the king and from his officials,

The *couriers* were swift runners who carried the *letters from the king and from his officials* to every part of *Israel and Judah*, reading them in the streets and marketplaces of all the towns. There must have been several couriers for them to have reached all the towns quickly, for hardly a month remained until the time in the second month for the Passover to be observed.

C. Content of the Invitation (vv. 6b-9)

6b. . . . which read:
"People of Israel, return to the Lord, the God of Abraham, Isaac and Israel, that he may return to you who are left, who have escaped from the hand of the kings of Assyria.

This was more than an invitation to a feast. It was a call to *return to the Lord, the God of* the ancestors of the *people of Israel*. At this point *the kings of Assyria* had conquered a substantial part of Israel's territory, taking captive many Israelites. In making a promise to the Israelites who were *left* that God would *return* to them if they would *return* to him, Hezekiah set a theme that is echoed frequently by the prophets (for examples, see Jeremiah 3:12; Joel

2:13; Zechariah 1:3; and Malachi 3:7). Again, as noted earlier, Hezekiah was attempting to end hostilities and build a bridge to those of the northern tribes who were perhaps questioning their own status as the people of God following the Assyrian onslaught of 722 BC.

> [7]*"Do not be like your fathers and brothers, who were unfaithful to the LORD, the God of their fathers, so that he made them an object of horror, as you see.*

The Israelites who had escaped capture could *see* the desolation that had come at the hand of the Assyrians. This had come about because their *fathers and brothers* had been *unfaithful to the Lord, the God of their fathers.* Would the remaining Israelites learn from this "visual aid" of *horror* and destruction?

> [8]*"Do not be stiff-necked, as your fathers were; submit to the LORD. Come to the sanctuary, which he has consecrated forever. Serve the LORD your God, so that his fierce anger will turn away from you.*

The Old Testament refers to the Israelite people as *stiff-necked* (meaning stubborn or obstinate) more than 30 times (Stephen used the same term of his Sanhedrin audience in Acts 7:51). Such an attitude toward God always leads to destruction.

The only way to prevent the pending judgment of God was for the Israelites to reject the stubborn ways of their *fathers* and *submit to the Lord.* The starting point on this road back to God was to *come* to the Lord's *sanctuary,* the temple in Jerusalem, and celebrate the Passover. This act would remind the people of their spiritual heritage—a heritage that many had forgotten.

> [9]*"If you return to the LORD, then your brothers and your children will be shown compassion by their captors and will come back to this land, for the LORD your God is gracious and compassionate. He will not turn his face from you if you return to him."*

Hezekiah's letter now returned to the promise of verse 6. Since *the Lord your God is gracious and compassionate,* he would rather bless than punish. He will not turn away from the Israelites if they *return to him* with genuine worship and faithful obedience. If they will do that, even those already in captivity *will be shown compassion by their captors and will come back to this land.* Hezekiah's promise reflected the words of Solomon in the prayer he offered at the dedication of the temple (1 Kings 8:46-51).

III. People Respond (2 Chronicles 30:10-12)

Drastic calls to action can draw mixed responses—and it was certainly a drastic change that Hezekiah was advocating. At this point, the people living in the northern tribes had never attended a Passover celebration in Jerusalem.

For generations, their government had promoted a state religion with worship centers at Bethel and Dan (1 Kings 12:26–33). Besides that, there were times when pagan worship had increased rapidly, especially during the infamous reign of Ahab (1 Kings 16:30-33).

A. Some With Animosity (v. 10)

¹⁰The couriers went from town to town in Ephraim and Manasseh, as far as Zebulun, but the people scorned and ridiculed them.

As *the couriers* traveled from *Ephraim* to *Manasseh* to *Zebulun,* they were moving progressively northward throughout Israel. Asher (mentioned in verse 11) was the northernmost of the tribal territories. King Hezekiah was serious that all Israelites be invited. (See the map on page 78.)

The sad fact is, however, that Hezekiah's invitation was met with scorn and ridicule. Perhaps that is not too surprising, for many in that territory probably still regarded Judah as an enemy. They remembered the bloody war in the time of King Ahaz when Israel and Aram had formed an alliance to oppose the growing might of Assyria and had tried to conquer Judah to add her to their coalition (Isaiah 7:1-4). They had failed in that effort (because Ahaz had sided with the Assyrians and called on them for help), and that had made them hate Judah all the more. Now they reacted with contempt when they heard the king of Judah (who was the son of Ahaz) inviting them to come and join his people in worship.

B. Others With Acceptance (vv. 11, 12)

¹¹Nevertheless, some men of Asher, Manasseh and Zebulun humbled themselves and went to Jerusalem.

Apparently the history of the nation had been passed from generation to generation in at least some of the households of the northern kingdom. Such households, desiring to serve the one true God, welcomed the reinstitution of the Passover and humbly *went to Jerusalem* to join in the worship of the Lord.

¹²Also in Judah the hand of God was on the people to give them unity of mind to carry out what the king and his officials had ordered, following the word of the LORD.

Now the focus shifts to the southern kingdom. Although the call to observe the Passover was issued by *the king and his officials,* it was ultimately given according to *the word of the Lord.* Guided by *the hand of God,* the people of *Judah* were more united in answering that call than those of the northern kingdom. And so they poured into Jerusalem at the appointed time in the second month. They were so delighted to observe the Passover once again that they continued the celebration for 14 days instead of the required 7 (2 Chronicles 30:13-27). This had happened during King Solomon's dedication of the temple, held in conjunction with the Feast of Tabernacles (2 Chronicles 7:9). Second Chronicles 30:26 states of Hezekiah's celebration: "There was great joy in Jerusalem, for since the days of Solomon son of David king of Israel there had been nothing like this in Jerusalem."

HEZEKIAH AND THE ASSYRIAN THREAT (2 KINGS 19:14-20, 32-34)

Establishing the Groundwork

The previous study concentrated on one aspect of Hezekiah's positive spiritual influence not only on Judah but on the northern tribes as well. But Hezekiah was also forced to confront some serious political realities during his reign, involving primarily the Assyrians. The Assyrians had, as already noted, conquered the northern kingdom in 722 BC and had taken nearly 30,000 of its people captive. The Assyrians, however, had Judah in their sights as well. Most of Hezekiah's dealings with the Assyrians occurred while Sennacherib was in power. It is likely that the time when Hezekiah "rebelled against the king of Assyria and did not serve him" (2 Kings 18:7) took place after Sennacherib came to power in 705 BC. (Often a change in the ruler of an empire such as that of the Assyrians was considered a prime opportunity for rebellion by subject peoples.)

Of course, Sennacherib did not intend to allow such an act to go unpunished. In 701 BC the Assyrian was able to turn his attention to Judah and to Hezekiah. He came to Judah with such an impressive show of strength that he could send a "large army" to threaten Jerusalem while he himself was leading a campaign against the town of Lachish (2 Kings 18:17). The field commander who was sent to Jerusalem by Sennacherib gave three reasons why the people of Judah should surrender to the Assyrians:

1) The people could not expect help from Egypt, for Egypt at this time was too weak to help anyone (2 Kings 18:19-21).

2) Sennacherib promised to treat the people of Judah well if they chose to surrender (vv. 31, 32)

3) The people could not expect help from the Lord, for the gods of the other peoples conquered by the Assyrians had not been able to save them.

Why should the people of Judah think that their god would be powerful enough to do what other gods had failed to do (vv. 33-35)?

The Assyrians were right when they said that Egypt would not be able to come to Judah's aid, but a threat from that direction did divert them for a time. They heard that "the Cushite king of Egypt" was marching out against them (2 Kings 19:9). Cush was the territory located just south of Egypt, and kings from there were ruling Egypt at this time. Sennacherib decided to gather his forces to meet this challenge, but he sent messengers to Hezekiah with a letter repeating his threat against Jerusalem and telling once again why Judah should surrender (vv. 10-13). The next passage to be examined begins with Hezekiah's reception of this letter.

Examining the Text

I. Hezekiah's Prayer (2 Kings 19:14-19)
A. The Power of the Lord (vv. 14-16)

14Hezekiah received the letter from the messengers and read it. Then he went up to the temple of the Lord and spread it out before the Lord.

After Hezekiah had *read* the *letter from* the Assyrian *messengers*, he *went up to the temple of the Lord*. His decision to go *before the Lord* in this manner recognized the importance of the temple and echoed the thoughts of Solomon in his prayer at the temple's dedication: "May your eyes be open to your servant's plea and to the plea of your people Israel, and may you listen to them whenever they cry out to you" (1 Kings 8:52).

Of course, Hezekiah did not need to *spread* the letter *out* before the Lord so that he could read its contents; but doing so was a gesture symbolic of Hezekiah's reliance on the Lord in this critical situation. Judah's army was no match for the massive forces of Assyria, but all the armies of earth were no match for the Lord.

15And Hezekiah prayed to the Lord: "O Lord, God of Israel, enthroned between the cherubim, you alone are God over all the kingdoms of the earth. You have made heaven and earth.

Hezekiah was fully aware of the structure of the temple and that in the Most Holy Place (or Holy of Holies) was the ark of the covenant with the Ten Commandments in it (2 Chronicles 5:10). On the cover of the ark were two *cherubim* with outstretched wings. (For a discussion of these, see the comments on 2 Chronicles 5:8 in chapter 7.) Only the high priest was permitted to go into the Most Holy Place and did so once every year on the Day of Atonement (Leviticus 16:11-17). Hezekiah acknowledged that the Lord was not confined to that sacred place that symbolized his presence with his people, nor was he only the *God of Israel*. He is *God over all the kingdoms of the earth*. He *made heaven and earth*. The armies of Assyria were a part of his creation, and he could control them.

16"Give ear, O LORD, and hear; open your eyes, O LORD, and see; listen to the words Sennacherib has sent to insult the living God.

Hezekiah pleaded with God to both look and *listen*—that is, to give full attention *to the words* of *Sennacherib*. This Assyrian has dared *to insult the living God* by declaring that he could no more save Judah than the imaginary gods of other nations could save those nations (vv. 10-13).

B. The Power of Assyria (vv. 17, 18)

17"It is true, O LORD, that the Assyrian kings have laid waste these nations and their lands.

Sennacherib's boasting about his triumphs was *true*. He and other *Assyrian kings* had conquered various *nations* situated between Jerusalem and the Assyrian capital of Nineveh.

18"They have thrown their gods into the fire and destroyed them, for they were not gods but only wood and stone, fashioned by men's hands.

In the process of their conquests, the Assyrians had *destroyed* in the *fire* the so-called *gods,* or idols, of the defeated nations. Sennacherib had boasted that these gods had not saved their worshipers; therefore, the Lord could not be expected to save his people. Hezekiah had a clearer understanding. He knew that these gods were only images *fashioned by men's hands* from *wood and stone*. They were made by men, and they were destroyed by men.

The Lord, however, was not made by men. Instead, he made men and everything else. He could destroy the men he had created, but they could not destroy or overpower him. The power of Assyria had crushed many nations, and it was enough to crush Judah alone; but it was helpless against Judah's God.

C. The Plea of Hezekiah (v. 19)

19"Now, O LORD our God, deliver us from his hand, so that all kingdoms on earth may know that you alone, O LORD, are God."

Certainly the Creator of heaven and earth could *deliver* Hezekiah and his people from the Assyrians. Hezekiah begged that the *Lord* would do this, but not for Judah's sake alone. A decisive victory over the mighty Assyrians would bring honor to the Lord and send a clear message to the pagan people of the world. It would let *all kingdoms* know that the Lord was not like the powerless idols worshiped in pagan nations. He *alone* is *God*, the one whose power cannot be overcome by any human force, no matter how large or impressive.

II. The Lord's Answer (2 Kings 19:20, 32-34)
A. "I Have Heard" (v. 20)

20Then Isaiah son of Amoz sent a message to Hezekiah: "This is what the LORD, the God of Israel, says: I have heard your prayer concerning Sennacherib king of Assyria."

God said yes to Hezekiah's *prayer* for help. He sent the prophet *Isaiah* to announce the promised deliverance before it was given. The advance announcement would make it plain that the defeat of *Sennacherib* was an act of God, not some accident of nature.

B. "I Will Act" (vv. 32-34)

32"Therefore this is what the LORD says concerning the king of Assyria:
"He will not enter this city
or shoot an arrow here.
He will not come before it with shield
or build a siege ramp against it.

Sennacherib had hoped to *enter this city*, Jerusalem, and take possession of it. Usually such an undertaking began by driving the defenders of the city from the top of the wall with a shower of arrows. Then some of the troops would advance on the wall, protecting themselves with large shields in order to raise scaling ladders, undermine the walls, or set fire to the city gates. If none of these strategies achieved the desired result, the attackers would *build* a bank of earth as a *siege ramp* up to the wall and then use battering rams to make a breach in the wall. But the Lord's plans were different. He said that Jerusalem would *not* witness any of these frightening actions.

33"By the way that he came he will return;
he will not enter this city, declares the LORD.

Sennacherib had sent an envoy to threaten Jerusalem and demand its surrender, but the Lord declared that he would *not* even *enter this city*. He would not be able to achieve his desired goals in Judah; humiliated, he would *return* to Assyria by the same *way*, not coming near Jerusalem again.

34"I will defend this city and save it,
for my sake and for the sake of David my servant."

Hezekiah had prayed for help for the Lord's sake, not for Hezekiah's or Jerusalem's (v. 19). The Lord answered by promising just what was asked: he would *defend this city and save it, for my sake.* But Jerusalem would also be saved *for the sake of David,* who had conquered the city and made it Israel's capital (2 Samuel 5:6-10). The Lord had promised special blessings to David and to Jerusalem, referring to that city as "chosen" (1 Kings 11:13).

That very night the Lord fulfilled his promise and carried out his judgment against the army of Sennacherib. The angel of the Lord put to death 185,000 Assyrian troops. With his army thus decimated, Sennacherib could do nothing but return in humiliation to his homeland. Eventually the proud Assyrian was murdered by his own sons while worshiping in the temple of his god (2 Kings 19:35-37).

THE REFORMATIONS OF JOSIAH
(2 KINGS 22:8-13; 23:21-23)

Establishing the Groundwork

Hezekiah was succeeded as king of Judah by his son Manasseh. Manasseh proved to be as bad as his father was good. Manasseh's reign was the longest of any king in either Israel or Judah—55 years. So pervasive was the presence of wickedness during his kingship that Judah and Jerusalem's eventual downfall is traced to his sinfulness (2 Kings 21:10-16; 24:1-4).

Manasseh's evil course was halted abruptly when Assyrian invaders captured him and took him to Babylon, which was then ruled by Assyria. During his captivity, Manasseh "sought the favor of the Lord his God and humbled himself greatly before the God of his fathers" (2 Chronicles 33:12). Eventually Manasseh was set free and was restored to power in Judah, where he led in undoing much of the evil that he had promoted (vv. 13-17). But when he died, his son Amon restored much of that evil (2 Kings 21:19-22).

Then came a popular uprising. It began when Amon's officials, apparently dissatisfied with his rule, assassinated him in his palace. "The people of the land" then rose up against these officials and put them to death. They made Amon's son Josiah king of Judah (2 Kings 21:22-24).

Josiah was only eight years old when he became king (2 Kings 22:1). We can only wonder who the power behind the throne was at this point. Perhaps the same person who led the uprising that placed Josiah in power became the tutor and guide of the boy king. Perhaps it was one of the priests (recall from a previous study how a godly priest, Jehoiada, guided Joash when he became king of Judah at age seven). Someone of strong faith and high character must have helped Josiah, for "he did what was right in the eyes of the Lord and walked in all the ways of his father David" (2 Kings 22:2). Josiah, in fact, became one last glimmer of hope for Judah—one Hezekiah-like king who attempted to call the nation back to its spiritual roots.

Second Chronicles 34 records more details concerning Josiah's heart for the Lord. As a teenager, "in the eighth year of his reign, . . . he began to seek the God of his father David" (v. 3). At age 20, in the twelfth year of his reign, he led an initiative that swept the idols from Judah and from much of Israel (the northern kingdom) as well (vv. 3-7). In the eighteenth year of his reign, at the age of 26 and thus still a young man, Josiah ordered a renovation of the neglected temple of the Lord. (Most likely the temple had suffered from neglect during the reigns of Manasseh and Amon.) The high priest Hilkiah had been instructed by Josiah, through the king's secretary Shaphan, to make certain that the workers involved in the project were paid correctly. They were also to be provided with the funds to purchase any materials necessary for the rebuilding.

Apparently, after Shaphan had conveyed these instructions to Hilkiah, the high priest informed Shaphan of a surprising discovery.

Examining the Text

I. Discovering a Book (2 Kings 22:8-10)
A. Hilkiah Informs Shaphan (v. 8)

⁸Hilkiah the high priest said to Shaphan the secretary, "I have found the Book of the Law in the temple of the Lord." He gave it to Shaphan, who read it.

Just what constituted *the Book of the Law* found by *Hilkiah* has been the subject of much discussion. Some believe it comprised all of Genesis through Deuteronomy (the Pentateuch). Others suggest that it was made up of a smaller portion of those five, specifically the book of Deuteronomy. The phrase *Book of the Law* is used in Deuteronomy 31:24-26 to refer to the contents of that particular book. A third possibility is suggested by 2 Kings 23:2, which states that Josiah read in the people's hearing "all the words of the Book of the Covenant." The term *Book of the Covenant* is used in Exodus 24:7 to describe (most likely) the material included in Exodus 20–23.

The contents of Deuteronomy certainly would be enough to generate the kind of intense response that Josiah later spearheaded. For example, the references to the "Lord's anger" (2 Kings 22:13) and the promises to bring disaster (vv. 16, 20) would fit with the list of curses pronounced in Deuteronomy 28:15-68 as a punishment for disobeying God's law. In addition, Deuteronomy 17:18 stipulates that a king, upon beginning his reign, should "write for himself on a scroll a copy of this law." Perhaps it was a copy of this law produced under these circumstances that was ignored by kings such as Manasseh and Amon. Now, by the providence of God, it had been found. Its discovery came during the reign of a king who took its message seriously. First, however, *Shaphan the secretary* read its contents. As secretary, he would have been especially interested in any written records such as the book discovered by Hilkiah.

B. Shaphan Informs Josiah (vv. 9, 10)

⁹, ¹⁰Then Shaphan the secretary went to the king and reported to him: "Your officials have paid out the money that was in the temple of the LORD and have entrusted it to the workers and supervisors at the temple." Then Shaphan the secretary informed the king, "Hilkiah the priest has given me a book." And Shaphan read from it in the presence of the king.

After reading the contents of the book, *Shaphan* then returned to King Josiah and reported on his conversation with Hilkiah. Shaphan first mentioned the matter that Josiah had instructed him to address concerning the *money that was in the temple*. This was to make sure that *the workers and supervisors* received proper compensation for their labors. Then Shaphan proceeded to inform Josiah about Hilkiah's discovery. He *read from* the book *in the presence of the king*.

II. Demanding Action (2 Kings 22:11-13)
A. Josiah's Distress (v. 11)

¹¹When the king heard the words of the Book of the Law, he tore his robes.

King Josiah's reaction upon hearing the contents of *the Book of the Law* reflected his anguish and remorse: *he tore his robes*. This is especially worth noting because Josiah's son, Jehoiakim, would later exhibit a brazen contempt for the Lord's message that came through Jeremiah by cutting it up, tossing it into the fire, and refusing to tear his robes (Jeremiah 36:22-24).

B. Josiah's Demands (vv. 12, 13)

¹²He gave these orders to Hilkiah the priest, Ahikam son of Shaphan, Acbor son of Micaiah, Shaphan the secretary and Asaiah the king's attendant:

The importance of the upcoming inquiry is indicated by the importance of the men chosen to make it. *Hilkiah* was the high *priest* (vv. 4, 8), the primary leader of Judah's religious life. Ahikam was influential in the government for many years (Jeremiah 26:24) and was the father of Gedaliah, who was later appointed governor of Judah by the Babylonians following the fall of Jerusalem (2 Kings 25:22). The son of *Acbor*, Elnathan, was an official in the administration of Josiah's son Jehoiakim (Jeremiah 26:22; 36:12). The role of *Shaphan the secretary* has already been noted. Nothing more is known of *Asaiah* than of his position as *the king's attendant*.

> [13]*"Go and inquire of the L*ORD *for me and for the people and for all Judah about what is written in this book that has been found. Great is the L*ORD*'s anger that burns against us because our fathers have not obeyed the words of this book; they have not acted in accordance with all that is written there concerning us."*

Josiah did not send these men to determine whether or not *this book* that had been found was authentic. Of that there was no question. Rather, the king's primary concern seems to have been whether or not the words of judgment within the book were to have an immediate fulfillment. Josiah was gravely concerned, not only for himself but *for the people* of Jerusalem *and for all Judah* because their *fathers* had *not obeyed the words of this book*. As noted previously, some reforms had already been instituted under Josiah's direction prior to Hilkiah's discovery of the book; but the book had revealed even more areas that needed to be addressed. Perhaps Josiah was made aware of the curses that accompanied disobedience of the Lord's commands (Deuteronomy 28:15-68). Josiah realized that the nation stood in danger of divine retribution. In fact, one reason he may have looked for an immediate word from the Lord was that he believed punishment was long overdue. Could the anger of the Lord be avoided, or was it too late?

The desired inquiry was made of Huldah, a prophetess in Jerusalem (vv. 14-20), and the king's worst fears were justified. Through Huldah the anger of the Lord against Judah because of its sins was indeed confirmed, but mercy and forbearance were extended to Josiah because of his desire to know and to do the Lord's will. Josiah was assured that the national destruction threatened in the Book of the Law would not occur during his reign. He himself would be "buried in peace" (v. 20). In fact, it was some three years after Josiah's death that the divinely appointed agents of the Lord's judgment (the Babylonians) made their first appearance in Judah.

III. Declaring a Passover (2 Kings 23:21-23)

Second Kings 23 gives an account of the various steps taken by Josiah in obedience to the law of the Lord. Pagan shrines of worship were destroyed.

Pagan priests were removed from office. Josiah's efforts included the fulfillment of a prophecy given some 300 years earlier by an anonymous man of God from Judah (2 Kings 23:15-18). That man of God had even mentioned Josiah by name (1 Kings 13:2).

A. Command (v. 21)

²¹The king gave this order to all the people: "Celebrate the Passover to the Lᴏʀᴅ your God, as it is written in this Book of the Covenant."

Another important phase of Josiah's rededication of all the people involved the observance of the Passover. Instructions are found in Exodus 12:1-20, 43-49 and Deuteronomy 16:1-8. The Exodus passage deals with how families were to observe this feast, while the Deuteronomy passage deals more with observing the Passover on a national level. The latter of these two circumstances fits the occasion described in the passage before us. This may support the view that the book discovered in the temple by Hilkiah was Deuteronomy.

B. Comparison (vv. 22, 23)

²²Not since the days of the judges who led Israel, nor throughout the days of the kings of Israel and the kings of Judah, had any such Passover been observed.

These verses provide an assessment of the significance of this Passover observance. Josiah's celebration surpassed any that had taken place since the days of the judges or during the time of the divided monarchy.

Why was this so? What was so special about the way Josiah observed the Passover? Second Chronicles 35:1-19 provides additional details about Josiah's celebration and includes an evaluation similar to that found in 2 Kings: "The Passover had not been observed like this in Israel since the days of the prophet Samuel; and none of the kings of Israel had ever celebrated such a Passover as did Josiah with the priests, the Levites and all Judah and Israel who were there with the people of Jerusalem" (v. 18). Josiah's compliance with the law's requirements is especially noted; for example, the Chronicles account records that all the Passover lambs were slaughtered exclusively by the Levites, as the law stipulated (2 Chronicles 35:3, 5, 6).

Josiah's devotion to the Law of Moses is also emphasized in 2 Kings 23:25. That passage provides this evaluation of one of Judah's most godly kings: "Neither before nor after Josiah was there a king like him who turned to the Lord as he did—with all his heart and with all his soul and with all his strength, in accordance with all the Law of Moses."

Such a one-of-a-kind tribute may appear to contradict what is said of Hezekiah, who receives similar praise in 2 Kings 18:5. However, as noted in the "Background" comments on 2 Chronicles 30:1-12 in this chapter, Hezekiah is specifically commended for his trust in the Lord, while Josiah's scrupulous observance of the law of Moses is stressed. Each king was exemplary in a different area of devotion to the Lord. Such kings were a primary reason why Judah lasted approximately 135 years longer than the northern kingdom, Israel.

23But in the eighteenth year of King Josiah, this Passover was celebrated to the Lord in Jerusalem.

This verse notes the time that *this Passover* celebration occurred: it was in the *eighteenth year of King Josiah*. Mentioning the time frame at this point serves to call attention to the urgency of Josiah's efforts at spiritual renewal in Judah since that was the same year that the Book of the Law was found (2 Kings 22:3, 8).

The discovery of the Book of the Law in that same eighteenth year, along with Josiah's wholehearted commitment to its contents, gave Judah a reprieve from the judgment of God. Sadly, it was only a reprieve; for Josiah was the last of Judah's godly kings.

THE FALL OF JERUSALEM
(2 KINGS 25:1-7; 2 CHRONICLES 36:15-21)

Establishing the Groundwork

Conditions in Judah deteriorated rapidly following the death of Josiah in 609 BC. Here is a summary of the reigns of Judah's last four kings:

Jehoahaz, also called Shallum, was a son of Josiah. He reigned over Judah only three months. He was taken captive to Egypt, where he died (2 Kings 23:31-34; Jeremiah 22:11, 12).

Jehoiakim was put on the throne by the Egyptians after they had removed Jehoahaz from power. This was another son of Josiah. He ruled for eleven years (609-598 BC). He was a striking contrast to his father. Jehoiakim lived in personal extravagance (Jeremiah 22:13-15), pursued dishonest gain, and set his eyes and his heart "on shedding innocent blood and on oppression and extortion" (22:17). During Jehoiakim's reign, King Nebuchadnezzar came to power in Babylon as Egypt declined in influence. Jehoiakim switched his loyalty to Babylon in an attempt to keep up with the times, but rebelled after three years (2 Kings 24:1). The Scriptures do not indicate how Jehoiakim died; many students believe he was assassinated.

Jehoiachin, Jehoiakim's son, ruled for only three months. He was taken captive to Babylon by Nebuchadnezzar in 597 BC. His later release from prison and elevation to a position of honor in Babylon is mentioned in 2 Kings 25:27-30 and Jeremiah 52:31-34.

Zedekiah, the last king of Judah, was another son of Josiah. Zedekiah reigned for eleven years until Jerusalem fell in 586 BC. Weak and unstable, he refused to heed the counsel of Jeremiah to surrender to the Babylonians (Jeremiah 27:12-15; 38:17, 18). When the Babylonians finally overtook Jerusalem, Zedekiah was forced to watch as they slaughtered his own sons. The Babylonians then put out his eyes and took him to Babylon (39:5-7), where he most likely was at the time of his death.

The two Scriptures in this next section of study examine the fall of Jerusalem from two perspectives. The first, from 2 Kings, covers some of the historical details of the event. The second, from 2 Chronicles, summarizes why this tragedy occurred. It also provides a somber description of the Babylonians' destruction of the city and the exile of its residents.

Examining the Text

I. Portrayal of a Siege (2 Kings 25:1-7)

King Zedekiah had made a trip to Babylon in the fourth year of his reign (Jeremiah 51:59). It is sometimes thought that he and others who plotted against Babylon were compelled to make this journey in order to give personal expressions of allegiance to Nebuchadnezzar.

A few years later, however, Zedekiah rebelled (2 Kings 24:20). Nebuchadnezzar then moved to subdue the disloyal nations, and Judah was first on his list.

A. Start of the Siege (v. 1)

¹So in the ninth year of Zedekiah's reign, on the tenth day of the tenth month, Nebuchadnezzar king of Babylon marched against Jerusalem with his whole army. He encamped outside the city and built siege works all around it.

The *ninth year of Zedekiah's reign* would have been, according to the dating system we use, around 588 BC. The *tenth month* would have occurred in winter, during our month of January. This shows the determination of *Nebuchadnezzar* as he began the military blockade of Jerusalem. Usually warfare occurred in spring (see 2 Samuel 11:1). To move an army and its equipment into position during the rainy, cold months of winter was a hardship. In addition, Nebuchadnezzar engaged *his whole army* in this effort. We are not told how many soldiers this involved, but surely the number was so overwhelming that the men of Judah would not dare to meet them in open battle. The people of Judah could only seek refuge behind the walls of *Jerusalem.*

The Babylonians *encamped outside the city and built siege works all around it,* so that no one could sneak in with food for the starving defenders or escape from the increasingly desperate conditions within the city. The siege works consisted of some kind of movable scaffolding or towers that were pushed up against the city walls, enabling archers to shoot their arrows at defenders along the walls or at people within the city itself. Sometimes these structures included battering rams used to break through the walls.

B. Severity of the Siege (vv. 2, 3)

2, 3The city was kept under siege until the eleventh year of King Zedekiah. By the ninth day of the fourth month the famine in the city had become so severe that there was no food for the people to eat.

The dates given in our text indicate that the *siege* of Jerusalem lasted 18 months. The conditions inside the city grew increasingly worse as those months progressed. The words of Lamentations 4:10 indicate that some of the people actually resorted to cannibalism to survive: "With their own hands compassionate women have cooked their own children, who became their food when my people were destroyed."

C. Success of the Siege (vv. 4-7)

4Then the city wall was broken through, and the whole army fled at night through the gate between the two walls near the king's garden, though the Babylonians were surrounding the city. They fled toward the Arabah,

While the famine was weakening the people inside Jerusalem, the Babylonians were persistently trying to breach the city's defenses from without. Finally *the city wall was broken through* (perhaps at a point in the north wall where the ground would have been nearly level). This signaled, of course, that the city was doomed and any further resistance was futile. The soldiers who had defended Jerusalem tried to escape the city at night through the gate between the two walls near the king's garden. This would have been located at the southeastern corner of the city, at the other end from where the breach had occurred. King Zedekiah went with them (Jeremiah 39:4), likely accompanied by other officials of Judah, and they *fled toward the Arabah*—downward from the heights on which Jerusalem was situated toward the Jordan River plain.

5, 6a *. . . but the Babylonian army pursued the king and overtook him in the plains of Jericho. All his soldiers were separated from him and scattered, and he was captured.*

Those who escaped the city had a head start while the pursuers were gathering their forces. The fugitives, however, were weak from hunger and in no condition to maintain the small lead they had on the *Babylonian army*.

It was about 20 miles from Jerusalem to *the plains of Jericho*. Possibly dawn had come by the time the men of Judah reached this territory. No doubt they could see the Babylonians gaining on them. Most likely the morale of those in Judah's army was so low at this point that the *soldiers* simply deserted their king and *scattered*, with every man looking out for himself. The *king* and other important officials were an easy capture.

6b*He was taken to the king of Babylon at Riblah, where sentence was pronounced on him.*

By this time in history, Nebuchadnezzar dominated all the countries at the eastern end of the Mediterranean Sea. It appears that he began the siege of Jerusalem (v. 1), then left his generals to conduct it while he made his headquarters at *Riblah*, some 200 miles to the north in what is now Syria. King Zedekiah was *taken* there as a prisoner and tried, judged, and condemned. Having broken his oath of allegiance to Nebuchadnezzar, he was considered a traitor.

7*They killed the sons of Zedekiah before his eyes. Then they put out his eyes, bound him with bronze shackles and took him to Babylon.*

The punishment Zedekiah received was severe. The last thing he was allowed to see was the death of his *sons*. Then he was blinded, perhaps with hot coals. Some years earlier, Ezekiel had made an interesting prophecy about Zedekiah: he was to be brought to Babylon, but he was not to see it (Ezekiel 12:13). The judgment on him by Nebuchadnezzar fulfilled this prophecy. Other leaders of Judah also experienced death at Riblah (2 Kings 25:18-21; Jeremiah 39:6). Zedekiah was then taken to *Babylon*—a dismal journey of nearly a thousand miles.

II. Pleas of the Prophets (2 Chronicles 36:15, 16)

As noted in the "Groundwork" section of this study, the following passage from the final chapter of 2 Chronicles focuses on why the disaster that befell Jerusalem and God's people occurred. Verses 11-14 summarize what took place during the reign of Zedekiah, the last king of Judah. In particular, it is noted that "all the leaders of the priests and the people became more and more unfaithful, following all the detestable practices of the nations and defiling the temple of the Lord" (2 Chronicles 36:14).

A. God's Mercy (v. 15)

15The LORD, the God of their fathers, sent word to them through his messengers again and again, because he had pity on his people and on his dwelling place.

The Lord had given his people fair and frequent warning of the judgment they would face if they continued in their sinful practices. God is described as repeatedly sending his faithful *messengers*, or prophets, to issue these warnings. Notice that God's *pity* extended not only to *his people*, but also to *his dwelling place*. God had promised to put his name in Jerusalem after the temple had been completed (1 Kings 9:3; 2 Kings 21:4). In addition the identity of the people was so closely bound to the temple in Jerusalem that God knew that its destruction would be an especially devastating burden for them to bear. Yet, as 2 Chronicles 36:14 tells us, the people had defiled that temple through their pagan practices. The time had come when God's judgment could no longer be avoided.

B. People's Mocking (v. 16)

16But they mocked God's messengers, despised his words and scoffed at his prophets until the wrath of the LORD was aroused against his people and there was no remedy.

Here is how God's people received his efforts to reach out to them in pity: *they mocked God's messengers, despised his words and scoffed at his prophets*. What patience God has! While he endured that for a time, eventually such callous treatment of the Lord's messengers could no longer be tolerated. His *wrath* was *aroused against his people and there was no remedy*. No remedy was available, not because God could not supply one, but because the people's sinfulness had reached the stage where they were not willing to accept any remedy.

III. Power of Babylon (2 Chronicles 36:17-21)

The Babylonians defeated the Egyptians at the Battle of Carchemish in 605 BC (see 2 Chronicles 35:20; Jeremiah 46:2). This epic battle changed the balance of power in the ancient world. Afterward the Babylonians turned their attention to Judah.

A. Lives Lost (v. 17)

17He brought up against them the king of the Babylonians, who killed their young men with the sword in the sanctuary, and spared neither young man nor young woman, old man or aged. God handed all of them over to Nebuchadnezzar.

Both the beginning and the conclusion of this verse highlight a pivotal truth: it was the Lord who *brought up against* his people *the king of the Babylonians,* and *God handed* his people *over to Nebuchadnezzar.* A secular historian may explain the Babylonian triumph over Jerusalem as the exercise of sheer political and military supremacy. The Bible reveals the primary cause to be the Lord's deliverance of his people to be judged.

B. Treasures Taken (v. 18)

18He carried to Babylon all the articles from the temple of God, both large and small, and the treasures of the Lord's temple and the treasures of the king and his officials.

The pagan mindset of this time would ask why Israel's God had refused to come to the rescue of his *temple* and its *treasures.* One might conclude that this reflected his weakness and his inferiority to the gods of other nations such as Babylon. The answer, however, had nothing to do with the weakness of the Lord. He allowed these tragedies to occur in fulfilling his promises of judgment.

C. Buildings Burned (v. 19)

19They set fire to God's temple and broke down the wall of Jerusalem; they burned all the palaces and destroyed everything of value there.

The two main structures of many cities of this time were the *temple* (a spiritual landmark) and the *wall* (the primary source of defense). The Babylonians destroyed both. The *palaces*—symbolic of status and wealth—suffered the same tragic end.

D. Remnant Removed (v. 20)

20He carried into exile to Babylon the remnant, who escaped from the sword, and they became servants to him and his sons until the kingdom of Persia came to power.

The doctrine of the *remnant* is one of the most important in Old Testament prophecy. In spite of God's judgment, he did not completely destroy his people. Just as he issued warnings through his prophets (v. 15), so also he spoke words of hope and promise. In time a remnant would return (Isaiah 10:21; Jeremiah 23:3; Ezekiel 6:8; Micah 2:12). That remnant eventually would be the source from which the Messiah came to offer to all peoples deliverance from the captivity of sin.

This verse reveals another important truth: the Babylonians' days on the center stage of world history would reach their limit—just as the Assyrians reached theirs before being overthrown by Babylon. Eventually, the Persians took control of the Babylonian Empire.

E. Rest Remembered (v. 21)

²¹The land enjoyed its sabbath rests; all the time of its desolation it rested, until the seventy years were completed in fulfillment of the word of the LORD spoken by Jeremiah.

The law of Moses prescribed a *sabbath* year for the promised land—a time (every seventh year) during which the land was to be given a rest. It was not to be cultivated or harvested. The people were instead to eat what grew in the sabbath year (Leviticus 25:1-7). Such a procedure gave the land the opportunity to be replenished for further use. This law also reminded the people of Israel that they were caretakers who cared for the land according to the giver's stipulations.

However, like many of the laws God gave to his people, this one had been ignored. In a sense the land cried out for God's judgment to be administered, for it had not been treated according to the Giver's directives. The punishment for violating God's covenant is found in Leviticus 26:14-43, including a promise to give the land its Sabbath rest. The language there (see vv. 34, 35, 42, 43) is very similar to the wording found here in 2 Chronicles.

The prophet *Jeremiah* had declared that the people's captivity would last for *seventy years* (Jeremiah 29:10). If one multiplies seventy by seven (since a sabbath year occurred every seventh year), the result is 490. If one adds 490 to 586 BC (the year Jerusalem fell), the resulting date is 1076 BC, which was during the time Samuel lived. Perhaps the people had not observed the sabbath year law properly since those days—just as they had not properly kept the Passover law since the time of Samuel (2 Chronicles 35:18).

The 70-year period of captivity would allow the land to "catch up" on the sabbaths missed because of the people's negligence. Once this had occurred, the land would be prepared, not only agriculturally, but also spiritually, to welcome back God's people in fulfillment of his promise. That return is the subject of the first passage to be covered in the next chapter.

How to Say It

ACBOR. *Ak*-bor.

AHAZ. *Ay*-haz.

AHIKAM. Uh-*high*-kum.

AMON. *Ay*-mun.

AMOZ. *Ay*-mahz.

ARABAH. *Ar*-uh-buh.

ASAIAH. As-*ay*-uh.

ASSYRIANS. Uh-*sear*-e-unz.

BAAL. *Bay*-ul.

BABYLON. *Bab*-uh-lun.

BABYLONIANS. Bab-ih-*low*-nee-unz.

BEERSHEBA. Beer-*she*-buh.

CARCHEMISH. *Kar*-key-mish.

EPHRAIM. *Ee*-fray-im.

GEDALIAH. *Ged*-uh-*lye*-uh. (G as in get; strong accent on *lye*).

HEZEKIAH. Hez-ih-*kye*-uh.

HILKIAH. Hill-*kye*-uh.

HULDAH. *Hul*-duh.

JEHOAHAZ. Jeh-*ho*-uh-haz.

JEHOIACHIN. Jeh-*hoy*-uh-kin.

JEHOIADA. Jee-*hoy*-uh-duh.

JEHOIAKIM. Jeh-*hoy*-uh-kim.

JEROBOAM. Jair-uh-*boe*-um.

JEZEBEL. *Jez*-uh-bel.

JOSIAH. Jo-*sigh*-uh.

LACHISH. *Lay*-kish.

MANASSEH. Muh-*nass*-uh.

MICAIAH. My-*kay*-uh.

NEBUCHADNEZZAR. *Neb*-yuh-kud-*nez*-er (strong accent on *nez*).

NINEVEH. *Nin*-uh-vuh.

RIBLAH. *Rib*-luh.

SANHEDRIN. *San*-huh-drun or San-*heed*-run.

SENNACHERIB. Sen-*nack*-er-ib.

SHALLUM. *Shall*-um.

SHAPHAN. *Shay*-fan.

ZEBULUN. *Zeb*-you-lun.

ZEDEKIAH. Zed-uh-*kye*-uh.

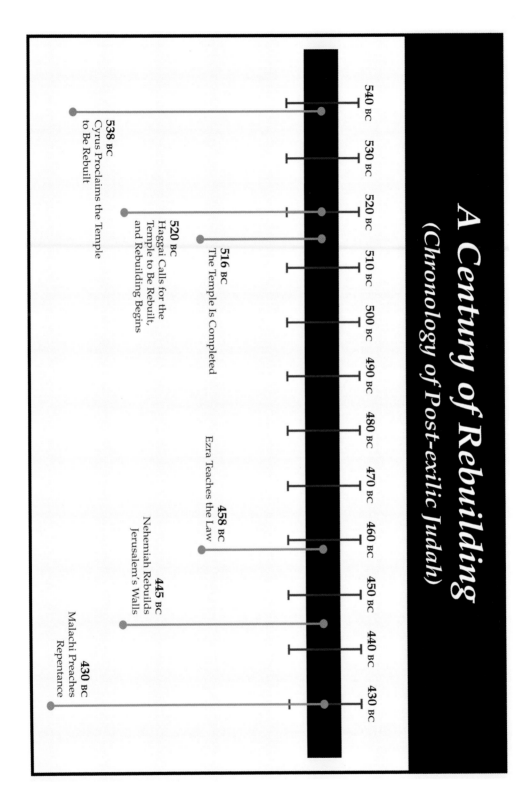

A Century of Rebuilding
(Chronology of Post-exilic Judah)

538 BC
Cyrus Proclaims the Temple to Be Rebuilt

520 BC
Haggai Calls for the Temple to Be Rebuilt, and Rebuilding Begins

516 BC
The Temple Is Completed

458 BC
Ezra Teaches the Law

445 BC
Nehemiah Rebuilds Jerusalem's Walls

430 BC
Malachi Preaches Repentance

540 BC · 530 BC · 520 BC · 510 BC · 500 BC · 490 BC · 480 BC · 470 BC · 460 BC · 450 BC · 440 BC · 430 BC

Chapter 12

Return from Exile:
The Leadership of Ezra and Nehemiah

Ezra 1:1-7; 3:1-3, 10-13; 6:14-16;
Nehemiah 1:1-4; 2:1-8, 17, 18; 4:15-20; 6:15, 16

RETURNING AND REBUILDING (EZRA 1:1-7)

Establishing the Groundwork

The final two chapters in this series of studies on the history books of the Old Testament will focus on what is usually called the post-exilic period, covering the history of God's people after the Babylonian captivity had ended and those who desired to do so returned to the promised land. The previous chapter concluded with a passage from the final chapter of 2 Chronicles. This passage provided an explanation why the exile to Babylon occurred and served a purpose similar to that of 2 Kings 17:6-18 concerning the northern kingdom of Israel. (See the study of that passage in chapter 10.)

Second Chronicles, however, concludes with a note of hope. In fact, the final two verses of 2 Chronicles and the first three verses of the book of Ezra are virtually the same. Because of this, some have proposed that Ezra may have been the author of the books of Chronicles as well as the book that bears his name. Certainly Ezra was well suited for such a task, being a man of great learning (see Ezra 7:6, 10).

The book of Ezra consists of two main parts. The first six chapters cover a period beginning in 538 BC, when Cyrus issued his decree permitting the exiles to return to Jerusalem if they desired, and ending with the dedication of the second temple in 516 BC. The remaining four chapters of the book record the arrival of Ezra and his party in Jerusalem in 458 BC and go on to tell of his subsequent activities. Of the period of nearly sixty years between these two sections we know very little. (See the chart on the opposite page.)

The destruction of Jerusalem and of Solomon's magnificent temple was a devastating series of events that set the faith of many of God's people reeling. Perhaps some questioned whether these tragedies meant that God had turned his back completely on his chosen people. The post-exilic period, as recorded in the three books of Ezra, Nehemiah, and Esther, provides the answer; and it is a resounding no! God still had a purpose for his people, and this is the note of hope with which 2 Chronicles ends and Ezra begins.

Examining the Text

I. Decree Ordained (Ezra 1:1-4)
A. God's Working (v. 1)

¹In the first year of Cyrus king of Persia, in order to fulfill the word of the Lord spoken by Jeremiah, the Lord moved the heart of Cyrus king of Persia to make a proclamation throughout his realm and to put it in writing:

Cyrus king of Persia was the human instrument whom God used to keep his promise to bring his people home. Persia came to power in 539 BC through the series of events described in Daniel 5.

King Cyrus possessed a discernment and fair-mindedness that many rulers in the ancient world lacked. He understood that it would enhance his reputation and get his reign started on a positive note if he provided some measure of relief from the cruel tactics of the Babylonians. So he demonstrated an attitude of diplomacy and tolerance in his dealings with conquered peoples. He gave these peoples a wide latitude in allowing them to practice their religions. Thus one should keep in mind that what the Scriptures describe Cyrus as doing for the Jews, he did also for other peoples: permitting them to return to their respective homelands. There they could reestablish themselves and be free to practice their religious beliefs.

Secular historians may view Cyrus's actions as simply the exercise of capable and discerning leadership. The Scripture, however, is clear in emphasizing that the Lord used this policy of *Cyrus* to accomplish his own purpose. This was all part of his plan as announced by *the word of the Lord spoken by Jeremiah*. That word describes the captivity as lasting 70 years (Jeremiah 29:10). Cyrus was not acting alone; the Lord, the heavenly king, *moved the heart* of the earthly *king* to implement a program of restoration for the Lord's people. It is noteworthy that another prophet (Isaiah) gave Spirit-inspired insight into the Lord's master plan some 100 years before Jeremiah uttered his prophecy (Isaiah 44:28; 45:1).

B. Cyrus's Words (vv. 2-4)

²,³"This is what Cyrus king of Persia says:

"'The Lord, the God of heaven, has given me all the kingdoms of the

earth and he has appointed me to build a temple for him at Jerusalem in Judah. Anyone of his people among you—may his God be with him, and let him go up to Jerusalem in Judah and build the temple of the Lord, *the God of Israel, the God who is in Jerusalem.*

As noted above, Cyrus allowed other captive peoples to return to their homelands—not just the Jews. Thus the acknowledgment of *the Lord* as *the God of heaven* should not be considered as a sign of any kind of conversion to the God of Israel on Cyrus's part. Nevertheless, it is clear that Cyrus was indeed God's instrument to carry out his purpose.

Following the claim to be authorized by the Lord, Cyrus's decree granted permission to any of the Lord's *people* to *go up* to *Jerusalem.* There they could participate in the rebuilding effort. The Hebrew word translated as *go up* occurs elsewhere in the Old Testament in the context of another significant movement of God's people: the exodus from bondage in Egypt (see Exodus 3:8, 17; 33:1). To *go up* thus had a special meaning for God's people and gave them a sense of kinship with the exodus event that established them as a "holy nation" (Exodus 19:5, 6). In a sense they could consider themselves reborn as a nation, for they were coming out of bondage in Babylon much as they had come out of Egypt under Moses. The promise of God's presence (*may his God be with him*) was also a key source of encouragement during the exodus and subsequent events (Exodus 3:11, 12; 33:14-17; Numbers 14:9). Now that promise offered hope to a captive people and assured them that God was still on his throne and they were still his chosen people.

⁴"And the people of any place where survivors may now be living are to provide him with silver and gold, with goods and livestock, and with freewill offerings for the temple of God in Jerusalem.'"

The final part of Cyrus's edict addressed the *people* who would choose not to return to Judah. Every Israelite was commanded to take part in the rebuilding program involving *Jerusalem* and its *temple.* A project of this scope would demand great resources; and each person must do his or her part, either by going or by giving *silver and gold* and *goods and livestock*—the last item being necessary for sacrifices and food.

II. Decree Obeyed (Ezra 1:5-7)
A. God's Action (v. 5)

⁵Then the family heads of Judah and Benjamin, and the priests and Levites—everyone whose heart God had moved—prepared to go up and build the house of the Lord *in Jerusalem.*

This verse lists those who *prepared to go up and build the house of the Lord in Jerusalem* (just as Cyrus's decree had stated). The *family heads* were probably the leaders of the various tribal clans, or extended families, within the tribes of *Judah and Benjamin*. These two tribes provided the primary makeup of the southern kingdom of Judah, which the Babylonians had conquered and taken captive.

Included in those who returned were the *priests and Levites*. Their spiritual leadership would be necessary in guiding and mentoring those who chose to return. Sadly, some of these priests and Levites eventually committed sin by marrying women from outside the covenant people. This caused great distress to Ezra and others among those who returned (Ezra 9:1-4).

In this verse it is also important to note the guidance of the Lord's hand. Those who chose to return included *everyone whose heart God had moved*. The same God who has "moved the heart" of a pagan king (Ezra 1:1) now moved among his people to stir them to action. This also meant that the same God who had brought the king of Babylon against his people (2 Chronicles 36:17) was now working for his people. He was fulfilling his promise to bring them home.

B. Neighbors' Assistance (v. 6)

⁶*All their neighbors assisted them with articles of silver and gold, with goods and livestock, and with valuable gifts, in addition to all the freewill offerings.*

In previous comments, the return from captivity was considered as a kind of "second exodus." Here one sees another parallel to the events surrounding the exodus of some 900 years before. Exodus 11:2 records these instructions given by the Lord to Moses: "Tell the people that men and women alike are to ask their neighbors for articles of silver and gold." And now, as this "second exodus" unfolded for God's people, *all their neighbors assisted them* with numerous contributions and *offerings*.

C. Cyrus's Assistance (v. 7)

⁷*Moreover, King Cyrus brought out the articles belonging to the temple of the Lord, which Nebuchadnezzar had carried away from Jerusalem and had placed in the temple of his god.*

Furthermore, *King Cyrus brought out the articles* that rightfully belonged to *the temple of the Lord*. This showed his personal support for the return home. Second Chronicles 36:18 describes how *Nebuchadnezzar had carried away* these items to Babylon. That king's successor had used some of those articles in a most unholy way (Daniel 5:1-4).

Now these actions were reversed, as the temple articles were removed from Babylon and taken to their original, rightful home in *Jerusalem*. This gave the returning captives some sense of continuity with the past when they were in a position to place these items in the new temple.

The removal of articles from a conquered people's place of worship was a significant religious statement in the ancient world. It was interpreted as a sign of the superiority of the conqueror's gods. In this case, *the Lord*, God of Israel, who had allowed the Babylonians to remove the articles from his temple, now allowed the Persians to send them back!

BUILDING THE SECOND TEMPLE
(EZRA 3:1-3, 10-13; 6:14-16)

Establishing the Groundwork

The verses of Ezra 1 that follow those covered in the previous section of study provide an inventory of the articles of gold and silver that were taken from Babylon to Jerusalem. The second chapter provides a record of those individuals who returned from Babylon to Judah. About 50,000, including servants, made this trip (Ezra 2:64, 65). Chapter 3 resumes the account of the returning exiles and describes the various steps taken upon their arrival in Judah. These included building an altar, offering the first sacrifices on it, and the laying of the foundation of the second temple. The return trip occurred in 536 BC.

Examining the Text

I. Rebuilding the Altar (Ezra 3:1-3)
A. Assembling in Jerusalem (v. 1)

¹When the seventh month came and the Israelites had settled in their towns, the people assembled as one man in Jerusalem.

The *seventh month* (our late September and early October) was a special month on the Israelites' calendar. The first day of this month was the day the Feast of Trumpets began (Leviticus 23:23-25), heralding the beginning of the Jewish civil year. This is observed today as Rosh Hashanah, the beginning of the Jewish New Year. (The first month of the Jewish religious year was the month during which the Passover was celebrated, as indicated in Exodus 12:1-11.) The tenth day of the seventh month was the Day of Atonement—the only day in the entire year when the high priest could enter the Holy of Holies. The observance of this day included special sacrifices and the sending of the scapegoat, on which was placed the sins of all the Israelites, into the wilderness (Leviticus 16; 23:26-32).

The fifteenth day of the seventh month was the beginning of the Feast of Tabernacles (or Booths). This week-long event was one of Israel's major festivals. Its purpose was to remind the Israelites of their 40 years of living in booths during the wilderness wanderings (Leviticus 23:33-36, 39-43).

That the people who had returned from captivity *assembled as one man in Jerusalem* emphasizes the sense of unity that was present among them. Although Jerusalem lay in ruins, a grim reminder of the penalty their fathers had paid for rebelling against God, it was still the holy city, the city of David. The people were determined to restore it to its place as the center of the nation's worship.

B. Accomplishing the Task (vv. 2, 3)

²Then Jeshua son of Jozadak and his fellow priests and Zerubbabel son of Shealtiel and his associates began to build the altar of the God of Israel to sacrifice burnt offerings on it, in accordance with what is written in the Law of Moses the man of God.

Jeshua and *Zerubbabel* held impressive credentials for leadership. Jeshua was in the lineage of the high priests. His grandfather Seraiah had been the high priest and was executed by the Babylonians when Nebuchadnezzar destroyed Jerusalem (2 Kings 25:18, 21). Jeshua is spelled "Joshua" in Haggai 1:1, and there he is called the high priest. His father, *Jozadak*, apparently was high priest during most of the Babylonian captivity. (Jozadak is the same as "Jehozadak" in 1 Chronicles 6:14, 15 and Haggai 1:1.)

Zerubbabel was a grandson of Jehoiachin, one of the last kings of Judah. They are listed in the genealogy of Jesus in Matthew 1:12, where Jehoiachin is called "Jeconiah." The returning captives thus had qualified leaders in two important areas: they had a religious leader who was a priest, and they had a civil leader who was of the Davidic line. (Zerubbabel may be another name for Sheshbazzar, mentioned in Ezra 1:8, 11 and 5:14; but this is not certain.)

The two leaders mentioned here were not left to do the work by themselves. Constructing the altar of the God of Israel was a community project. This new altar was built on the precise spot where the former altar for the temple had been (v. 3). David had built an altar there even before it became the site for the temple (2 Samuel 24:25). Such sites were considered very sacred, and its location would have been easily determined.

> **³Despite their fear of the peoples around them, they built the altar on its foundation and sacrificed burnt offerings on it to the LORD, both the morning and evening sacrifices.**

The *peoples around* the Israelites were peoples who had originated through the intermarriage of Israelites with Assyrians. This had occurred as the result of the Assyrians' having brought foreigners to Israel following the fall of Samaria (2 Kings 17:24; Ezra 4:9, 10), some of whom intermarried with the few Israelites who had been left behind when most Israelites were deported. These peoples were the equivalent of the Samaritans, although that term is not used in the Old Testament. They were likely influenced by the Assyrians' pagan beliefs. They resented the returnees, who were considered intruders.

The returnees were probably outnumbered and thus feared their neighbors. Some commentators suggest that the site on which the people *built the altar* had been used by others during the 50 years since the temple was destroyed. As the Israelites cleared away all semblance of pagan worship, their neighbors resented the intrusion.

However, those returning were convinced that there is only one God and that this altar was only for him. These people were keenly aware that their forefathers had attempted to blend the worship of God with pagan worship, and captivity was the result. This captivity accomplished one very important thing: it cured the Israelites of yielding to the practice of idolatry. These returnees determined to have no other gods, just as the First Commandment instructs (Exodus 20:3; Deuteronomy 5:7).

The law of Moses decreed that *burnt offerings* were to be made each *morning* and *evening*, one animal each time. On the Sabbath Day, two animals were sacrificed in the morning and two in the evening (Numbers 28:1-10).

II. Laying the Temple's Foundation (Ezra 3:10-13)

Verses 4-9 of Ezra 3 record that the people celebrated the Feast of Tabernacles, which, as noted earlier in the comments on verse 1, was to be celebrated during the seventh month. Then work began on laying the foundation for the new temple. Verse 8 states that this took place "in the second month of the second year after their arrival." This would have been in our late April or early May of 536 BC. Interestingly, the building of Solomon's temple also began in the second month of the Jewish year (1 Kings 6:1).

Other similarities of this construction to that of Solomon are striking (see 1 Kings 5:1-11). In both instances cedar logs were taken from the mountains of Lebanon to the Mediterranean Sea, formed into giant rafts, and floated to Joppa, Israel's primary seaport. From there they were transported overland to the hills of Jerusalem, a distance of about 40 miles. And in each case the workers were paid with food.

A. Preparations (v. 10)

¹⁰When the builders laid the foundation of the temple of the Lord, the priests in their vestments and with trumpets, and the Levites (the sons of Asaph) with cymbals, took their places to praise the Lord, as prescribed by David king of Israel.

The laying of *the foundation* for this new *temple of the Lord* was a time for great celebration and worship. We may very well compare it to a dedication service that we would hold at the laying of a cornerstone for a church building. The people were gathered *to praise the Lord* for his blessings on the building effort.

The *priests* wore their special apparel, certainly appropriate for such an occasion as this. The clothing that was originally designed for the priests was to "to give them dignity and honor" (Exodus 28:40). The people had earlier provided these garments for the priests (Ezra 2:69). The priests led the worship with their *trumpets*—long, straight horns that were flared or turned up at the end. They were accompanied by *Levites* who were specifically in charge of certain aspects of the temple music. Their ancestor, *Asaph*, had been a prominent musician appointed by *David* to lead in praising the Lord before the ark of the covenant, after it was brought to Jerusalem (1 Chronicles 16:4-6). Apparently this family had maintained its skills and standing across many generations.

David had done much to incorporate music into the life of Israel's worship, not only through his appointment of certain Levites when the ark was brought to Jerusalem, but also through later preparations made for Solomon's temple (1 Chronicles 23:1-5; 25). Now, as the second temple was being constructed, music was being reinstituted after the pattern David had prescribed. This served to emphasize the continuity between the first temple and the second.

B. Praises (v. 11)

¹¹With praise and thanksgiving they sang to the Lord:
  "He is good;
    his love to Israel endures forever."
And all the people gave a great shout of praise to the Lord, because the foundation of the house of the Lord was laid.

The words used in this time of *praise and thanksgiving* call to mind the ceremony at the dedication of Solomon's temple (2 Chronicles 5:13). The leaders may have deliberately patterned their worship after what occurred at the dedication of the first temple in order, again, to emphasize the continuity with an earlier time of celebration.

The Hebrew word translated *sang* indicates antiphonal singing on this occasion: two groups singing in response to each other. Then *all the people gave a great shout of praise to the Lord*—a response similar to that given when David brought the ark of the covenant to Jerusalem (1 Chronicles 15:28).

C. Perceptions (vv. 12, 13)

12, 13But many of the older priests and Levites and family heads, who had seen the former temple, wept aloud when they saw the foundation of this temple being laid, while many others shouted for joy. No one could distinguish the sound of the shouts of joy from the sound of weeping, because the people made so much noise. And the sound was heard far away.

The *former*, or first, *temple* had been destroyed about 50 years earlier; thus, some of the older priests and Levites remembered how it had looked. In their eyes the second temple appeared greatly inferior (see Haggai 2:1-3). They could see the material that had been collected for this second project, and it was obvious that their temple could never measure up to the majesty and splendor of Solomon's. They also knew that, despite the various offerings of gold and silver that had been given toward building the temple, it could not even remotely match the amount of gold and silver that had adorned Solomon's magnificent structure.

Many others, however, *shouted for joy*. Presumably, these were the younger ones among those gathered. Having not seen Solomon's temple, they could not contrast it with the one currently being built. For both old and young, this was a deeply emotional moment; and those of each group expressed their feelings with great intensity.

III. Completing the Project (Ezra 6:14-16)

Previously it was noted that those who returned to Judah from captivity in Babylon went to work building an altar on which to offer sacrifices, "despite their fear of the peoples around them" (Ezra 3:3). These peoples later expressed a desire to assist in building the second temple; but the Jewish leaders refused their offer, apparently because of the pagan influences that had affected the religion of these people. Those returning from Babylon were especially sensitive to such pagan influences, because they were painfully aware that those influences had resulted in the captivity from which they had just been set free. In addition, these other peoples had not returned to Judah with the captives. The right to rebuild the temple belonged only to the returning Jews.

Angered by such a response, these peoples then began to hinder the work on the temple in any way they could (Ezra 4:4, 5). For approximately sixteen years, the temple lay partially completed—a sad testimony to the failure of God's people to complete the project they had begun so willingly.

Then, as often happened during critical periods in Old Testament history, God raised up prophets to challenge his people. On this occasion, Haggai and Zechariah came forward to stir up an indifferent people to resume work on the long-neglected temple and give first place to the things of God. As a result the people resumed building in the year 520 BC (Ezra 5:1, 2; Haggai 1:14, 15).

That action brought questions from the Persian officials in the area. A project of such proportions could have subversive designs. The situation was explained to the regional governor, and he was told that permission for the construction had been received from Cyrus shortly after he conquered Babylon in 539 BC (Ezra 5:3-17).

The new king, Darius, upon hearing the report, ordered that a search be made for the original decree. It was found in Ecbatana (Ezra 6:1, 2)—the summer home of the Persian rulers, situated in the mountains of Media almost 300 miles northeast of Babylon. Darius then ordered that the work must continue and that the royal revenues of the area be used to assist in the project and insure its completion (vv. 6-12).

A. Resuming the Work (vv. 14, 15)

14So the elders of the Jews continued to build and prosper under the preaching of Haggai the prophet and Zechariah, a descendant of Iddo. They finished building the temple according to the command of the God of Israel and the decrees of Cyrus, Darius and Artaxerxes, kings of Persia.

As Ezra wrote this account, perhaps up to 80 years after the events he was describing, he recorded the fact that many people were responsible for the rebuilding of the temple. It involved the work of *the elders of the Jews* as well as the forceful exhortations of *Haggai the prophet and Zechariah*. But behind them all was *the God of Israel*.

The influence of three Persian *kings* is also cited. They include *Cyrus* (who gave the original decree for the project in 538 BC), *Darius* (who enforced the decree of Cyrus when it was found), and *Artaxerxes*. This Darius was not the Mede who "took over the kingdom" on the night Belshazzar was slain in fulfillment of the handwriting on the wall (Daniel 5:31). Apparently that Darius served as a governor under the authority of Cyrus. The Darius mentioned in the verse before us was another man, who ruled the Persian Empire from 521 to 486 BC. He was the ruler who ordered the search for Cyrus's decree authorizing the rebuilding of the temple.

The mention of Artaxerxes may seem surprising, for his reign was much later, from 465 to 424 BC, during the time when Ezra and Nehemiah carried out their ministries. Ezra, however, was likely making a very wise gesture by including the name of the king of his own time; for Artaxerxes also provided significant assistance to the Jews (Ezra 7:11-28; Nehemiah 2:1-8). This also served to introduce Artaxerxes in preparation for his part in the remainder of the book of Ezra.

¹⁵The temple was completed on the third day of the month Adar, in the sixth year of the reign of King Darius.

The precise date is given for the completion of this important project. *Adar* was (and still is) the twelfth *month* of the year in the Jewish calendar. It did not come at the beginning of winter as our twelfth month of December does, but at the end of winter—around the last part of February and the first part of March. *The sixth year of the reign of King Darius* was 516 BC.

B. Rejoicing in the Achievement (v. 16)

¹⁶Then the people of Israel—the priests, the Levites and the rest of the exiles—celebrated the dedication of the house of God with joy.

Everyone joined in *the dedication of the house of God*. The work itself had been a cooperative effort, and the celebration was for all. When the foundations of the temple were laid, two sounds had been heard: joy and weeping (Ezra 3:12, 13). This time only the emotion of *joy* was expressed. A significant milestone had been reached.

NEHEMIAH PREPARES TO REBUILD THE WALLS OF JERUSALEM (NEHEMIAH 1:1-4; 2:1-8, 17, 18)

Establishing the Groundwork

Nehemiah was a contemporary of Ezra. This is clear from reading Nehemiah 8:9 and 12:31-36. (No doubt they had more contact with one another than on just these two occasions.) Both were born into families that had been carried into captivity by the Babylonians. After the Persians overthrew the Babylonians in 539 BC, many Jews took advantage of the decree of King Cyrus and returned to their homeland. But others chose to remain in Babylon, where God used some of them to carry out his purpose on behalf of his people. Daniel is perhaps the best example of this. He (and his three friends) were promoted to high positions in the Babylonian government (Daniel 2:48, 49). Then when the Persians conquered Babylon, they promptly gave Daniel a position of great authority among them (Daniel 6:1-3).

Another example is Nehemiah, who gained a prominent post in the service of the Persian king, Artaxerxes. He describes himself as a "cupbearer" (Nehemiah 1:11), but he was not a menial servant as such a title might seem to suggest. In this position, Nehemiah enjoyed the king's trust and had ready access to his ear. These advantages Nehemiah was able to use to the benefit of his people.

Examining the Text

I. Request for News (Nehemiah 1:1-4)
A. Discouraging Report (vv. 1-3)

¹The words of Nehemiah son of Hacaliah:
In the month of Kislev in the twentieth year, while I was in the citadel of Susa.

The account of Nehemiah's life began as autumn was turning to winter, for *the month of Kislev* corresponds to the last part of November and the first part of December on our calendars. The *twentieth year* of Artaxerxes, king of Persia (2:1) was 445 BC. Nehemiah describes himself as being *in the citadel of Susa*, which was the winter capital of Persia. (There were actually four capital cities in the Persian Empire; the Persian kings often went to Susa to reside during the winter because of the milder climate there.) More than 90 years had now passed since the Jews were released from captivity in Babylon. Approximately 70 years had passed since the completion of the temple in Jerusalem.

²Hanani, one of my brothers, came from Judah with some other men, and I questioned them about the Jewish remnant that survived the exile, and also about Jerusalem.

At some point, *Hanani*, one of Nehemiah's *brothers*, had chosen to make the nearly 1,000 mile journey to *Judah* and back again along with *some other men*. Hanani's return offered the opportunity to learn about the status of two matters in particular: *the Jewish remnant that survived the exile* and was now living in Judah and the condition of the city of *Jerusalem*.

> ³**They said to me, "Those who survived the exile and are back in the province are in great trouble and disgrace. The wall of Jerusalem is broken down, and its gates have been burned with fire."**

The answer Nehemiah received was most disheartening. The Jews, now in their old homeland, were *in great trouble and disgrace*. The primary source of that trouble and disgrace was the fact that *the wall of Jerusalem* remained *broken down* and its *gates* were in disrepair. This damage may have been the result of Nebuchadnezzar's troops ravaging the city, when they "set fire to God's temple and broke down the wall of Jerusalem" (2 Chronicles 36:19. But that event had taken place nearly a century and a half earlier. Some suggest a more recent series of events was behind Jerusalem's plight. Ezra 4:8-16 records a letter from certain Persian officials to Artaxerxes at some point during his reign, reporting that the Jews were rebuilding the walls of "rebellious" Jerusalem, undoubtedly seen as prelude to revolt. Artaxerxes responded by giving those officials permission to stop that rebuilding (Ezra 4:17-23). It is possible that the Persian authorities not only stopped construction of new walls (v. 23), but also ended up tearing down those walls that had been rebuilt to that point (v. 12). This series of events may be what Hanani and his colleagues were describing to Nehemiah.

Whatever the circumstances, for the city to remain in such a deplorable state was devastating news to hear. Obviously the residents were under constant threat of being attacked by outsiders and having their possessions stolen, because a city without walls was an easy target.

B. Dramatic Reaction (v. 4)

⁴**When I heard these things, I sat down and wept. For some days I mourned and fasted and prayed before the God of heaven.**

Nehemiah's concern for the land of his forefathers was profound. His weeping, mourning, fasting, and prayer did not last for hours, but *for some days!* Some suggest that Nehemiah was ashamed because he had stayed in the East to live in the king's palace instead of going to help restore his homeland. The text gives no hint of this, however.

The remainder of chapter 1 includes Nehemiah's passionate prayer for his people. Nehemiah acknowledged God as "great and awesome" (v. 5). He confessed the sins of not only the nation of Israel but of himself and his father's house as well (vv. 6, 7). He concluded his plea with a request that he be granted "favor in the presence of this man"—a reference to King Artaxerxes, before whom Nehemiah served as cupbearer (v. 11). It is clear from this request that Nehemiah was already thinking of doing something to remedy the desperate conditions in his homeland. He knew he could not take such a step without the king's approval.

II. Request for Help (Nehemiah 2:1-8)
A. Nehemiah's Sadness (vv. 1-3)

1aIn the month of Nisan in the twentieth year of King Artaxerxes, when wine was brought for him, I took the wine and gave it to the king.

The reference to *the month of Nisan* indicates that four months had passed since Nehemiah first heard the news about Jerusalem's distress. Thus Nehemiah had had a lot of time in which to think, weep, and pray before his encounter with the king. He also must have been waiting for an appropriate time to mention his concerns to the king.

Nehemiah had previously described himself as "cupbearer to the king" (Nehemiah 1:11). This was an important office but also risky. The cupbearer had to taste any *wine* brought before *the king*. Thus, if it had been secretly poisoned by an enemy of the king, the king would know it before drinking the wine himself. The cupbearer had to be someone whom the king trusted completely, and so he often became a confidant and informal counselor of a king, and someone who could influence a king's decisions. Like Esther in the book that bears her name, God had placed one of his people at the right place at the right time in order to help all of them.

1b, 2aI had not been sad in his presence before; so the king asked me, "Why does your face look so sad when you are not ill? This can be nothing but sadness of heart."

One's face can divulge what a person is feeling. The fact that Nehemiah *had not been sad* in the king's *presence before* means that Nehemiah had been able to disguise his feelings over the past four months—putting on a happy face, as it were. But on this particular day, his anguish over his people's condition showed.

King Artaxerxes showed genuine concern over the emotional state of his cupbearer. This may say something about the king's capacity for empathy. It also says something about the character of Nehemiah that he was the kind of person about whom the king genuinely cared.

At the same time, the king may have had another motive for asking his question. A gloomy appearance could be evidence of a plot against the king. The courts of ancient kings were often hotbeds of intrigue. (Indeed, the king's own father had been assassinated by a member of the court.) So a king had good reason to be suspicious of any change in mood among his servants.

> ²ᵇ, ³*I was very much afraid, but I said to the king, "May the king live forever! Why should my face not look sad when the city where my fathers are buried lies in ruins, and its gates have been destroyed by fire?"*

The fact that Nehemiah *was very much afraid* about saying why he was sad was not unreasonable. Artaxerxes had the power of life and death over Nehemiah. If indeed the gates of Jerusalem had earlier been burned in conjunction with a real or imagined revolt against Persian authority (see the earlier comments on Nehemiah 1:3), then the showing of sympathy for Jerusalem might be taken by the king as treason.

We should pause to note the rather discerning way in which Nehemiah described Jerusalem. He said nothing of the reasons why Jerusalem's gates came to be burned (whether originally in 586 BC or more recently). Instead he emphasized the fact that *the city where my fathers are buried lies in ruins.* This fact may have been designed to tug at the king's emotions. Often the way a matter is presented determines how it is received.

B. Nehemiah's Strategy (vv. 4-8)

> ⁴*The king said to me, "What is it you want?"*
> *Then I prayed to the God of heaven,*

In those days, one did not ask kings for favors as easily as people in Western countries make demands of their elected officials. The proper protocol was to wait for the king's invitation. Artaxerxes could tell Nehemiah wanted something, so he invited him to make his request.

Nehemiah had an answer ready, but before giving it he offered a quick prayer to the greater King. If his petition displeased the king, Nehemiah might be demoted, fired, jailed, or even executed. So he *prayed* as he made his request. (Throughout this book, Nehemiah is pictured as a man of prayer: 1:4; 4:4, 9; 5:19; 6:9, 14; 13:14, 22, 29, 31).

> ⁵ *. . . and I answered the king, "If it pleases the king and if your servant has found favor in his sight, let him send me to the city in Judah where my fathers are buried so that I can rebuild it."*

Nehemiah not only wanted time off; he also wanted the king to *send* him to *rebuild* Jerusalem. This meant that the Persian government would assume the cost of the trip and of rebuilding the ruined walls and gates.

⁶Then the king, with the queen sitting beside him, asked me, "How long will your journey take, and when will you get back?" It pleased the king to send me; so I set a time.

The king's reaction was favorable. Though he had previously opposed having the walls of Jerusalem rebuilt (Ezra 4:20, 21), there were a number of reasons for him to grant Nehemiah's request. It would be good for the Persian Empire to have a well-fortified city in Judah. It could provide additional defense against the armies of Egypt or cut off an alliance between the Greeks (who by this time had become a force to be reckoned with) and Egyptians. Though Persia was currently at peace with both those nations, this arrangement was tentative at best. The king knew that Nehemiah was capable and loyal—the kind of man who could administer the building of a city and not betray him to his enemies. So the king was *pleased* to send Nehemiah, and his question was practical and businesslike: how long would it take to do the job?

In response Nehemiah *set a time*. This is another indication that Nehemiah had thought much about this project. He was able to estimate how long it would take to do what he wanted to do. The text does not tell us the specific time set by Nehemiah, but his absence ended up being 12 years (see Nehemiah 5:14; 13:6). His stay may well have extended beyond his original estimate, but if so he could have corresponded with the king and received permission to extend his visit.

⁷I also said to him, "If it pleases the king, may I have letters to the governors of Trans-Euphrates, so that they will provide me safe-conduct until I arrive in Judah?

Again we see that Nehemiah had been thinking and planning. All *the governors of Trans-Euphrates* (a term describing territories east of the Euphrates River) were subject to the king. Nehemiah needed letters ordering them to allow him to pass safely through their territories until he arrived in *Judah*.

⁸"And may I have a letter to Asaph, keeper of the king's forest, so he will give me timber to make beams for the gates of the citadel by the temple and for the city wall and for the residence I will occupy?" And because the gracious hand of my God was upon me, the king granted my requests.

Nehemiah then asked for a more costly favor. He needed *timber* from *the king's forest*. Some students think that this refers to a woodland near Jerusalem; but earlier rebuilders of Jerusalem had brought timber from Lebanon, far to the north (Ezra 3:7). It seems probable that Nehemiah would do the same. Stone for the walls was available at Jerusalem, but there would be several *gates* in the walls. Probably each gate would be enclosed in a tower. Heavy timber would be needed for the upper floor of a tower and for the large doors.

The citadel was a fort that overlooked the temple. It, too, would need timber for upper floors and for doors. In addition, Nehemiah planned a house for himself. This would probably include not only his *residence*, but also offices for himself and other officials of Jerusalem. All told, this was no small amount of timber for which Nehemiah was asking; but the king promptly granted it. Nehemiah had been praying for just such a response, and now he gave credit to *the gracious hand of my God.*

III. Request for Action (Nehemiah 2:17, 18a)

Having received the king's permission and support, Nehemiah proceeded to Judah with a military escort ordered by the king. His arrival brought no little measure of grief to Sanballat and Tobiah, leaders of neighboring peoples who did not want to see the Jews succeed.

After arriving in Jerusalem, Nehemiah waited three days, probably resting up from his long trip (vv. 9-11). Verses 12-16 then record how Nehemiah, accompanied by a few trusted men, went out secretly by night to survey the ruined walls.

A. Recommendation (v. 17)

¹⁷Then I said to them, "You see the trouble we are in: Jerusalem lies in ruins, and its gates have been burned with fire. Come, let us rebuild the wall of Jerusalem, and we will no longer be in disgrace."

Then does not necessarily mean the day after Nehemiah's survey of the city. We do not know how long Nehemiah and his men consulted and planned before deciding that the time was right to make their plans known. At that point Nehemiah spoke to *them*. This can mean any or all of the people listed in verse 16: the priests, nobles, officials, and others of the Jews. Perhaps Nehemiah spoke first with some of the leaders, and then met with all the people.

Nehemiah's presentation was in three parts. First was the need: *You see the trouble we are in.* A quick glance at the ruins all around them made this clear. Second was the remedy: *Come, let us rebuild the wall of Jerusalem.* The people will not have a wall unless they go to work and build it. Third was the result of rebuilding: *we will no longer be in disgrace.* Until the rubble of the old wall was cleared away and a new wall was built, *Jerusalem* could not have the dignity, respect, and protection of an important city.

18ªI also told them about the gracious hand of my God upon me and what the king had said to me.

Nehemiah cited two factors that would encourage his hearers in the work of rebuilding the walls. First, he was sure that *the gracious hand* of *God* was helping him. Evidence of this was seen in the success of his project thus far. Second, he had the support of *the king*. Standing before him was yet another factor. This was the people whose strong hands could build a city—if only their hearts were as strong as their hands.

B. Response (v. 18b)

18ᵇThey replied, "Let us start rebuilding." So they began this good work.

Nehemiah got the response he wanted. We need not suppose it came instantly or even unanimously. There may have been questions, discussion, or even some opposition. But Nehemiah's careful, prayerful preparation silenced any critics and ignited a fire in the hearts of any who had previously been discouraged at a task such as Nehemiah was proposing. *So they began this good work.*

FACING OPPOSITION AND FINISHING THE TASK (NEHEMIAH 4:15-20; 6:15, 16)

Establishing the Groundwork

The enemies of the Jews ridiculed their project of rebuilding the wall of Jerusalem (Nehemiah 2:19, 20; 4:1-3). The Jews, however, took it seriously. Quickly they organized the workers and began the task, assigning certain portions of the wall to the various groups (Nehemiah 3). With enthusiasm and energy they built the wall to half its intended height, "for the people worked with all their heart" (Nehemiah 4:6). But the opposition remained as determined as those who were engaged in the rebuilding effort. Nehemiah 4:6-9 records the efforts of certain individuals and groups to thwart the undertaking. Verse 9 notes the use of both divine and human resources in protecting the people: "But we prayed to our God and posted a guard day and night to meet this threat."

Verse 10 cites another source of discouragement—one that came from among the workers themselves, as some voiced concern over both the stamina of the workers and the size of the task that lay ahead. Again, Nehemiah responded with careful planning: he stationed people at the most vulnerable portions of the wall and armed them with swords, spears, and bows (v. 13). He then encouraged them not to forget their spiritual "armor": "Remember the Lord, who is great and awesome" (v. 14).

Examining the Text

I. Equipping the People (Nehemiah 4:15-20)
A. Weapons Supplied (vv. 15-18)

15When our enemies heard that we were aware of their plot and that God had frustrated it, we all returned to the wall, each to his own work.

God had frustrated the *plot* to attack and even murder the workers (vv. 11, 12) by seeing that a warning reached the workers, thus giving them the opportunity to arm themselves.

16, 17aFrom that day on, half of my men did the work, while the other half were equipped with spears, shields, bows and armor. The officers posted themselves behind all the people of Judah who were building the wall.

Those whom Nehemiah describes as *my men* may refer to a special group of *officers* or workers who worked closely with him. Some of them may have accompanied him from Persia. Previously they had been assigned to construction work, but now, in light of the increasing threats to the people's safety, their efforts were divided between working and defending. *Half* of them *did the work* on the wall, *while the other half were equipped with* the weapons of war normally used in that day. The other Jews at work on the wall are called *the people of Judah*. Most likely they were working in the family groups and trade groups as described in Nehemiah 3. *The officers* were the leaders of each group. They *posted themselves behind* the builders to act as both foremen and guards, and were prepared to assume a military role if necessary.

17bThose who carried materials did their work with one hand and held a weapon in the other,

Some of the men were doing work that could be done *with one hand*. For example, some must have been clearing rubble out of the way (v. 10). A man could pick up trash with one hand and put it in a basket. Then two men could carry the basket between them, each holding a side of it with one hand while his other hand held a sword or spear or bow.

18a . . . and each of the builders wore his sword at his side as he worked.

Some of the work, of course, could not be done one-handed. If a man needed both hands to do his job, he had a sword fastened to his belt so that he could become a soldier at a moment's notice.

18bBut the man who sounded the trumpet stayed with me.

As supervisor of the entire project, Nehemiah was constantly moving about to keep in touch with all that was going on. Workers at the other end of the city might be half a mile away. Nehemiah had no radio to communicate with them, but he had a trumpeter. That man *stayed* beside Nehemiah continually.

B. Words Spoken (vv. 19, 20)

19Then I said to the nobles, the officials and the rest of the people, "The work is extensive and spread out, and we are widely separated from each other along the wall.

Alone on its section of the wall, a small group of workers would be easy prey for a band of guerrilla fighters that might charge through a nearby space where a gate was to be built. Nehemiah did not want any group to face such an assault alone.

20"Wherever you hear the sound of the trumpet, join us there. Our God will fight for us!"

At this point the wall was only half as high as it was going to be (v. 6), but it was high enough so that someone on top of it would have a clear view of the surrounding territory. Nehemiah could not be everywhere at once, but armed men could be spaced around the city to keep watch in all directions. If one of them saw a hostile party coming, he could wave or send a runner across town to Nehemiah. The trumpeter could then run swiftly to the threatened point, and the trumpet call would bring other armed men to that point. Explaining this plan, Nehemiah added that the men would not be alone in battle: *Our God will fight for us!* Once more we see illustrated Nehemiah's blend of both wise planning and steadfast trust in the Lord.

II. Ending the Project (Nehemiah 6:15, 16)
A. Finished Wall (v. 15)

15So the wall was completed on the twenty-fifth of Elul, in fifty-two days.

At last *the wall* was finished! Both the completion date and the time the project took are mentioned here: *the twenty-fifth of Elul, in fifty-two days.* This would have been in our month of October, in the year 445 BC. Within six months after Nehemiah received approval for his project from King Artaxerxes, the job was *completed.*

Some doubt that such a project as this could have been completed in such a short time. But we need to remember several factors. First, the city of Jerusalem at this time was smaller than modern Jerusalem. Second, the Babylonians probably had not completely torn down the entire wall. Third, the people doing the task did not have to quarry the stones; they had to dig them out of the rubble. Fourth, the people were working under considerable pressure; and people will often work harder and faster under those conditions. Finally, and most important, the blessing of God on this effort should not be minimized in any way. The entire effort had been undergirded with prayer from the very start. Even Nehemiah's enemies could not deny this, as the next verse states.

B. Frustrated Enemies (v. 16)

16When all our enemies heard about this, all the surrounding nations were afraid and lost their self-confidence, because they realized that this work had been done with the help of our God.

The *enemies* of God's people from *all the surrounding nations* had been watching closely the progress on the wall and had done all they could to intimidate the workers and frustrate their efforts. Earlier Nehemiah had encouraged the workers not to be afraid (Nehemiah 4:14). Now it was the enemies who *were afraid and lost their self-confidence*. They could attribute the success of the undertaking to nothing except the *help* of *God*.

The completion of the wall did not solve all of the Jews' problems. The remainder of the book of Nehemiah chronicles a series of issues within the city that Nehemiah had to confront, including the failure to bring tithes to support the Lord's work, the conducting of business on the Sabbath, and the marriages of men of Judah to women from pagan peoples. In each situation, Nehemiah demonstrated the kind of courageous leadership that he had exercised in spearheading the rebuilding of the wall of Jerusalem. Leaders of the Lord's people today can learn much from Nehemiah's example.

How to Say It

ADAR. *Ay*-dar.

ARTAXERXES. Are-tuh-*zerk*-seez.

ASAPH. *Ay*-saff.

ASSYRIANS. Uh-*sear*-e-unz.

BABYLONIAN. Bab-ih-*low*-nee-un.

BELSHAZZAR. Bel-*shazz*-er.

CYRUS. *Sigh*-russ.

DARIUS. Duh-*rye*-us.

ECBATANA. Ek-buh-*tahn*-uh.

ELUL. *Ee*-lull or Eh-lool.

EUPHRATES. You-*fray*-teez.

HACALIAH. Hack-uh-*lye*-uh.

HANANI. Huh-*nay*-nye.

IDDO. *Id*-do.

JECONIAH. *Jek*-o-*nye*-uh (strong accent on *nye*).

JEHOIACHIN. Jeh-*hoy*-uh-kin.

JEHOZADAK. Jeh-*hoz*-uh-dak.

JESHUA. *Jesh*-you-uh.

JOZADAK. *Joz*-uh-dak.

JUDAH. *Joo*-duh.

KISLEV. *Kiss*-lev.

NEBUCHADNEZZAR. *Neb*-yuh-kud-*nez*-er (strong accent on *nez*).

NISAN. *Nye*-san.

ROSH HASHANAH. Rawsh Huh-*shaw*-nuh.

SAMARIA. Suh-*mare*-ee-uh.

SAMARITANS. Suh-*mare*-uh-tunz.

SANBALLAT. San-*bal*-ut.

SERAIAH. Se-*ray*-yuh or Se-*rye*-uh.

SHEALTIEL. She-*al*-tee-el.

SHESHBAZZAR. Shesh-*baz*-ar.

SUSA. *Soo*-suh.

TOBIAH. Toe-*bye*-uh.

ZECHARIAH. *Zek*-uh-*rye*-uh (strong accent on *rye*).

ZERUBBABEL. Zeh-*rub*-uh-bul.

Chapter 13

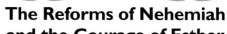

The Reforms of Nehemiah and the Courage of Esther

Nehemiah 8:1-12; 9:32-38; Esther 3:1-6; 4:7-16; 8:3-8; 9:17-23

READING GOD'S LAW TO THE PEOPLE (NEHEMIAH 8:1-12)

Establishing the Groundwork

As important as the completion of the wall around Jerusalem was, it did not insure the safety of the city. Nehemiah 7:4 notes, "Now the city was large and spacious, but there were few people in it, and the houses had not yet been rebuilt." Because the city had so few residents (and therefore defenders), special care had to be taken to guard the wall and the city gates. Nehemiah had delegated some of his leadership duties to two men: Hanani, his brother who had first informed him of the dismal conditions in Jerusalem (Nehemiah 1:1-3), and Hananiah, who is described as "a man of integrity [who] feared God more than most men do" (Nehemiah 7:2). He told these men to appoint some of the residents of the city as guards to assist in protecting the city from any attackers (v. 3).

The remainder of chapter 7 is largely a record of the families who had returned to Judah from the Babylonian captivity. The list is practically a duplicate of the one found in Ezra 2. Probably Nehemiah used it as a starting point for taking a census and organizing the people for the defense and development of Jerusalem. Nehemiah recognized that a critical ingredient of the city's stability was the people's knowledge of and adherence to God's law. The wall had been completed in the sixth month of Elul (Nehemiah 6:15). The seventh month included several significant religious celebrations for God's people, including the Day of Atonement and the Feast of Tabernacles. This emphasis was used to call the people to rededicate themselves to God's law.

It will be noted in the following study that Ezra was present for this time of rededication. Ezra's reputation as a "teacher well versed in the Law of Moses" (Ezra 7:6) has already been cited. The following text records that he was also a priest (Nehemiah 8:2, 9). He had come to Judah in 458 BC and was quite upset to see the degree to which that law was being ignored. A particularly disturbing matter involved men of Judah who had taken wives from among the pagans who lived nearby (Ezra 9:1-15). Ezra confronted the men who had done this, and they agreed that they must end these marriages that God's law had forbidden (Ezra 10:1-17).

Some students believe that Ezra at some point returned to the East for a time, and that in his absence injustice and lawbreaking increased. When Nehemiah came to rebuild Jerusalem's wall in 445 BC, he had to deal with the problems that were mentioned at the conclusion of the preceding chapter. By the time the wall was completed, it is believed that Ezra had returned to Judah; and the people were looking to him for further teaching about the law. Perhaps he encouraged organizing the kind of observance that is described in the following passage.

Examining the Text

I. Public Reading of the Law (Nehemiah 8:1-6)
A. The Audience (vv. 1, 2)

¹All the people assembled as one man in the square before the Water Gate. They told Ezra the scribe to bring out the Book of the Law of Moses, which the Lord had commanded for Israel.

The fact that *all the people assembled* together *as one man* reflects a unity of purpose. The same phrase was used when the returnees gathered together and made plans to restore proper worship (Ezra 3:1). The place where they met, *in the square before the Water Gate*, was located at the east wall of Jerusalem. It had that name because the people went through it to bring water from a spring outside the wall. The street leading to that gate widened into a square inside the wall. A great number of armed men could gather there to oppose enemies who might try to smash the gate with a battering ram. The same square provided space for a peaceful assembly (such as this one) when no enemy was in sight.

The people gathered on this occasion because they wanted *Ezra the scribe* to teach them more about the law. Literally, the word scribe means "writer." But when a writer painstakingly made copies of the Scriptures by hand, naturally he came to know those Scriptures very well and could teach them to others. Thus the word *scribe* came to signify a scholar and teacher. That is what Ezra had proved himself to be; in fact, the Hebrew word translated "teacher" in Ezra 7:6 is the same as that translated *scribe* in the verse before us. In addition, the Hebrew word for *Book* comes from the same root word as that for *scribe*.

The *Book of the Law of Moses* used by Ezra on this occasion should not be thought of as hundreds of flat pages bound between hard covers like a modern book. Rather, it was a long strip, probably of parchment, and perhaps about 18 inches wide. It could be rolled up for storage and unrolled for reading. Moses had received the law from God and had written it down some 1,000 years before (though we do not know the age of the copy Ezra used). Although very old, that *which the Lord had commanded for Israel* had not lost any of its authority; it was still the Word of God in Ezra's day.

> *²So on the first day of the seventh month Ezra the priest brought the Law before the assembly, which was made up of men and women and all who were able to understand.*

The inclusion of *women and all who were able to understand* (that is, older children) showed the seriousness of the occasion. Moses had commanded that the words of *the Law* be read every seven years during the Feast of Tabernacles and that "men, women and children, and the aliens living in your towns" be assembled for this reading (Deuteronomy 31:9-13). We do not know that this was a seventh year, but perhaps the reading of the law had been neglected during the captivity and return. It was deemed appropriate at this time—*the first day of the seventh month*, which coincided with the Feast of Trumpets (Leviticus 23:23, 24; Numbers 29:1-6) and the beginning of the Jewish year on the civil calendar. Also, the wall had been completed on the 25th day of the previous month of Elul (Nehemiah 6:15); so this occasion provided a welcome respite from that effort.

B. The Reader (vv. 3-6)

> *³He read it aloud from daybreak till noon as he faced the square before the Water Gate in the presence of the men, women and others who could understand. And all the people listened attentively to the Book of the Law.*

This was no 20-minute sermon! *From daybreak until noon* would have covered at least five hours. Perhaps *all the people listened attentively* because God was very prominent in their thoughts as they looked around with amazement and gratitude at the newly rebuilt walls of the city.

We have no way knowing exactly what was included in the *Book of the Law* that Ezra *read*. The term *Law* sometimes refers to the Pentateuch, the first five books of the Old Testament. But that does not seem to be the case here, for Ezra could read what he read and others explain it (v. 8) in half a day. Perhaps he read only those portions of the Pentateuch that applied to the situation at hand or to the specific issues confronting the people.

⁴Ezra the scribe stood on a high wooden platform built for the occasion. Beside him on his right stood Mattithiah, Shema, Anaiah, Uriah, Hilkiah and Maaseiah; and on his left were Pedaiah, Mishael, Malkijah, Hashum, Hashbaddanah, Zechariah and Meshullam.

The biggest part of the preparation for this event may have been the building of a *high wooden platform*. It had to be big enough and strong enough to support Ezra and the other men listed in this chapter. We suppose the 13 cited here were Ezra's fellow priests or other men of influence who took their place with Ezra to indicate their support of what he was doing. Ezra *stood* in the middle of the group, with six of the men *on his right* and the other seven *on his left*. This was an appropriate place for him to be, given his part in reading the law.

⁵Ezra opened the book. All the people could see him because he was standing above them; and as he opened it, the people all stood up.

Apparently most of the people had been sitting on the ground while Ezra and his companions assembled on the stage. Then Ezra held the sacred scroll on which the law was written and started to unroll it. *All the people* rose to their feet to show respect for the Word of God.

⁶Ezra praised the LORD, the great God; and all the people lifted their hands and responded, "Amen! Amen!" Then they bowed down and worshiped the LORD with their faces to the ground.

Before beginning his reading, *Ezra praised the Lord*. This may have been something similar to what we call an invocation. The people *lifted their hands* in worship, perhaps symbolizing their longing for God (much as a child raises his or her hands to a parent when in need). Their twofold response of *"Amen! Amen!"* showed their intensity of emotion. Then in humility *they bowed down . . . with their faces to the ground*. It is obvious that their worship of the Lord as *the great God* was genuine.

II. Public Explanation of the Law (Nehemiah 8:7, 8)
A. The Teachers (v. 7)

⁷The Levites—Jeshua, Bani, Sherebiah, Jamin, Akkub, Shabbethai, Hodiah, Maaseiah, Kelita, Azariah, Jozabad, Hanan and Pelaiah—instructed the people in the Law while the people were standing there.

The meeting began with worship that was united, fervent, and reverent. But the people had come primarily to listen to the Word of God and to learn from it. Well might their opening prayer be that of the psalmist: "Open my eyes that I may see wonderful things in your law" (Psalm 119:18).

In verse 4, we counted 14 people on the platform (including Ezra). Now we see there were many more. (The term *the Levites* includes those individuals listed here, but there are additional names listed in Nehemiah 10:9-13.) These men *instructed the people in the Law* in the manner described in the next verse.

B. The Technique (v. 8)

⁸They read from the Book of the Law of God, making it clear and giving the meaning so that the people could understand what was being read.

The first step in this task of teaching the people the *Book of the Law of God* was *making it clear*. All of us need additional help in understanding the Bible at one time or another. Some of this need can be attributed to changes in the English language. For this reason, some of the many new Bible translations that have come out can be very useful to us. This matter of change in language was even truer in Ezra's situation. Moses wrote the law about a thousand years before Ezra read it to the people, so imagine how the Hebrew language had changed in that span of time! In fact, the Hebrew language by this time was beginning to fade out of common use; and Aramaic was taking its place. The Jews in this post-exilic period needed a lot of help understanding a book that was a thousand years old, and Ezra had a lot of help in explaining it.

The second step involved *giving the meaning*. After making sure that the text itself was understood, the readers offered the proper interpretation of what they read, carefully explaining a particular statement or section of text and then telling how that passage applied to the audience. This is preaching and teaching at its finest! When we study and learn from godly teachers today and apply the Bible to our lives, then we can become students who "correctly [handle] the word of truth" (2 Timothy 2:15).

III. Public Reaction to the Law (Nehemiah 8:9-12)
A. Call to Joy (vv. 9-11)

⁹Then Nehemiah the governor, Ezra the priest and scribe, and the Levites who were instructing the people said to them all, "This day is sacred to the LORD your God. Do not mourn or weep." For all the people had been weeping as they listened to the words of the Law.

As the people listened to the words of the Law, they began weeping. Apparently they realized how far they had strayed from the divine standards within it. Their reaction was similar to King Josiah's when he heard the law read by his secretary Shaphan. Josiah even tore his robes in his anguish over the people's disobedience of the law (2 Kings 22:10, 11). On this occasion in Nehemiah's day, when the law was made clear to the people, many realized how badly they had been violating it. They were overcome with shame, grief, and fear.

However, there is a proper time for grief and a proper time for joy (Ecclesiastes 3:4). The reading of the law had convicted the people of their sin. But this was also a time to celebrate God's goodness. The first day of any month on the Jewish calendar was observed with special religious ceremonies (see Numbers 28:11-15). However, as previously noted, the first day of the seventh month (which this day was, according to verse 2) had added meaning because it marked the first day of a new year on the civil calendar. Mourning and *weeping* were not appropriate for such a *sacred* day. One wonders if the people's lack of familiarity with the law meant that they did not realize the special nature of this day and had not celebrated it, for example, with trumpet blasts as prescribed by the law (Leviticus 23:23-25).

> ¹⁰Nehemiah said, "Go and enjoy choice food and sweet drinks, and send some to those who have nothing prepared. This day is sacred to our Lord. Do not grieve, for the joy of the Lᴏʀᴅ is your strength."

From daybreak until noon the people had been listening attentively, becoming increasingly convicted of their sinful ways. Now Nehemiah encouraged them to *go* and use the rest of the day in joyous celebration. But they were not to be selfish—the finest of *food* and *drinks* were to be shared with people too poor to prepare the best for themselves. And as the people resolved to leave sin behind, they were to remember that *the joy of the Lord* was their *strength* for avoiding future disobedience and its terrible consequences. Some mistakenly believe that the religion of the Old Testament was gloomy and austere, but that was not the case. Joyous festivals were a regular part of the people's religious activity.

> ¹¹The Levites calmed all the people, saying, "Be still, for this is a sacred day. Do not grieve."

The *Levites* mentioned in verse 7 *calmed all the people*. Perhaps they did this by going out among the people gathered to give personal messages of encouragement to those most distressed.

B. Celebration of Learning (v. 12)

> ¹²Then all the people went away to eat and drink, to send portions of food and to celebrate with great joy, because they now understood the words that had been made known to them.

All the people proceeded to follow the instructions given in verse 10. At first the people had wept when the *words* of the law were read, because they realized that they had not kept them. Those same words, however, offered forgiveness and hope to the repentant. Understanding of God's Word still brings joy to all who come to it with an attitude of reverence and a willingness to do what it says—although we may first be challenged to do some serious soul searching as this audience was.

A PRAYER OF CONFESSION (NEHEMIAH 9:32-38)

Establishing the Groundwork

The half day of teaching mentioned in the previous passage apparently only whetted the appetites of those who were present. The next day the people came back for more (Nehemiah 8:13). Later in the same month (the seventh month) came the week-long Feast of Tabernacles, and the law was read every day of the week (vv. 17, 18). And every day the people continued to be confronted by how far they had wandered from the law.

When the Feast of Tabernacles was over, the penitent people decided to set aside additional time for confession of sin. The Feast of Tabernacles was celebrated from the 15th through the 22nd days of the seventh month. On the 24th day of the month, "the Israelites gathered together, fasting and wearing sackcloth and having dust on their heads" (Nehemiah 9:1). Nehemiah 9:3 says, "They stood where they were and read from the Book of the Law of the Lord their God for a quarter of the day, and spent another quarter in confession and in worshiping the Lord their God." Several of the Levites then led in a lengthy prayer, confessing to the Lord that their fathers had forsaken God's law and that they themselves had done no better. They had suffered punishment from God, and they admitted that they deserved it. The next passage focuses on the conclusion of that earnest prayer.

Examining the Text

I. Review of the Past (Nehemiah 9:32-35)
A. Difficult Punishment (v. 32)

32 "Now therefore, O our God, the great, mighty and awesome God, who keeps his covenant of love, do not let all this hardship seem trifling in your eyes—the hardship that has come upon us, upon our kings and leaders, upon our priests and prophets, upon our fathers and all your people, from the days of the kings of Assyria until today.

The Levites who led in prayer understood that God is *great, mighty and awesome*, and that they must approach him reverently. There was nothing casual or flippant about their attitude as they called upon a God before whom they knew they deserved nothing but punishment. Yet they were also aware that this God *keeps his covenant of love*. Earlier in this prayer the Levites had referred to the covenant God had made with Abraham (vv. 7, 8). Then they cited various examples of God's faithfulness toward Abraham's descendants, the children of Israel (vv. 9-15). Those examples, however, were interspersed amidst examples of Israel's disobedience and failure to keep their part of the agreement. The people "became arrogant and stiff-necked, and did not obey your commands" (v. 16). Other examples of this attitude are found in verses 17, 18, and 26-30.

Still, God "did not put an end to them or abandon them" for God is "a gracious and merciful God" (v. 31). The Levites pointed out how God had extended mercy to his people in the past. Their prayer was that he would also show mercy to them in their present desperate situation.

The Levites also noted the *hardship* that they had been through *from the days of the kings of Assyria until today*. These hardships had affected all the *people*, including both the national officials (*kings and leaders*) and the religious leaders (*priests and prophets*). In the middle of the ninth century BC, the northern kingdom of Israel had first come into contact with Assyria. King Jehu of Israel had paid tribute to the Assyrian king at that time, Shalmaneser III. In 722 BC, the Assyrians had captured Samaria, the capital of Israel; and their king, Sargon II, had taken more than 27,000 citizens captive. Later the Assyrians under Sennacherib had turned their aggression toward the southern kingdom of Judah and set their sights on Jerusalem. The Assyrian army, however, never set foot in the city; for God destroyed their army (2 Kings 19:35, 36).

Judah's respite from the Assyrian threat did not mean the end of her hardships. The Assyrians were followed by the Babylonians, and it was they who finally conquered Jerusalem in 586 BC. Many Jews were carried away to exile in Babylon, and those who remained behind felt the heavy hand of the oppressor. After the Persians conquered Babylon in 539 BC, the Jews were allowed to return home; but they still had to pay tribute to Persia. By the time of this event recorded in our text, the hardships that God's people had experienced since the time of the kings of Assyria had lasted some 400 years.

B. Deserved Punishment (vv. 33-35)

33"In all that has happened to us, you have been just; you have acted faithfully, while we did wrong.

The reference to the many hardships in the previous verse was not a complaint against God. The Levites were quick to add that God was entirely *just* in his actions. They deserved all the suffering that God had allowed to come upon them. God had done what was right; they had done what was *wrong*.

34"Our kings, our leaders, our priests and our fathers did not follow your law; they did not pay attention to your commands or the warnings you gave them.

The confession of guilt continued. Here many of the same groups cited as having suffered hardships in verse 32 are declared to be guilty of not following God's *law* or paying *attention* to his *commands* and *warnings*. These groups (*our kings, our leaders, our priests*) were people in positions of authority. They should have set an example of faithful obedience for their people to follow.

35"Even while they were in their kingdom, enjoying your great goodness to them in the spacious and fertile land you gave them, they did not serve you or turn from their evil ways."

God had blessed the people by bringing them into a *spacious and fertile land*. That land was a gift God *gave* the people, and it was to be maintained according to the Giver's terms. But in spite of their many blessings, they forgot God—a warning that Moses had voiced prior to the people's entrance into Canaan (Deuteronomy 8:10-20).

II. Renewal in the Present (Nehemiah 9:36-38)
A. Bitter Conditions (vv. 36, 37)

36"But see, we are slaves today, slaves in the land you gave our forefathers so they could eat its fruit and the other good things it produces.

This portion of the prayer highlighted yet another contrast. When the people of Israel had entered the promised *land*, they were a free people. Now, because of their sins, they were *slaves*. It is true that the Persian yoke they now had to bear was light in comparison to that of the Assyrians and the Babylonians; but still, as a nation they were not free and independent.

37"Because of our sins, its abundant harvest goes to the kings you have placed over us. They rule over our bodies and our cattle as they please. We are in great distress.

The productive land that God had given to the children of Israel still yielded its *abundant harvest*, but not to them. Instead, the productivity went *to the kings you have placed over us.* (Moses had issued a warning of this as well in Deuteronomy 28:33.) This was the present sad plight of Israel, although the Levites had the courage and insight to place the blame squarely where it belonged: *because of our sins.* They also confessed that they were *in great distress.* The Persian rulers drafted their subjects into military service, a practice that may be inferred from the phrase *they rule over our bodies.* Many of the people, in order to pay the tribute exacted by the Persian overlord, were forced to borrow from the rich, at high interest. When they were unable to repay the loans, they would lose the small holdings of land that were theirs. Some even saw their children sold to satisfy their creditors (Nehemiah 5:4, 5).

B. Binding Covenant (v. 38)

[38]*"In view of all this, we are making a binding agreement, putting it in writing, and our leaders, our Levites and our priests are affixing their seals to it."*

Appalled by their history of sin and punishment, the people were ready to add some concrete action to their prayer. They made *a binding agreement* and put it *in writing.* Those who affixed their *seals* to this document (thus making their agreement to it official) and the various groups that supported it are listed in Nehemiah 10:1-29. The specific contents of the agreement are found in verses 30-39. The people recognized that any hope for their future lay in looking to the past—acknowledging their spiritual heritage—and resolving "to follow the Law of God given through Moses the servant of God and to obey carefully all the commands, regulations and decrees of the Lord our Lord" (v. 29).

HAMAN'S PLOT AGAINST THE JEWS (ESTHER 3:1-6; 4:7-16)

Establishing the Groundwork

In our study of the post-exilic period of Old Testament history thus far, we have highlighted three major journeys from the region of the captivity to Judah. The first was in 536 BC under the leadership of Zerubbabel and Jeshua; the second was in 458 BC under Ezra; and the third was in 445 BC under Nehemiah. The story of Esther and her uncle Mordecai took place approximately 20 years before the second return. The presence of these two individuals in Persia is another indication that not all Jews chose to return home from Babylon when King Cyrus issued the decree in 538 BC that allowed them to do so. (See the chart on page 258.)

The Persian king in the book of Esther is Xerxes, who ruled from 486 to 465 BC and was also known by the Greek name of Ahasuerus. The earliest date mentioned in the book is the third year of Xerxes' reign (483 BC) in Esther 1:3, which dates the occasion on which Vashti was deposed as queen. In the seventh year (479 BC), Esther was chosen as queen to replace Vashti. The latest date mentioned is the twelfth year (474 BC), when Haman began his murderous scheme against Mordecai and all the Jews.

One of the unusual characteristics of the book of Esther that is often discussed is the absence of the name of God from the book. In fact, Esther is the only book in the Bible that does not mention God. Yet it is clear from the manner in which the events take place that the hand of God is most certainly at work on behalf of his chosen people. Mordecai's challenge to Esther in Esther 4:14 ("And who knows but that you have come to royal position for such a time as this?") implies that she is not where she is by accident or any "stroke of luck." No doubt the Jews could look back on the events recorded in the book of Esther and see clearly that it was the hand of God that had protected his people from the "vile Haman" (Esther 7:6).

Examining the Text

I. Haman's Hatred (Esther 3:1-6)
A. Haman's Rise to Power (v. 1)

¹After these events, King Xerxes honored Haman son of Hammedatha, the Agagite, elevating him and giving him a seat of honor higher than that of all the other nobles.

The second chapter of the book of Esther mentions two *events* in particular: Esther's selection as queen to replace the deposed Vashti (vv. 1-18) and Mordecai's uncovering of a plot to kill King Xerxes (vv. 19-23). During the process through which Esther was eventually chosen as queen, she had been commanded by Mordecai not to reveal her nationality (Esther 2:10, 20), apparently out of his concern for her safety. That concern was justified. The sinister and murderous intentions of Haman become clear in the text before us. No reason is given for why Haman was elevated and *given a seat of honor higher than that of all the other nobles in Xerxes' court*. Mordecai's unrewarded kindness at the close of chapter 2 is followed with Haman's unexplained promotion.

B. Mordecai's Refusal to Bow (vv. 2-4)

[2, 3]*All the royal officials at the king's gate knelt down and paid honor to Haman, for the king had commanded this concerning him. But Mordecai would not kneel down or pay him honor.*

Then the royal officials at the king's gate asked Mordecai, "Why do you disobey the king's command?"

In ancient Near Eastern courts, it was a common practice for *royal officials* to bow or prostrate themselves before their superiors. We wonder, then, why *the king* had to issue a special order that *Haman* be honored this way. Perhaps Haman had been elevated over other officers that he had previously served, and thus needed the king's command in order to receive the new treatment that was "due" him.

In stark contrast to the vast majority of the officials, *Mordecai would not kneel down or pay him honor*. Why Mordecai would not bow to Haman is not explained in the Scripture. Bowing to a superior out of respect is not forbidden in the Bible; in fact, it gives several examples of Israelites bowing before kings (1 Samuel 24:8; 2 Samuel 14:4; 1 Kings 1:16; and 1 Chronicles 21:21) and other individuals (Genesis 23:7; 33:1-3; and 44:14).

Some students believe Mordecai's refusal involves the long-running hostility between the Israelites and the Amalekites. The description of Haman as "the Agagite" (v. 1) may point in this direction. Agag was an Amalekite king put to death by Samuel after Saul's failure to do so (1 Samuel 15:8, 32, 33). Some believe the name *Agag* was a royal title, as Abimelech was for Philistine kings and Pharaoh for Egyptian kings. If so, then Haman was descended from the royal line of the Amalekites. Roots of antagonism between Amalek and Israel can be traced to the time of the exodus. Not long after their departure from Egypt, the Israelites were viciously attacked by the Amalekites (Exodus 17:8). After the Lord provided victory to his people, he declared to Moses, "I will completely blot out the memory of Amalek," and "The Lord will be at war against the Amalekites from generation to generation" (Exodus 17:14, 16). Mordecai, probably aware of this "holy war," might have refused to kneel before someone identified with a people whom the Lord had purposed to destroy.

Other students believe there was more to Mordecai's refusal than hostility toward a particular race or nation. While Israelites did bow to kings and others, according to the custom of the day, pious Israelites would not bow to false deities (cf. Daniel 3). These students believe there was something of a proclamation of deity attached to the elevation of Haman. This would explain why the court officials had to be commanded to bow to Haman, and it would explain why righteous Mordecai refused.

⁴Day after day they spoke to him but he refused to comply. Therefore they told Haman about it to see whether Mordecai's behavior would be tolerated, for he had told them he was a Jew.

Day after day, Mordecai's fellow officials *spoke to him* about his refusal to bow to Haman. It appears that initially they were concerned about possible consequences. Eventually they informed Haman, *to see whether Mordecai's behavior would be tolerated.* Noted in this verse is the fact that Mordecai had *told* the other officials that *he was a Jew.* Apparently Mordecai linked his refusal to bow before Haman to his being a Jew, though again the specifics of this refusal are not given. (This would be significant in either explanation given above for Mordecai's refusal to bow.) Perhaps Mordecai's companions did not understand his Jewish beliefs, or possibly they also harbored some antagonism toward the Jews. In any event, they told Haman about Mordecai.

C. Haman's Rage Against the Jews (vv. 5, 6)

⁵When Haman saw that Mordecai would not kneel down or pay him honor, he was enraged.

Haman made a point to observe Mordecai's behavior. When he *saw that Mordecai would not kneel down or pay him honor*, he was furious.

⁶Yet having learned who Mordecai's people were, he scorned the idea of killing only Mordecai. Instead Haman looked for a way to destroy all Mordecai's people, the Jews, throughout the whole kingdom of Xerxes.

Haman's immediate thought was to seize Mordecai and have him executed. But when he learned that Mordecai was a Jew, *all* of Mordecai's *people* became a target of his rage. It should be noted that God's redemption plan for the world was at stake, for the Jews were the people through whom the promised Messiah was to come. The same issue was at stake when wicked Queen Athaliah of Judah attempted to destroy the entire royal family upon seizing power (2 Kings 11:1).

II. Esther's Hesitation (Esther 4:7-11)

Haman set his plan in motion "in the twelfth year of King Xerxes," or in 474 BC (Esther 3:7). Esther had been queen for five years (2:16) by the time Haman went to the king with his charge that "a certain people" did not keep the king's laws and that it would be in the king's best interest to eliminate them (3:8, 9).

Xerxes went along with the proposal. The appropriate documents were drawn up and dispatched to the far reaches of his empire (3:12-15), with the massacre scheduled to be carried out on a set day. It is noteworthy that Haman determined to annihilate the Jews during the first month of the Jewish year (3:7) and cast a lot at that time to determine the time when the scheme would be carried out. The lot fell on the twelfth month (3:7). Clearly the result of the lot was providentially guided by the Lord to allow the Jews the maximum amount of time to prepare to respond in whatever way they could. Haman's plan was to include "all the Jews—young and old, women and little children" (3:13). The king apparently did not realize that this decree was a death sentence for his own wife as well!

When Mordecai heard the news, he immediately went into mourning. He tore his clothes and put on sackcloth and ashes (4:1). There was similar mourning by Jews throughout the empire (4:3). When Esther learned of Mordecai's distress, she sent him appropriate clothes so that he could enter the king's gate. But he refused them (4:4). Then Esther sent "Hathach, one of the king's eunuchs" to find out what was troubling Mordecai (4:5).

A. Danger to the Jews (vv. 7, 8)

7Mordecai told him everything that had happened to him, including the exact amount of money Haman had promised to pay into the royal treasury for the destruction of the Jews.

Mordecai gave Hathach all the bad news, mentioning *the exact amount of money Haman had promised to pay* the king to allow *the Jews* to be slaughtered. There is nothing at this point to suggest that Hathach or anyone else in the king's court knew that Esther was Jewish.

It may seem surprising to us that Esther knew nothing about Haman's plot to kill her people. But we need to keep in mind that the harem of an ancient Near Eastern ruler was virtually isolated from the world of politics and from most other activities as well.

8He also gave him a copy of the text of the edict for their annihilation, which had been published in Susa, to show to Esther and explain it to her, and he told him to urge her to go into the king's presence to beg for mercy and plead with him for her people.

Mordecai *gave* to Hathach *a copy of the text of the edict* authorizing the *annihilation* of the Jews. Hathach was to *show* the copy to Esther and explain it to her so that she would know the implications of this decree for Esther's *people* and for Esther herself. The decree *had been published in Susa*, the winter capital of the Persian. Then Hathach was to *urge* Esther to go before the king to *plead* on behalf of her people that they would be spared.

B. Dilemma for Esther (vv. 9-11)

⁹Hathach went back and reported to Esther what Mordecai had said.

Hathach faithfully did as he was told. Now, as we say, "the ball was in Esther's court." She could, of course, ignore Mordecai's request. At first glance this would seem to be the safest course. But to ignore his request might not actually be all that safe. There was always the possibility that her heritage would eventually be revealed, a fact that Mordecai later mentioned to her (vv. 13, 14). But more important than doing the *safe* thing was doing the *right* thing.

> *¹⁰, ¹¹Then she instructed him to say to Mordecai, "All the king's officials and the people of the royal provinces know that for any man or woman who approaches the king in the inner court without being summoned the king has but one law: that he be put to death. The only exception to this is for the king to extend the gold scepter to him and spare his life. But thirty days have passed since I was called to go to the king."*

Even if Esther chose to do as Mordecai asked, actually taking such a step was quite risky. Anyone who approached *the king in the inner court without being summoned* faced the death penalty. This seems like a very severe law, but ancient Near Eastern rulers were surrounded with all kinds of intrigue and plots against their lives. (One may recall that this is why King Artaxerxes had a "cupbearer" like Nehemiah to taste the king's wine before the king did.) Under such conditions, a policy such as this seems to have been a reasonable precaution. Indeed, we know from reading Esther 2:21-23 that one assassination plot had already been foiled. (The king's precautions, however, did not prevent his eventual murder in 465 BC.)

There was one *exception* to the death penalty of the king: if the person seeking an audience found favor in his sight, *the king* would *extend* his *gold scepter* and the law would be suspended. But there was another problem where Esther was concerned. She had not been *called* into the presence of the king for *thirty days*. Such a lengthy period of time may have made Esther wonder if she had fallen out of favor with the king.

III. Mordecai's Hope (Esther 4:12-16)
A. Mordecai's Challenge (vv. 12-14)

¹²When Esther's words were reported to Mordecai,

Did Esther hope that her situation would relieve her of further responsibility in the matter? Or did she hope that the king would eventually summon her? Of course, if she waited until he called it could be too late.

Or did she hope that Mordecai would come up with another plan that had a better chance of succeeding?

> *13* . . . *he sent back this answer: "Do not think that because you are in the king's house you alone of all the Jews will escape.*

Most of us try to avoid situations in which we have to make hard decisions, but sometimes in life they are unavoidable. Mordecai reminded Esther that she could not hope to find safety *in the king's* palace because of her royal position. Hathach would know that she was Jewish since he had been conveying Mordecai's message to her; and sooner or later others were bound to find out, sealing her fate along with that of *all the Jews.*

> *14"For if you remain silent at this time, relief and deliverance for the Jews will arise from another place, but you and your father's family will perish. And who knows but that you have come to royal position for such a time as this?"*

Mordecai's plan seemed like the best idea at the time. But even if Esther did not cooperate, he firmly believed that God would provide *relief and deliverance for the Jews* in some other way. He knew enough history to recognize that in times past God had delivered his people in various ways and could certainly do so again.

The question facing Esther at this point was which sovereign (heavenly or earthly) she would honor. She should not assume that her status would exempt her from Haman's decree. Her loyalty was to another, greater King whose "decree" was responsible for her being in her *royal position* at this specific moment in history. She was not where she was by accident, but *for such a time as this.*

B. Esther's Courage (vv. 15, 16)

> *15, 16Then Esther sent this reply to Mordecai: "Go, gather together all the Jews who are in Susa, and fast for me. Do not eat or drink for three days, night or day. I and my maids will fast as you do. When this is done, I will go to the king, even though it is against the law. And if I perish, I perish."*

Esther was determined not to "go it alone" once she had made her decision. Knowing that *all the Jews* of *Susa* were joining her in a three-day *fast* would provide moral support. Although prayer is not specifically mentioned, we can be certain that those fasting hours were filled with numerous requests offered up to God for deliverance.

Esther's words *if I perish, I perish* were not a shoulder-shrugging surrender to fate. They reflect the courage of someone determined to do what was right, even though it was risky.

HAMAN'S DECREE IS REVERSED (ESTHER 8:3-8; 9:17-23)

Establishing the Groundwork

Following the three days of fasting, Esther came into the king's presence, dressed in her royal robes. The king did extend the gold scepter to her, inviting her to approach him and to touch the tip of the scepter (Esther 5:1, 2). King Xerxes offered to grant any request made by Esther, "even up to half the kingdom" (v. 3). Eventually Esther spoke up on behalf of her people at a banquet she hosted for the king and Haman. There she exposed Haman as the instigator behind the scheme to annihilate the Jewish people (Esther 7:1-6). Before that banquet, however, Haman had ordered a huge gallows to be built upon which to execute Mordecai (Esther 5:14). At about that same time and without Haman's knowledge, Xerxes decided to honor Mordecai for foiling an assassination plot mentioned earlier (2:21-23; 6:1-3).

The supreme irony came when the king asked Haman (who had just arrived to request the death of Mordecai) how to reward "the man the king delights to honor" (6:6). Haman, thinking that he himself was the one to be rewarded, replied that such a man should be dressed in some of the king's finest clothes and be paraded through the streets, mounted on one of the king's own horses led by a leading citizen (6:6-9). Imagine Haman's chagrin when he learned that Mordecai was the one to be honored and that he (Haman) was to be the one to lead the horse!

During the banquet that followed, Esther told the king about the plight of her people (7:1-6). In another notable irony, the king ordered Haman hanged (or more accurately, "impaled") on the gallows that Haman had built for Mordecai (7:9, 10). However, the decree that the king had issued earlier declaring the extermination of the Jews was still in force. Such a decree of the king could not be set aside (8:8; compare Daniel 6:8, 12, 15). The Jews remained in grave danger.

Examining the Text

I. Reversing a Decree (Esther 8:3-8)

A. Esther's Plea (v. 3)

3Esther again pleaded with the king, falling at his feet and weeping. She begged him to put an end to the evil plan of Haman the Agagite, which he had devised against the Jews.

The first two verses of Esther 8 tell how King Xerxes gave to Esther the estate of Haman and gave to Mordecai his signet ring, the symbol of royal authority. But this did not give Mordecai the power to revoke the decree that called for the death of his people. According to the law of the Medes and Persians, a decree once issued could not be withdrawn. (See Daniel 6:8-15.)

For this reason Esther once more had to step forward on behalf of her people. Emboldened by her earlier success, she approached *the king* a second time. This time she fell prostrate before him *weeping* to plead for protection against the scheme Haman *had devised against the Jews.*

B. Xerxes' Permission (v. 4)

4Then the king extended the gold scepter to Esther and she arose and stood before him.

Once again *the king extended the gold scepter to Esther* (as in Esther 5:2), indicating permission to come *before him.*

C. Esther's Proposal (vv. 5, 6)

5"If it pleases the king," she said, "and if he regards me with favor and thinks it the right thing to do, and if he is pleased with me, let an order be written overruling the dispatches that Haman son of Hammedatha, the Agagite, devised and wrote to destroy the Jews in all the king's provinces.

Like a lawyer pleading a case, Esther carefully laid out her argument point by point. Her first appeal to the king was a personal one: *if he regards me with favor.* She already had clear evidence (since the gold scepter had been extended to her) that she had found such favor, but a reminder would not hurt. She later repeated the thought in the phrase *if he is pleased with me.*

The phrase *and thinks it is the right thing to do* indicates Esther's appeal to the king's sense of justice. In requesting that the king overrule *the dispatches* prepared by Haman, Esther placed the blame for the evil decree on Haman rather than on *the king.* Xerxes had trusted Haman completely when Haman had described "a certain people" as troublesome without specifying who they were (Esther 3:8, 9). Consequently, when the schemer presented the king with a decree to destroy these people, the king had agreed with the understanding that it would be beneficial to his empire. Little did he realize that the decree was rooted in Haman's personal desire to get revenge against Mordecai and Mordecai's people for a personal slight.

⁶"For how can I bear to see disaster fall on my people? How can I bear to see the destruction of my family?"

At the time he had approved the death decree, the king had no idea that Esther was Jewish. Now, of course, he realized the impact that it was certain to have on not only her but on her *people* and her *family*.

D. Xerxes' Provision (vv. 7, 8)

⁷, ⁸King Xerxes replied to Queen Esther and to Mordecai the Jew, "Because Haman attacked the Jews, I have given his estate to Esther, and they have hanged him on the gallows. Now write another decree in the king's name in behalf of the Jews as seems best to you, and seal it with the king's signet ring—for no document written in the king's name and sealed with his ring can be revoked."

Once the king understood the situation, he wasted no time in providing a remedy. He gave Mordecai the authority to *write another decree* as he saw fit—one that would counter the decree of Haman. The king's trust in Haman had been misplaced. Now, however, the king was certain that Mordecai could be trusted. He had good reason to conclude this, because it was Mordecai who earlier had reported a conspiracy against the king (Esther 2:21-23). Verses 9 and 10 record that Mordecai "wrote in the name of King Xerxes" a decree to be announced throughout the empire. One could suggest that Mordecai was also writing in the name of the King of kings, who was carrying out his sovereign plan for the defense of his people and the continuation of his messianic plan.

II. Remembering a Day (Esther 9:17-23)

Mordecai lost no time in using the king's authority to carry out his plan to save his people. He first summoned the "royal secretaries" to make copies of the new decree that was to be dispatched to the remote corners of the Persian Empire. The empire included 127 provinces, stretching from India to Cush, located just south of Egypt. Many languages were spoken throughout the empire; so the scribes not only copied the decree, but they also translated it into the language appropriate to each province and people (Esther 8:9).

Once the translations were made and sealed, Mordecai dispatched them throughout the empire. The Persians had one of the best postal systems in the ancient world. Riding "fast horses especially bred for the king" (v. 10), they quickly and efficiently delivered their message. Getting the message out swiftly was essential to providing the Jews time to prepare for their defense.

A. A Celebration Commences (vv. 17-19)

¹⁷This happened on the thirteenth day of the month of Adar, and on the fourteenth they rested and made it a day of feasting and joy.

The second decree issued by Xerxes gave the Jews throughout the empire the authority to defend themselves against their enemies on the day Haman had arranged for their destruction: *the thirteenth day of the month of Adar* (Esther 3:13). (This would be the equivalent of late February or early March on our calendar.) On that day 500 men and the 10 sons of Haman were put to death in Susa (9:12). Esther then asked the king that the decree be extended a day to allow the Jews an additional opportunity to defend themselves. This request was granted, and on the fourteenth day of Adar an additional 300 men were put to death (9:15).

Beyond Susa, Jews in the remainder of the empire put to death 75,000 enemies on the thirteenth day of Adar (9:16), then on the fourteenth day these Jews *rested* and celebrated their triumph with *feasting and joy*. The plan by which the enemies of the Jews hoped to destroy them became an event that bound the Jews throughout the empire closer together.

¹⁸The Jews in Susa, however, had assembled on the thirteenth and fourteenth, and then on the fifteenth they rested and made it a day of feasting and joy.

The Jews in Susa followed a slightly different schedule in setting aside time for celebration. As already noted, Jews in Susa *assembled* to defend themselves *on the thirteenth and fourteenth* days of Adar. They then *rested* on the *fifteenth* day and made this their time for *feasting and joy*.

¹⁹That is why rural Jews—those living in villages—observe the fourteenth of the month of Adar as a day of joy and feasting, a day for giving presents to each other.

Throughout this account of the Jews' defense of themselves, the text emphasizes that the Jews did not take any plunder from their enemies, even though Xerxes had given them permission to do so (Esther 8:11; 9:10, 15, 16). As if to highlight that part of their deliverance, the Jews' commemoration, celebrated on *the fourteenth of the month of Adar* by the Jews of the *villages* (or *rural* areas), was marked, not by taking anything, but by *giving presents to each other*. Some suggest that the Jews' refusal to take any plunder was rooted in the possible link between Haman and the Amalekites (see the discussion of this in the earlier comments on Esther 3:2). Just as King Saul was told to take no plunder when he destroyed the Amalekites (1 Samuel 15:1-3), so these Jews took no plunder when they destroyed their enemies.

B. A Celebration Continues (vv. 20-23)

20-22Mordecai recorded these events, and he sent letters to all the Jews throughout the provinces of King Xerxes, near and far, to have them celebrate annually the fourteenth and fifteenth days of the month of Adar as the time when the Jews got relief from their enemies, and as the month when their sorrow was turned into joy and their mourning into a day of celebration. He wrote them to observe the days as days of feasting and joy and giving presents of food to one another and gifts to the poor.

These verses record Mordecai's action to make "official" what had been explained in the previous verses: *all the Jews* in the Persian Empire were to observe *the fourteenth and fifteenth days of the month of Adar* as *days of feasting and joy.* This declaration specified that the Jews were to give *presents of food to one another and gifts to the poor.*

23So the Jews agreed to continue the celebration they had begun, doing what Mordecai had written to them.

As noted later in the book of Esther, these days came to be called Purim, derived from *pur* (the Hebrew word for lot), because Haman had cast the *pur*, or lot, in order to arrange for the Jews' destruction (Esther 9:24-26). This feast is still observed by Jews on the fourteenth day of Adar except in Jerusalem, where it is observed on the fifteenth. In our calendar, Purim usually falls in the month of March. While the Jewish historian Josephus mentions this festival, it is not mentioned in the New Testament, perhaps because it was not one of the major Jewish feasts, and, being celebrated only locally, was not a factor in the ministry of Jesus.

Purim may be considered a celebration of God's ability to work all things for the good of his people and to counter the evil intentions of others so that his good purposes may result (see Genesis 45:7, 8; Romans 8:28). Certainly we have seen this illustrated quite often in our study of the history of God's people. May we take to heart these and other lessons, "so that through endurance and the encouragement of the Scriptures we might have hope" (Romans 15:4).

How to Say It

ABIMELECH. Uh-*bim*-eh-lek.

ABRAHAM. *Ay*-bruh-ham.

AGAG. *Ay*-gag.

AGAGITE. *Ay*-guh-gite.

AHASUERUS. Uh-haz-you-*ee*-rus.

AKKUB. *Ak*-ub.

AMALEK. *Am*-uh-lek.

AMALEKITES. *Am*-uh-leh-kites or Uh-*mal*-ih-kites.

ANAIAH. Uh-*nye*-uh.

ARAMAIC. *Air*-uh-*may*-ik (strong accent on *may*).

ASSYRIA. Uh-*sear*-ee-uh.

ATHALIAH. Ath-uh-*lye*-uh.

AZARIAH. Az-uh-*rye*-uh.

BABYLONIAN. Bab-ih-*low*-nee-un.

BANI. *Bay*-nye.

ELUL. *Ee*-lull or Eh-lool.

HAMAN. *Hay*-mun.

HAMMEDATHA. Ham-med-*day*-thuh.

HANAN. *Hay*-nuhn.

HANANI. Huh-*nay*-nye.

HANANIAH. Han-uh-*nye*-uh.

HASHBADDANAH. Hash-*bad*-duh-nuh.

HASHUM. *Hay*-shum.

HATHACH. *Hay*-tak.

HILKIAH. Hill-*kye*-uh.

HODIAH. Ho-*dye*-uh.

JAMIN. *Jay*-min.

JESHUA. *Jesh*-you-uh.

JOSEPHUS. Jo-*see*-fus.

JOSIAH. Jo-*sigh*-uh.

JOZABAD. *Jaws*-ah-bad.

KELITA. *Kel*-ih-tuh.

MAASEIAH. May-uh-*see*-yuh.

MALKIJAH. Mal-*kye*-uh.

MATTITHIAH. Mat-ih-*thigh*-uh.

MESHULLAM. Me-*shul*-am.

MISHAEL. *Mish*-a-el.

MORDECAI. *Mor*-dih-kye.

PEDAIAH. Peh-*day*-yuh.

PELAIAH. Pe-*lay*-yuh or Pe-*lye*-uh.

PHARAOH. *Fair*-o or *Fay*-roe.

PHILISTINE. Fuh-*liss*-teen or *Fill*-us-teen.

PURIM. *Pew*-rim.

SAMARIA. Suh-*mare*-ee-uh.

SARGON. *Sar*-gon.

SENNACHERIB. Sen-*nack*-er-ib.

SHABBETHAI. *Shab*-ee-thigh.

SHALMANESER. Shal-mun-*ee*-zer.

SHAPHAN. *Shay*-fan.

SHEMA. *She*-muh.

SHEREBIAH. *Sher*-ee-*bye*-uh (strong accent on *bye*).

SUSA. *Soo*-suh.

URIAH. Yu-*rye*-uh.

VASHTI. *Vash*-tie.

XERXES. *Zerk*-seez.

ZECHARIAH. *Zek*-uh-*rye*-uh (strong accent on *rye*).

ZERUBBABEL. Zeh-*rub*-uh-bul.